Gendering American Politics

Perspectives from the Literature

Karen O'Connor
Professor of Government
American University

Sarah E. Brewer
American University

Michael Philip Fisher
Rutgers University and Hunter College-CUNY

PEARSON
Longman

New York San Francisco Boston
London Toronto Sydney Tokyo Singapore Madrid
Mexico City Munich Paris Cape Town Hong Kong Montreal

Executive Editor: Eric Stano
Senior Marketing Manager: Elizabeth Fogarty
Production Manager: Eric Jorgensen
Project Coordination, Text Design, and Electronic Page Make-up:
    Electronic Publishing Services Inc., New York City
Cover Design Manager: Wendy Ann Fredericks
Cover Designer: Kay Petronio
Cover Photo: © Kenneth C. Zirkel/iStockphoto
Manufacturing Manager: Mary Fischer
Printer and Binder: R.R. Donnelley & Sons
Cover Printer: Phoenix Color Corp.

For permission to use copyrighted material, grateful acknowledgement is made to the copyright holders on pp. 337–339, which are hereby made part of this copyright page.

Library of Congress Cataloging-in-Publication Data
Gendering American politics : perspectives from the literature / [edited by]
Karen O'Connor, Sarah E. Brewer, Michael Philip Fisher.
    p. cm.
Includes bibliographical references.
ISBN 0-321-09086-1
1. Women in politics—United States. I. O'Connor, Karen II. Brewer, Sarah E. III. Fisher,
Michael Philip.
HQ1236.5.U6G465 2006
320'.082'0973—dc22
                        2005014341

Visit us at www.ablongman.com.

ISBN 0-321-09086-1

1 2 3 4 5 6 7 8 9 10—DOC—08 07 06 05

Contents

Preface   ix

CHAPTER 1   Opening the Debate   1

1   **Virginia Sapiro.** 1981. "When Are Interests Interesting? The Problem of Political Representation of Women"   **1**

2   **Irene Diamond and Nancy Hartsock.** 1981. "Beyond Interests in Politics"   **11**

WRAPPING UP   17

CHAPTER 2   Confronting the Constitution   19

3   **Ellen Carol DuBois.** 1987. "Outgrowing the Compact of the Fathers: Equal Rights, Woman Suffrage, and the United States Constitution, 1820–1878"   **19**

4   **Eileen Lorenzi McDonagh.** 1990. "The Significance of the Nineteenth Amendment: A New Look at Civil Rights, Social Welfare, and Woman Suffrage Alignments in the Progressive Era"   **25**

5   **Jane J. Mansbridge.** 1986. "Why We Lost the ERA"   **33**

6   **Catharine A. MacKinnon.** 1989. "Toward Feminist Jurisprudence"   **39**

WRAPPING UP   42

CHAPTER 3   Participating in the Process   43

7   **Susan Welch.** 1977. "Women as Political Animals? A Test of Some Explanations for Male-Female Political Participation Differences"   **43**

8   **Anne N. Costain.** 1992. "A New Women's Movement Emerges"   **49**

9   **Kay Lehman Schlozman, Nancy Burns, and Sidney Verba.** 1994. "Gender and the Pathways to Participation: The Role of Resources"   **57**

10   **Carol Hardy-Fanta.** 1999. "Discovering Latina Women in Politics: Gender, Culture, and Participatory Theory"   **67**

WRAPPING UP   74

CHAPTER 4   Aiming for Office   75

11   **Susan J. Carroll.** 1985. "Political Elites and Sex Differences in Political Ambition: A Reconsideration"   **75**

12   **Edmond Costantini.** 1990. "Political Women and Political Ambition: Closing the Gender Gap"   **79**

13   **Richard L. Fox and Jennifer L. Lawless.** 2003. "Family Structure, Sex-Role Socialization, and the Decision to Run for Office"   **87**

14   **Barbara Palmer and Dennis Simon.** 2003. "Political Ambition and Women in the U.S. House of Representatives, 1916–2000"   **97**

WRAPPING UP   102

CHAPTER 5   Listening for Women's Voices   103

15   **Patricia Gurin.** 1985. "Women's Gender Consciousness"   **103**

16   **Pamela Johnston Conover.** 1988. "Feminists and the Gender Gap"   **111**

17   **Elizabeth Adell Cook and Clyde Wilcox.** 1991. "Feminism and the Gender Gap—A Second Look"   **121**

18   **Barbara Norrander.** 1997. "The Independence Gap and the Gender Gap"   **127**

19   **Karen M. Kaufmann and John R. Petrocik.** 1999. "The Changing Politics of American Men: Understanding the Sources of the Gender Gap"   **133**

20   **Ronnee Schreiber.** 2002. "Injecting a Woman's Voice: Conservative Women's Organizations, Gender Consciousness, and the Expression of Women's Policy Preferences"   **141**

WRAPPING UP   151

CHAPTER 6   Finding a Place in the Political Parties   153

21   **Ellen Boneparth.** 1977. "Women in Campaigns: From Lickin' and Stickin' to Strategy"   **153**

22   **Diane L. Fowlkes, Jerry Perkins, and Sue Tolleson Rinehart.** 1979. "Gender Roles and Party Roles"   **161**

23   **Jo Freeman.** 1986. "The Political Culture of the Democratic and Republican Parties"   **167**

24   **Kira Sanbonmatsu.** 2002. "Political Parties and the Recruitment of Women to State Legislatures"   **175**

WRAPPING UP   181

CHAPTER 7   Running for Office   183

25   **R. Darcy and Sarah Slavin Schramm.** 1977. "When Women Run against Men"   **183**

26   **Charles S. Bullock III and Susan A. MacManus.** 1991. "Municipal Electoral Structure and the Election of Councilwomen"   **189**

27   **Leonie Huddy and Nayda Terkildsen.** 1993. "Gender Stereotypes and the Perception of Male and Female Candidates"   **195**

28   **Kim Fridkin Kahn.** 1994. "The Distorted Mirror: Press Coverage of Women Candidates for Statewide Office"   **203**

29   **Kathleen Dolan.** 2001. "Electoral Context, Issues, and Voting for Women in the 1990s"   **213**

WRAPPING UP   218

CHAPTER 8   Legislating for Women   219

30   **Emmy E. Werner.** 1966. "Women in Congress, 1917–1964"   **219**

31   **Sue Thomas.** 1991. "The Impact of Women on State Legislative Policies"   **227**

32   **Lyn Kathlene.** 1994. "Power and Influence in State Legislative Policy Making: The Interaction of Gender and Position in Committee Hearing Debates"   **235**

33   **Cindy Simon Rosenthal.** 2000. "Gender Styles in State Legislative Committees: Raising Their Voices in Resolving Conflict"   **245**

34   **Michele L. Swers.** 1998. "Are Women More Likely to Vote for Women's Issue Bills than Their Male Colleagues?"   **251**

35   **Mary Hawkesworth.** 2003. "Congressional Enactments of Race-Gender: Toward a Theory of Raced-Gendered Institutions"   **257**

WRAPPING UP   267

CHAPTER 9   Judging Women   269

36   **John Gruhl, Cassia Spohn, and Susan Welch.** 1981. "Women as Policymakers: The Case of Trial Judges"   **269**

37   **Donald R. Songer, Sue Davis, and Susan Haire.** 1994. "A Reappraisal of Diversification in the Federal Courts: Gender Effects in the Courts of Appeals"   **275**

38   **Phyllis Coontz.** 2000. "Gender and Judicial Decisions: Do Female Judges Decide Cases Differently than Male Judges?"   **281**

39   **Karen O'Connor and Jeffrey A. Segal.** 1990. "Justice Sandra Day O'Connor and the Supreme Court's Reaction to Its First Female Member"   **287**

WRAPPING UP   292

CHAPTER 10   Governing Women   293

40   **Myra Marx Ferree.** 1974. "A Woman for President? Changing Responses: 1958–1972"   **293**

41   **Kathleen A. Frankovic.** 1988. "The Ferraro Factor"   **297**

42   **Georgia Duerst-Lahti.** 1997. "Reconceiving Theories of Power: Consequences of Masculinism in the Executive Branch"   **307**

43   **MaryAnne Borrelli.** 1997. "Gender, Credibility, and Politics: The Senate Nomination Hearings of Cabinet Secretaries-Designate, 1975–1993"   **315**

44   **Karen O'Connor, Bernadette Nye, and Laura van Assendelft.** 1996. "Wives in the White House: The Political Influence of First Ladies"   **323**

45   **Julie Dolan.** 2001. "Political Appointees in the United States: Does Gender Make a Difference?"   **331**

WRAPPING UP   335

Credits   337

Preface

I entered the J.D./Ph.D. program at the State University of New York at Buffalo in 1973, just two years after Congress had sent the proposed Equal Rights Amendment to the states for their ratification, and the same year that *Roe* v. *Wade* was decided. I knew that I wanted to study women and politics, especially women and the law, but at that time, the Women's Studies Department on campus offered only an M.A. No women and politics classes were offered at Buffalo, although pioneers on women and politics such as Roberta Siegel taught there, but she was soon to leave to go to Rutgers University. Only a handful of places, most notably the new Center for the American Woman in Politics (CAWP) at the Eagleton Institute of Politics at Rutgers University, offered any courses on women and politics. It was only a few years earlier, in 1969, that the Women's Caucus for Political Science was founded to urge better treatment of women political scientists and to fight for recognition of women and politics as a legitimate field of inquiry. Indeed, it is hard to imagine that a standard text that many women of my generation learned from was called *Political Man*, with few questioning Robert Lane's near exclusion of women from his seminal discussion of citizens engaged in or disengaged from the political process.

In spite of not having taken any courses on women and politics (but having taken four courses on women and the law at the law school), I requested and was allowed to elect women and politics as a Ph.D. comprehensive examination area in 1975. Looking back, to be honest, I chose women and politics not only because of my interest in the subject, but, more relevant to the project at hand, there wasn't that much out there for me to read, analyze, and remember. There had been a few major books by authors such as then Georgetown University Professor Jeane Kirkpatrick (who was to go on to become the first female U.S. ambassador to the United Nations), a few book chapters, most notably in Louise Young's *Notable American Women*, and a few articles, several of them included in this volume. It wasn't until 1980 that *Women & Politics*, a scholarly journal designed to publish research about women and politics, was founded. During the 1960s and 1970s, it was rare for mainstream political science journals to publish work by or about women, and *Women & Politics* became an outlet for many men and women working in the area, be it American politics, comparative politics, or feminist theory. Several articles in this collection first appeared there.

During the mid to late 1970s, when I was first studying political science, the first generation of a core of women and politics scholars emerged, often guided by pioneers in the field including, in no particular order, Marianne Githens, Jewell Prestage, Susan Welch, M. Margaret Conway, Naomi Lynn, and Cornelia Flora. Male scholars such as M. Kent Jennings and Theodore Lowi were urging their female students to explore issues of women and politics, be it socialization processes or the women's movement. These women, including Jo Freeman and Virginia Sapiro, were soon to produce true classics in the field of women and politics. Freeman's and Sapiro's dissertations ultimately were published as widely heralded books, *The Politics of Women's Liberation* and *The Political Integration of Women: Roles, Socialization, and Politics*, respectively, which continue to be classics in the field. Other books, including Virginia Gray and Pamela Johnston Conover's *Feminism and the New Right: Conflict over the American Family* and Barbara Deckard Sinclair's *The Women's Movement: Political, Socioeconomic, and Psychological Issues*, as well as Marianne Githens and Jewell Prestage's *A Portrait of Marginality: The Political Behavior of American Women*, among others, were to make it easier for women of my generation to teach women and politics classes, although they often were not treated with much respect by colleagues.

I joined with Nancy E. McGlen, who as a professor at SUNY Buffalo served on both my Ph.D. examination and dissertation committees, to write *Women's Rights: The Struggle for Equality in the 19th and 20th Centuries*, which was completed in 1983, after more years of work on it than either of us would care to admit. Later, we realized the rapid development of the subfield while working on *Women, Politics, and American Society* (1993) and its second edition. In but a two-year period, as more and more scholars began to recognize how understudied women were as their numbers increased on city councils, in statehouses, and in Congress, and as women's participation was finally noted as key to the successes or failures of social movements as well as political candidates, the body of outstanding work, both in scholarly journals and in book form, skyrocketed. In fact, for the third edition, faced with the daunting task of sifting through the voluminous literature of what was now an organized research section designated by the American Political Science Association, we were happy to welcome as co-authors Laura van Assendelft, who was a student of mine at Emory University, and Wendy Gunther-Canada, who was trained at Rutgers and CAWP.

Gendering American Politics: Perspectives from the Literature is a logical outgrowth of *Women, Politics, and American Society*, as well as my four years as editor of *Women & Politics*. It is an effort to bring together the multitude of works that I have used in class and, more importantly, provide scholars and students with easy access to important works in the field. While no one volume can include all the major works, this edited collection attempts to include some of the best early work in the field along with representative samples in a host of areas to allow students to begin to appreciate how the study of women in American politics has evolved, and to offer suggestions for future research. We apologize in advance to those whose important work could not be included in this volume, and we thank those authors whose work is included for permitting us to use their work, as well as allowing us to edit their works to manageable lengths for a collection of this sort.

Some of the research represented in this collection contains highly sophisticated statistical methodological analyses. To make this collection as student friendly as possible, we have made every effort to omit complex discussion of methods and mathematics. Similarly, text references and footnotes also are excluded. Full citations to each article, however, are included for those who wish to read an article in full. Many of these works are available on JSTOR or ProQuest.

The pieces that make up this volume are grouped in ten chapters that focus on topic areas ranging from the opening of the debate about women in politics and constitutional issues to women in judiciary and governing roles. Each piece is preceded by introductory material that attempts to situate the work within the literature and to highlight its contributions and innovations to the development of our understanding of women and American politics. Each chapter concludes with "Wrapping Up" questions designed to encourage students to think about where the field of women and politics has been and where it is going.

We expect that some professors will use all of the sections in this collection, while others will use fewer sections, or use the sections in a different order, as best fits the outline of their individual courses. Thus, these sections may be used out of order and individual readings within each section can stand on their own, although many do make reference to other works in the volume to engage students further in the debate. Moreover, this collection can be used as a supplement to McGlen et al. *Women, Politics, and American Society*, or any of the host of other excellent works that now exist for use in the hundreds of women and politics courses that are offered under a variety of names in colleges and universities across the nation.

The outstanding work that Laura and Wendy do on updating *Women, Politics, and American Society* has allowed me to co-edit this volume with two outstanding former students, each with different interests in women and politics. Sarah E. Brewer received her Ph.D. from American University in 2003 after extensively documenting the role of women as professional political campaign consultants in American elections. As associate director of the Women & Politics Institute at American University, she teaches the courses Women and Politics and Women and Political Leadership, as well as a variety of other more specialized courses on women and politics. Michael Philip Fisher graduated from American University, where he was managing editor of *Women & Politics* for some of the time that I served as editor of that journal. He is now pursuing doctoral studies at Rutgers, concentrating in feminist political theory. Sarah and Michael brought differing perspectives on what scholarship should be included in this collection, as well as how it should be organized. And, as someone who has worked in this field for years, I was delighted to learn more about the field from their fresh eyes and more recent efforts to grapple with many of the issues posed by works contained in this collection. I cannot thank them enough for their fully equal contributions to this volume. I would also like to thank Dean William E. LeoGrande of the School of Public Affairs for his support of the Women & Politics Institute, under whose auspices we were able to take time to work on this collection. Finally, I would like to thank the reviewers who provided feedback on the manuscript for this book during its development: Nikki R. van Hightower; Kimberly Nalder, California State University-Sacramento; Susan M. Behunick; Kendra Stewart, Eastern Kentucky University; Terri S. Fine, University of Central Florida; Susan Johnson, University of Wisconsin-Whitewater; Toni Marzotto, Towson University; and Stacy G. Ulbig, Southwest Missouri State University.

It is now more than thirty years since I read my first works on women and politics and used them to argue with my professors to include more about women in their classes on politics more generally. Still, sad to say, many in the discipline continue to view women and politics as separate from mainstream political science. But, more than half of the electorate, the growing number of women in political positions, and the effects of that growth cannot be ignored. This volume, hopefully, will go far to document, without question, the high caliber and importance of the work in the field.

KAREN O'CONNOR

CHAPTER 1
Opening the Debate

READING 1

When Are Interests Interesting?
The Problem of Political
Representation of Women

(1981)

Virginia Sapiro

In this seminal essay from the prestigious *American Political Science Review*, Virginia Sapiro sets out the major challenges she sees facing those who study women in American politics. For her and other scholars working at the intersections of empirical research and political theory, a number of deeply related theoretical puzzles loom on the horizon: What is power and who wields it? What counts as politics? And, for that matter, what counts as democracy, feminism, equality, or justice? Throughout this essay, her predominant concern is to bring together these and seemingly more disparate strands of research conducted under the rubric of "feminism" or "feminist theory" into a unified analytic framework, tailored here to her professional home in political science. As one of the first scholars to lay out such a vision for feminist political scientists—and certainly the first to do so in so high-profile a publication—Sapiro asks important foundational questions. Do women have an essential interest or perspective that deserves representation? Must this interest be represented by women, or is it enough that those representing women's interests of whatever gender be sensitive and responsive to their needs? And, just what difference will it make if women and their interests are adequately represented?

You will see that as she addresses these and related questions, two conceptual touchstones continually crop up—*interest* and *representation*. These twin ideas are central theoretical building blocks of political science, especially for liberal political theory and the study of liberal nation-states such as the United States. So perhaps, it is not surprising that Sapiro crafts her analysis around them. And, indeed, they do provide a great payoff for her and the field. These concepts provide a bridge between philosophical and scientific approaches to the state. Claims made in those terms simultaneously can be empirical (documenting the failure of a particular state to represent women adequately) and normative (judging any such state of affairs to be unjust). This type of doubled argument is what feminist theorists sometimes call "transformative knowledge." In many ways, it is what sets feminist inquiry apart from traditional political science methodologies—and what makes it such a potent political tool.

In the beginning there was no problem of political representation of women. The reason was not that everyone agreed that women should not be represented; rather, the argument was that women *were* represented. . . . The most serious legal objections to women's participation in electoral politics, both at citizen and elite levels, was that the male is the head of the family (the "head of household," as he is still known), and in him was invested the authority to rule his family and to represent his family's interests in the "outside" world. The question many opponents of women's suffrage asked was how it could be possible for a woman to have interests separate and distinct from those of her husband; that is, how could a woman be considered an individual citizen with the rights of a distinct individual?

[* * *]

New demands by feminist movements have opened a different question. Women (as well as many others) ask not for representation as individual citizens, but as members of a group. They ask not only that citizens who happen to be women be represented, but also that women be represented *because* they are women. What does this demand mean? On what grounds can we argue that women are entitled to representation as members of a group rather than, simply, as individuals? Is the demand for representation of women simply or necessarily a demand for more women in political office? . . .

[* * *]

What Is to Be Represented?

One of the few truly obvious facts of political life is that the proportion of women among those designated as representatives is considerably smaller than the proportion of women found among the represented. This is the fact to which many people turn when they argue that women are underrepresented. This rationale frays under close scrutiny. Let us say, for example, that I am a redheaded woman. Why should I wish to be represented by a woman, indeed, a redheaded woman? I could say, as many people would, that such a person, resembling me, would represent my interests.

- "And how do you know that?" (the attentive reader asks).
- "Because she is in the same position I am in and could act for me. She would understand and feel the same way" (I answer).
- "When you say, 'the same position,' do you mean as a woman or as a redhead?"
- "As a woman, of course."

- "Why as a woman and not as a redhead?"
- "Because being a redhead is not politically relevant and being a woman is."

It is clear that the real question is not whether my representative looks like me—it is whether my interests are being represented. [As Hanna Pitkin argued,] what matters is whether my representative is "acting in the interest of the represented, in a manner responsive" to me.

In order to discuss representation of women we must consider whether women as a group have unique politically relevant characteristics, whether they have special interests to which a representative could or should respond. Can we argue that women as a group share particular social, economic, or political problems that do not closely match those of other groups, or that they share a particular viewpoint on the solutions to political problems? If so, we can also argue that women share interests that may be represented. Framing the working definition of "representable interests" in this fashion does not mean that the problems or issues are exclusively those of the specified interest group any more than we can make the same argument about other types of groups more widely accepted as interest groups. The fact that there is a labor interest group, for example, reflects the existence of other groups such as the business establishment, consumers, and government, which in a larger sense share labor's concerns, but often have viewpoints on the nature of, or solutions to, the problems which conflict with those of labor. That in the abstract "good wages," "fair prices," or "efficiency" sound good for everyone does not eliminate the differences of interest among the groups pursuing these goals. We would not suggest that business people or consumers can adequately represent the interests of labor simply because they too are somehow involved in the industrial enterprise. Nor does our working definition of an interest group mean that all of the potential members of that group are consciously allied, or that there is a clear and obvious answer to any given problem articulated by the entire group that differs substantially from answers articulated by others. In fact, I am not using "interest group" in the narrow sense generally found in political science, which seems to require an organized group of people interacting through conventional political channels in opposition to other organized interest groups. As we shall see, studies of women (and other oppressed groups) demonstrate that part of the political relevance of some groups is that they have been systematically denied the means with which to form themselves into an interest organization: self-consciousness and identification. The terms "interest group" and "interest organization" are therefore not interchangeable here, although the latter is formed primarily out of the former.

The term "women's issues" usually refers to public concerns that impinge primarily on the private (especially domestic) sphere of social life, and particularly those values associated with children and nurturance. But even within this domain "women's issues" can be interpreted in three distinct, although related ways. One interpretation is simply that women are more interested in these issues than in others as a result of their "parochial" domestic concerns. Another is that they are more interested in these issues than are men—that there is, in a sense, a division of labor in political attention. Finally, one could say that regardless of their relative level of concern with these issues, women have a "special" interest, or a particular (potential) viewpoint from which their positions or preferences might be derived. In discussing representation, we are more concerned with the latter two, and especially the final interpretation. In order to analyze women's interests, we will follow two lines of inquiry. The first is the problem of women's "objective situation" and its relevance to political interests; the other is the hardly less difficult question of women's consciousness of their own interests and the "subjective" condition of women.

Research in various fields of social science provides evidence that women do have a distinct position and a shared set of problems that characterize a special interest. Many of these distinctions are located in the institution in which women and men are probably most often assumed to have common interests, the family. Much has been made of the "sharing" or "democratic" model of the modern family, but whatever democratization has taken place, it has not come close to erasing the division of labor and, indeed, stratification, by sex. . . . We are accustomed to the idea that divisions of labor and stratification in public life define group interests in politics; can the same case be made for divisions of labor in private life? One can make such a case if these "private arrangements" are either determined at least in part by public policy or governmental organization, or if these arrangements affect objects of public policy and policy debate. Gender divisions of labor and stratification within the family meet these tests. . . .

Law and public policy continue to create and reinforce differences between women and men in property and contract matters (especially regarding marriage, divorce, and widowhood), economic opportunity (including employment, credit, and social security), protection from violence (rape and wife battery), control over fertility and child care, educational opportunities, and civic rights and obligations. Women and men have different relationships to pregnancy, childbirth, and lactation. These biological differences are exaggerated by women's having been given nearly total responsibility for reproduction, child care, and even child support. Marxist and non-Marxist scholars alike understand a group's relation to the mode of production, their relative control over both processes and products, as at least part of the basis for defining political interests. Children are perhaps the most important "products" of a society. Reproduction must be considered in a serious way as a factor in the political economy of governance.

The indicators generally used to describe differences in socioeconomic position also show that the politically relevant situations of women and men are different. Social and individual goods are very unevenly divided between the sexes. Women in almost all countries have less education than men, and where they achieve equivalent levels of education, segregation by field and therefore skills and market value remains. Women are less likely to be in the labor market. Men and women remain segregated in different sectors of the labor market and in jobs of different status within the same sectors. Wealth and credit are unevenly distributed. Men and women do not have the same access to physical and mental health, in large part because of sociopolitical factors. When we consider the half of the female population in paid employment, we find that they do not have equal access to leisure. Few groups in any society have a lower proportion of its members in positions accorded high status, value, or power. Only in life expectancy do women "outdo" men, a bonus that has little compensatory value in some countries, given the poverty of the aged and the inadequate support services available to them.

To say that women are in a different social position from that of men and there-fore have interests to be represented is not the same as saying that women are con-scious of these differences, that they define themselves as having special interests requiring representation, or that men and women as groups now disagree on policy issues on which women might have a special interest. Studies of public opinion on the status and roles of women show relatively few significant differences between the sexes, and do not reveal women to be consistently more feminist than men. . . .

. . . It is no coincidence that the women's movement has emphasized "con-sciousness raising" so heavily, using phrases such as "The personal is the political." These efforts are meant to increase awareness among women that what they might perceive as personal and isolated problems (such as underdeveloped skills, poor pay, or even feelings of "middle-aged depression") are widely shared problems that are due in large part to widespread social, economic, and political factors. . . .

[* * *]

When Does Representation Occur?

We have argued that there is a woman's interest to be represented. Let us, for now, limit the conception of this interest to the expansion of rights, liberties, and oppor-tunities for women where these have been denied or inhibited in comparison with those of men. We now turn to a new set of questions: Under what circumstances are political systems representative of women? Under what circumstances do they act in the interests of the represented—in this case, women? . . .

A. Political Economy. A careful examination of women's political history suggests that women's own actions have sometimes played only minor roles in some of the most profound legal or policy changes in comparison with other current problems and features of the political system. . . . Even in the instances in which women's movements were active, influential, and successful, as in the case of a number of suf-frage movements, it would be a mistake to analyze the movement activities without paying careful attention to the more general political context. . . . In many cases poli-cies that affect and even expand the status and opportunities of women appear to be propelled by sources other than women's interest organizations.

One rather commonplace assumption, based in the functionalist school of polit-ical development, is that modernization breeds secularization, mass communication, merit rather than parochially based social systems, and ultimately egalitarianism, including equality for women and men. As pleasant as such a parsimonious, com-prehensive theory might be, it is wrong in many respects and in many cases. It is also misleading or silent on the evolution of specific policies. . . . Although the sweeping view of development theory per se is of little help, comparative studies uncover cer-tain aspects of the needs and structures of the political economy that appear to sup-port or inhibit change in the status of women. What follows is merely a laundry list; the work that remains is to develop these into more coherent theory and, especially, to model their interaction.

1. *Economic needs.* Women constitute a marginal labor force whose status and specific activities fluctuate according to systemic needs for production, reproduction, and consumption. Changes in policies concerning women appear especially linked to the rise and fall of population needs. Among the policies most linked to population needs are those concerning birth control, child care, marriage and sexuality, and employment. Birth control policies offer an interesting example of this link. Many of the laws barring contraception and abortion (and, for that matter, homosexuality) were instituted in the nineteenth century and at times in the twentieth century when expansion of the population was needed. The legalization of contraception and abortion in many nations at about the same time as the boom of post-war babies reached adulthood, and the remarkable fluctuations in population policy in Nazi Germany and in the Soviet Union from the 1920s on testify to how the supply of labor (including military labor) influences policies that directly affect women.

   Fertility and employment of women are directly related; employment policies appear to have histories similar to that of birth control. Women were, in effect, drafted into traditionally male employment during World War II. When new sectors of the economy expand and, especially when auxiliary or lower-status workers are demanded for this expansion, women have often provided the new source of labor. . . .

2. *War.* Although war is supposed to be the domain of men, not to mention a major force shaping male life, war has often had profound effects on the status and roles of women. As a marginal labor force, women have been used as substitutes for men in the domestic labor force, which has meant both the expansion of female employment and, to some degree, expansion of the types of jobs in which women are employed. During and especially after wars, policies are also designed to restock the population, which means pushing women out of productive and into reproductive work. . . . Just as war encourages female entry into the labor force, war can develop new political roles for women, which are often institutionalized by law and policy after the war is over. In some cases governments have used women's part in the war as what amounts to an excuse for extending women's rights, as in the case of suffrage in Britain. . . .

3. *International Politics.* . . . One of the unstudied aspects of policy on women is the process by which international politics affects domestic policy. In some cases it appears that feminists of one nation use the example of policies discussed or employed in another, as in the case of the growing interest in American affirmative action policies in Europe. In others, the role of women may be used as a national sign of status or a symbol to other nations; in an odd sense, in this case the women represent the government rather than the reverse. One of the clearest examples is found in Germany at the turn of the century, when women were allowed into universities in part because German leaders felt they could not convincingly lead the world as a rational,

scientific nation as long as they were among the few "advanced" nations to bar women from higher education. . . .

4. *Federalism and International Organization*. One common observation in American politics in the 1960s and one of the assumptions of many political reform groups, is that alteration of civil liberties and rights is most easily accomplished at the federal rather than at the state level, that a federal structure is particularly conducive to change. American history offers numerous examples of this principle with regard to women. Land-grant colleges were among the leaders in extending higher education to women. The Nineteenth. Amendment to the Constitution accomplished what could have taken years longer in the South and much of the East. In the post–World War II era, the Supreme Court in particular, but also Congress and the executive branch, have pushed change far beyond what most states would initiate on their own. . . .

5. *Intergroup Tensions*. . . . Progress on the status of women appears to occur at times when the status of other social groups is under question as well, but it seems just as apparent that women's demands are often blocked by policy considerations involving those other groups. . . .

B. Ideology.   . . . There should be little doubt that ideology is an important factor as well, but its exact role is unclear. Parties of the left are not always remarkably different from parties on the right in their policy efforts toward women. Until 1980 Republican and Democratic parties alike gave the nod to the Equal Rights Amendment, and, despite his general recalcitrance on matters of civil rights, it was Richard Nixon who extended the executive order of affirmative action. . . .

[* * *]

. . . Religion and secularism have [also] played very important roles within nations, often in interaction with left-right politics that is well worth untangling and examining. . . .

C. Feminist Movements and Interest Organizations.   Thus far we have said little about feminism per se as an influence in policies on women. Although there are numerous worthwhile studies of women's movements, there are vast gaps in analysis of the role of women's movements and organizations in the policy-making process.

The very nature of patriarchalism makes the development of a woman's interest group and strategies for successful influence a complex and interesting problem. Conflict that may be understood as a battle between the sexes tears at the most basic structures of society as well as personal life. Pressures against such an interpretation make it difficult for women's interest organizations to define the grounds of political conflict over the status of women. Whereas most interest organizations would be loath to blame their socio-political problems on themselves (especially when members of their own group are notably absent from positions of power), women are under pressure to underscore their own participation in their oppression in order not to appear to be staging the battle for greater equality as a battle between women and men. Thus, women's organizations are caught in a dilemma regarding which strategies will suit the needs of *intra*group mobilization and *inter*group influence. If women's groups feel pressed to criticize themselves in the early stages of the development of a movement, they are unlikely to mobilize vast numbers of other women, particularly because a principal problem among women is low self-esteem and a relatively low sense of personal and political efficacy. On the other hand, if women's movements blame those in power, who tend to be men, they are often labeled as cranks and "man-haters," and on those grounds may again be easily dismissed by those—male and female—they attempt to influence. . . .

[* * *]

D. Women as Representatives.   Certainly one of the most often-voiced desires of the women's movement is placing women in positions of influence. The very term "representation of women" is usually taken very specifically to mean increasing the number of women in political office because of the assumption that women in power would be more responsive to women's interests than men would be. Questions about the validity of this assumption have led to a wealth of research on women in elite positions, much of which provides some clues, and much of which raises further questions.

The major questions posed in the literature on women as public officeholders are (1) are women different from men; and (2) if so (or not), why (or why not)? Research on these questions reveals considerably more similarity between the sexes than difference, although some of the differences are of great importance to the problem of representation. . . .

[* * *]

Although women might fare better, in terms of campaign strategy, not to discuss women's interests, or especially not to claim to represent them, female candidates and officeholders are forced into a "woman's role," or at least they are forced to be defined as "woman" candidates or politicians rather than simply as candidates or politicians. They are more often asked about their families than are men. Once women are in office, their committee assignments, initiation of legislation, and the topics on which they speak tend to reflect traditional women's concerns. What we do not know, however, is the degree to which these differences are attributable to self-initiation or to the constraints of organizations and other elites. . . .

 . . . Although women may not run "as women," they tend to be sympathetic toward feminism and may become partially concerned with women's issues once in office. Even when it appears that male and female officeholders share preferences on women's issues, it is often up to the women to do the real legislative work. Although sympathetic attitudes are important, legislative work is crucial.

With more research on elite behavior, it may become possible to determine the effects of organizational roles and structures on the ability of members of the elite to respond to women's interests. Although legislators may become most effective when they become specialists, or take a leading role on specialized committees, is the same true when the specialty is women's issues? Or, as suggested above, is this type of specialty interpreted as a narrow interest compared with, for example, the fortunes of the airplane industry in Washington? . . .

[* * *]

We may also look at formalization of the women's interest in terms of strategies of segregation and integration. Special offices within parties or governments have important symbolic meaning and they are generally, although not always, staffed by activists and specialists in women's problems. At the same time, however, segregation can "ghettoize" the problems; it can segregate the issues both from other related problems and from experts and leaders in other fields. How do these forces balance in the policy process?

These observations about the problems of women as representatives of women returns us to a question posed at the beginning: is an increase in the number of women in positions of power the key to representing women? We can now argue that it is a necessary condition, but it is not sufficient. We have seen that the presence of female officeholders is only one element among the factors determining the degree to which government responds to the interests of women. Moreover, the role of women in government is shaped by the effects of recruitment procedures and organizational constraints in a political system dominated by patriarchal norms. Not the least of the problems is the presence of many female leaders who, to varying degrees, accept and make decisions according to these patriarchal norms.

Can we argue that the presence of more women among public officeholders will mean women will be more represented than they were? Increasing the number of women in government is not sufficient, but it is necessary. First, we have seen that women in office do make some difference in government responsiveness to women's interests. Second, the mere presence of women in positions of power readjusts what is now a thoroughly inequitable distribution of political values in society: power, participation, and decision making. If we accept the democratic ideal that participation in governance is valuable, can we argue that systematic exclusion of a particular social group is acceptable? Finally, increased representation of people who "look like" women will effect powerful symbolic changes in politics. Women and men continue to think of politics as a male domain because the empirical truth at this moment is that politics *is* a male domain. People of both sexes find governance by women odd, remarkable, extraordinary, and even inappropriate. Can we consider a governing system to be representative of women if women are not considered "representative" of governance? . . .

Conclusion: When Women's Interests Are Interesting

The question of what is to be represented and under what circumstances are women represented has left us with a vast web that needs untangling. . . . The answers require new investigations of fundamental questions of politics, informed by a recognition that gender differentiation and stratification profoundly structure human life. . . .

[* * *]

Taking a serious interest in women and politics will also change some of the ways in which political scientists approach and discuss politics. Women's studies research has already pointed out flaws and gaps in accepted political theories and models. It has also revealed many pieces of conventional wisdom to be false, usually by transforming common and sometimes unstated assumptions into questions and hypotheses. Research on women uncovers critical problems in democratic theory and research which are of direct relevance to the problem of representation.

Women's studies research also criticizes and refines the basic tool of any type of research: language. We have already suggested that analysis of women and representation offers an opportunity to scrutinize the "political," the core concept in our vocabulary. We have made many of our words more blunt tools than they need be. "What is the nature of man, what are his needs and wants? How do these relate to political interests, goals, strategies, and structures?" If we ask these questions of our political philosophers and psychologists, the answers depend in large part upon whether we understand "man" to be a generic term or one that refers to a specific gender. Most of our great philosophers held that the nature of males and females is very different. What do we mean, then, when we ask about the political implications of the "nature of man"? Political scientists have difficulty incorporating women into the political world because they lack or reject the appropriate language. "Patriarchy," "sexism," "feminist," and "male-dominated" appear to be emotionally charged words, the tools of the polemicist rather than the scholar. But are these words necessarily more charged than "monarchy," "democratic," "Democratic," or "authoritarian"?

For now, the root of the study of politics is, as an eminent political scientist has argued, "man." In politics the sum of the parts is not equal to the whole. The argument of women's studies scholars is that by focusing our attention primarily on half of humanity, assuming that that half speaks for—represents—all, we have done worse than understanding half of politics. Political science can only benefit by expanding its view. . . .

TOWARD CRITICAL THINKING

1. Virginia Sapiro focuses throughout her essay on women's demands for representation. Can all the various political phenomena that scholars of women in American politics want to explain be resolved as questions of representation? What important topics *cannot* be explored in such terms? What other concepts would you make central to your own analysis?

2. Sapiro argues that gender is a more salient characteristic than, for example, hair color. What makes women's demands for representation more important than demands that could be made on behalf of redheads? What implications does this suggest for the future of gender politics? Do you think gender will always be a salient political characteristic? Explain.

READING 2

Beyond Interests in Politics

(1981)

Irene Diamond and Nancy Hartsock

In this response to Virginia Sapiro's "When Are Interests Interesting? The Problem of Political Representation of Women" (Reading 1), Irene Diamond and Nancy Hartsock take on the very ideas we identified earlier as the source of power in Sapiro's argument—interest and representation—in this article in the same issue of the *American Political Science Review*. For Sapiro, these ideas provide a conceptual way of making arguments that are simultaneously scientific and critical, and objectively valid but subjectively powerful. But, for scholars such as Diamond and Hartsock, coming from a more radical tradition within feminist theory, these conventional categories are more limiting than empowering. They have long been the pillars of the political and legal theory that excluded women. And, in Sapiro's model, Diamond and Hartsock see the potential for them to once again force important perspectives out of our basic picture of what women are, need, do, and represent.

So what, though? Sapiro's argument that women have a common interest worthy of representation has proven convincing to many scholars. Indeed, as you will see, Sapiro is hardly alone in her conviction that representation and interest should be the foundational categories of political analysis. But, to stop here misses the import of Diamond and Hartsock's intervention. To them, the transformative knowledge produced by feminist scholars is radical not simply because it allows women to move out into the rarefied public world of men. Instead, it must criticize, engage, and celebrate. It should tear at the very fabric of our political culture, creating opportunities for us to reconsider our most simple sense of what is *possible* in politics—or might be. It is this struggle to redefine our nation's basic political vocabulary and to remake the lives of its citizens—not the relatively elitist effort to gain representation in the halls of government—that Diamond and Hartsock ask us to explore. But, as you read, note the many goals—political and scholarly—they share with Sapiro. Their differences run deep, but so, too, does their shared commitment to producing critical, transformative, and *convincing* knowledge about the social and political lives of women.

In "When Are Interests Interesting?" Virginia Sapiro makes a number of stimulating and important arguments. Her article is particularly useful because it both suggests new research directions and serves as an example of the difficulties of approaching the study of women and politics within the conventional categories of political analysis. We disagree with Sapiro on a number of points, but rather than addressing these here, we hope to expand the discussion by focusing on the ways in which Sapiro's arguments illuminate the problems created by attempting to make do with the conventional categories.[1] Recent developments in feminist theory have begun to uncover fundamental weaknesses in the categories of political analysis themselves, thus forcing researchers to move beyond the positions Sapiro has taken.

Sapiro's treatment of women's representation underscores the major problem her article presents: on the one hand, she holds that women are an interest group, but on the other, she states that conflict over the issues raised by including women in politics "tears at the most basic structures and conceptions of society." If women are simply another interest group, however seriously one may take their interests, they remain a special interest group not fundamentally different from others, and in discussing their concerns one need raise no important new political or methodological questions. But if the inclusion of women in politics threatens the most basic structures of society, one cannot fit their concerns into the framework of interests. These inconsistent positions are an inevitable consequence of trying to work within the conventional categories of political analysis. Here we will point to the new directions which research can take if one follows the implications raised by the question of women's political representation.

If women have common interests, as both we and Sapiro believe they do, any attempt to ascertain these interests involves one in the difficult problem of understanding objective social situations and their relevance to political interests. In addition, one must recognize that the different objective situations of the sexes may not necessarily be clearly reflected in women's consciousness of these differences. While Sapiro understands these things, she is vague about which characteristics are most salient and how they relate to women's objective interests.[2]

---

[1]Among our specific points of disagreement with Sapiro are her claim that women have accepted a denial of equality as in their interest, that separatism is best understood as related to self-help and involving self-contained services to other women, that the major goal of the women's movement has more than anything else been to put women in positions of influence, and that women developed as political persons and women's roles became policy questions in the context of the twentieth-century expansion of social welfare. We hold instead that there is a centuries-old tradition of female resistance to inequality, that separatism must be understood as more strategy and philosophy than as delivery of services to other women, that important parts of the women's movement have as their goal the creation of a just society for all human beings rather than the installation of women in powerful positions, and finally, that women's roles have been policy questions in political theorizing at least as far back as Plato's *Republic*.

[2]There are two important difficulties with Sapiro's description of what it means to share common interests. First, her definition of what it means to (objectively) share an interest is so vague that it cannot even differentiate the interests of labor from capital. Second, she fails to address the several important methodological problems presented by the concept of objective interests. An adequate ground for attributing common interests to a group must address issues such as (1) control over the political agenda, (2) latent possibilities for conflict as well as observable conflict, (3) the relation of "real" to subjectively held interests, and (4) the relation of interests and desires to human needs. The attribution of common interests requires an understanding of human nature and social structure which can satisfactorily account for the systematic failure of large groups to perceive and act on politics from which, arguably, they would benefit. Whether or not one finds the Marxian account of political and economic domination persuasive, it does at least meet these formal requirements for an attribution of objective interests.

Instead of a consideration of these issues—all of them presenting complicated problems for research—Sapiro's essay offers a mixed list of factors and social indicators which may be politically relevant, and some references to the few significant differences between women's and men's attitudes as these emerge from public opinion data. The attribution of common concerns to women needs a firmer institutional foundation than this.

If women's issues have been defined by the division of labor in private life, as Sapiro and others have suggested, why not base an account of women's common concerns on a more thoroughgoing analysis of this division of labor? We hold that despite the real differences among women, there are commonalities which grow from women's life activity of producing and sustaining human beings. At the level of grand theory, it may be fruitful to proceed on the basis of the radical-feminist hypothesis that all forms of oppression and domination are modeled on male/female oppression. However, the power relations of race and class which mediate this common female experience remain important for middle-level theory and empirical accounts; failure to take account of them will lead to errors and may even undermine the legitimacy of feminist scholarship.

In schematic and simplified terms, "women's work" occurs in a context characterized by concrete involvement with the necessities of life rather than abstraction from them, a context in which the specific qualities of individuals and objects are central, and in which the unification of mind and body, of mental and manual labor, is inherent in the activities performed. In this context, relations with others take a variety of forms which transcend instrumental cooperation for the attainment of joint ends. Feminist theorists have pointed out that the depth and variety of a woman's relations with others grows both from her socialization as a female human being and from the biological fact of living in a female body. In the face of menstruation, coitus, pregnancy, childbirth, lactation—all challenges to bodily bounds—a female cannot maintain in any simple way the distinction Freud saw as central to human existence—the clear disjunction between me and not-me. And the social circumstance that typically women, but not men, nurture the young has meant that the child's task of differentiating from the mother follows different patterns in each sex; this differentiation reinforces boundary confusion in female egos and boundary strengthening in males. Psychoanalytic evidence suggests that as a result of these early experiences, women tend to define and experience themselves relationally, while men are more likely to form a sense of self as separate and disconnected from the world.

We hypothesize that these different psychic experiences both grow out of and in turn reinforce the sexual division of labor. And different male and female life-activity leads toward profoundly different social understandings. For men, "masculinity" can only be attained by means of opposition to the concrete world of daily life, by escaping from contact with the "female" world of the household into the "masculine" world of public life, and at least in the *polis*, politics. This experience of two worlds—one considered valuable, if largely attainable, the other considered useless and demeaning, if concrete and necessary—organizes what might be termed *phallocentric* social existence. In contrast, women's relationally defined existence, as constructed through the sexual division of labor, results in a social understanding in which dichotomies are less foreign, everyday life is more valued, and a sense of connectedness and continuity with other persons and the natural world is central.

Our argument is that female experience not only inverts that of the male but also forms a basis on which to expose the traditional conceptions of masculine existence and the political community men have constructed as both partial and fundamentally flawed. Throughout Western history the life-activities most important to survival—motherwork, housework, and, until the rise of capitalism, any work necessary to basic subsistence or survival—have been held to be unworthy of those who are fully human.

[* * *]

A systematic examination of the psychic and institutional consequences of the sexual division of labor could provide the necessary base for the attribution of common interests to women. The processes which both create and reinforce the sexual division of labor and translate its psychic and institutional consequences into hierarchical relations of power would need to be specified. Clearly this is no small task. Yet pursuing this line of inquiry becomes even more compelling when one recognizes that while the meanings of "public" and "private" have changed over time, women as a group have remained excluded from public authority. What feminist theorist Mary Daly has labeled "gynephobia" may be inherent in the very construction of state societies in the West.

Attention to the sexual division of labor also calls into question the appropriateness of the language of interests for understanding political life. As [political scientist] Christian Bay has remarked, this language fails to assign priorities to human wants, needs, objectives, and purposes, and in so doing implicitly supports the "right of the strong to prevail in every contest." We should remember that the language of interests emerged along with the changes in the division of labor in production and reflected society's understanding of itself as dominated by rational economic men seeking to maximize their satisfactions. But human beings are moved by more than interests. The reduction of all human emotions to interests and interests to the rational search for gain reduces the human community to an instrumental, arbitrary, and deeply unstable alliance, one which rests on the private desires of isolated individuals. An account of social life such as this is clearly partial: certainly a mother's characteristically nurturing relationship to her child is difficult to describe in terms of instrumental interests in individual gain. Close attention to women's activity rather than men's and the consequent thoroughgoing focus on whole human beings necessitates the development of *more* encompassing categories of analysis for political life.

A focus on the expansion of rights for women leads to similar questions. But here too Sapiro's discussion of the circumstances where political systems have responded to the expansion of the rights previously denied women in comparison with men does not go far enough. By focusing the discussion as she does, Sapiro perpetuates the belief that women are primarily seeking to catch up with men; instead she should address the fact that much of what women want and need is not the same as what men want and need. Reproductive freedom and access to abortion are perhaps the most prominent examples. Perhaps the best way to determine whether a public issue is concerned with advancing the representation of women is to establish whether it merely advocates extending to women rights established for men, or whether the discussion moves into new territory. Our outline of the sexual division of labor points to why issues centering on the reproduction of life cannot be covered by agendas which take account only of the demands appropriate to male individuals.

The problems feminism poses for the conventional understanding of individual rights can, ironically, be found in their shared intellectual roots in the seventeenth and eighteenth centuries: not only has feminism used the theory as far back as the eighteenth century, where feminism was based on the conception of the independent and autonomous self, but also at the same time it has argued for a recognition of women as a sexual class. More recently feminist theory has challenged the use of the rights framework on the issue of abortion and forced sterilization. For example, while liberal, pro-choice activists in the U.S. articulated the need for abortion in terms of rights, recent work argues that the achievements of this struggle have had contradictory impacts, and that failures are partly attributable to the inappropriateness of the language of rights and the problematic nature of communities constructed around rights.

Sapiro's implicit adherence to the language of interests and rights and the assumptions of individualism which this language carries makes her discussion of the conditions that permit women to control the quality of their lives less useful than it might be. Her discussion is both too comprehensive and too narrow, since we are offered a bibliography of explanations at a variety of levels of analysis with no suggestion about their relative importance or interrelationships. Sapiro's unwillingness to focus on the importance of any group, female or otherwise, leads her to ignore the influence of three of the most significant factors that structure social relations—sex, race, and class. This blank in the midst of comprehensiveness grows from her failure to make a clean break with the assumptions of the interest group framework. Though Sapiro clearly holds that the state is not neutral vis-à-vis women, her conceptual tools do not permit her to develop this insight. Where can she put her own recognition of the important ways in which gender differentiation and stratification structure human life? Indeed, her very use of the term "responsiveness" carries with it the hidden and untested assumption that women's demands can be integrated into political systems. Before one accepts this assumption, or the counter-claim of the inherent impenetrability of political life, one must have more precise empirical specification of the dynamics of representation, the tensions which emerge in response to demands, and the contradictions which accompany policy success.

Marxists have long argued that state policy is intimately linked to the social divisions deriving from productive activity. We are suggesting, with Sapiro, that this concept should be expanded to recognize the profound implications of the social divisions deriving from *reproductive* activity. The task at hand is to begin to take seriously the full complexity of state power and state policies. Within ongoing states, the entire policy process—from identifying legitimate needs to implementing specific policies that affect the lives of women—is shaped by a social fabric in which hierarchies based on gender, class and race are heavily intertwined. Empirical work needs to dissect the changing character of these interconnections, and thus we propose more systematic investigations both of the different phases of the policy process and the survival strategies of women of different classes and races. Once issues have been defined and political coalitions have been mobilized, the votes of female and male legislators do not differ substantially. Men seem to be able, in these circumstances, to represent and "act for" women. Our hypothesis, however, is that the ability of men to act for women varies considerably through the different phases of the policy process: only women can "act for" women in identifying "invisible" problems affecting the lives of large numbers of women. At the same time, women's ability to "act for" women must be understood in the context of the survival strategies women have created in response to their powerlessness. Thus, in dealing with policy changes made without the agitation of women, such as the Married Women's Property Acts, one must recognize that this advance was of little material consequence for the survival of the vast majority of women in nineteenth-century America. In contrast, the current attention public officials are giving to the abuse of women in the family is a direct outcome of women's collective action on "invisible" problems. A focus on women's survival strategies which takes account of women's lack of access to resources and information would also be useful for understanding how differences in consciousness among women develop during periods of change, and why women's own actions sometimes conflict with their own welfare and survival. For instance, early pregnancy among black teenage girls lacking job opportunities might be examined as their way of achieving adult status and a sense of self-worth. In a somewhat different vein, women's participation in right-wing political activities concerning the family and sexual issues might be better viewed as efforts to achieve human dignity in the face of change: these women's opposition to the routine assaults on female sexuality in the contemporary news and entertainment media has taken the form of banning sex education in public schools, and their response to the socioeconomic changes undermining survival strategies appropriate to family-based patriarchy has been to attack feminism.

The most fundamental question to be addressed, one which has been only hinted at in our discussion thus far, is the extent to which inclusion of questions regarding reproduction and sexuality may change the political process itself. We believe that taking women's lives seriously would have far-reaching and profound consequences, and that the very concepts of what is political and what is public may be threatened by the inclusion of women's concerns in political life.

From women's perspective, one sees the intimate interconnections between the purportedly separate private and public realms. Yet the origins of Western politics in the Greek city-states provides a forceful reminder of the extent to which politics has been structured by the exclusion of women's concerns. In ancient Greece the public, political world was constructed as an arena in which participants were freed of the constraints of necessary labor, and political power rested on courage in war and courage in speech. Women, slaves, and all the concerns associated with the household and the world of necessity were excluded from the public world. This public world of course in reality depended on and could not have existed without the private world of household production. Yet this dependence was rarely recognized by political thinkers. While the content of the public world has changed, and the formal barriers between the spheres have been removed, the refracted impact of the ancient dualities still structures much of our thinking about politics. That the ancient understanding of the citizen as warrior is still with us is illustrated by the depth of opposition in the United States to authorizing women to serve in combat. Civic personality is not yet separate from military capacity, but the need to re-think the relationship between war and politics is made more urgent by the present technological possibilities for total destruction.

In sum, we are not saying, as Sapiro does, that recent scholarship in women's studies can show that political science has been studying the actions of only half of humanity, and that the subject matter of political science should be expanded. Instead, we are suggesting that the focus on the activity of only half of humanity is fundamental to what has been understood as political life for the last 2500 years. To include women's concerns, to represent women in the public life of our society might well lead to a profound redefinition of the nature of public life itself.

TOWARD CRITICAL THINKING

1. Irene Diamond and Nancy Hartsock argue that their focus on the sexual division of labor allows, among other things, a more careful attention to race and class than are possible with Virginia Sapiro's interest-based approach. Are you convinced? Why, or why not? To what issues does Sapiro's approach allow more careful attention?

2. Diamond and Hartsock conclude their essay with the observation that "to represent women in the public life of our society might well lead to a profound redefinition of the nature of public life itself." How has the nature of public life changed in the decades since this piece was published? How hasn't it changed?

WRAPPING UP

1. Virginia Sapiro's and Irene Diamond's and Nancy Hartsock's primary disagreement is over how we might learn about the content of American women's inherent "interest" vis-à-vis the government—in other words, what do women want, need, or deserve from the state simply by virtue of being women? What interests do you think all women share? Among your responses, are there any interests that might not be shared by lesbians? Women of color? Women who choose not to have children? Poor women? Or older women? If so, can you still think of them as being in "women's interests"?

2. If Diamond and Hartsock are right that the exclusion of women from politics is a central part of our conception of public life and the result of 2500 years of practice and coercion, the pace of recent changes in the status of women across the globe should give us pause as social scientists—however slow they might sometimes seem in coming. What explains this apparent revolution? Or have things changed less than they seem to have?

READING 3

Outgrowing the Compact of the Fathers: Equal Rights, Woman Suffrage, and the United States Constitution, 1820–1878

(1987)

Ellen Carol DuBois

In this essay from a 1987 special issue of the *Journal of American History* on "The Constitution and American Life," Ellen Carol DuBois focuses in on a critical moment in American political history—the end of the Civil War. Before this moment, woman suffrage leaders and abolitionists could see their causes as tightly linked. They had grown from the same organizational roots and both groups worked, after all, for the principle of equality. But, when the war ended and attention turned to the suddenly urgent question of suffrage, the relationship between the two allied movements dramatically collapsed. What happened?

As you will see, DuBois's answer centers on changes within the ideology of the woman suffrage movement—that is, the ideas and concepts that were the suffragists' tools for action. Prominent early woman suffrage and abolition activists spoke of the right to vote as a *natural* right that both women and slaves ought to have simply by virtue of being human. But, after the passage of the Fifteenth Amendment, which enfranchised black men while it left women of every color behind, activists working for woman suffrage understandably felt betrayed. Many of them reversed course. Where they had once waxed philosophical about the natural rights of the citizen, they soon learned to speak instead of the tremendous "degradation" of seeing black men—their supposed social and moral inferiors—elevated above them. Black women, in the meantime, were forgotten in the arguments made by both black men and white women. The result was a women's movement that would never look the same to people of color—of either gender.

[* * *]

The notion of political equality for women was so radical that for a long time it was virtually impossible even to imagine woman suffrage. Within the democratic political tradition, the emphasis on independence as a condition for possession of the suffrage worked to exclude women, who were dependent on men almost by definition. Women had an honored place in early republican thought, but they were never considered men's equals, nor was it regarded as appropriate to demand political rights for them. During the 1820s and 1830s, as popular political passions increased, so did the obstacles to the political inclusion of women. Who besides women could provide the "virtue" needed to protect the republic from the rampant but necessary self-interest of men?

The barrier to the proposition of equal political rights for women was broken within a movement that was not initially political, but within which female activism flourished—abolitionism. . . .

In its first decade, radical abolitionism repudiated the political arena as fundamentally corrupt and the Constitution as inherently proslavery; that hostility to politics helped women's activism to flourish within the movement. But, as [historian] Eric Foner has made clear, abolitionism had eventually to reconcile itself with popular reverence for the Constitution, with the republican political tradition in its radical form. The rise of political abolitionism in the 1840s temporarily increased women's isolation from politics but eventually lessened it. When the American Anti-Slavery Society split in 1839, political abolitionists, largely male, were on one side, and women abolitionists, mostly Garrisonian, were on the other.

Within a decade, however, that seeming impasse had generated the demand for woman suffrage. The woman who articulated the proposition that women should have the same political rights as men had equally strong links to female and to political abolitionism. She was Elizabeth Cady Stanton, protégé of Lucretia Mott, cousin of Gerrit Smith, and wife of Henry B. Stanton. She came to understand that a fundamental change in women's political status was the key to their comprehensive equal rights. Just as her husband was participating in the development of a political and constitutional approach to antislavery, she was inventing a political and constitutional approach to women's rights. In the summer of 1848, while Henry Stanton was organizing the Free Soil party in Buffalo, New York, Elizabeth Cady Stanton called together the first women's rights convention in Seneca Falls.

[* * *]

The demand for political equality could inspire a women's rights movement among women from 1848 on because political democracy was simultaneously a widely held belief and a radical assertion when applied to women. Political equality for women rested on the popular republican tradition that insisted on equal rights for all, with the franchise the crowning jewel of individual freedom. Women's rights advocates could speak of their demands in terms of the "rights, for which our fathers fought, bled, and died," seeking only to claim women's place in the glorious American political experiment. They enjoyed the confidence of appealing to a virtually hegemonic republican tradition. . . .

As the demand for woman suffrage became linked with a widely held republican faith, it also expressed the desire of some women for a radically different position in society than women's traditional one. Woman suffrage carried with it the unmistakable message of women's desire for independence, especially from men within the family. "The Right of Suffrage for Women is, in our opinion, the cornerstone of this enterprise," resolved the 1851 women's rights convention, "since we do not seek to protect woman, but rather to place her in a position to protect herself." . . .

[* * *]

The new focus on political equality did not narrow the scope of the women's rights movement but enlarged it, particularly to include the issue of wives' subordination to their husbands. Ideologically, the women's rights consensus that centered around woman suffrage emboldened egalitarians like Ernestine Rose and Stanton to elaborate the implications of individual rights principles for the family. Women's position in marriage was criticized, in language borrowed from abolitionism, as a violation of the most elementary individual right, the right to control the uses of one's body. Throughout the 1850s Lucy Stone spoke repeatedly against the common law of marriage because it "gives the 'custody' of the wife's person to her husband, so that he has a right to her even against herself." When contracting her own marriage, she protested against all manifestations of coverture by taking the unheard-of step of refusing her husband's name. During the decade legislative gains gave married women rights to their own earnings and property, rights that constituted a fundamental challenge to the economic inequalities of marriage.

Finally, at the Tenth National Woman's Rights Convention in 1860, Stanton made equal rights criticisms of the marriage relation explicit by reintroducing the old Owenite demand for liberalization of divorce laws. What was important about Stanton's resolution was not her vehement indictment of the miserable underside of women's married lives—previous women's movements had targeted domestic violence, and Stanton used those traditions in attacking the "legalized prostitution" of coerced marital intercourse and unwilling maternity. What was new was that Stanton based her indictment of women's position in marriage on the supremacy of individual rights, and on the systematic violation in marriage of "the inalienable right of all to be happy," and that she advocated divorce and remarriage, not resignation, as the solution to women's marital misery. . . .

Participants in the 1860 convention engaged in a heated debate over Stanton's resolutions. . . . The issue at the heart of the 1860 debate—the fact that women are equally at economic risk in and outside marriage—continues to plague feminists today. But even in the mid-nineteenth century, Stanton's equal rights approach established basic principles that Blackwell had to concede, in particular, the principle of a woman's right to self-determination over her own body.

[* * *]

Women's Rights and Universal Suffrage, 1863–1869

In the wake of the Civil War, equal rights was elevated to the level of constitutional principle. . . . The faith in constitutional revision and interpretation among believers in equal rights during Reconstruction was virtually unlimited, for if amending the Constitution could abolish slavery, what could it not do? The women's rights movement, already committed to an egalitarian and political version of individual rights, shared deeply in that reverent, yet activist, attitude toward the Constitution. . . .

Thus in 1863 congressional radicals turned to the women's rights movement for support in passing the first of the Reconstruction amendments, the constitutional abolition of slavery. Women's rights leaders ... were eager to help and organized a campaign of popular support, the first such effort on behalf of a proposed constitutional amendment. They collected over four hundred thousand signatures [and they were given] much of the credit for the ultimate passage of the Thirteenth Amendment.

Once slavery was abolished, the political status of the former slaves became the crucial constitutional question. Black suffrage was the key, both to the freedmen's own future and to the fortunes of the Republican party. Women's rights leaders were determined to take advantage of the constitutional crisis that swirled around black suffrage. In their work on behalf of the Thirteenth Amendment, they took every opportunity to point out that the principle of unconditional emancipation led directly to that of universal enfranchisement. In Stanton's memorable metaphor, the black suffrage issue opened the "constitutional door," and women intended to "avail ourselves of the strong arm and blue uniform of the black soldier to walk in by his side."

[* * *]

The belief that the right to vote was the individual's natural right made the case for woman suffrage much stronger, more self-evident than it had ever been. "In considering the question of suffrage," Stanton declared in 1867, "there are two starting points: one, that this right is a gift of society, in which certain men, having inherited this privilege from some abstract body and abstract place, have now the right to secure it for themselves and their privileged order to the end of time. . . . Ignoring this point of view as untenable and anti-republican, and taking the opposite, that suffrage is a natural right—as necessary to man under government, for the protection of person and property, as are air and motion to life—we hold the talisman . . . to point out the tyranny of every qualification to the free exercise of this sacred right."

Given those premises, it was only necessary to appeal to the natural rights women held in common with all other persons. Rather than argue that women had a special need or capacity for the franchise, women's rights advocates regarded any mention of race or sex as suspect, as a reference to the inferiority of women and Negroes. . . . In the Reconstruction-era approach to women's enfranchisement, race and sex were, in Olympia Brown's words, "two accidents of the body" unworthy of constitutional recognition. "The terms 'male' and 'female' simply designate the physical or animal distinction between the sexes," explained Ernestine Rose, who had always insisted that the distinction of sex was the enemy of women's freedom. "Human beings are men and women, possessed of human faculties and understanding, which we call mind; and mind recognizes no sex, therefore the term 'male,' as applied to human beings—to citizens—ought to be expunged from the constitution and laws as a last remnant of barbarism."

While the Republican party discussed the constitutional disposition of black suffrage, women's rights leaders insisted that the nation be reconstructed not on the basis of special cases designed for "anomalous beings" but on the fundamental principle of universal suffrage. "To bury the black man and the woman in the citizen," they organized the American Equal Rights Association with the goal of incorporating black suffrage and woman suffrage into the overarching demand for universal suffrage.

The Reconstruction-era tendency to regard the difference of sex, and of race, as "incidental" simultaneously advanced and retarded the women's rights movement.

Undoubtedly it lent a certain abstraction to the discussion of women's rights, which can be measured by the paucity of discussion of concrete grievances—sexual, economic, domestic—from women's rights platforms in those years. Yet, the emphasis on the equal rights of all individuals carried with it the militant confidence of absolute principle and the intention to abolish female subordination as totally as slavery.

[* * *]

Given the Republican party's determination to draw the line at black suffrage, however, the political claims of women and of freedmen were increasingly antagonistic. Within reform circles, former allies—Elizabeth Cady Stanton and Wendell Phillips, Susan B. Anthony and Frederick Douglass—divided bitterly over whether to base Reconstruction on black suffrage or on universal suffrage. Each faction staked its claim on different ground. The champions of black suffrage spoke in terms of freedmen's historically specific needs as a group and of the ballot as an instrument for their protection. Douglass's position was that when women were "dragged from their houses and hung upon lamp-posts"—he meant white women—their need for the ballot would be as great as that of the black man.

[* * *]

The failure of the universal suffrage campaign in the face of the political realities of Reconstruction can be read in the language of the Fourteenth Amendment. The amendment included the first reference in the Constitution to the distinction of sex and to the inferiority of women by specifying the number of "male citizens" as the basis of congressional representation. The comparison with the Constitution's three-fifths clause, written eighty years earlier, is obvious. . . .

The Fifteenth Amendment represented a more powerful defense of the freedmen's political rights, but that only underlined the Republicans' refusal to include discrimination by sex with that by race, color, and previous condition of servitude in the constitutional guarantee of political rights. Even Ernestine Rose, an especially strong advocate of equal rights, had to admit at this point that the universal suffrage approach had failed women and that they might do better to find new grounds for their claim for political rights. "Congress has enacted resolutions for the suffrage of men and brothers. They don't speak of the women and sisters," she declared. "I propose to call [our movement] Woman Suffrage; then we shall know what we mean." Women's rights leaders abandoned the American Equal Rights Association and formed a new organization, the National Woman Suffrage Association (NWSA), to assert a new version of their demand.

The impact of the defeat of universal suffrage began to generate new kinds of arguments for women's political rights. Previously the case for suffrage had consistently been put in terms of the individual rights of all persons, regardless of their sex and race. Angered by their exclusion from the Fifteenth Amendment, women's rights advocates began to develop fundamentally different arguments for their cause. They claimed their right to the ballot not as individuals but as a sex. . . .

[* * *]

The argument that women should be enfranchised to bring the "feminine element" into government had a decidedly nationalist edge, which reflected the Fifteenth Amendment's transfer of control over the right of suffrage from the state to the national level. Part of the argument for black suffrage was that enfranchising the freedmen would keep the Republican party in power, thus preserving the victories of the war and strengthening the nation. In arguing that the "feminine element" would elevate national life and "exalt purity, virtue, morality, true religion," woman suffrage partisans were trying to match that nationalist argument and go it one better. Enfranchising the freedmen only promised partisan advantage; enfranchising "woman" would uplift the nation at its very heart, the family. . . .

The new suffrage arguments also contained a strong theme of race antagonism, a reaction to the strategic antagonism between black suffrage and woman suffrage. Whereas the advocates of universal suffrage had claimed comradeship between men of the disfranchised and despised classes and all women, woman suffrage advocates now claimed that the enfranchisement of black men created "an aristocracy of sex" because it elevated all men over all women. Woman suffragists criticized the Fifteenth Amendment because "a *man's* government is worse than a *white* man's government" and because the amendment elevated the "lowest orders of manhood" over "the higher classes of women." The racism of such protests was expressed in hints of sexual violence, in the suggestion that women's disfranchisement would mean their "degradation," "insult," and "humiliation." Those overtly racist arguments reflected white women's special fury that men they considered their inferiors had been enfranchised before them.

[* * *]

By the end of the 1870s, such arguments would dominate woman suffrage ideology. The impact of that ideological change was complex. The demand for woman suffrage, in that it claimed the vote for women as women, permitted the cultivation of sex-consciousness far more than had the equal rights and universal suffrage approach. The call for woman suffrage, therefore, was much more effective in forging women into a group with a common status and with a common demand—a group that would form the popular basis for a women's rights movement. Yet the emphasis on sexual difference steered the women's rights movement away from its egalitarian origins; the movement would ultimately become more compatible with conservative ideas about social hierarchy.

[* * *]

TOWARD CRITICAL THINKING

1. Ellen Carol DuBois shows that women's rights activists historically have been associated with both abolition and white supremacy. What effects, if any, did this dissonance within the women's rights community have on the movement's prospects for success? Do you think that a universalist solution might really have found majority support in a political environment so readily mobilized against the freed slaves?

2. The civil rights activist community still struggles today to heal the divisions sown during this period between activists working to further women's rights and those working against racism. Indeed, the struggles against racism and sexism have sometimes seemed to fit together in a zero-sum game—a situation in which one side can gain only at the expense of the other. But *must* we see the two struggles as a zero-sum game? How else might the future successes in the two struggles be fundamentally related? In what instances have the two causes been advanced together?

READING 4

The Significance of the Nineteenth Amendment: A New Look at Civil Rights, Social Welfare, and Woman Suffrage Alignments in the Progressive Era

(1990)

Eileen Lorenzi McDonagh

Like Ellen Carol DuBois's essay, this article by Eileen Lorenzi McDonagh was published in a special issue on the Constitution, this time in the political science journal *Women & Politics*. Here, McDonagh looks at the ideological and political coalitions that drove the suffrage movement to victory in Congress. As DuBois shows, the activist community pushing for woman suffrage after the Civil War drew strong connections between the cause of suffrage and the racist attitudes that pervaded the day's political scene. But, turning our attention from the activists to the legislators they worked to sway, McDonagh tells a very different story. Her research demonstrates that the members of Congress who voted for woman suffrage were in fact the same legislators behind other civil rights and social welfare initiatives, not the racists voting against them. This pattern suggests that, at least for the legislators involved, support for woman suffrage may indeed have been part of an overarching commitment to continued expansion of rights and justice—hardly the portrait DuBois paints.

How can the same period in American history seem so different from one study to the next? In this case, the difference comes first and foremost from the data the two studies analyze. DuBois was working primarily with historical narratives—letters, publications, and speeches. McDonagh, on the other hand, is analyzing voting data from legislation related to woman suffrage and civil rights for blacks, which allows her to sort out at a highly factual level just what positions went together in the behavior of legislators. Indeed, this kind of attention to empirical data is one of the many strengths of political science relative to other disciplines such as history. But, McDonagh's use of voting data also has its shortcomings. Votes are only recorded as yeas or nays, not with the rich detail and the relatively clear connections among issues that could be drawn by a speech or a pamphlet. As you read this study, think critically about what other strengths and limitations this quantitative approach might have. What questions does it close off for us? And, as in this case, what new ways of answering old questions does it open up?

[* * *]

Woman Suffrage: Issue Connections

Scholarship to date has depicted the woman suffrage issue in a number of conflicting ways. First, there is the important [historian] Aileen Kraditor thesis that argues that at the turn of the century the campaign for women's rights was based almost exclusively on expediency arguments stressing the utilitarian values of admitting women to complete participating status in the polity. Chief among such utilities was the promise that women would bring into the electorate "educated, responsible" female voters who could counterbalance what was assumed to be the threatening, if not destructive, impact of newly enfranchised "uneducated, irresponsible" immigrant and black male voters.

In this interpretation, not only does the expediency argument replace earlier "rights and justice" arguments for woman suffrage, but these utilitarian principles become associated with what can only (distressingly) be labeled as racist arguments for woman suffrage. An example of the rhetoric, if not logic, associated with this view of woman suffrage is captured in the following resolution passed by the National American Woman Suffrage Association (NAWSA) at its convention in Washington, D.C., in 1893:

> *Resolved.* That without expressing any opinion on the proper qualifications for voting, we call attention to the significant facts that in every State there are more women who can read and write than the whole number of illiterate male voters; more white women who can read and write than all negro voters; more American women who can read and write than all foreign voters; so that the enfranchisement of such women would settle the vexed question of rule by illiteracy, whether of homegrown or foreign-born production.

Such arguments about the political power of adding women's vote to the electorate as a way of neutralizing the "unwanted" impact of immigrant and black (male) votes were made even more explicit in appeals to enfranchise women in the South, the one region where woman suffrage barely mustered any support at all. In the words of Belle Kearney in her address to the NAWSA in 1903, "the enfranchisement of women would insure immediate and durable white supremacy, honestly attained, for upon unquestioned authority it is stated that in every southern State but one there are more educated women than all the illiterate voters, white and black, native and foreign, combined." . . .

. . . Kearney's speech was received enthusiastically . . . and the above quotes exemplify why many historians to date have associated the woman suffrage issue with "expediency," if not with racist orientations. However, we will be examining the degree to which such issue connections operated at the level of voting patterns on legislation in the national Congress. Did House members who supported woman suffrage also support such legislation as immigration restriction and denial of black rights? Put another way, can we discern in the congressional roll-call voting patterns support and opposition to the woman suffrage amendment related to such racist orientations?

The focus on utilitarian arguments proffered by some leaders of the woman suffrage movement places the Nineteenth Amendment in the same issue domain as another major legislative battle of the Progressive Era: prohibition. The Eighteenth Amendment, prohibiting the manufacture, sale, transportation, import, and export of all intoxicating liquors, was ratified in 1919 just a little more than a year prior to the ratification of the Nineteenth Amendment enfranchising women. Even more significant than this juxtaposition in time, however, is the long history linking these two pieces of legislation.

At the level of social movement leadership, the earlier temperance campaigns of the nineteenth century provided many women with their first experiences in political organization, which later served them well as the woman suffrage organizations emerged as a distinct and separate concern. The leadership overlap between woman suffrage and temperance organizations bolstered a public perception of a connection between these two issues. The perception was deeply reinforced by liquor interests prophesying that a vote for woman suffrage would be a vote for prohibition. Intensive campaigning by liquor interests to prevent passage of prohibition legislation— and instrumentally, to prevent passage of woman suffrage legislation—produced at the very least a legacy in which there was a perceived connection between these two legislative goals. Furthermore, this connection is affirmed in just about every historical account of these two issues.

However, again our question focuses on the actual voting patterns on prohibition and woman suffrage in the national Congress where legislators are empowered to enact laws. If prohibition and woman suffrage are linked, do we find House members supporting both and opposing both, as historians' accounts would lead us to expect? . . .

The expediency arguments cited above suggest a congruity of woman suffrage, prohibition, and immigration and racial issue positions. In this formulation, the chief value entailed in the enfranchisement of women is the provision of new votes instrumental for social and political control of the behavior of such "undesired" groups as immigrants and blacks. We want to suggest that this formulation, if correct, would involve not only a transformation of woman suffrage, from a civil rights issue in the nineteenth century to an instrumental expediency issue in the twentieth, but also the metamorphosis of woman suffrage from a positive civil rights issue for women to a negative civil rights issue for immigrants and blacks.

If the Kraditor thesis is correct—and that, of course, is the question—we argue here that civil rights and civil liberties principles are intimately involved in so-called expediency and status consistency goals. We argue this because the goal of social control in the case of prohibition, for example, was not one of regulation but rather one of an absolute and universal legal ban on the use of all alcoholic beverages. . . .

The repeal of the Eighteenth Amendment suggests not only the practical failure entailed in its implementation but also the original distortion involved in its formulation. It was not merely a regulatory issue involving "social control" but an infringement of the individual rights and liberties of American citizens. As such, prohibition needs to be classified as a "negative civil rights and civil liberties" issue, and any alignment it might have had with woman suffrage is clearly problematic, not merely from the standpoint of instrumental expediency but also from the standpoint of the heritage of woman suffrage as a civil rights issue in its own right.

Thus the definition of prohibition as a civil rights, civil liberties issue, along with what has been its assumed relationship to woman suffrage, raises some serious questions about the nature of the woman suffrage issue in the Progressive Era. The serious-ness of these questions is only more evident in the context of the racist element involved in expediency logic, as cited above. Did the view that woman suffrage was a means to accomplish "white supremacy" translate into a connection between sup-port for woman suffrage and support for negative civil rights legislation in the national Congress? This question will be examined by analyzing patterns of sup-port for woman suffrage in the House of Representatives in relation to voting pat-terns on such negative civil rights legislation as the prohibition of interracial marriage in the District of Columbia and the ban on all black and African immi-gration. In this way the Kraditor thesis is extended by asking not merely whether woman suffrage had become an expediency issue by 1900 but whether, in fact, clas-sification as an expediency issue in this time period invokes basic civil rights and civil liberties issue positions as well.

Equally important to the above analysis, however, is the attachment of the woman suffrage issue to the innovative social welfare and social justice legislation of its time period. Another potential promise embedded in the rhetoric of suffrage leaders seeking to garner support for enfranchising women was the claim that women would add to the public sphere of politics what researchers today would call the "emotion-work" and "car-ing-work" most often associated with the private sphere of the family. . . .

[* * *]

The importance of women's contribution of this caring, if not maternal, orien-tation to the public sphere was most apparent, perhaps, in regard to legislation designed to restrict child labor. . . . Women's involvement and concern about this issue was one example of how the enfranchising of women was viewed as an impor-tant way of adding to the electorate a huge group of voters who would push for and support such basic social welfare legislation as child labor restriction.

[* * *]

Thus, we see two very different bases for assessing the significance of the woman suffrage issue in the Progressive Era. On the one hand, we interpret expediency argu-ments for woman suffrage legislation as linking it with the attempt to constrict politi-cally the exercise of civil liberties and civil rights of immigrants and blacks. According to our analysis, the social control goals involved in immigration restriction and prohi-bition legislation went beyond mere regulatory concerns. Rather, such legislation embod-ied the negation of basic civil rights and civil liberties of the target groups involved. If woman suffrage is linked as an instrumental means to negate the civil rights and civil liberties of "unwanted" elements in the American political system—and that remains a prime question—then Kraditor's thesis takes on new import. Suffrage becomes not merely an expediency issue by the turn of the century but, rather, an issue dramatically changing from an embodiment of positive civil rights in the nineteenth century to one meant to implement negative civil rights legislation in the twentieth century.

On the other hand, women were viewed during the Progressive Era as the pro-prietors of that special morality of personal, caring relationships associated with the private sphere of the home. At the time in American history when the concept of the welfare state was beginning to be formulated, the entry of women into the political system as voters held special power for catalyzing the processes that began to "make the personal political."

In the midst of these conflicting interpretations, we . . . must remember that the most fundamental fact of the woman suffrage issue was its legislative formulation. . . . [T]he ultimate goal was to get laws passed at the state and national level enfranchising women. That it took great efforts to get the woman suffrage issue on the legislative agenda has been established by much historical scholarship. However, our question here is: What happened at that point when the woman suffrage issue was voted on in the national Congress?

[* * *]

Data Definition

Woman suffrage legislation was first voted on in the House of Representatives in 1915 in the 63rd Congress, where it was soundly defeated by a margin of 204 against to 174 in favor. In the 65th Congress in 1918, it was voted on again, where it passed in the House but was defeated in the Senate. Finally, in the 66th Congress in 1919, the woman suffrage amendment easily passed in the House by a margin of 304 in favor to 90 against, squeaked by a two-thirds majority in the Senate, and survived a cliff-hanging ratification process to become the Nineteenth Amendment to the Constitution on August 26, 1920.

To examine woman suffrage in relation to issues relevant to its interpretation as a "negative civil rights" issue or "social welfare" issue, we will look at roll call voting patterns in the 63rd, 65th, and 66th Congresses. All floor votes on woman suffrage, prohibition, black civil rights, child labor, and general labor issues will be considered. . . . Paired yeas and paired nays are added to the number of yeas and nays respectively cast; those absent or not voting are omitted from analysis. All votes on relevant issues are included if the division supporting and opposing the legislation is at least an 85%–15% split.

Status consistency connections with the woman suffrage issue will be examined by paying particularly close attention to how voting on the Nineteenth Amendment correlated with voting on Prohibition, immigration restriction, and black civil rights issues. The status consistency thesis suggests that the rural, Protestant, nativist American interests would package support for woman suffrage together with support for prohibition, immigration restriction, and restriction of black civil rights. However, if woman suffrage remains connected to civil rights concerns, we should find evidence to the contrary in the associations between these issues areas.

Analysis: Civil Rights and Social Welfare Issues Connections

. . . [Vote data analyzed here present] a striking picture bringing into serious question the validity of the Kraditor thesis. . . . One of the first surprises is the extremely low degree of association between woman suffrage and prohibition. Though these two issues have long been connected in historical accounts, it does not appear that House members voting for woman suffrage were in any way necessarily the same House members who were voting for prohibition. . . .

We also note with interest . . . the lack of consistency among the immigration votes. The first three immigration votes are positively associated with prohibition, but the fourth immigration vote clearly stands apart. This is the proposal to restrict all immigration of blacks and of those of African descent. As indicated above, this categorical racial discrimination, in the face of no economic threat to labor interests, can be evaluated as a civil rights issue rather than an immigration issue per se. Indeed, [the data support] such an interpretation. The fourth immigration vote is positively associated with the three votes on black civil rights (involving the right of interracial marriage in the District of Columbia). Furthermore, we see that this fourth immigration vote and black civil rights legislation are all positively associated with woman suffrage. Most importantly, however, this association is not in the direction predicted by the Kraditor thesis: Those who voted for woman suffrage consistently voted against racist exclusionary immigration legislation.

When we expand this analysis to look at black civil rights issues per se, we find additional supporting evidence: Those who vote for woman suffrage also vote against the effort to outlaw interracial marriage in the District of Columbia. What is more, there is no statistically significant relationship between support for immigration restriction and the woman suffrage issue. . . . Thus, there is no evidence . . . that rhetorical appeals to enfranchise women in order to stave off the inundation of uneducated immigrant voters, much less to ensure white supremacy, had any impact on the voting decisions of House members. . . .

We noted above that the first three immigration votes were positively associated with prohibition. It seems apparent that those who were seeking to control the number and type of immigrants to this country also were those who were more inclined to vote to outlaw all drinking for all inhabitants. This is very much as we would expect, and by comparison it throws into even greater relief the detachment of woman suffrage and other civil rights issues from prohibition and immigration legislation.

The analysis above calls into question the validity of linking the woman suffrage issue with other status consistency issues, and especially with racist orientations. Instead, we see support for considering the woman suffrage issue in terms of social justice concerns that also are reflected in black civil rights voting orientations. Prohibition, on the other hand, is highly associated with voting on immigration restrictions based on characteristics such as literacy, but is not strongly associated with the one immigration issue excluding all blacks, nor with voting on black civil rights. Thus, not only are prohibition and woman suffrage patterns unrelated to each other, they are differentially linked to immigration and black civil rights issues. . . .

[* * *]

When we turn to the issue connections between woman suffrage and social welfare legislation, we see the somewhat complicated patterns that we would expect. . . .

[T]he strongest relationship is between support for woman suffrage and support for child labor restrictions. . . .

When it comes to the welfare of laborers, we see that there is a positive and statistically significant relationship between support for woman suffrage and for the social welfare of laborers. However, the degree of association is not as strong, and it is not difficult to understand why that is the case. American labor interests most often were ambivalent, if not hostile, to the woman suffrage issue. Not only were women typically viewed by labor union leaders as competitors to male labor interests, but woman suffrage was popularly associated with support for prohibition, . . . a policy American labor vehemently opposed. . . .

[* * *]

Conclusion

. . . We find that suffrage does not connect with status consistency issues designed to exert social control—if not restriction of civil rights and civil liberties—in the American political system. Rather, woman suffrage was unconnected to immigration and prohibition legislation and was positively associated with support for black civil rights. This is immensely important to the debate over the "rights and justice" versus "expediency and utility" arguments that characterize suffrage analysis.

In addition, this research leads us to an important recognition: We must begin to differentiate between woman suffrage as a social movement and as a legislative issue. As a social movement, much was said and done on behalf of the suffrage cause, and it remains a problematic debate to distinguish between what suffrage leaders really thought about immigration and racial issues and what they were willing to say in order to win support in the battle to get legislation enacted. Though this in no way excuses what is basically unpardonable racist rhetoric in the suffrage legacy, it nevertheless raises the question whether such sentiments were the result of deeply felt biases or were pragmatic tolls viewed as necessary to pay the price of enfranchisement.

However, when we switch to woman suffrage as a legislative issue, it is not so much the rhetoric of lobbying as the decision-making process itself that becomes the focus of attention. The long-neglected arena of legislative activity is where we can determine not only the partisan, regional, and constituency influences related to suffrage support but also the characteristic alignments between woman suffrage and the civil rights and social welfare legislation also considered throughout the same time period.

When we look at the legislators who voted on suffrage—rather than the activists who lobbied for suffrage—and the relations to voting positions on other issues, we find a pattern of issues connections very different from what has been identified heretofore. We do not find support for connecting suffrage to a status consistency package; rather, we find evidence that suffrage was associated until the very end with issues of rights and justice.

[* * *]

TOWARD CRITICAL THINKING

1. If we are to believe Eileen Lorenzi McDonagh's finding that a general orientation toward civil rights existed among legislators, why do we not see more support for universal civil rights efforts such as the pre–Civil War push for universal suffrage?

2. McDonagh makes a vigorous attempt to discredit historian Aileen Kraditor's "expediency" thesis—and the historical connection between feminism and racism that it suggests. Why do you think that this part of American history has become the ground for such heated debate?

Reading 5

Why We Lost the ERA

(1986)

Jane J. Mansbridge

In this chapter from her book of the same title, Jane J. Mansbridge argues that the failure to secure passage of the Equal Rights Amendment (ERA) to the Constitution resulted in part from the strategies and structure of the pro-ERA movement. Arguing that ERA supporters had little need and even less desire to present the ERA as the relatively humble provision that it was, Mansbridge makes clear the unique set of conditions that led this broadly supported measure to fail once sent to the state legislatures for ratification. In short, many state legislators in what we would now call "swing states" were scared—by supporters and opponents of the ERA alike—into voting against it. Unfounded fears of a sudden military draft for women, integrated bathrooms, and abortion on demand that ERA opponents worked to proliferate were only bolstered by feminists' own conditions that the amendment would redraw the battle lines in the war for gender equality. With state legislators facing increasingly acute electoral pressures from the organized Right and little of concrete importance to be gained or lost from the Left, supporters of the ERA quickly lost momentum.

The somewhat subtler theme to emerge from Mansbridge's analysis, though, is the privileged position that the status quo enjoys in American politics and political culture, and the particular repercussions this phenomenon has for women. In this case, opponents of the ERA were able to overcome an impressive majority coalition behind the amendment by making the changes it would bring seem too lofty, too radical, and too extreme for the pleasantly middle-of-the road American political temperament. Note that ERA opponents did not risk a parallel danger of seeming too conservative for the country. As you ask yourself why this is the case, pay careful attention to Mansbridge's observations about the importance of decision-making structures. While based here on what might seem like the now distant history of the 1970s, Mansbridge's theoretical framework has much to teach us about how to handle—and to analyze—political opportunities for major progressive change today and in the future.

1. Equality of rights under the law shall not be denied or abridged by the United States or by any State on account of sex.

2. The Congress shall have the power to enforce, by appropriate legislation, the provisions of this article.

3. This amendment shall take effect two years after the date of ratification.

—Complete text of the Equal Rights Amendment

In March 1972 the Equal Rights Amendment to the United States Constitution— the ERA—passed the Senate of the United States with a vote of 84 to 8, seventeen votes more than the two-thirds required for constitutional amendments. In the ensuing ten years—from 1972 to 1982—a majority of Americans consistently told interviewers that they favored this amendment to the Constitution. Yet on June 30, 1982, the deadline for ratifying the amendment passed with only thirty-five of the required thirty-eight states having ratified.

How did this happen?

If the ERA had been ratified, the Supreme Court would have been unlikely to use it to bring about major changes in the relations between American men and women, at least in the foreseeable future. Nor did the American public want any significant change in gender roles, whether at work, at home, or in society at large. The groups that fought for the ERA and the groups that fought against it, however, had a stake in believing that the ERA *would* produce these kinds of changes. With both the proponents and the opponents exaggerating the likely effects of the ERA, legislators in wavering states became convinced that the ERA might, in fact, produce important substantive changes—and the necessary votes were lost. Considering the large number of legislative votes required to amend the Constitution, the puzzle is not why the ERA died but why it came so close to passing.

Contrary to widespread belief, public support for the ERA did not increase in the course of the ten-year struggle. In key wavering states where the ERA was most debated, public support actually declined. Much of the support for the Amendment was superficial, because it was based on a support for abstract rights, not for real changes. Many nominal supporters took strong antifeminist positions on other issues, and their support evaporated when the ERA became linked in their minds to feminist positions they rejected.

The irony in all this is that the ERA would have had much less substantive effect than either proponents or opponents claimed. Because the ERA applied only to the government and not to private businesses and corporations, it would have had no noticeable effect, at least in the short run, on the gap between men's and women's wages. Furthermore, during the 1970s, the Supreme Court began to use the Fourteenth Amendment to the Constitution to declare unconstitutional almost all the laws and practices that Congress had intended to make unconstitutional when it passed the ERA in 1972. The exceptions were laws and practices that most Americans approved. Thus, by the late 1970s it was hard to show that the ERA would have made any of the substantive changes that most Americans favored.

While the ERA would have had few immediate, tangible effects, I nonetheless believe that its defeat was a major setback for equality between men and women. Its direct effects would have been slight, but its indirect effects on both judges and legislators would probably have led in the long run to interpretations of existing laws and enactment of new laws that would have benefited women. The lack of immediate benefits did, however, deeply influence the course of the public debate. Because ERA activists had little of an immediate, practical nature to lose if the ERA was defeated, they had little reason to describe it in a way that would make it acceptable to middle-of-the-road legislators. As a consequence, the most influential leaders in the pro-ERA organizations and many of the activists in those organizations chose to interpret the ERA as delivering radical results.

Most proponents contended, for example, that the ERA would require the military to send women draftees into combat on the same basis as men. ERA proponents adopted this position even though it reduced their chances of achieving the short-run goal of passing the ERA and despite the fact that the Court was not likely to interpret the ERA as having this effect. They did so in part because their ideology called for full equality with men, not for equality with exceptions. In a somewhat similar manner, certain feminist lawyers argued in state courts that state ERAs required states to fund medically necessary abortions if they were funding all medically necessary services for men. Such arguments also reduced the chances that legislators in the key unratified states would vote for the federal ERA.

The struggle reveals how impossible it is, even in the most favorable circumstances, to dispense with "ideology" in favor of practical political reasoning when the actors in the drama give their energies voluntarily, without pay or other material incentives. Volunteers always have mixed motives, but most are trying to do good and promote justice. As a result, most would rather lose fighting for a cause they believe in than win fighting for a cause they feel is morally compromised.

Because the ERA offered its supporters no tangible benefits, activists worked hard for it only if they believed strongly in equality for women. They had no reason to "betray" that principle by compromise for compromise offered no concrete benefits, either to them personally or to women generally. ERA opponents took relatively extreme positions for similar reasons. But their "radicalism" cost them less, because they had only to disrupt an emerging consensus, not to produce one.

Refusing to compromise is, of course, often better than winning. It is not the focus on principle rather than practice that should give the reader of this story pause. It is the difficulty both sides had assimilating information about the struggle in which they were engaged. This institutionalized deafness meant that neither the activists nor the general public could make even an informed guess about what passage of the ERA would accomplish. As a result, there was no serious national debate about whether the Amendment was the best way of accomplishing what the proponents sought or whether it really threatened the values that opponents sought to defend. Nor did the proponents, who ran the gamut from feminist lawyers to grass-roots activists, ever engage one another in a wide-ranging discussion of strategy.

The only possible way to have persuaded three more state legislatures to ratify the ERA would have been to insist—correctly—that it would do relatively little in the short run, and to insist equally strongly—and correctly—on the importance of placing the principle in the Constitution to guide the Supreme Court in its long-run evolution of constitutional law. In addition, the pro-ERA movement would have had to develop an ongoing, district-based political network capable of turning generalized public sympathy for reforms that benefit women into political pressure on specific legislators in the marginal unratified states. But even this strategy might not have worked. Comparatively few state legislators were open to persuasion on this issue, and the troops for district-based organizing were often hard to mobilize—or keep mobilized.

The movement away from principle and the increasing focus on substantive effects was probably an inevitable result of the ten-year struggle for the ERA. Inevitable or not, the shift did occur. In the near future, therefore, the only way to convince legislators that the ERA would not have undesirable substantive effects would be to add explicit amendments limiting its application to the military, abortion, and so on. No principled feminist, including myself, favors an ERA that includes such "crippling" amendments. In the present political climate, therefore, the future of the ERA looks even dimmer than its past.

The death of the ERA was, of course, also related to broader changes in American political attitudes. Two of these changes were especially relevant: growing legislative skepticism about the consequences of giving the U.S. Supreme Court authority to review legislation, and the growing organizational power of the new Right.

Suspicion of the Supreme Court, and of the role of lawyers and judges generally, certainly played a significant role in the ERA's demise. For its advocates, the ERA was a device for allowing the Supreme Court to impose the principle of equality between the sexes on recalcitrant state legislators. For legislators, that was precisely the problem. They did not want their actions reviewed, much less reversed, by federal judges whom they did not even appoint. There was a larger problem as well. The ERA embodied a principle, which was supposed to apply, without exception, to specific pieces of legislation. But most people—including most legislators—do not derive their preferences from principles. Instead, they derive their principles from their preferences, endorsing principles they associate with outcomes they like. Because the justices of the Supreme Court of the United States put somewhat more weight than ordinary citizens do on the principles they have evolved from the Constitution, they often find themselves taking controversial or even unpopular stands. As a result, much of the public has come to view the Court as "out of control." Although the Court's unpopular decisions have not yet reduced its power, they took their toll on the ERA. If the primary cause of the ERA's defeat was the fear that it would lead to major changes in the roles of men and women, a major subsidiary cause was legislative backlash against "progressive" Court decisions, starting with the 1954 school desegregation decision. Many state legislators were unwilling to give the Court "new words to play with," rightly fearing that this could eventually have all sorts of unforeseeable consequences they might not like and would not be able to reverse.

The same sense of impotence in the face of national changes that fueled the reaction against the Court also fed the conservative backlash against feminism and the growth of the "new" Right. For many conservative Americans, the personal became political for the first time when questions of family, children, sexual behavior, and women's roles became subjects of political debate. Leaders of the "old" Radical Right, who had traditionally focused on national defense and the Communist menace, became aware of the organizing potential of these "women's" issues only slowly. Once assimilated, however, the "new" issues turned out to have two great organizational virtues. First, they provided a link with fundamentalist churches. The evangelizing culture and the stable geographic base of the fundamentalist churches made them powerful actors in state legislatures once they ventured into the political process. Second, "women's issues" not only gave a focus to the reaction against the changes in child rearing, sexual behavior, divorce, and the use of drugs that had taken place in the 1960s and 1970s, they also mobilized a group, traditional homemakers, that had lost status over the two previous decades and was feeling the psychological effects of the loss. The new women's issues, combined with improvements in computer technology that reduced the cost of processing large numbers of names, made it feasible for the first time to contact by direct mail and thus bring into concerted political activities many who had previously been concerned only with a single issue or not been involved in politics at all.

State legislators were predisposed to oppose a constitutional amendment that gave the federal government power in one of the few areas that was still primarily in the province of the states, namely, family law. The entry of new conservative activists into the political process enhanced this "natural" resistance. As fundamentalist women became more prominent in the opposition, the ERA came to be seen as an issue that pitted women against women and, moreover, women of the Right against women of the Left. Once the ERA lost its aura of benefiting all women and became a partisan issue, it lost its chance of gaining the supermajority required for a constitutional amendment.

There are two lessons to be learned from the story told here. The first is a lesson about the politics of promoting "the common good." We have known for a long time of the extraordinary inequities built into the way different groups can influence legislators in a pluralist democratic system. We have also known that because it is harder to organize for the general interest than for particular interests, the general interest will—all other things being equal—count less in the political process than most people want it to. The story of the ERA struggle reveals a third, less widely recognized, obstacle to promoting the common good. Organizing on behalf of the general interest usually requires volunteers, and mobilizing volunteers often requires an exaggerated, black or white vision of events to justify spending time and money on the cause. Ironically, the greatest cost in organizing for the public interest may be the distortion, in the course of organizing, of that interest itself.

A second, practical lesson follows from the first. While organizations that depend on volunteers to promote the common good seem to have an inherent tendency toward ideological purity and polarized perceptions, they can develop institutions that help correct these tendencies, ranging from small-group techniques through formal systems of representation. Although ongoing organizations are susceptible to the temptations of speaking only to themselves, they are also our main repositories of past experience and our main mechanism for avoiding the endless repetition of past errors. Effectively promoting the common good thus requires that we keep such organizations strong and consistently funded, while at the same time trying to ensure internal dialogue on substantive issues.

TOWARD CRITICAL THINKING

1. As Jane J. Mansbridge notes, federal courts had largely accomplished by means of constitutional *interpretation* what the ERA was designed to accomplish by means of constitutional *amendment*—and have gone still farther today. Given these successes, and setting aside for a moment the very real possibility of judicial retrenchment of those rights, is there any reason to continue pursuing an Equal Rights Amendment? What rights might women still have to gain from an ERA?

2. What commonalities do you perceive between the failure of the ERA and the failure of the universal suffrage amendment as described by Ellen Carol DuBois? What lessons emerge for those who would try to amend the Constitution for feminist ends in the future?

READING 6

Toward Feminist Jurisprudence

(1989)

Catharine A. MacKinnon

This short but sweeping essay is the final chapter in Catherine A. MacKinnon's landmark book *Toward a Feminist Theory of the State*. In only a few pages, MacKinnon builds a biting critique of liberal law, unmasking the ways in which the American judicial system enshrines and reproduces male privilege and power over women. But how?

For MacKinnon, famous as a lawyer but also trained at Yale as a political scientist, the complicated answer to this question begins with the liberal legal system. In this type of system, each citizen is treated as an autonomous and equal subject before the law, who must be treated by the law just as every other citizen is. But, MacKinnon's point—perhaps obvious to those of us who never lived before a feminist movement but hardly so obvious at the time—is precisely that this model cannot be accurate. Liberal political theories have assumed that all citizens were roughly similar before the state became involved in their problems—often by insisting that individuals meet certain gender, racial, economic, and cultural criteria before they could count as "citizens" at all. Just the opposite, MacKinnon starts from the knowledge that no law has heretofore been necessary to allow women to be beaten down, either literally or metaphorically. Rather, the state's studied absence from women's enforced domestic privacy is what has allowed them to be subjected to the very injustices for which women now seek remedy. But, the standards governing what counts as a legal matter, what courts can do, and who has standing to insist that a court do anything at all were, as MacKinnon notes, fully formed while women were less than full citizens. Thus, women face the apparently impossible task of convincing a court (and typically a male judge) that a particular defendant can be held responsible for injuries that have been centuries in the making. The limits this puts on women's legal activism are great, but so, too, is the energy with which MacKinnon rises to the challenge of imagining another way to go about the practice of the law.

A jurisprudence is a theory of the relation between life and law. In life, "woman" and "man" are widely experienced as features of being, not constructs of perception, cultural interventions, or forced identities. Gender, in other words, is lived as ontology, not as epistemology. Law actively participates in this transformation of perspective into being. In liberal regimes, law is a particularly potent source and badge of legitimacy, and site and cloak of force. The force underpins the legitimacy as the legitimacy conceals the force. When life becomes law in such a system, the transformation is both formal and substantive. It reenters life marked by power.

In male supremacist societies, the male standpoint dominates civil society in the form of the objective standard—that standpoint which, because it dominates in the world, does not appear to function as a standpoint at all. Under its aegis, men dominate women and children, three-quarters of the world. Family and kinship rules and sexual mores guarantee reproductive ownership and sexual access and control to men as a group. Hierarchies among men are ordered on the basis of race and class, stratifying women as well. The state incorporates these facts of social power in and as law. Two things happen: law becomes legitimate, and social dominance becomes invisible. Liberal legalism is thus a medium for making male dominance both invisible and legitimate by adopting the male point of view in law at the same time as it enforces that view on society.

Through legal mediation, male dominance is made to seem a feature of life, not a one-sided construct imposed by force for the advantage of a dominant group. To the degree it succeeds ontologically, male dominance does not look epistemological: control over being produces control over consciousness, fusing material conditions with consciousness in a way that is inextricable short of social change. Dominance reified becomes difference. . . . In the liberal state, the rule of law—neutral, abstract, elevated, pervasive—both institutionalizes the power of men over women and institutionalizes power in its male form.

From a feminist perspective, male supremacist jurisprudence erects qualities valued from the male point of view as standards for the proper and actual relation between life and law. . . . Those with power in civil society, not women, design its norms and institutions, which become the status quo. Those with power, not usually women, write constitutions, which become law's highest standards. Those with power in political systems that women did not design and from which women have been excluded write legislation, which sets ruling values. Then, jurisprudentially, judicial review is said to go beyond its proper scope—to delegitimate courts and the rule of law itself—when legal questions are not confined to assessing the formal correspondence between legislation and the constitution, or legislation and social reality, but scrutinize the underlying substance. Lines of precedent fully developed before women were permitted to vote, continued while women were not allowed to learn to read and write, sustained under a reign of sexual terror and abasement and silence and misrepresentation continuing to the present day are considered valid bases for defeating "unprecedented" interpretations or initiatives from women's point of view. Doctrines of standing suggest that because women's deepest injuries are shared in some way by most or all women, no individual woman is differentially injured enough to be able to sue for women's deepest injuries.

Structurally, only when the state has acted can constitutional equality guarantees be invoked. But no law gives men the right to rape women. This has not been necessary, since no rape law has ever seriously undermined the terms of men's entitlement to sexual access to women. No government is, yet, in the pornography business. This has not been necessary, since no man who wants pornography encounters serious trouble getting it, regardless of obscenity laws. No law gives fathers the right to abuse their daughters sexually. This has not been necessary, since no state has ever systematically intervened in their social possession of and access to them. No law gives husbands the right to batter their wives. This has not been necessary, since there is nothing to stop them. No law silences women. This has not been necessary, for women are previously silenced in society—by sexual abuse, by not being heard, by not being believed, by poverty, by illiteracy, by a language that provides only unspeakable vocabulary for their most formative traumas, by a publishing industry that virtually guarantees that if they ever find a voice it leaves no trace in the world. No law takes away women's privacy. Most women do not have any to take, and no law gives them what they do not already have. No law guarantees that women will forever remain the social unequals of men. This is not necessary, because the law guaranteeing sex equality requires, in an unequal society, that before one can be equal legally, one must be equal socially. So long as power enforced by law reflects and corresponds—in form and in substance—to power enforced by men over women in society, law is objective, appears principled, becomes just the way things are. So long as men dominate women effectively enough in society without the support of positive law, nothing constitutional can be done about it. . . .

[* * *]

Equality will require change, not reflection—a new jurisprudence, a new relation between life and law. Law that does not dominate life is as difficult to envision as a society in which men do not dominate women, and for the same reasons. To the extent feminist law embodies women's point of view, it will be said that its law is not neutral. But existing law is not neutral. It will be said that it undermines the legitimacy of the legal system. But the legitimacy of existing law is based on force at women's expense. Women have never consented to its rule—suggesting that the system's legitimacy needs repair that women are in a position to provide. It will be said that feminist law is special pleading for a particular group and one cannot start that or where will it end. But existing law is already special pleading for a particular group, where it has ended. The question is not where it will stop, but whether it will start for any group but the dominant one. It will be said that feminist law cannot win and will not work. But this is premature. Its possibilities cannot be assessed in the abstract but must engage the world. A feminist theory of the state has barely been imagined; systematically, it has never been tried.

TOWARD CRITICAL THINKING

1. Catharine A. MacKinnon frequently repeats that male supremacy succeeds epistemologically—that is, through the manipulation of knowledge—by seeming to be an ontological truth—that is, an essential feature of being and no mere construct. The argument can be difficult to follow for those unaccustomed to legal jargon, but it boils down to this: does hiding the socially constructed nature of gender reinforce male supremacy? Do you agree or disagree? Why or why not?

2. MacKinnon argues that many forms of oppression that violate the principle of sex equality in the Constitution's equal protection clause are supported by tradition and social power, not specific positive actions of the state. Historically, though, the reach of *courts* has been limited to the judgment of just such positive actions, while *legislatures* have been charged with identifying policy problems and crafting the government's response to them. Why, then, does MacKinnon seem to prefer judicial remedies? In your view, is she correct?

WRAPPING UP

1. In her conclusion, Eileen Lorenzi McDonagh argues for a theoretical distinction between woman suffrage as a legislative issue and woman suffrage as a social movement. Do you think that this distinction would clarify the issue, or do you think that separating the two might lead to further confusion? What do you suppose Ellen Carol DuBois or Jane J. Mansbridge would think of McDonagh's argument?

2. If one thing is clear after reading Catharine A. MacKinnon's piece, it is that structural change in the way law is practiced is necessary to achieve the true emancipation of women. Are these the same kinds of changes for which the suffragists and the ERA activists fought? If MacKinnon could rewrite the Nineteenth Amendment and the proposed ERA, how would those texts be reworded?

READING 7

Women as Political Animals?
A Test of Some Explanations
for Male-Female Political
Participation Differences

(1977)

Susan Welch

In this article published in the *American Journal of Political Science,* Susan Welch looks at three common arguments about why women participate in politics at lower rates than do men— although you will see that her findings challenge even that basic assertion. Welch settles the various arguments about participation differences between men and women into three basic classes of explanations. The socialization explanation focuses on the differing ways in which women and men are raised to think of politics and of their role as citizens. The situational explanation, on the other hand, looks at the time constraints faced by women, imagining that a nation of dutiful wives must decide whether or not to join a campaign while surrounded by their crying children and challenged by the difficulties of keeping house for their husbands. Finally, the structural explanation looks at the socioeconomic positions that women tend to occupy. Because historically women have been less educated and less likely to work outside the home than men, it seemed reasonable to suggest that women might simply be predisposed by the structure of the society to participate less in a range of political activities.

Using data from a major study regularly repeated by political scientists—here called the Survey Research Center (SRC) study but now better known as the National Election Studies (NES)—Welch comes to some surprising conclusions about women's political participation. She uses political science methods to reverse the common wisdom about political participation just as Eileen Lorenzi McDonagh (Reading 4) revised her colleagues' opinions about the Reconstruction–era suffrage movement.

An Overtime Comparison of Female and Male Political Participation

While current evaluations of sex differences in American political participation are contradictory, the dominant finding over the years has been that women participate less in political activities than do men. While these differences have been reasonably consistent, though in many cases small, explanations for the differences have been untested to a surprising extent. Two explanations have been prominent: first, that women are socialized into a more politically passive role than men; second, that women have special family responsibilities that prevent their full participation in politics. A third and less frequently explicit explanation is sometimes offered. This structural explanation contends that women are less likely to be found in those sectors of society with structural characteristics that enhance political participation: particularly highly educated parts of the community. These three explanations will be referred to as the political socialization, the situational, and the structural explanations, respectively. These explanations are neither contradictory nor mutually exclusive. All might be working together, or the situational variables may contribute to and perpetuate the distinct political socialization patterns. Further, socialization patterns that have nothing to do with politics directly may influence the educational or occupational choices of females and thus contribute to the sex differences in these categories which then allow for the structural explanation. Despite this, these explanations seem conceptually distinct and would have different policy implications if similarity in male-female participation is a desired end. . . .

[* * *]

An Overview of Past Research

Political Socialization

The stereotype of the politically passive woman has persisted despite the fact that participation of women has never been found to be much less than that of men; early voting studies found about a ten percent difference, and when education was controlled, even those differences decreased. The interpretation placed upon the slightly lower rates of participation by women has frequently been a psychological one. [Hence,] the political socialization explanation [concludes] that the relative nonparticipation of women does not, in general, stem from restrictions imposed on women. It results in large part from a set of norms that women hold that they should not participate as much as men, that politics is a man's game. . . .

[* * *]

The Situational Explanation

. . . The situational explanation argues that traditionally women have been kept busy within the home taking care of husband and children. They have little time to participate fully in politics, as this would involve being away from home and neglecting their familial responsibilities. Furthermore, by not working outside the home, a woman has less opportunity to become interested in politics, to expose herself to political argument and discussion, and so forth. Thus, this argument hypothesizes that it is the presence of children and the absence of an outside the home work role that inhibits women's political participation.

[* * *]

The Structural Explanation

There have been many partial tests of the structural explanation[, showing] that controlling for education removes some of the differences between male and female voting participation rates; among the highly educated, few differences remained. . . .

[* * *]

Hypotheses, Data, and Methods

Our analysis of comparative male-female participation will explore, for a variety of political acts, three alternative conditions, or hypotheses.

[* * *]

1. Male and female participation are essentially similar. This condition would of course support the structural hypothesis. If it is true, then male-female discrepancies are due to the different distribution of males and females throughout age, regional, income, and education categories.

2. Male participation is higher than that of females, but when situational factors are controlled, male-female rates become similar. The existence of this condition supports the situational explanation: that family ties and home-boundedness limit female political participation.

3. Male participation is consistently higher than that of women, even controlling for situational factors. The existence of this condition would give support to a socialization explanation, through it does not prove it directly or suggest how this socialization is done, since the childhood results have been so minimal.

[* * *]

Data and Methods

The basis for our analysis will be three SRC election studies: 1952, 1964, and 1972. These three were chosen in order to examine changes over time. They are relatively evenly spaced over the twenty-year period, and they reflect elections with Democratic and Republican victors. Thirteen forms of political participation are examined.

Five deal with attention to and interest in political campaigns. The other eight are voting and campaign acts that a respondent could perform: registering to vote, voting, trying to influence others, writing a public official, giving money, going to a political meeting, working for a party or committee, belonging to a political club. . . .

Findings

[* * *]

The Structural Explanation

. . . Males were more likely than females to try to influence others to vote a certain way, to follow campaign activities on the radio, and to express a high or moderate interest in the election campaign. Women, on the other hand, are significantly more likely than men to belong to a political club. Other forms of activities display only slight differences between males and females.

Controlling for the structural variables does reduce male-female participation differences in most, if not all instances. The reductions, however, are generally small; this is not surprising since the original differences in most cases were also small.

In only a few cases do structural factors eradicate male-female participation differences, though in most cases they reduce the differences to statistical insignificance. . . .

In sum, structural factors are important in explaining male-female participation differences, but do not account for the entire difference.

The Situational Explanation

[* * *]

. . . [W]hen situational and structural characteristics are accounted for, by 1972 females participate more than males in 6 of the 8 activities, while slightly lagging behind males in 5 of 6 forms of attention to the campaign. The one activity where men participate significantly more than women is an interesting one: whether the individual has tried to influence another person's vote. In this one particular case, it does appear that women are indeed more politically passive than men, in that they are not as aggressive as men in trying to influence another person's vote. It could be of course, that they simply do not perceive and/or report themselves as trying to influence votes as often as do men, but that is a measurement problem beyond the scope of this paper. Those 2 activities where women participate more than men are equally interesting. Women more often belong to political clubs and do party work than do men. This finding should not be surprising, in that observers have often noted that women seem to be the backbone of many political campaigns, even though they are not found in the leadership positions.

The impact of situational factors was also assessed separately for each sex. The predominant pattern is that the situational factors of marriage and children (controlling for the structural variables) generally affect male and female participation in the same way. Marriage, in general, has a slight or negligible effect on participation in most forms of political activity. Where it does have effects, they are the same for both sexes. In only one instance does marriage seem to have contradictory effects. It slightly improves the likelihood of females writing letters to public officials, but slightly decreases the likelihood of males doing so. In no case does marriage produce a statistically significant increase in the participation of one sex and a statistically significant decrease in the other.

The presence of children in the home has even less effect on participation than does marriage. Again, most of the minimal effects have a similar impact on both men and women. The presence of children did diminish the propensity to vote by men in 1972, but had no effect on women in that year or on people of either sex in previous years. In 1964, women with children were significantly less likely to follow the campaign on radio and TV than those without children, but in 1972 the effect on these variables of having children was similar for males and females.

Contrary to the effects of marriage and children, the third situational factor, work outside the home, produces a dramatic increase in female voting and on other forms of activity. The positive effect on participation of employment outside the home has increased over time. The effect was not as great in 1964, and in 1952, working actually diminished female participation slightly. The effect of employment on males, on the other hand, was small and insignificant. In 1964 and 1972, employment by males decreased their attention to the campaign, though it did not impede voting or other activities.

Two explanations seem plausible for the differential effect of employment on males and females. First, the woman who goes to work outside the household may be a more adventurous, self-confident person than one who stays at home, and this self-confidence could carry over into the political arena; or, conversely, the work experience itself may produce confidence which transmits itself into increased political efficacy. For males, there may not be such a pronounced self-selection process. Second, it may be that for most males, unemployment is a temporary condition, such as short-term loss of work, or a relatively new condition, such as retirement. Under these conditions, patterns of behavior learned while working may simply carry over to the unemployed stage. The unemployed woman, however, is almost always a housewife; a status that may provide a long-term set of behavior and attitudinal patterns. . . .

[* * *]

In the employed category, college educated women participate more than college educated men in most activities. Exceptions include trying to influence the vote of someone else, and three of the spectator activities. Among employed high school graduates, women tend both to follow the media and participate in the campaign acts slightly more than males, though the differences are minute. The less educated employed males and females participate fairly equally in most activities.

The pattern among the unemployed group is more mixed. Part of the problem in interpretation is that in all cases the number of unemployed high school educated males is less than 50, and in some cases the number of unemployed college educated males is also less than 50. Despite this, some tentative conclusions can be drawn. Among the college educated, participation by the jobless of both sexes is almost as great as their employed counterparts. The unemployed high school graduates vote less than their employed counterparts, but in other types of participation they do not lag far behind (and in some cases exceed) those who are employed. Females among this group exceed male participation in 7 activities, and males exceed in 6. The females participate more than males in voting and campaign acts, where males are generally more active in 16 spectator activities. . . .

Discussion

Our analysis has shown that the stereotype of the politically passive woman simply is untrue. . . . Women participate in the aggregate less than men not because of some belief that they hold about the role of women in politics, but largely because they are less likely to be found in those categories of people who participate in politics: the employed and highly educated in particular. . . .

We did not directly deal with the validity of the socialization explanation. However, by showing that males and females are little different in their participation as adults, the socialization explanation becomes rather irrelevant, except for the one category of adults where women do continue to participate less than men. Even in 1952, the overall participation differences between males and females were very small in most activities, leading one to question whether the socialization explanation was valid even then.

Viewing the 13 activities categorized as "voting," campaigning, and spectator acts, we again see little to support the socialization explanation. Women may lag slightly behind in spectator or passive activities, but they are equals in voting and campaigning roles. The socialization explanation would certainly not predict this outcome. Why many political scientists favor the childhood political socialization explanation as a reason for so much of adult political behavior is unclear.

[* * *]

TOWARD CRITICAL THINKING

1. If the differences between men and women in political participation can be almost entirely explained by structural and situational variables, what role remains for political socialization? It seems counterintuitive—even just wrong—to conclude that the way women are raised to think of their "proper roles" has no consequences for such a nontraditional activity for women as participating in politics, but that is where Susan Welch's findings seem to point us. Has she taken some wrong turn?

2. Welch leaves out of her analysis a number of important factors, including (as she notes in a passage omitted from this selection) overt discrimination. Why do you think this is? Is the term perhaps too vague, considering that it could potentially bring structural, situational, and socialization explanations under one umbrella? How could you rise above this challenge to research the role overt discrimination has played in depressing women's political participation?

READING 8

A New Women's Movement Emerges

(1992)

Anne N. Costain

Around the time that Susan Welch (Reading 7) and other scholars began to struggle with the differences between men's and women's political participation, the twentieth-century women's movement began in earnest. No similar structure—at once ideological, social, cultural, therapeutic, and political—existed to mobilize men around issues of personal-turned-political import, suggesting that comparisons of the kind Welch sought might simply miss the distinctiveness of women's collective struggle altogether. Instead, Anne N. Costain and other women's movement scholars have opened up the possibility that there is something historically specific about this kind of activism, that the movement politics of the 1960s and 1970s gave some women the kinds of opportunities and goals that would make the comparison of their activities with men's inappropriate.

In this piece from Costain's book *Inviting Women's Rebellion,* her particular focus is the role played by mobilizing organizations within the women's movement as a mediator between men and women in the government and feminists at the grass roots. These organizations are a critical piece in the participation puzzle: they brought new participants into politics, structured the way they behaved politically, and coordinated their efforts even at a mass level. They helped build the connections between women and "high politics" that made change appear possible, as well as the connections among activist women and feminists inside the government that were needed for change actually to occur. Costain argues that the scholarly analysis of the movement—and its internal politics—will have to be integrated into our theories to make sense of women's political participation, both in the past and the present.

After receiving substantial assistance from political institutions in the early sixties, by the mid-sixties, women's groups were ready to seize the initiative in organizing a new movement. By starting NOW in 1966 to increase and focus public pressure on government to change its policies toward women, feminists began the process of bringing together traditional women's groups and newer movement groups. The founding of NOW has been recognized as a seminal event in the development of the contemporary women's movement, but its equally important role of reconciling diverse groups with widely divergent objectives and members has not been emphasized sufficiently. NOW played a bridging role between the more radical new "liberation" groups springing up on the left and the more conservative, traditional women's groups, which were in the process of rediscovering feminism.

New Organizational Strength

NOW's founding was both carefully planned and somewhat spontaneous. Betty Friedan, whose widely read book *The Feminine Mystique* first alerted many women to their collective discontent, was actively recruited to take steps to organize a group representing women and their interests. Richard Graham and Sonia Pressman of the EEOC, Mary Eastwood of the Justice Department, and Catherine East of the Citizens' Advisory Council on the Status of Women, wanted Friedan to form a group to bring pressure on government to listen to women's concerns about public policy. In addition to these government-linked activists, Friedan's mail was filled with pleas from the general public to do something concrete. Many people felt that the barriers keeping women from full participation in society needed to be challenged and that Friedan was an ideal person to organize this challenge.

[* * *]

The decisive moment came when Catherine East invited Friedan to attend the Third Conference of the Commissions on the Status of Women in Washington. . . . It had become clear to them that the government was unwilling to allow commissions that it created and controlled to be used to apply pressure on other parts of the government.

By the end of the conference, Friedan headed a twenty-eight member organization called the National Organization for Women (NOW). Despite the founding members' disappointment with the conference, they were careful to deny even "implied criticism of any existing group or conference, but rather a realization of the limitations of various organizations." NOW members also took pains, initially, not to go further in their stated goals than the recommendations of the Presidential Commission on the Status of Women. In its first year, NOW neither endorsed the ERA nor supported loosening restrictions on abortion. What NOW did was apply pressure on the executive branch of government. Within hours of NOW's founding, its leaders had sent telegrams urging the reappointment of Graham to the EEOC, mailed letters asking the EEOC to rescind its directive on "help wanted" listings in the newspaper, which allowed private employers to specify "male" or "female" positions, and contacted House and Senate offices supporting legislation mandating equal federal jury service for women and men.

Despite meetings throughout this first year with high government officials, . . . concrete accomplishments were relatively modest. . . .

Dissatisfaction was apparent at the second national conference of NOW, held in November 1967. Members passed a NOW Bill of Rights, which for the first time endorsed both a woman's right to have an abortion and the passage of the ERA. They had now moved substantially beyond the more cautious recommendations of the presidential commission. The immediate impact of these actions was fragmentation within NOW, as many labor-union women left the group over its stand on the ERA, which organized labor continued to oppose. Politically conservative NOW members quit after the conference because of NOW's endorsement of abortion. These desertions allowed NOW to move to the left politically, bringing it closer to the women's liberation groups that were forming across the United States in the late sixties.

Friedan's priorities for NOW are clear from a 22 September, 1969 memorandum to NOW board members and chapter presidents. Friedan warned them that those under 40 years old would be more central to NOW's future development than would those over 40. Consequently, she urged that they take care to bring young people into the organization's leadership. She also cautioned that the current leaders of NOW should pay more attention to those who criticized NOW for not doing enough rather than to those who complained that it was doing too much.

Despite NOW's move to the left and its vision of attracting younger (and often more radical) movement adherents, it suffered a further schism in 1968 as Ti-Grace Atkinson, president of the New York City chapter of NOW, resigned along with several other NOW members over what they saw as the hierarchical, undemocratic character of the organization. Atkinson organized the women's liberation group, "The October 17th Movement," later called "The Feminists."

After its second national conference, NOW not only adopted a more radical agenda of issues, but its tactics became less conventional. In 1967, members of NOW started picketing EEOC offices throughout the United States to pressure the commission to stop sanctioning sex-segregated want ads. In 1968, NOW sponsored a number of protest actions, including a week of sit-ins, picketing, and demonstrations against male-only public accommodations, a "Fast to Free Women from Poverty Day" on May 18, and—to protest religious bias against women—a "national unveiling," burning veils that women wore to church. The year 1969 was unofficially dubbed "the year of protest" for NOW. The week before Mother's Day was designated "Freedom for Women Week." A Washington march sponsored by NOW was the largest demonstration for women's rights in America since the early 1900s. NOW members met in front of the White House "to dramatize—with chains, aprons and a skit by the New Feminist Theater—that women are bound to the home and to the lowest rung jobs, as well as second class status."

During the late sixties, NOW members sometimes joined with members of liberation groups like the Society to Cut Up Men (SCUM) to stage protest events. The periodical press in this period covered the women's movement more for its sensationalist value than its political significance. Consequently, magazine articles in the late sixties focused on the more extreme liberation groups rather than on the more moderate organizations such as NOW. . . .

[* * *]

The leadership of NOW was sufficiently alarmed at being identified with some of these more radical groups for the board of directors of NOW, who met in December 1968, to lay down "Guidelines on Public Relations" that forbade anyone speaking for NOW to offer an opinion on any issue that was not already official NOW policy if there was "any chance that it would be controversial."

NOW's more extensive organizational base, with a national membership of over four thousand by 1970, attracted women from many of the liberation groups. These new and predominantly young members brought new issues, such as lesbianism, to

NOW, along with enthusiasm for unconventional political activities, which expanded the repertoire of tactics within NOW.

At the same time, more conservative groups became more accepting of both the agenda and tactics of NOW. Among these groups was WEAL, formed in 1968 after its founder Elizabeth Boyer left NOW in protest over its support for abortion rights. As NOW was increasingly willing to join with younger, more radical women in protest, WEAL tried to preserve NOW's earlier tradition of applying conventional pressure for change. . . .

[* * *]

WEAL became involved in litigation in the late 1960s and early 1970s, trying to force government agencies, including the Departments of Labor and Health, Education and Welfare, to begin monitoring laws prohibiting sex discrimination. Its most striking successes were a series of legal challenges to universities' hiring, promotion, and termination practices based on President Johnson's executive order that prohibited sex discrimination by federal contractors.

By the early 1970s, WEAL, a holdout in adopting disorderly tactics, had also changed. In 1970, Boyer had told the press, "We do not picket or chain ourselves to the White House gates. . . . And we are not a clutch of people getting together for group therapy." Boyer sent a letter in March 1971 assuring members that "we are not oriented to demonstrations nor to flamboyant publicity tactics." But by 1973, WEAL had reversed its stand on abortion, now supporting it, and had become more tolerant of protest. . . . By 1973, consciousness raising, borrowed from liberation groups, had become an accepted activity within WEAL. . . .

New York Times coverage of the women's movement in the late sixties and early seventies gives hints of this convergence among movement groups. . . . Women's groups seem to have agreed that unity was the key to bringing about social change.

While the increased acceptance of consciousness raising and public protest moved the separate wings of the women's movement closer, the start of coordinated lobbying in Washington by women's movement groups, such as NOW, the National Women's Political Caucus (NWPC), and WEAL, solidified cooperation with traditional women's groups. Serious efforts to establish an ongoing, well-organized lobby to pressure Congress and the executive branch on behalf of women's concerns did not begin in earnest until 1972. Members of women's groups had to see concrete legislative benefits coming out of Congress such as Title IX of the Education Amendments Act of 1972, which barred discrimination based on gender in federally funded education programs, and the ERA before they were willing to commit the resources and take the risks inherent in participating in coordinated Washington lobbying.

Lobbying creates a need for groups to accept common strategies to achieve legislative objectives. Since movement groups attracted individuals whose primary commitment was to feminism and ending the oppression of women, the compromises necessary to accomplish purely legislative ends seemed to many of their members like selling out. Further, the women's movement had, historically and in the early 1970s, experienced serious factionalism, ranging from the decades-long controversy over the ERA to recent splits precipitated by the abortion issue. As evidence that the groups' fears were not without foundation, when NOW and NWPC opened Washington legislative offices in 1973, both groups became ensnarled in internal dissent, ranging from dues protests to leadership struggles.

Despite the problems these controversies created for the expansion of lobbying activity in both groups in the early 1970s, a structure of cooperative effort to foster women's interests was established that linked older organizations such as the National Federation of Business and Professional Women's Clubs and the American Association of University Women to the newer groups. In interviews conducted in 1974–75 with lobbyists and officers from many of the women's groups active in Washington, it was evident that the older organizations played a major role in helping the newer women's movement groups organize to start lobbying. The League of Women Voters (the League) held training sessions for lobbyists from NOW and the NWPC. The American Association of University Women and the National Federation of Business and Professional Women's Clubs shared information with women's movement groups about people to contact on Capitol Hill. . . .

However, the representatives of many of these traditional groups reported that working on women's rights had a very beneficial effect on their members. . . .

The newer movement groups experienced more conflict within their organizations than did the older groups. Internal disagreement in NOW and the NWPC over the amount of national legislative work they should undertake limited NOW and the NWPC's ability to work with other women's groups that were lobbying Congress. Many of their members felt that the application of pressure in states and communities was more effective than national lobbying. Still others believed that protest would gain more attention than lobbying.

Conflict between women's groups erupted occasionally as each competed with the others for the membership of committed feminists. When one organization seemed to be less effective than another, it feared loss of members to other groups. By contrast, such traditional organizations as the League and the American Association of University Women were able to attract women from the younger generation through their successful lobbying on feminist issues—women who, otherwise, would have likely not joined either the League or the American Association of University Women or the more strident movement-oriented groups.

In summary, by the early 1970s, there was a marked convergence of women's groups from the left, right, and center of the political spectrum. Organizationally this meant that significant resources were now available to mount an effective challenge to the status quo. Most of these resources were drawn from traditional women's organizations. The League, United Methodist Women, the National Woman's Party (the original drafters of the ERA), the American Association of University Women, and the National Federation of Business and Professional Women were among the established women's groups that contributed significant resources to ERA ratification efforts. The spectrum of women's movement groups, ranging from liberation groups such as WITCH and The Feminists to "conservative" movement groups like WEAL, brought new recruits and fresh ideas to the feminist cause. Although nonfeminist groups, including Common Cause, the American Civil Liberties Union, and the National Education Association, also materially aided women's efforts to achieve legal change, their assistance, although beneficial, was not crucial to the movement. Protest, consciousness raising, and ongoing Washington lobbying were all a part of the organizational repertoire of the movement in the early seventies. The structure of political opportunity within this period, while favorable on balance, was more mixed than in the early sixties, with a blend of government facilitation and tentative efforts at repression.

[* * *]

Psychological Change

Available evidence suggests that there was a dramatic increase in egalitarian attitudes towards women in the early 1970s, just as women's organizations began to take the initiative in pushing for change in public policy on gender. The longest across-time measure of prejudice toward women is a question that has been repeated periodically since 1937: Were individuals willing to vote for a qualified woman for president? As [Myra Marx] Ferree (Reading 40) argued persuasively, this question probably tells less about people's likely behavior, if given the opportunity to vote for a woman president, than about their willingness openly to express prejudice toward women. It is also at least a rough indicator of their degree of discomfort with the idea of women playing a serious political role.

After twenty years (between 1949 and 1969) in which there was little change in public attitudes toward voting for a woman president (roughly 55 percent of the population would), suddenly, between 1969 and 1971, women's willingness to vote for a woman for president jumped a full 18 percentage points, from 49-percent approval in 1969 to 67-percent approval in 1971. Men's approval in this period increased from 58 percent in 1969 to 65 percent in 1971.

The abruptness of this change has been variously attributed to the rise of a women's movement and to increasing public awareness of the egalitarian legislation Congress passed in the mid-1960s, including the Equal Pay Act of 1963 and the Civil Rights Act of 1964. Both events are presumed to have made prejudice against women less socially acceptable. This new tolerance of a greater political role for women can itself be viewed as creating the preconditions for further growth in the women's movement. As women revised their earlier view that they were not suited to play a strong political role because of their sex, they began to develop the type of political consciousness that allowed them to work for change in their own situation.

During this same period, more women were both entering the work force and changing their attitudes about the suitability of married women working. In 1960, 38 percent of adult women were in the labor force. By 1970, this figure had risen to 43 percent. By 1980, the figure was 52 percent. As [political scientist] Burstein noted, the available evidence indicates that public opinion on this issue changed rapidly starting in the late 1960s. Between 1946 and 1969, popular approval of married women working increased at a rate of just 0.7 percent per year. From 1969 to 1975, this rate of increase more than doubled to a 1.9 percent rise in public approval.

Women's lives were in the process of changing from their previous narrow focus on home and family, as more entered the work force. Their opinions were also being transformed as they became more likely to approve of wider political and employment roles for women. These changes began to be reflected in the growing recognition among women that they faced discrimination because of their sex. In 1970, 54 percent of women felt that women of equal ability to men have less chance of becoming corporate executives, 50 percent believed that they faced discrimination in attaining executive-level jobs in business, and 40 percent expressed the view that there was discrimination against women in the professions. As attitudes toward sex roles became more egalitarian and awareness of discrimination grew more pervasive, the stage was set both for the women's movement to grow in size, as new recruits were added to its ranks, and for government to respond to an increasingly public and popular issue.

[* * *]

TOWARD CRITICAL THINKING

1. The National Organization for Women (NOW) was attacked both from within and without as too conservative and as too radical. At the time Anne N. Costain discusses, its perceived middle position in the women's community helped NOW find its niche as a coordinator for many of its sister organizations. Today, though, these attacks are more often than not followed up with accusations of irrelevance. What has changed? Why might NOW no longer be able to command the audience and support it once did? Think back to the questions raised in Chapter 1 about the theoretical possibility of a singular "women's interest."

2. The women's movement and other political movements of the 1960s and 1970s changed our notion of what it means to participate in politics. How have our definitions of political participation changed over time?

READING 9

Gender and the Pathways to Participation: The Role of Resources

(1994)

Kay Lehman Schlozman, Nancy Burns,
and Sidney Verba

In this article published in the *Journal of Politics,* Kay Lehman Schlozman, Nancy Burns, and Sidney Verba take the opportunity to examine gender differences in the same way that Susan Welch (Reading 7) did. Through the analysis of mass public survey data, with attention to the potentially deficient assumptions that had guided the earlier empirical research, they expand the working definition of what counts as political participation. Here they include community and church organizing, sectors of community activism in which women historically have been prominent. This type of change at the stage of operationalization—the political science term for defining and delimiting the behavior we plan to examine—meant that Schlozman, Burns, and Verba did not find as strong a set of differences between the men and women in their study as they might have otherwise expected.

A second and possibly more important methodological step forward that this article presents is the decision to conceive of political actions in terms of the resources necessary actually to accomplish them. In other words, the researchers controlled not only for education and so on, as Welch and other scholars had, but also for three broad categories of underexamined potentially political participatory activities such as the time, money, and civic skills associated with campaign volunteering or church organizing. Once they controlled for these three factors, Schlozman, Burns, and Verba are able to bring much more evidence to bear than did Welch on the same conclusion she reached—that the explanation for women's different levels of political participation lay in their unequal access to necessary resources.

Among the recurrent questions in the study of citizen political behavior in America are the extent and sources of gender differences in participation. In this article, we use a new data set to probe whether a gender gap exists with respect to a variety of kinds of civic activity. We also apply a resource model of political participation to inquire whether disparities in activity can be explained by inequalities in the resources that facilitate participation and whether there are differences in the way in which these resources work for men and women to influence levels of involvement.

Survey research once seemed to demonstrate the existence of a disparity in citizen participation with men more, and women less, likely to take part in political life, a disparity usually construed as the natural outgrowth of distinctive processes of social learning and adult roles that centered women in the private domain of the home and men in the world outside. These early studies soon came in for criticism on many grounds, several of which are germane to our inquiry. First, scholars pointed out that small—and sometimes not statistically significant—differences were invested with too much importance. A related criticism took issue with the very definition of what constitutes political activity, arguing that overemphasis upon voting and other electoral activities leads scholars to underestimate women's political involvement because it ignores alternative modes of participation—for example, organizational, protest, and grassroots community activity—in which women have always taken part. Were the understanding of political participation to encompass modes of involvement less formal, less conventional, and less nationally centered the findings would differ.

Second, critics argued that these early studies ignored the pivotal role of differential access to political resources. Women may be less politically active, these critics argued, because they are disadvantaged with respect to the resources that facilitate political activity—for example, because they may have lower levels of education, earn less money, or have less free time—and not because of a learned lack of interest in politics.

Finally, scholars argued that the processes of politicization might be different for men and women. Gender differences in the patterns of citizens' lives might mean not only differences in the amounts of resources accumulated by women and men but also differences in the utility of various resources for political activity. . . .

[* * *]

In this [article], we use data from a recent survey of the American public to assess these arguments systematically: to discern whether the paths to politics are gender-specific and to evaluate whether differences in resources are responsible for the disparity between men and women in political activity. . . .

The Citizen Participation Study

We employ data from the Citizen Participation Study, a large-scale, two-stage survey of the voluntary activity of the American public. The first stage consisted of more than 15,000 telephone interviews of a random sample of American adults conducted during the last six months of 1989. These 20-minute screener interviews provided a profile of political and nonpolitical activity as well as basic demographic information. In the spring of 1990, we conducted much longer, in-person interviews with a stratified random sample of 2,517 of the original 15,000 respondents chosen to produce a disproportionate number of both those active in politics as well as African Americans and Latinos. The data in this article are from the 2,517 respondents in the followup survey. . . .

For several reasons, this study is unusually well suited for probing the questions we have posed here. First, the survey was designed to contain more extensive measures of political resources than have been available in the past. The survey included measures not only of standard demographic variables but also of such potentially relevant political resources as vocabulary skill, the amount of time devoted to various activities, and the communications and organizational skills exercised in the nonpolitical institutions of adult life. Thus, we are able to investigate in ways not before possible the relationship of political resources to men's and women's political participation.

Moreover, the Citizen Participation Study is based on a very broad construction of what constitutes participation allowing us, for the first time, to subject to empirical test the contention that women and men specialize in different kinds of voluntary activity. With respect to political participation, the survey asked about an array of citizen activities: modes of participation that require money as well as those that demand inputs of time; unconventional as well as conventional activity; electoral activities as well as more direct forms of the communication of messages to public officials; and activities done alone as well as those undertaken jointly. Thus, we can move beyond voting and electoral activity to encompass contacts with government officials, attendance at protests, marches, or demonstrations, involvement in organizations that take stands in politics, informal efforts to address community problems, and voluntary service on local governing boards or regular attendance at meetings of such boards. In addition, we asked about volume of activity—not only whether respondents had engaged in the activity but how much they had done.

Even more unusual than the range of political acts covered by the Citizen Participation Study is that the survey also asked about voluntary activity outside of politics—in churches, secular charities, and nonpolitical organizations. The questions about organizations were unusually detailed, encompassing several questions about the respondent's involvement in each of no fewer than 20 categories of organizations—fraternal groups, unions, political issue organizations, hobby clubs, neighborhood or homeowner associations, and so on—and an extensive battery about the single organization that is most important to the respondent. With respect to religious participation, we asked about not only attendance at religious services but also activity in educational, charitable, and social activities associated with a church or synagogue—apart from attendance at services. . . .

[* * *]

Gender Difference in the Amount of Participation

When we expand the scope of what we mean by political participation, what are the differences between women and men in the amount and kind of activity they undertake? . . . For each kind of activity except for attending protest, there is a consistent gender difference with women less active than men. The differences for voting, working in a campaign, serving on a local board, or attending a protest are statistically insignificant. Statistically significant gender differences are found in relation to making a campaign contribution, working informally in the community, contacting an official, and affiliation with a political organization—that is, membership in or contributions to organizations that take stands in politics. . . . Summing across all eight acts on our scale of activity, we find that women engage in an average of 2.0 acts, men in an average of 2.3, a statistically significant difference that would appear to be of moderate substantive significance.

. . . If the percentage of citizens who engage in a particular political activity is a measure of how hard or easy it is, the size of the gender gap is not related to the difficulty of the act. Furthermore, gender differences do not disappear when we expand the scope of participation beyond electoral participation. The exception is protesting; women are as likely to attend a protest as men. The data suggest that women participate a bit less than men in community activity. Contrary to what might be expected, there is less gender difference in the formal political activity of serving on a local government board than there is in more informal, ad hoc activities such as working with others in the community or getting involved in a political organization. . . .

Voluntary Activity Outside Politics

. . . [T]here is virtually no difference between women and men when it comes to voluntary participation in nonpolitical organizations and charities that are secular. What is striking, however, is that the arena in which women are clearly more active than men is one that is rarely mentioned in discussions of gender differences in participation—religious institutions. Not only are women more likely than men to go to services regularly, they are also more likely to give time to educational, charitable, or social activities associated with their church or synagogue and to contribute money to their religion. The differences are statistically significant and fairly substantial. Only when it comes to serving on the board or holding an official position in a religious institution are men about as active as women.

So far we have a pattern of small differences with men more active than women in politics, rough gender equality in voluntary activity in the secular domain outside politics, and women more active than men in religious institutions. A different pattern emerges if we consider the volume of activity—the average number of hours or dollars contributed in the political, secular nonpolitical, and religious domains of voluntary participation—by women and men who are active in each realm. . . . The striking contrast in these data is not among the three realms of voluntary activity, but rather between time and money as voluntary inputs. With respect to time, there is no consistent gender difference in the average number of hours dedicated to voluntary action among those who are active. Surprisingly, once active, men give on average more hours to church than do women—even though women are more likely to be active in their churches. Equally surprising, *women* give more hours to politics, once active, than do men. With respect to money, however, the pattern is quite uniform. Money is different from time: among donors, men make larger contributions than do women in each of the three domains—even though it is only in politics that they are more likely than women to be donors. These data suggest, then, that the patterns of difference have less to do with whether an activity falls into the realm of conventional, formalized electoral participation and more to do with whether the contribution to civic life is money or time. . . .

The Resources That Facilitate Political Involvement

In this section we investigate whether there are gender differences in the resources that might facilitate political activity: time, money, or civic skills. These resources derive from experiences at home and in school as well as from adult commitments—family circumstances, position in the work force, and affiliations with voluntary associations and churches or synagogues. Insofar as the life patterns of men and women differ systematically with respect to family responsibilities, work, and nonpolitical voluntary participation, their ability to acquire civic resources will also differ.

Money

. . . Given gender differences in both work-force participation and earnings, it is not surprising to find that, by every measure, women have less income than men: they live in households with smaller average incomes and earn less on average, even if they are working full time.

When it comes to using family money for political purposes, what might matter, as suggested earlier, is not simply the level of household income but also control over income. . . . [We analyzed data for] all married couples, for married couples in which the respondent works fulltime for pay, and for married couples in which both partners work fulltime for pay, [to determine] measures of the extent to which the respondent's earnings contribute to family income. Consistent with the lower wages of women, in families where both spouses are employed fulltime, men reported that they contributed 62% of family income and women reported that they contributed 43%. As a consequence of both lower family incomes and lower contributions to family incomes, we should *expect* women to contribute less money to political, charitable, and religious causes than men.

Time

Most forms of political involvement—working in a campaign, taking part in a community activity, attending a protest—require an investment of at least some time. Because women's and men's lives have traditionally been patterned by different commitments to home and the workplace, time may be quite inequitably distributed. We asked our respondents to estimate the time they devote to certain necessary activities: working for pay, including commuting and necessary work at home; doing household chores including child care; studying or attending classes toward a degree; and sleeping. The time remaining in a 24-hour day after accounting for these necessary activities is our measure of free time.

[O]nce obligatory activities have been taken care of, men and women have in the aggregate the same amount of free time left over. Free time varies, not with gender, but with such life circumstances as working fulltime or having preschool children at home. However, these life circumstances do not, on average, affect the time available to men and women in quite the same way. Men, who are more likely than women to be employed fulltime, put in longer hours on the job, even when compared to women who are employed fulltime. In contrast, women take disproportionate responsibility for caring for home and children, even when both husband and wife are employed fulltime. The net effect is that overall gender equality with respect to free time masks substantial differences among subgroups—with women who have fulltime jobs and preschool children at home having the fewest free hours to spare.

Civic Skills

Civic skills, the communications and organizational abilities that allow citizens to use time and money effectively in political life, constitute a third resource for politics. These skills are acquired throughout the life cycle beginning at home and in school. In many ways, the process is cumulative: education not only produces such skills, but it also affects the likelihood that an adult will be in a position to develop skills even further. Those with high levels of education tend to enter occupations offering greater opportunities for honing civic skills and to be more likely to exercise civic skills as part of their activity in nonpolitical organizations and churches.

Since the acquisition of civic skills begins early in life in school, gender differences in levels of formal education may contribute to participation differences. The men in our sample reported somewhat more education, an average of 13 years of schooling, than did the women, who reported an average of 12 and one-half years. In particular, men are more likely than women to have graduate training and, especially, doctoral or other professional degrees. In contrast, there is no advantage to either men or women when it comes to two other education-related measures of civic skills: participation in high school student government and vocabulary ability.

[* * *]

. . . Let us begin with job-based civic skills. Considering all respondents, whether working or not, men report more opportunities to practice such job-based civic skills: they average 1.72 skills; women average 1.10. The process that produces the difference is a cumulative one. First, men are more likely than women to have jobs and, if working, to work fulltime. Furthermore, men are more likely than women to hold the kinds of jobs requiring formal education and on-the-job training that might be expected to provide opportunities to develop civic skills. This relationship obtains even when education is held constant. . . . To summarize, it seems that men's advantage with respect to civic skills exercised on the job results from a process by which men have differential access to jobs that require education and training and not from differential access to skill opportunities in these jobs.

Civic skills relevant to politics can also be exercised in nonpolitical voluntary associations. . . . [W]e asked about affiliations with a wide variety of types of voluntary associations. For the organization with which the individual was most involved, we asked a series of questions including items about opportunities to practice civic skills. As we have seen, in contrast to men's greater work-force participation, there is no gender gap in affiliation with a nonpolitical organization. Furthermore, among those in organizations, men report no more opportunities to practice civic skills than do women.

The pattern for church-based skills differs somewhat from that for skills developed on the job or in nonpolitical voluntary associations. Because they are more likely than men to be church members or to attend services regularly at the same church, women have, on average, somewhat more opportunities to exercise civic skills in the religious domain. However, in a pattern that echoes what we found for nonpolitical organizations, among church members women and men have similar opportunities to practice skills.

. . . First, for both men and women, but especially for men, the workplace provides by far the largest number of opportunities for the development of civic skills. Secular nonpolitical organizations and religious institutions provide roughly equivalent opportunities to practice civic skills—but many fewer in comparison to jobs. If there is a gender difference in skill acquisition, it depends on the different rate of institutional affiliation of women and men; that is, the proportion working, in an organization, or involved with a church or synagogue. With respect to work, it also depends on the fact that men, on average, hold more highly skilled jobs. Within each institution—that is, among the affiliated—the likelihood of acquiring skills is equal. Since women are less likely to be working than men and, if working, to have less skilled jobs, they get fewer skills from the workplace than men. Since women are more likely to be affiliated with a church or synagogue than men, they get more skills from religious institutions. However, since the workplace produces on average more skills than do religious institutions, men wind up advantaged in terms of civic skills.

Are the Paths to Participation Gender-Specific?

We have seen that there are disparities of varying sizes in the resources that men and women bring to politics, disparities that reflect their roles and experiences in family, workplace, and society. In this section of the article we investigate whether, apart from these differences in resources, the path to participation is different for women and men. We address this question twice—once for the overall level of political activity and once for the amount of money individuals give to politics.

Overall Political Activity

[* * *]

The results contain some surprises. We had expected the amount of free time available and the presence of school-age children to have consequences for the amount of political activity. They do not—for either men or women. Preschoolers, on the other hand, do diminish activity.

While the broad outlines of the explanation of political participation are the same for men and women, one difference in the paths to participation deserves further discussion. Affiliation with nonpolitical organizations, apart from the politically relevant skills exercised there, has an impact on activity for women, but not for men. Part of the explanation for this gender difference lies in the fact that the effect of organizational affiliation is especially strong for nonworking women for whom the broader exposure outside of the household may play a special role. . . .

Political Money

In all three domains of voluntary activity—politics, charities, and churches—among those who make donations, women give, on average, significantly smaller amounts than men. While women are no less likely than men to make contributions to charitable or religious institutions, in the political domain, not only do women contribute less when they give but they are less likely to make political contributions in the first place. In an era when political money has assumed greater significance, this is a gender difference that merits fuller exploration. As we have seen, differences in income and in the percentage of contributions to the family income were among the larger resource differences between men and women. . . .

. . . [T]he basic pattern is similar for women and men, but very different from the pattern for overall political activity. When it comes to giving money, most of the measures of resources that proved powerful in explaining overall activity—in particular, measures of education and most civic skills—are irrelevant. The single variable that matters most for both men and women is family income—the effect is strong and the same for women and men. In addition, for both men and women, contributions seem to rise with the proportion of family income attributable to their earnings. For each additional percentage of family income a respondent brings in, political contributions increase by about a dollar.

[* * *]

Conclusion

[* * *]

Our results suggest that, among the multiple implications of women's much publicized economic disadvantage, are political consequences that have been largely overlooked. Recent scholarship has focused upon the extent to which women's traditional responsibilities in the home have robbed them of the free time necessary for political involvement. Our results demonstrate not only that, in the aggregate, women have as much free time as men but also that the availability of free time seems not to be critical for the decision to take part—although, among activists, it affects significantly the amount of time given to politics. In contrast, women have less money in their housholds and less control over the money in their households than men do, disadvantages that matter crucially for a form of participation, making political contributions, that has become increasingly important in recent decades.

Our results add another dimension to the widespread concern about the role of money in American politics, a concern that has thus far not been focused at all on issues of gender. With respect to the disparities in economic resources between men and women, however, the question is not only with the meaning of market-place inequalities for the principle of democratic equality among citizens but also with the way that the domestic political economy of the family exacerbates those marketplace inequalities when it comes to mode of citizen involvement of increasing significance is contemporary American politics.

TOWARD CRITICAL THINKING

1. To broaden the definition of what constitutes participation, Key Lehman Schlozman, Nancy Burns, and Sidney Verba include church attendance and charity work. What does the inclusion of these types of activity add to our understanding of the gender differences in political participation between men and women? Why should we consider these activities political? Are there any organized group activities that are not political? What about bowling leagues or book clubs? What about online communities? Explain your answers.

2. The researchers conclude that significant differences exist between men and women in terms of the amount of money they contribute to political causes, and they argue that in the current political climate this difference places women at a political disadvantage. Women simply cannot afford to wield the kind of influence in politics that men do. Do these researchers convince you that this is a problem for American politics? Think back to Virginia Sapiro's and to Irene Diamond's and Nancy Hartsock's effort to make a place within scientific analysis for social critique. How effective is it in this case?

READING 10

Discovering Latina Women in Politics: Gender, Culture, and Participatory Theory

(1999)

Carol Hardy-Fanta

In this opening chapter of her book, *Latina Politics, Latino Politics: Gender, Culture, and Political Participation in Boston,* Carol Hardy-Fanta directly takes on the challenges to political science's definitions that scholars such as Susan Welch (Reading 7) and Kay Lehman Schlozman, Nancy Burns, and Sidney Verba (Reading 9) have tried to work out within the framework of their more conventional analyses. Hardy-Fanta's work here flies in the face of convention, noting that the traditional ways of explaining diversity among political actors have resulted not only in the widespread invisibility of Latinas in politics but also in the popular image of Latinas as passive, submissive, and weak.

Hardy-Fanta begins her novel analysis with an old observation among feminist political scientists: we must reconsider our definition of what counts as politics. But, here, Hardy-Fanta adds a unique touch, focusing on both Latina involvement in traditional, or what she calls "titular," politics as well as Latina work among *la gente del pueblo,* or the common folks. More importantly, though, unlike many scholars before her, she does not simply insist that this community work is political. Instead, no doubt aware that her work would come in for criticism from the conservative center of the discipline, she uses rich personal anecdotes to show how Latinas' work among *la gente del pueblo* fills a gap within mainstream politics between atomized citizens and the liberal city government—as connectors among Hispanics, as connectors between their communities and the city government of Boston, as *portavoces* carrying the needs and desires of their people to the City Hall politicians eager to display smiling Latina/o faces in their publicity photos and to claim credit for "Latino outreach." She works especially through one story—that of Josefina Ortega—to develop a provocative model of political participation that challenges more effectively than any of the work we have read so far just how we must ask and answer questions about women and politics.

To talk about "discovering" Latina women in politics is a little like Columbus "discovering" America: just as the land already existed for its original peoples, Latina women know they have been active politically in Boston for years. Latina women in Boston demonstrate the full range of traditional political roles: running for office, mobilizing voters, mobilizing communities for concrete benefits, and providing political education for new members of the community. In addition, when the definition of "What is political?" is expanded beyond the traditional behaviors of electoral politics, Latina women consistently are the force behind political participation and mobilization in the Latino community. In this [chapter,] I challenge the invisibility of Latina women as political actors, a common perception in mainstream political science literature, first by revealing their numbers in traditional political roles and then by examining the ways Latina women's politics broaden the definition of the nature of politics. . . .

[* * *]

[One] explanation for why Latina women are invisible in mainstream literature may be found in the very way politics is defined. When gender differences are scrutinized, researchers typically compare women to men on those behavioral measures of politics that either are dominated by men or defined by men as politics: organizational membership, voting rates in elections, and attitudes about political participation. While there is nothing inherently wrong with such a comparison, an understanding of the political life of women is constrained by male definitions of politics.

Ignored—or rendered invisible—Latina women have been denied recognition of their political roles in the mainstream literature. One might ask at this juncture why I am focusing so much attention [in my research] on Latina women in political roles that reflect traditional conceptions of political life, especially if one of my major points is that the definition of politics in these terms is a gendered construct, as I will discuss shortly. There are two answers to this question.

First, my point here is *not* that what Latina women do as candidates, as ward leaders, or as promoters of Latino voting is necessarily different from non-Latina women, or even from men (although gender differences in these roles do exist). My point here is "simply" that Latina women are political actors in Boston. They are participating in traditional political roles with great enthusiasm, effectiveness, and dedication.

The fact that Latina women demonstrate activism in electoral politics—traditional politics—is not really a simple point, however. It runs counter to the prevailing view of the apolitical Latina woman, the passive and submissive Latina woman. These are *Latina* women—the very women who are identified in the literature as submissive, passive, subordinated, and oppressed. Puerto Rican women, Dominican women, Mexican-American women, and Central American women in Boston—with their actions, their words, and their perspective on politics—challenge the ingrained image of the apolitical Latina woman. We cannot underestimate the importance of rendering visible the contribution of these women to the political mobilization of Latino communities.

Second, what is more important for this discussion of Latina women and the nature of politics is that, in addition to their activism in *traditional* political roles, Latina women were identified by both men and women as being the driving force for pulling Boston's Latinos into political participation. In addition to their roles as connectors between City Hall and the community, Latina women are connectors among members of the community to help the community solve its problems. As several Latinos said, "There's more to politics than just voting." If politics is more than elections and public office—if politics is about people joining together participating at all levels of community and government life—the role of Latina women in mobilizing Latinos becomes more visible. If [in the words of political theorist Benjamin Barber] "the challenge is to envision the human future and then to inspire a passion in others for that vision" the question to be asked is: If there is more to politics than electoral politics—that is, the politics of representation—then how do gender and culture shape our understanding of this alternative?

Gender and the Construction of "What Is Political?"

How does gender limit or enhance the definition of politics? One is reminded of Simone de Beauvoir's observation that men "describe the world from their own point of view, which they confuse with absolute truth." Some suggest that part of the reason politics is defined in terms of public behaviors and formal organizations is that public life *is* the male life, and so politics has become defined in masculine terms as the public politics of elections, office holding, and political party. . . .

Within the "absolute truth" of politics as constructed by men exists the essentially hierarchical ladder of representative government, in which a few are elected to represent the interests of the many. And within much of current political theory there exists a parallel hierarchy of political behaviors in which electoral politics is identified as "politics" while a whole wealth of political life is called a variety of other names: community organizing, community politics, and grassroots politics, to name a few. . . .

A vision of participatory democracy is very different. Participatory democracy is firmly rooted in beliefs about community, collective organization, self-government, and, above all, opportunities for participation by the many, not restricted to the elite few. Empirical examples of such participation in action, and how an increase in participatory experiences is brought about, are rare. Another limitation of existing theories of participatory democracy is that the role of gender, again, receives little attention.

The term *grassroots politics* is often used to reflect a more community-focused type of politics that involves greater opportunities for self-government and self-direction and that increases participation by connecting private problems to public issues. One of the major splits in how politics is defined is between "politics" and "grassroots politics" or "community organizing." Political participation in a participatory model, however, is the politics of local efforts to achieve change. The tension between local efforts on local issues and efforts to elect representatives to tackle larger issues is a false tension in participatory theory. In contrast to [political scientist E.E.] Schattschneider's hierarchical view of "experts" and "ignorants" is a vision of people becoming self-governing at all levels of government and in the workplace through the act of participating.

Latina Women and Participatory Theory

This alternative vision of blending self-government, grassroot community efforts, and personal/private issues with public issues plays a central role in current feminist political theory. In particular, the political lives of women, and of Latina women specifically, are examined with a less biased eye in the feminist press. . . .

[* * *]

In their efforts to mobilize the community, Latina women in Boston embody key elements of a more participatory vision of political life. The . . . ability to generate Latino political participation is linked to gender. When I developed a list of reputational leaders to interview that emphasized people in the news and individuals with official titles, 60 percent of the names were men. However, when these individuals were asked, "Who draws Latinos into participation?" the lists reversed themselves to 60 percent women. In fact, when the list excluded agency directors and people who hold jobs in city or state government, the vast majority (over 75 percent) of the people considered able to influence or draw people into the political process were Latina women.

Latina women in Boston provide empirical evidence of a broad expanse of political activism at the grassroots level. Julio Rojas, for example, is a community activist and an organizer of the Puerto Rican National Congress Convention that took place in Boston in May 1989. He describes the presence of women at the grassroots level of politics in Boston: "I say that women have been a major force at the grassroots level in the Hispanic community—from the day we came here, from the day we came to the United States." Nelson Merced, the first Latino state representative in Massachusetts, states that Latina women are just as crucial at the electoral level of politics but ties the women's political skills to their relationships within the community.

> I think, more than anything else, women have a lot more potential; Hispanic women have a lot more potential for getting elected. They're more involved in the community, they're organized—they're better organizers. I don't want to make these general statements, but they communicate better with people, they're there in the community, they're in the trenches all the time, they deal with the children, they deal with the household and they may work, but they have—I think they have a stronger network, where men have—sort of—these networks, but I think they're weaker, whereas the women have a stronger network.

[* * *]

One of the central debates in feminist theory, with implications for the present study of politics, is the question whether women see the world in ways different from men—in more relational terms. [Psychologist Carol] Gilligan, for example, reexamines women's moral base and brings to light the caring and relationship orientation of women in resolving social and personal issues. She argues that women view the world differently from men. The apparent differences between an ethics of care and an ethics of justice has implications for the interactive aspects of politics. [Nancy] Chodorow and [Deborah] Tannen claim that, for women, personal interrelationships and connection are more important than for men. They also suggest that men view the world in positional terms, in terms of personal status rather than connections and intimacy. The question may be raised whether such differences are rooted in biology, or whether they are socially constructed. Regardless of the source of these apparent differences, however, the implication for political mobilization is that if political mobilization is more likely to occur when interpersonal relationships rather than access to hierarchically determined positions are the basis for politics, then how women view politics is an essential element in any struggle for a more participatory America.

In suggesting that gender differences stressing relationships (for women) and positions and status (for men) exist, the question remains, then, whether these differences represent the *result* of gender construction or whether they represent a *normative prescription* for a more democratic society. As evidenced from the stories recounted throughout [interviews for this project], the experiences of Latina women in Boston suggest that a more personally connected politics and a vision of politics as an interactive process based on personal relationships *are* more effective in mobilizing the Latino communities than a male vision of politics as access to power, positions, and formal structures.

A second debate that frames the issue of gender differences and participatory theory is the permeability of the boundary between private and public politics. Juanita Fonseca, in her office at City Hall, said to me, "The personal is political. . . . What happens every day is politics. What's going on right now—whether I agreed to meet you today—is politics." And Carmen Gómez, a South American who runs a social service agency, quietly declared: "Everything is political." These views support [one] contention about personal politics—that the distinction between the personal and the political is artificially constructed.

These views are not supported, however, in most writings by male theorists. Even Barber, in *Strong Democracy*, finally comes down on the side that politics must be considered to be public, not private (although he admits the boundary between the two is frequently hard to distinguish). Public politics, private politics, the personal and the political is one of the theoretical themes that permeates the definition of politics discussed in this book, and gets at the heart of my next point.

For Latina women in Boston, politics is an *interpersonal politics*—a politics that blends personal relationships into political relationships. By weaving politics into the fabric of daily life, Josefina Ortega illustrates how connectedness and mutual relationships increase Latino political participation. She also illustrates how electoral politics are not in a hierarchical relationship with participatory politics but form an inseparable thread, perhaps a continuum, one dependent on the interpersonal relationships of everday life.

Portrait of Josefina Ortega: Connection and Mutual Relationships

Doña Fina, as she is often referred to, was born in a "humble family" in Puerto Rico. Now in her sixties, she came to New York when she was twenty-three years old and became a professional singer of Puerto Rican folklore. She moved to Boston in 1966 and has spent much of her time here organizing and conducting dance classes for children in a studio in the basement of her modest home.

When I introduced myself on the phone, she made comments like *"Pues, yo no tengo mucho que ver con eso de la política"* ("I'm not very involved in things like politics"). But with little encouragement, she revealed that she does know many people who are politicians and that they have called and said, "Fina, we need a hundred people at this meeting." They count on her ability to bring people to political events—an ability based on her connections to people in the community, to *la gente del pueblo.*

Josefina Ortega has numerous plaques and awards on her dining-room wall honoring her community contributions, but she has not used her political connections to distract her from her community connections. Her major focus continues to be on dance and on helping Latino children maintain their folklore, culture, and artistic heritage. Her dream is to develop a truly community-oriented cultural center. She does not use her political connections for personal gain; she has never moved into any official position, and she continues to relate to the community as a dance instructor, as an organizer of cultural events, and as a volunteer at a program for *los ancianos* (the elderly) at a local community center. By serving traditional Latin meals and joining them in traditional Latin songs, she encourages *los ancianos* to come out of their isolation. Because she knows so many people and is trusted by them, when she calls and urges them to join her to work on community problems, they respond.

Doña Fina and her daughter, who was present at the interview, also participate in electoral politics. Both attended the Democratic Party caucuses in February 1990. Ortega votes consistently and sees the vote as a crucial tool for community betterment. She also works on getting people registered and urging them to vote. She is one of the women who put a megaphone on the top of her car to publicize election day, as described previously by Marta Correa. This portrait suggests several important lessons for political analysts and mobilizers: connections must exist within a relationship built on mutuality and reciprocity. Because Josefina Ortega *gives* of her time and energy to the children, when she calls on the parents for a political rally they respond. She donates much of her time, often charging no money for the dance classes in her basement, and perceives herself as not being in it for herself. She does not use her connections for personal gain but instead because of a belief that something needs to be done to help people.

Her more conservative or "old-fashioned" view of solutions to social problems creates somewhat of a generation gap with younger activists, but this probably endears her to the common folk, who may have more conservative leanings than are desired by the more liberal or radical leaders in the community. For example, one of the important issues in the community is teenage pregnancy, and there are few social service programs for pregnant Latina girls. She had the idea of bringing the girls into peoples' homes and teaching them something (her idea was embroidery—a somewhat passé occupation, but one that many Latina mothers probably remember from their youth). The program later implemented by other Latina activists did not incorporate Ortega's ideas; instead, it stressed counseling and education.

For Ortega, a political life consists of intertwining cultural activism, everyday relationships, dance instruction, and electoral politics. Latina women, in fact, often mobilize around issues related to their daily lives. Women's roles in the family may stimulate rather than inhibit political activism. . . . And this may not be unique to Latina women in Boston. [The research] suggests that "patterns of female political participation across Latin America reveal that women's roles in the family, although typically perceived as obstacles to participation, also serve as rationalizations for leadership roles as well as catalysts for mobilization."

Doña Fina also dispels the notion that alternative forms of politics suppress electoral politics; she is intimately involved with voting and elections. In many ways, she reflects women's way of combining everyday relationships and political activism. Her life as a political mobilizer clearly challenges the distinction between private and public spheres of politics and suggests that this distinction is a social construct rather than a reflection of a universal political reality. Her success in increasing Latino participation, even in electoral politics, is due precisely to her personal relationships.

Political participation is thus *woven into the fabric of daily life*. The boundary between public and private becomes blurred. . . .

[* * *]

TOWARD CRITICAL THINKING

1. Carol Hardy-Fanta was only able to study women including Josefina Ortega and the others she discusses here because of her nontraditional, one-on-one methods. How could you find evidence for theories such as hers in data from mass public behavior studies of scholars including Kay Lehman Schlozman, Nancy Burns, and Sidney Verba's Citizen Participation Survey? What advantages come from having such a large database upon which to support one's conclusions?

2. How have women of other cultures played the roles that Hardy-Fanta discusses— *portavoz*, connector, and so on? Think back to earlier readings about suffrage politics, for example.

WRAPPING UP

1. Despite Susan Welch's preliminary findings to the contrary, many scholars continue to expect that childhood socialization is a major barrier to women's advanced political participation. How do you see the attitudes instilled in children about gender and politics changing today? Do you predict that women will "catch up" to men within the next generation? Might they go even farther?

2. What value might there be in looking at women's involvement in electoral politics separately from all their other kinds of activism within their communities? What is special about elections that warrants our particular attention? Give some examples of unique circumstances that accompany activism around elections.

READING 11

Political Elites and Sex Differences in Political Ambition: A Reconsideration

(1985)

Susan J. Carroll

In her classic article first published in the *Journal of Politics*, Susan J. Carroll examines the differences between men and women in their levels of political ambition. Early research in the 1970s consistently found women were significantly less likely to express an interest in seeking elected office. For example, the research by Diane L. Fowlkes, Jerry Perkins, and Sue Tolleson Rinehart (Reading 22) on women and men party activists found that women were less likely to desire to run for office than their male counterparts. This difference generally was attributed to gender-role socialization. In addition, scholars found that there were institutional barriers to potential women candidates, such as lack of recruitment by the political parties, which inhibited women from running for office.

In this article, Carroll seeks to clarify what the causes are for women's lower levels of political ambition. She compares the differences between the levels of political ambition of men and women party activists and men and women office holders. In addition, using survey data of national convention delegates from the 1972, 1976, and 1980 presidential election cycles, she is able to ask if women's level of political ambition changed during those critical years of the women's movement. This work moved scholars from questions that resulted in explanations rooted in either institutional or socialization theories and demonstrated that both explanations are useful when trying to explain women's lower interest in running for elected office.

[* * *]

The numbers of women holding local, county, and state legislative offices have increased significantly in recent years. The proportion of women among state legislators increased from 4% in 1969 to 15% in 1985. The proportion of mayors and local council members who were women more than doubled from 4% to 10% in the years between 1975 and 1981. The proportion of women among county commissioners grew from 3% in 1975 to 8% in 1983. However, increases in the numbers and proportions of women among local, county, and state legislative officeholders have not been paralleled by increases among congressional and major statewide officeholders. In 1985 women hold twenty-four, or 4.5%, of the 535 seats in Congress; this is only four more seats than they held in 1961–62. Only two women currently serve as governors of states.

If women among political elites are less ambitious for public officeholding than their male counterparts, then the paucity of women at higher levels of office despite increases at lower levels might well be largely a function of an "ambition gap" among women and men at lower levels of office. . . .

A substantial body of research on sex differences in ambition would seem to point to the conclusion that the discrepancy between the numbers of women at higher and lower levels of office is in large part a product of the constrained aspirations of political women relative to those of political men. Study after study has found women in political elites to be considerably less ambitious for public officeholding than their male counterparts.

However, most previous studies have focused on the political ambitions of delegates to national party conventions or other party activists. The ambitions of representative national samples of male and female public officeholders have not been examined. Moreover, despite the fact that much larger proportions of male than female party activists had held public office, previous analyses of sex differences in ambition have not controlled for officeholding status. Consequently, most findings of sex differences in ambition have been based on a comparison of the ambitions of a group of women, few of whom had held office, with a group of men, many of whom had held office. Yet ambition theory clearly points to current political position as a variable that is likely to influence officeholding aspirations.

This study examines the political ambitions of representative national samples of women and men holding comparable elective offices in 1981. Because the findings are strikingly different from those of the earlier party activist studies, two possible explanations for the differences in results are tested. The first is that the findings of earlier studies were misleading; the failure of these studies to control for a critical variable, officeholding status, may have masked underlying similarities in the ambitions of women and men who had similar levels of officeholding experience. The second possible explanation is that change has occurred over time; perhaps an actual increase in the political ambitions of political women, relative to those of political men, accounts for discrepancy between the earlier delegate study findings and 1981 public officeholder findings.

[* * *]

Ambitions of 1981 Elective Officeholders

Contrary to the findings of past research examining the ambitions of delegates to national party conventions, women and men serving in comparable elective offices in 1981 were very similar in their political ambitions. Across most levels of office, women and men were about equally as likely to want another term in the office in which they were serving in 1981, to aspire to some other elective or appointive position, and to desire ultimately to serve in a national or state gubernatorial office, thereby reflecting a "high" level of aspiration.

In the few cases where there were small (but statistically insignificant) differences between women and men, the differences generally pointed in the direction of greater ambition among women. Women state legislators were slightly more likely than their male counterparts to desire both another term in the state house and another office. Similarly, female country commissioners slightly more often than male county commissioners expressed a desire to seek another term on country governing boards. The major exception to this pattern of women's ambitions equaling or exceeding those of men occurred among state senators. Women state senators were somewhat less likely overall than their counterparts to express interest in another term in the state senate; however, women in the state senate nevertheless were more likely than men to say they definitely (rather than probably) desired another term (34.7% to 29.4%).

[* * *]

Officeholding Status as a Possible Explanation

[* * *]

To test for the possibility that earlier studies found differences only because they failed to control for officeholding status and thus masked underlying similarities in the ambitions of women and men who had comparable officeholding experience, the relationship between ambition and sex was examined for both those delegates in 1972 who held or had held public office and those who had not. . . . [A]mong officeholders, women did not lag as far behind men in their interest in serving in a future office as they did among nonofficeholders. Nevertheless, sizable sex differences in public officeholding are apparent for both officeholders and nonofficeholders.

. . . [T]he effect of sex on ambition is both strong and statistically significant even when the effects of officeholding status and other variables are taken into account. While officeholding status has a statistically significant effect on ambition, its effect and that of other variables do not overpower that of sex. Thus, sex differences in ambition among 1972 convention delegates clearly existed independent of differences between the sexes in their public officeholding experience. The failure of previous research using the *1972 Convention Delegate Study* to control for officeholding status did not lead to erroneous conclusions about sex differences in ambition.

Change over Time as a Possible Explanation

As increasing numbers of women moved into elective positions and other positions of political power during the 1970s, the political opportunity structure may have been perceived by women as increasingly receptive to their participation. If so, perhaps political women's ambition grew in response to their changing perceptions, and perhaps a real increase in ambition over time is the underlying reason for the discrepancy in findings between the 1981 public officeholder study and earlier research.

[* * *]

The public officeholding ambitions of male and female delegates to the 1980 conventions are strikingly similar to those of their counterparts among delegates to the 1972 conventions. Morever, the 1980 ambition levels of 1972 delegates of both sexes closely parallel their 1972 ambition levels. Both women delegates to the 1980 conventions and women delegates to the 1972 conventions resurveyed in 1980 were much less likely to have aspirations reflecting a "high" level of ambition and much more likely to desire no elective office than were their male counterparts. Women who had held public office among both 1980 delegates and resurveyed 1972 delegates were slightly more likely than women officeholders among delegates in 1972 to exhibit "high" ambition. Nevertheless, women officeholders in both cohorts of delegates also continued in 1980 to be notably less ambitious than their male counterparts.

These findings suggest that the political ambitions of political women, relative to those of political men, did not increase greatly during the 1970s. If officeholder data from the early 1970s were available, it is possible that a different pattern might emerge. However, existing data offer little evidence that the findings of sex differences among 1972 delegates who had held public office but no sex differences among 1981 elective officeholders are a consequence of real increases in political women's ambition.

[* * *]

TOWARD CRITICAL THINKING

1. What do you think accounts for there being differences in the levels of political ambition between men and women party activists but not between men and women office holders?

2. Susan J. Carroll found that the level of political ambition of women national convention delegates did not change over the three election cycles that she studied. Why, despite the changes brought by the women's movement, were women party activists not more likely to desire elected office in 1980 than in 1972?

READING 12

Political Women and Political Ambition: Closing the Gender Gap

(1990)

Edmond Costantini

Instead of measuring the differences between men's and women's interest in seeking elected office, Edmond Costantini changes the measure of political ambition to a question of motivation. He argues that pursuit of higher office is just one of many acts that are part of a self-enhancing political motivation, which also could include a desire for personal influence and profit independent of office holding. Drawing on literature that identifies the motivations for individuals to join and participate in interest groups, Costantini categorizes political motivation into four groups: sociality, purposive, allegiance, and personalist. Costantini identifies a motivational theory that goes beyond a personal quest for power as he details multiple reasons why party activists are involved in politics.

Costantini's research uses survey data of men and women party activists in California from 1964 to 1988. Not only does he test to see if there continues to be a gap between men and women activists' desire to pursue elected office, but he also compares the motivations for their involvement in party politics. And, like Susan J. Carroll (Reading 11), he is able to compare women's level of political ambition over time to further test the impact of the women's movement on women's interest in running for office.

Costantini's work, published in the *American Journal of Political Science*, suggests that traditional political science has defined political ambition from the perspective of men. When women did not express their political interests in the same way as their male counterparts, researchers did not question the definition of ambition but instead concluded that women were less ambitious. This and subsequent research recognizes that women may have different political motivations, and that they may express their ambition in a different way than men.

This inquiry explores what female political party activists "want" from politics—recognizing, of course, that not all women (nor all men) want the same thing and that it is unlikely that any given activist will want only one thing. The central focus is upon political ambition, or those declared political motives that bespeak an interest in an ascendant political career and in using politics as a vehicle for personal self-enhancement. Gender differences in levels of ambition will be considered, and motivational trends during the 20-year period encompassed by the analysis will be documented. The discussion will also probe the characteristics associated with ambition among the women being studied and contemplate the implications of the trends and associations identified.

[* * *]

. . . The analysis considers how male and female activists differ in what they want from politics beyond what is revealed with respect to the ambition dimension. Of particular interest is the way these data suggest the special contributions that women have been making to the parties in which they participate, notwithstanding any shortfalls in political ambition and in the achievement of political power. Accordingly, the analysis contemplates party organizational consequences—not necessarily salutary—should female party activists succeed in closing the possible gender gap in ambition.

Data Base

The present data derive from questionnaires completed by 3,000 California political leaders and activists who responded at one time or another to survey questionnaires mailed at approximately four-year intervals from 1964 to 1986. Respondents were selected for study because they had been members of the state's delegation to their party's most recent presidential nominating convention or had unsuccessfully attempted to become members by serving on delegation slates entered in California's presidential primary. . . .

[* * *]

Measuring Political Motives and Identifying the Political Ambition Dimension

Two series of . . . questions included in our survey instruments have probed political motives, one inquiring into the respondents' reasons for becoming involved in politics, the other into why they wished to become delegates to their party's most recent national convention. . . .

Political ambition: The desire for political power, prestige, and profit.

Sociality: An interest in the opportunities that politics offers for friendship, fun, and conviviality.

Purposive: A concern for policy issues and the state of the society.

Allegiance: An obligation to fidelity or loyalty to party, party leaders, and the community in general.

Personalist: The importance of particular individuals—proximate (friends) or remote (candidates)—in inducing political activity.

. . . "Political ambition" is used as [a] label, even though its [definition extends] beyond the office-seeking goals with which the term is conventionally associated. Indeed, the present data suggest that a desire for public office—which, after all, may be affected by place-specific opportunity structures—is only part of a more multifaceted inclination to use political activity as a vehicle for self-enhancement. . . .

[* * *]

Political Motives and Political Power

Mentioned with increasing frequency but rarely explored in quantitative gender-and-politics studies is a motivational explanation for male political dominance and the claim that one important reason women have less political power than men may be that they are less likely to value, or to aspire to its achievement. . . . For the activists studied here, such a shortfall would most clearly implicate the *socialization explanation* of male political dominance—in many ways the "bedrock" explanation of this dominance—and the acceptance (by males and females) of traditional understandings of gender roles vis-à-vis politics or the belief that the pursuit of political power is an inappropriate endeavor for women.

Other explanations may also be implicated. The *structural explanation* focuses upon the inequality of resources (e.g., differing levels of education, income, employment experience) that men and women may bring to politics and the relative absence of women in the socioeconomically defined eligibility pool from which leaders and candidates for public office are typically drawn. The *situational explanation* emphasizes how the responsibilities associated with homemaking and motherhood mean that women "do not have the time or energy to pursue political activities [and do not] have the political contacts to get started in the political arena." A recognition (or perception) of structural or situational liabilities may deter women from developing (or pursuing) political ambitions, conventionally understood.

The present study's female participants have already passed the threshold where structural and situational factors are likely to serve as major barriers to political activity. Their mere presence in the sample signifies the achievement of some level of leadership. Further, there are numerous indications in the data that they—like their male counterparts—have been making substantial commitments of time and energy to politics, even if those commitments do not appear to translate well into the holding of public office. At the same time, women respondents in each party have significantly lower educational achievements and family incomes than men and are less likely to be engaged in the professions, business, or other prestige occupations. . . .

The *gatekeeping explanation* of male political dominance turns to the way in which voters may be less receptive to female candidates for public office and to the way males who dominate positions of power may use that dominance to perpetuate their superordinate political status. Surely the reluctance—or perceived reluctance—of strategically well-situated players to admit women into the inner sanctums of power affects the aspirations of politically interested women. However, a number of recent studies have shown that once women become candidates for elective office—at least lower-level office—they are as electable as men, other things (e.g., district competitiveness) being equal. . . .

Environmental explanations illuminate the reasons for geographic variability in female political success, especially differences in state legislative membership. Thus, states with "traditional" political cultures are considered to be relatively inhospitable and those with "moralistic" cultures relatively conductive to the entry of women into positions of power. Also explored has been the relationship between female officeholding and such place-related factors as extent of party competition, urbanization, legislative professionalism (e.g., salaries, staff), the presence of multimember electoral districts or nonpartisan election systems, state population relative to number of legislative seats, and population concentration in proximity to the locus of governmental authority.

Certainly, the levels of political ambition exhibited by the women studied here are likely to be affected by the California environment, including the nontraditional nature of the state's political culture. However, not only is this particular state important in its own right, but we have no *a priori* reason to believe that the relationships found between gender and ambition and between female ambition and other variables are limited to the study's locale.

In any event, the motivational explanation for gender differences in political power is not necessarily an alternative to any of the other explanations commonly proffered. With respect to the present study, support for such an explanation merely requires a showing that the reasons underlying the political activity of men and women respondents are substantially different, with the latter less likely to be driven by ambition or impelled by self-enhancing goals. The analysis turns first to the task of meeting this requirement. To the extent that there is an ambition gender gap, that gap may be a manifestation of any or all of the nonmotivational factors suggested above.

The Political Ambition Gender Gap

The present data provide powerful confirmation for the notion that male and female political activists want different things from politics. Female activists are less likely to be motivated by political ambition as operationally defined here. . . . Both [women and men], regardless of party, provide identical rankings for [the five motivational] dimensions, with scores on the ambition scale being the lowest. However, female scores are lower than male scores only on the ambition scale. Only on this scale do male-female differences achieve significance . . . for each party's respondents. And it is on the ambition scale that the gender gap is widest.

[* * *]

Moreover, the gap manifests itself with particular clarity and over time consistency on the scale item that measures interest in seeking elective public office—the item most directly invoking conventional understandings of political ambition and most likely to threaten the sort of contentious activity that commentators identify as distasteful to women. It is interesting that the gender gap is relatively small on the item that regards interest in being *appointed* to government office—an ambition that can be fulfilled without engaging in such contentious activity or making the long-term or fulltime commitments more typically associated with elective office.

The [data] indicate that Republican women evince somewhat lower levels of political ambition than their Democratic counterparts. . . .

Closing the Ambition Gender Gap

While gender differences in political ambition persist over the life of the project, [there is] a marked over time increase in political ambition among women respondents. Democratic female scale scores rise monotonically across the six phases, just as they do among the Republicans. . . .

The present data permit tracking individuals who participated in the study more than once. Of the 86 resurveyed female respondents who produced different ambition scale scores, approximately two-thirds have higher scores at their most recent point of participation. . . . In contrast, male repeaters with different scores are as likely to produce lower as higher scores. . . . The tendency of resurveyed female respondents to become more ambitious over time is especially notable when it is considered that (1) age and ambition among respondents—male as well as female—are inversely related and (2) six of the seven items that compose the scale involve the respondent's recollection of what originally inspired his or her political involvement and thus should elicit the same answers. . . . For some female repeaters, it may be surmised, expanding ambition affects recollection; present motives are the prism through which original motives are reconstructed. For others, ambition that may have been understood [earlier] to be gender inappropriate and thereby unexpressed (presumably in their political behavior as well as in their survey responses) was seen as more acceptable and hence more freely revealed [later]. In either case, the pattern of changing scale performance among repeater females suggests an awakening of political ambition and an expansion of the sorts of self-enhancing behaviors likely to be associated with that ambition.

[* * *]

Increases in ambition among female respondents are not matched by increases among males. Thus, the male-female difference in ambition scale scores—while consistent in direction and significant in magnitude throughout—tends to become progressively smaller over the life of the project. . . .

[* * *]

In sum, we find clear evidence of continuity and change regarding gender differences in political ambition. Women activists at each stage of the project and in each party are markedly less likely than their male counterparts to base their political involvement on an interest in self-enhancement. Thus, the present data are consistent with a motivational explanation of female underrepresentation in positions of political power and provide evidence of a factor—proximate in nature—which may contribute to that underrepresentation. At the same time, the data indicate that the ambition gender gap has narrowed over the life of the project as women activists have become increasingly impelled by self-enhancement considerations. This narrowing has been particularly evident among the Democrats and is distinctive in that there is no notable over time change in male-female differences on the other four motivational dimensions.

Political Women and Political Ambition:
Social Background

The analysis turns here to a consideration of the variations in ambition among women respondents and to a delineation of the nonpolitical characteristics that likely contribute to their adoption of aspirations that run counter to traditional political and social norms—to their "countersocialization."

Social Background

[* * *]

. . . What background characteristics seem to lead some politically active women to be more ambitious than other politically active women?

[* * *]

What *does* explain ambition among the project's female participants? Two sorts of variables seem to be at work. The first suggests the importance of social integration or community anchorage. Being employed outside the home, having a religious affiliation, and being civically active each proves to be independently predictive of political ambition. . . . Indeed, politically ambitious women may see civic activism as a means of overcoming whatever structural disadvantages they suffer vis-à-vis their male competitors and as an alternative to the social prestige and political skills associated with the occupational and educational achievements that are more typically associated with political men. Such a formulation would suggest that ambition precedes civic activism for political women. . . .

Employment outside the home is another manifestation of social integration that may both reflect and contribute to the sort of self-confidence from which political women benefit as they contemplate activities more typically associated with political men. . . .

. . . [A]mbitious women appear, in social background terms, to be the sorts of women who have been at the leading edge of contemporary changes in gender role understandings. The fact that, among these predominantly middle-class women, being employed rather than being a housewife is independently associated with ambition may be seen in this light and not only as an indicator of the explanatory significance of social integration. The independent importance of year of participation in the project reinforces the previous showing that ambition among political women increases as we move to its more recent phases. Similarly, the fact that the younger the respondent—regardless of year of participation—the more politically ambitious she is likely to be also points to modernity's effects, although in this case the variable is also independently associated with ambition among male respondents . . . .

Ambition and the Feminist Impulse

[* * *]

. . . [The] feminist impulse has contributed to the closing of the ambition gender gap. . . .

The relationship between age, year of project participation, and ambition is also suggestive of feminism's import. Age and ambition scale scores are inversely related among female respondents regardless of when they participated in the project, and those who participated in the last three project phases tend to be more ambitious than earlier participants regardless of age. One would expect that the feminist impact movement's—including as a spur to ambition—would be particularly powerful among female respondents coming of political age as its blossoming occurred or during those three recent phases. Indeed, it is among the post–1970 participants under 40 years of age that ambition scale scores (as well as ERA support and membership in feminist organizations) prove to be distinctively high among female respondents and that the ambition gender gap is narrowest.

Finally, interparty differences in female performance on the ambition scale may reflect how the Republican leadership cadre has been relatively impervious to women with feminist perspectives. Only 12% of Republican 1976–84 female respondents compared to 46% of their Democratic counterparts indicated they were members of feminist organizations. In 1980–84 only 21% of Republican women compared to 93% of Democratic women indicated that they very much or somewhat favored ERA passage. . . .

[* * *]

TOWARD CRITICAL THINKING

1. Is there a problem with defining political ambition strictly in terms of office-seeking behavior? Do you believe that all types of motivations—including sociality, purposive, allegiance, and personalist—could be measures of political ambition? Why or why not?

2. The findings of this research are based on the activities and beliefs of party activists in the state of California over a twenty-year period. Would the findings be different had Edmond Costantini looked at party activists from states in the South, Northeast, or Midwest then or in 2005? Why or why not?

Reading 13

Family Structure, Sex-Role Socialization, and the Decision to Run for Office

(2003)

Richard L. Fox and Jennifer L. Lawless

Women and politics research has argued that the lower numbers of women serving in elective office is the result of a lower number of women running for office. In 1976, Marcia Manning Lee's "Why Few Women Hold Public Office: Democracy and Sexual Roles" in *Political Science Quarterly* noted that, contrary to popular opinion, women were as interested in politics as men and did not view politics as "dirty" or as a "man's business." However, she found that women's traditional roles as wives and mothers significantly inhibited them from running for office.

Similarly, in 2003, Richard L. Fox and Jennifer L. Lawless surveyed a group of potential men and women candidates and examined why women choose to (or not to) declare candidacy for public office. Relying on early research into the career paths of members of Congress, their work moves away from surveying party activists, who are already involved in politics, to a group of professionals who work in jobs traditionally used as launching pads for future political careers.

This research continues to draw on traditional gender-role theory used by Manning Lee, and on other research, including studies by Ellen Boneparth (Reading 21) and Diane L. Fowlkes, Jerry Perkins, and Sue Tolleson Rinehart (Reading 22). More than twenty-five years separate the 2003 survey and earlier, classic studies on potential women candidates, campaign workers, and party activists. But, Fox and Lawless's work published in *Women & Politics* shows the continued significance of traditional gender roles on women's interest in pursuing elective office.

Although the number of women serving in elective office has grown dramatically over the course of the last twenty years, women remain severely underrepresented in most elected offices. . . .

. . . [M]any gender politics scholars point to the small number of women candidates as the leading explanation for the small number of women holding elective office. More specifically, researchers attribute the dearth of women in politics to the small proportion of women in the pool of candidates generally considered "eligible" for political office. . . . According to this explanation, as women's presence in the fields of law and business increases, so, too, will their economic status and their likelihood of seeking elected positions.

An assumption on which the "eligibility pool" explanation is predicated is that men and women who are similarly situated in terms of socioeconomic status and professional accomplishment will be equally likely to decide to run for elective office. We argue that this assumption is potentially inaccurate and incomplete. . . . [V]irtually all information pertaining to political ambition and the decision to run for office yields from samples of candidates and officeholders. We know from the ambition theory literature that politicians tend to behave in ways that maximize their likelihood of attaining higher office, but the theory is relatively silent when asked to decide whether potential candidates, the majority of whom will never seek office, will actually enter a race.

Yet research on women who have actually sought public office suggests that the initial decision to run is often among the most formidable barriers to entering the political arena. A wide range of scholarly literature concerning gender socialization, for example, reveals that women and men, regardless of occupational status, continue to view their family responsibilities differently. Further, while the historical norm of men as providers and women as caretakers of the home has certainly declined, analysis of the political system continues to reveal prevalent stereotypes associated with these traditional roles. Thus, to assume that men and women in the eligibility pool will consider running for office at equal rates is to fail to take into account the potential force of traditional family structures and attitudes about gender-based roles that often accompany traditional socialization.

[* * *]

Central Hypotheses

For gender politics scholars, traditional sex-role socialization has played a prominent role in explaining the slow inclusion of women in electoral politics. Throughout the history of the United States, women and men have been taught, overtly and through inference, that politics is a business best left to men. . . . As we enter the twenty-first century, however, the extent to which socialized norms and traditional family structures persist among potential candidates for public office is not entirely evident.

Clearly, many of the barriers to women's advancement in formerly male fields are drastically changing; women now enter law schools and MPA programs at equal levels with men. Correspondingly, over the course of the last thirty years, women's presence in the fields of business and law has increased dramatically. Further, the conception of a rigid set of sex roles has dissipated with the increasing number of two-career families.

Despite these educational and occupational shifts, contemporary studies of family gender dynamics reveal that many traditional roles and attitudes persist. Women, even in two-career households, for instance, are more likely than their spouses to spend time raising children and completing household tasks, such as cleaning and laundry. . . .

If we are to gain a better understanding of the gender dynamics associated with the initial decision to run for office, it is critical to explore more thoroughly the manner in which family structures and traditional socialization have an impact on men and women's likelihood of launching a political candidacy. If certain aspects of gender socialization ultimately influence whether women and men consider running for office, then understanding the effects of traditional socialization is critical to exploring the likelihood that women and men in the eligibility pool will turn a consideration of a candidacy into an actual campaign. Thus, the effects of traditional socialization are key to understanding the long-term prospects for gender parity in elective office. . . .

. . . Rooted in literature that suggests that traditional gender socialization plays a significant role in men and women's decisions to enter the political arena, we identified two overarching hypotheses, each of which consists of two components. Our *Consider Running Hypothesis* posits that women in the eligibility pool who have traditional family structures, or hold traditional attitudes about gender roles, will be less likely than similarly situated men to consider running for public office. The *High Ambition Hypothesis*, related to the *Consider Running Hypothesis*, predicts that women in the eligibility pool who have traditional family structures, or hold traditional attitudes about gender roles, will express less ambition than similarly situated men to serve in high-level elective office, such as governor, member of the U.S. House of Representatives, or U.S. senator. Both hypotheses culminate to posit that historically socialized attitudes and roles, even among women in the pool of eligible candidates, will have an impact on the initial decision to seek elected office. Examining these hypotheses will allow us to begin to explore the interaction of gender and the decision to run for office, and the degree to which this interaction may be critical in assessing women's continued underrepresentation as candidates for elective office.

Methods and the Eligibility Pool Sample

[* * *]

In an attempt to test our two general hypotheses and explore the manner in which traditional socialization and family structure may have an impact on the initial decision to run for office, we randomly sampled men and women in occupations that match the professional backgrounds of members of the U.S. House of Representatives. We based our sample design on a breakdown of the five most common occupations of members of the U.S. House of Representatives before they entered politics: lawyers, business executives, legislative staff members, educators, and political activists (lobbyists and heads of interest groups). . . . We asked respondents about their familial arrangements, political activism, political outlook, and perceptions and willingness to run for office.

[* * *]

. . . Overall, the samples of men and women were similar in terms of age, race, religion, level of education, and occupation. Prior to assessing the manner in which traditional sex-role socialization and family structures may have an impact on the decision to seek office, though, it is important to note the manner in which historically socialized roles and attitudes may have already played a role in the formation of the eligibility pool.

Foremost, despite the fact that traditional family structures were prevalent in our sample, respondents' family arrangements indicate that women were less likely than men both to be married and to have children. Eighty-eight percent of men in the sample were married, compared to 70% of women. And men were 12% more likely than women to have children (84% of men compared to 72% of women). Certainly not all women in the sample felt forced to choose between devotion to family and devotion to career, but rather, managed to maintain both a traditional family structure and high-level occupational status. Consistent with earlier analyses of professional women, though, the lower likelihood of women in the eligibility pool being married and/or having children suggests that to achieve the professional accomplishment of this group, some women may have eschewed traditional family structures.

Another potentially important difference between the men and women in the sample of the eligibility pool is that men reported higher incomes than did women. Twenty-three percent of female respondents, compared to only 7% of males, had personal incomes of $50,000 or less. This gender difference indicates that traditional attitudes and family structures may have already influenced the pool of potential candidates, as women were more likely than men to earn less money, despite the fact that both men and women were chosen from the same tier of professional accomplishment. Because financial independence can be a significant determinant of whether a potential candidate actually runs for office, the men in our sample may have been advantaged in terms of seriously considering entering politics.

Finally, it is essential to note that men in the sample were more likely than women to characterize themselves as possessing traits typically considered appropriate for a political career. An extensive body of literature has found that preferences for "masculine" character traits influence candidate recruitment and self-selection. Stereotypical "masculine" traits, such as assertiveness and self-confidence, tend to be viewed as more desirable for activities such as campaigning and holding top elective office; "feminine" traits, including compassion and willingness to compromise, are linked to the traditional domain of family. . . . Thus the men in the sample were more likely to possess the characteristics that might be linked to a political career, whereas women who were socioeconomically and professionally positioned to consider a political candidacy may have had to transgress traditionally socialized norms, or be willing to exist in an electoral environment that tends not to embrace stereotypical "women's" traits.

Traditional Socialization, Family Structure, and the Decision to Run for Office

Our *Consider Running Hypothesis* asserts that among women in the eligibility pool, women with traditional family structures and historically socialized attitudes will be less likely than their similarly situated male counterparts to consider seeking public office. In an attempt to measure the impact of traditional socialization on the decision to run for office, we asked our respondents a series of questions regarding their level of interest and involvement in politics. Approximately 95% of both male and female respondents voted in the 1994, 1996, and 1998 elections; and 16% of the men and 17% of the women in the sample belonged to a political organization or interest group. . . . Somewhat surprisingly, women and men asserted, in roughly equal proportions, that they had seriously considered running for office; 40% of women and 38% of men in the sample expressed interest in seeking an elected position. This finding demonstrates some progress when compared to earlier research that found or hypothesized that women have less political ambition or inclination to seek elective office than do men. Despite equal levels of stated political ambition, however, it remains critically important to investigate the factors that influence the consideration of seeking office. Not only does the enduring legacy of gender role socialization in society make this an important endeavor, but the differences in family structures and sex-role attitudes between the men and women in our sample also suggest the importance of a fuller investigation.

[* * *]

When we turn to family structures and traditional attitudes about gender roles, the results . . . reveal clear support for our *Consider Running Hypothesis*. For all members of the eligibility pool, traditional gender socialization influenced whether or not respondents seriously considered running for office. . . . [P]otential women candidates seemed to feel particularly constrained by traditional family structures and socialized attitudes about women's roles. Although marital status did not have a statistically significant impact on considering a political candidacy, the results . . . suggest that men still perceived more freedom to enter the public realm of politics, regardless of family structure. As was the finding of earlier studies of actual candidates, the presence of children at home reduced the likelihood that women would consider running for office by approximately 27%, thereby suggesting that some vestiges of traditional family structures persist. For the men in our sample, the presence of children at home did not serve as a barrier to considering a run for office.

Family support was important to both men and women in the eligibility pool. For both men and women, a supportive spouse increased by more than 50% the likelihood that a respondent seriously considered running for office. In fact, family support was actually more significant for men than women. We attribute this seemingly counterintuitive finding to the fact that women were less likely to be married and, therefore, less likely to have the opportunity to rely on spousal support of a candidacy. After all, more married women (65%) than married men (53%) said they would be more likely to run for office if they were supported by a family member or spouse. It is quite plausible, therefore, that women rely on their families for external support of their non-traditional decision to think about running for office. Men, on the other hand, might rely on spousal support because dissipating sex-role stereotypes suggest to men that it is an appropriate consideration. Unquestionably, more research is needed in this area to investigate further the manner in which men and women conceptualize "family support."

It appears that overcoming sex-role socialization in terms of family structures is not the only pattern of traditional socialization that affects considering a run for office. For men, more traditional attitudes about gender roles, as well as a self-identification with "masculine" traits, substantially increased the likelihood of considering a run for public office. Otherwise a "typical" male respondent, a man with the most traditional outlook of gender roles (anti-choice, anti-ERA, negative impression of feminism, thinks men are better suited for politics than are women), was 60% more likely than a man with the most non-traditional attitudes about gender roles to consider a candidacy. Comparably, men who identified most strongly with "masculine" traits were 56% more likely than men who did not identify with traits of assertiveness, aggression, determination, and independence to consider a run for office. Whereas women who have considered running for office often must trump traditional attitudes about socially ascribed family structures, men are more likely to consider running for office when they subscribe to historically socialized roles.

Finally, we should note that Democratic party affiliation was a positive predictor of all respondents' prospects for considering to run for office, but the effects were more significant for women than men. Controlling for other variables, Democratic women were 26% more likely than non-Democrats to have seriously considered running for office. The propensity of women candidates to be affiliated with the Democratic party has been attributed, most notably, to the fact that the Democratic party's policy positions are more likely to coincide with a purported set of "women's issues." Thus, women might feel that the party serves as a venue through which to receive support for addressing "women's issues" and other policies that have traditionally been relegated to the private sphere of the home. Similarly, women were 57% more likely to consider running for office if they were members of political interest groups.

. . . [A] number of variables that influenced men and women's likelihood of considering a candidacy also had differential impacts on men and women. Most notably, as respondents aged, women were significantly less likely than similarly situated men to consider running for office. As mentioned earlier, considering that women in the sample had more child care responsibilities, this finding suggests that by the time women's family structures allow them to think about a political candidacy, their increased age detracts from their likelihood of considering the idea. Further, the same traditional attitudes about gender roles that bolstered men's likelihood of considering a candidacy made women significantly less likely to consider running for office. This finding suggests that perhaps both women and men who find themselves as the primary caretakers of children or the household engage in too many tasks to consider running for office. Because these roles have historically fallen on women, though, men are disadvantaged in terms of their political ambition only when they trump stereotypical roles. Finally, support from family was more important to men; as previously noted, though, the family structures of men and women in the sample differed, with women significantly less likely than men both to be married and to have children.

Together, these findings suggest that traditional gender socialization continues to be important in the electoral arena. Even women who have overcome a certain degree of traditional sex-role socialization, simply by virtue of the fact that they exist in the top tier of professional accomplishment, continue to be affected by family structure and traditional attitudes about gender roles in the initial decision to consider a political candidacy. Despite the fact that men and women express comparable levels of political ambition, the reality is that men and women in the eligibility pool face different decision criteria when considering a potential candidacy.

Traditional Socialization, Family Structure, and Interest in High-Level Office

Turning now to our *High Ambition Hypothesis*—traditional socialization leads fewer women than men to express interest in high-level office—we uncovered only marginal support. In examining this hypothesis, we asked respondents two questions: if they were to run for office, which office would be the first position they would most likely seek? And second, from a list of nine possible local, state, and national level offices, which, if any, would they be interested in holding? Surprisingly, the only statistically significant difference among responses regarding office preference was that women (12%) were more likely than men (3%) to prefer a judgeship as their first elected position. The remainder of the responses suggested that men and women were just as likely to consider legislative and executive positions, at all levels of government.

Again, though, if we are to gain a fuller understanding of men and women's office preferences, it is important to explore the extent to which traditional socialization affects eligibility pool members' choices. . . .

In the first set of equations, we considered only those respondents who said they had considered running for office. [We find] there were no statistically significant differences between women and men. In other words, among respondents who considered running for elective office, traditional family structures and adherence to gender roles did not influence interest in high-level office. This suggests that once women express an interest in seeking office, they are just as likely to aspire to hold the same types of offices as men. . . . .

[* * *]

. . . From the outset, it is important to note that for neither men, nor women, did interest in low-level political office predict interest in high-level office. More specifically, only 42% of respondents who expressed interest in high-level office also stated that they would be interested in seeking low-level office. This finding questions the degree to which potential candidates' interest or success in one office generates thoughts of a higher office. Perhaps more importantly, because men were more likely than women to express interest in high-level offices, we should be cautious in assuming that an increase in women high-office holders will ensue from an increase in the percentage of women holding local and state-level political positions.

. . . Turning to the family structure variables, traditional family structures played at least a marginal role. Our data suggest that, among women, the presence of children at home was a significant consideration that deterred women from expressing interest in high-level office by approximately 15%. Children at home did not have an impact on men's office preferences. A highly supportive family increased men's probability of expressing interest in high-level office by more than 35%; married men were more than 10% more likely than unmarried men to have expressed interest in running for Congress or a governorship. Neither support from family nor marital status was a statistically significant predictor among women. Once again, though, we cannot be certain as to whether "family support" meant the same thing to men and women in the sample. In a similar vein, it is quite possible that married men construed their marital status as evidence of family support and, therefore, received a boost in the propensity to express interest in running merely because they had a spouse who they perceived as unconditionally supportive. Women in the sample may not have confounded the presence of a husband with that of a supportive family member, perhaps because they were aware of the fact that transcending traditional roles might not be welcomed by their spouse.

Traditional attitudes and sex-role stereotypes also disparately affected the levels of office preferred by women and men respondents. Women who supported the ERA, abortion rights, feminism, and the notion that politics is not a male domain were 64% more likely than similarly-situated, but more traditional, women to express interest in high-level office. This finding suggests that a move away from traditional socialization was important for women who preferred high-level elective positions. Quite the contrary, no such move away from socialized norms was required for men in the sample. Neither disagreement with a feminist agenda, nor a belief in traditional roles and attitudes, increased men's interest in a high-level elected position.

Finally, it is important to recognize that traditional socialization may have manifested itself in one additional way in terms of the level of office members of the eligibility pool preferred. Consistent with research that associates economic independence with willingness to run for office, annual personal income was a significant predictor of whether men in the sample aspired to hold high-level political positions. Income was not a significant predictor of women's interest in these positions. This may be explained by the fact that women in the sample were less likely to have reached the highest levels of economic comfort, and accordingly, were less reliant on their financial state of affairs when thinking about the level of office they would aspire to hold. . . .

. . . [In sum,] traditional gender role socialization affected men and women in the eligibility pool differently, despite many of their socioeconomic and professional similarities. Women with fewer male traits were less likely than their male counterparts to express interest in high-level offices, as were women who held traditional attitudes about gender roles. . . . [T]he results are quite suggestive of the idea that traditional patterns of sex-role socialization make women less likely than their male counterparts to express interest in the highest levels of political office. Therefore, the increase of women in pipeline professions for political careers might not, in and of itself, generate a significant increase in the proportion of women serving as members of Congress or governors in years to come.

[* * *]

TOWARD CRITICAL THINKING

1. Richard L. Fox and Jennifer L. Lawless found that traditional gender roles continue to impede women from running for office. After twenty-five years of advances made toward women's equality, why is this still the case?

2. Research on women and politics has found that women candidates and legislators have historically had different career backgrounds than their male counterparts. Fox and Lawless focused primarily on careers that men have used to enter public life. What are the difficulties associated with attempting to define and survey a "potential" pool of candidates that is career-focused?

Reading 14

Political Ambition and Women in the U.S. House of Representatives, 1916–2000

(2003)

Barbara Palmer and Dennis Simon

Although women party activists are less likely than men to report an interest in running for elective office, Susan J. Carroll (Reading 11) found minimal differences between men and women office holders and their level of political ambition. Barbara Palmer and Dennis Simon move beyond the question of whether or not men and women have similar levels of ambition and ask whether political ambition theories effectively predict the decisions of women office holders to run for higher office. More specifically, these scholars test the seminal theory on political ambition outlined in 1966 by Joseph Schlesinger in *Ambition and Politics* on women in the U.S. House of Representatives.

Palmer and Simon examine the ambition of all women members who have served from 1916 to 2000 in this article published in *Political Research Quarterly*. By looking at the careers of thirty-nine widows who served during that period in the House and identifying over 200 opportunities that women members of the House had to run for the Senate, they were able to indicate the factors that contribute to whether or not congresswomen decide to run for reelection or for statewide office. In addition to testing specific theories of political ambition, Palmer and Simon identify significant variables that women consider when running for office in general.

By comparing the ambition of congressional widows to women members who came to Congress in their own right, Palmer and Simon contribute to the research that we have focused on in Chapter 4—the significance of traditional gender roles on women's level of political ambition.

Within the field of electoral studies, there is a rich literature devoted to understanding political ambition and how electoral incentives influence the behavior of office seekers and office holders. The classic work in this area is *Ambition and Politics* by Joseph Schlesinger (1966). His analysis, based upon extensive career data, showed that advancing in electoral politics was a product of ambition, party competition, and the structure of political opportunities. . . .

The appeal of ambition theory is its scope and generality. However, women as office seekers and office holders have received little attention in these works. This is largely because the incidence of females seeking and holding office, until recently, was relatively low. . . . [T]his study is designed to address two questions that arise from Schlesinger's typology of ambition. First, why do some "congressional widows" choose to seek a career for themselves in the House while others simply serve out the term of their deceased husbands? We focus upon congressional widows because this group constitutes an almost ideal natural experiment for examining the differences between discrete and static ambition. Our second question focuses upon the distinction between static and progressive ambition. Accordingly, we ask what prompts some female members of the U.S. House to run for the Senate while others elect not to pursue the opportunity for higher office.

Our analysis first shows that a meaningful distinction can be made between women who exhibit discrete and static ambition, a distinction that has been overlooked in the ambition theory literature. In fact, among congressional widows, there are measurable differences between those who seek reelection and those who step down, with independent political experience and political partnerships with husbands being especially important. Consequently, understood within the context of ambition theory, congressional widows are not a monolithic group. In addition, our analysis highlights the distinction between static and progressive ambition. We provide evidence that careerist women in the House are strategic when deciding whether to take advantage of an opportunity to run for the Senate. This decision to run for higher office incorporates the probability of winning, the value of the office, and the costs of running. As such, we are able to identify the distinct factors that influence whether women will exhibit discrete, static or progressive ambition.

A Typology of Ambition

" . . . *for women aspiring to serve in Congress, the best husband has been a dead husband.*"

"*Men are raised to play football, to bash their heads and come back for more. Women are raised to stand back. We aren't raised to be risk takers.*"

Representative Sue Myrick, R–NC

In his analysis of political careers, Schlesinger draws distinctions between discrete, static, and progressive ambition. In essence, this theory of political ambition reflects the hierarchy of political offices in the United States that functions as a "career ladder" or "opportunity structure" for ambitious politicians. The presumption is that lower level offices serve as a spring board into higher office, such as the decision to move from the House into the Senate. . . . Static ambition, on the other hand, manifests itself when the officeholder "seeks to make a long-run career out of a particular office" and continues to seek reelection. Finally, ambition is progressive "when the politician aspires to attain an office more important than the one" that is currently held, i.e. seeks election to a higher office to move up the career ladder.

... While discrete ambition is an integral part of the logic behind ambition theory, it has never been subjected to empirical scrutiny. In other words, we know why members of Congress want to climb up the career ladder, but we know nothing about those who decide to get off the ladder. Consequently, our analysis attempts to provide a more complete understanding of ambition theory and identify the factors associated with each type of ambition in Schlesinger's hierarchy.

Moreover, the extant research on women and political ambition is somewhat ambiguous. For example, there is evidence, at least in the 1970s and 1980s, that women were less ambitious than men, particularly among party activists. Other research, however, has shown that there is little difference in the political ambitions of men and women who have actually held political office. One of the problems within this literature is that there does not appear to be any coherence underlying the concept of political ambition. Thus, ... we seek to provide a more complete analysis of ambition theory in general as well as a foundation for understanding the political ambitions of women.

Discrete vs. Static Ambition: The Case of Congressional Widows

As late as the 1970s, much of the press and research attention devoted to women in Congress focused on the widow connection. As [political scientist] Diane Kincaid explained, the prevailing wisdom, particularly in the press, was that women who served in Congress got there "over their husband's dead bodies." After a member of Congress died, the "bereaved widow" was often recruited to run in a special election to fill her husband's vacant seat. . . . In many cases, the understanding, whether explicit or implicit, was that the widow would not seek to retain the seat during the next election cycle. Thus, congressional widows were presumed to be the quintessential example of discrete ambition.

The problem with this prevailing wisdom, Kincaid points out, is that it is based upon several problematic assumptions. Prior to World War II, 15 of the 28 women (53.6 percent) elected to the House had succeeded their spouses. Today, only 3 of the 60 women serving in the 107th Congress are widows. Further, if one looks at the number of members of Congress who died in office, very few were actually succeeded by their wives. From 1917 to 1976, for example, 487 members died in office, but only 35 (7.2 percent) were succeeded by their widows. This suggests that the congressional widow is not as common as typically presumed, particularly in light of the number of opportunities for widows to succeed their husbands.

A second consideration is the presumed behavior of widows as reluctant placeholders. The idea that women were "given" the seats earned by their dead husbands is simply inaccurate. Although vacant Senate seats can be filled by appointment, vacant House seats must be filled through a special election. . . . On the other hand, many of these women had advantages, such as inherited name recognition and a ready-made staff. Many of them had worked on their husbands' campaigns and, as a result, knew their districts well. Consequently, these congressional widows possessed resources and advantages similar to those enjoyed by incumbents. More importantly, many of these women did not step down after their initial terms expired. Without doubt, there are congressional widows who conform to the conventional wisdom, but there are many others, such as Edith Nourse Rogers (18 terms) and Frances P. Bolton (15 terms), who made long careers for themselves in the House.

It is clear then that congressional widows are not a monolith. Thus, they provide an identifiable group—in the sense of a natural experiment—which can be used to explore differences between discrete and static ambition. What are the differences between these women who retired after a single term as opposed to those who pursued congressional careers?

. . . [T]o explore the differences among congressional widows and differentiate among women who exhibited discrete and static ambition, we turn to the literature on the career paths of women in politics. This research identifies three factors associated with political ambition among women: working outside the home, the prevailing social and political culture, and age. In general, one of the most consistent predictors of political ambition among women was whether they worked outside the home. To refine the idea of "working outside of the home," two aspects are most relevant to our analysis. The first involves whether the woman worked closely (in either a paid or unpaid capacity) with her husband when he served as a member of the House. Such experience brings with it a familiarity not only with organizing an effective campaign but also with the responsibilities and routines of running a congressional office. A second aspect of "working outside the home" pertains to whether a woman was active in politics independent of her husband's political career. The nature of this independent experience may include holding elective office, appointive office, or serving in the organization of a local, state, or national party.

The literature also emphasizes the importance of cultural and social factors. Prior to the late 1960s, American culture itself treated politics as primarily a "man's game." Women were traditionally steered away, or even barred, from professions that typically led to political office, such as law and business. In the early 1970s, however, with the dawn of the Women's Movement, we see the sharpest increases in the number of women attending law school and more women entering the political arena. The unique role of women in the South, however, has made cultural barriers more restrictive in this region and is an important factor in understanding women's political participation. We also know that age has an impact on political careers, women are typically older when they first run for office. The motivation to start and then continue a political career is going to depend upon the age of the woman. . . .

Static vs. Progressive Ambition: Running for the Senate

[* * *]

There is a growing body of evidence that women are strategic in their initial decisions to run for the House. In particular, this decision is influenced by the opportunity structure. The biggest hurdle women face, a hurdle that all candidates face, is incumbency. There is some evidence that in the past, women were "sacrificial lambs" running in contests against incumbents that they had no hope of defeating. Recent analyses, however, show that this is no longer the case. Women are far more likely to run in races with open seats, where they have the highest chance of success. Given that women are strategic with regards to the initial decision to run for the House, we expect that they would be just as strategic in their decision to run for higher office. . . .

. . . [T]he decision to run for the Senate is presented as the product of an expected utility calculation. The expected utility of running for an office will be a function of the costs of running, the probability of winning, and the value of the member's current office. One indicator of cost is the size of the state. This reflects the coincidence or overlap of House and Senate constituencies; the smaller the state, the more a House district overlaps with the target electorate in a Senate race. The probability of winning is influenced by incumbency as well as party competition. Open seats are the most desirable because they present the highest chance of winning. Likewise, running against a safe incumbent of the opposite party is the least desirable. Finally, the value of a House seat to an incumbent varies as an inverse function of seniority. In general, the value of a House seat increases with the number of terms served, as both knowledge of the policy process and the internal influence of the member increases. As seniority increases, then, the Senate seat becomes less valued. . . .

[* * *]

Data and Measurement

To test these hypotheses, we constructed a database consisting of biographical and electoral data on all women elected to the U.S. House of Representatives between 1916 and 2000. . . .

We recorded any independent political positions held by the woman (e.g., state legislator) as well as the number of years she served in such positions. In addition, these sources reported whether a widow had worked for or with her husband over the course of his congressional career. . . .

These data contain 39 widows elected to the House during the period from 1916 to 2000. . . .

[* * *]

Results and Analysis

Discrete versus Static Ambition

. . . As expected, the probability of a widow exhibiting static ambition and pursuing a career increases when she has worked with her husband and with the number of years that the widow held office on her own. The probability decreases, as hypothesized, if the widow is from the South and if she is 60 or older. The probability that she will pursue a career has also increased since 1970. . . .

[* * *]

Static versus Progressive Ambition

The data used to estimate [static versus progressive ambition] consist of 213 opportunities to run for the Senate among female careerists in the House of Representatives. The low incidence of decisions to run given the opportunity (18 of 213 or 8.5 percent) has two consequences. First, running for the Senate is a rare event and, . . . standard estimation techniques will underestimate this probability. Second, obtaining the "best" possible estimates requires an alternative technique that adjusts for the skewed distribution of the dependent variable. . . .

[* * *]

... As expected, women who are risk takers are more likely to exhibit progressive ambition. Compared to their counterparts from medium-sized states, women from small states are also more likely to make a run for the Senate. And rather than sacrifice experience and seniority, women who are mid-career are more likely to run for Senate. In addition, women are more likely to take advantage of an open seat, where they have the highest probability of winning. ...

[* * *]

... More generally, the probability of running is substantially larger for risk takers when compared to their non-risk taking counterparts. Contrary to Representative Sue Myrick's observation, some women—like some men—are taught or acquire the ability to take electoral risks when entering congressional politics, and this attitude helps us to understand the difference between static and progressive ambition.

TOWARD CRITICAL THINKING

1. Barbara Palmer and Dennis Simon find that congresswomen have similar calculations for whether to run for a U.S. Senate seat as outlined by the ambition literature. What are some variables that were not explored by the researchers but that may be significant in the decision of women members of Congress to run for higher office, including governor and president?

2. Palmer and Simon discuss how congressional widows present a natural experiment to test the theory of discrete versus static ambition. Can you think of a case where there could be a comparable group of men? What are the implications on the significance of gender in politics?

WRAPPING UP

1. Why does the level of political ambition differ between men and women who have never run for elected office? What are the significant differences for women between their initial decisions to first throw their hat into the ring and their quests for higher office after they have competed in at least one election campaign that could account for their different levels of political ambition?

2. What explains the variation between women with higher levels of political ambition and women who do not wish to run for office? How do these variables compare with those that distinguish men who seek elected office from men who do not?

READING 15

Women's Gender Consciousness

(1985)

Patricia Gurin

Patricia Gurin—a psychologist whose work has been tremendously influential among political scientists—made quite a splash with this article published in *Public Opinion Quarterly*. Her concept of gender consciousness has illuminated the link between group identity and individual action for a variety of types of activists working in the broader field of identity politics. It not only provides a way for us to imagine how group identities become important in individual decision-making processes, but it also shows us how we might develop comparative predictions about varying levels of group consciousness among different demographic groups.

For example, Gurin makes the controversial argument that women are less likely than African Americans to feel a sense of group consciousness or connectedness to their group that could extend to political activities. Why? Because strong group consciousness, according to her theory, derives from frequent positive contact with fellow members of the group and relatively infrequent or negative contact with members of other groups. Consider, for instance, the different effects we might suppose family structure could have for the two groups. For African Americans (at least those in racially homogeneous families), the intimate world of family relationships is also a world of shared group membership. But for women (at least those in heterosexual families), these intimate relationships serve to link them and their fates to men.

Although Gurin's argument has been the subject of widespread critique—some of which follows in the rest of Chapter 5—it has also been the most widely influential and emulated model in the subfield. Perhaps this is because it is so intuitive and commonsensical; perhaps because it lends itself easily to the kind of empirical research rewarded by journal editors and book publishers. Either way, the theory merits your serious attention and continued consideration as you continue to read the entries in this volume.

Family life and the roles of women and men within and outside the family have changed impressively over the past 30 years. Large numbers of women, even those with young children, have moved into the labor force. By 1979 women comprised 51 percent of the students in higher education institutions, up from 38 percent in 1963. And while the division of labor within the family is far from equal, some changes toward equality have occurred. Attitudes toward gender roles are now more egalitarian; for example, they are more favorable toward women working outside the home, combining jobs with motherhood, and otherwise participating in the public arena. . . . Data from the last 30 years of election studies at the Institute for Social Research also show that the male edge in turnout has virtually disappeared and that women are now more active in electoral campaigns than they were in the 1950s.

To what extent have these status and attitude changes been accompanied by more general ideological awareness of how gender shapes the lives and fortunes of men and women? Do more women now recognize that they are objectively deprived economically and politically? Do more women believe that women are treated categorically? Have women become more aggrieved about their relative influence in the public arena? Have more begun to question the legitimacy of gender disparities, such as their continuing wage gap?

There is reason to suspect little change, despite the seemingly dramatic changes selectively depicted by the media. For one thing, the American scene does not promote group-conscious beliefs among deprived, subordinated social categories. During most of its history the United States has been characterized by an expanding economy, large geographical population shifts, and enough intergenerational mobility to allow Americans, aided by an ideology of meritocracy, to presume more status changes than have actually existed. These conditions all encourage individualism, not solidarity or the recognition of group disparities and awareness of structural forces that impede achievements for some social categories. Instead, Americans tend to morselize experience, fail to connect their own experiences to those of others of like status, and firmly believe in a just world where individuals largely receive what they deserve. Thus, the very idea of categorical treatment flies in the face of widely held values.

Current theory can help us understand why women have not developed group consciousness as readily as other subordinate categories in America. Women lack many of the structural conditions that promote bonds to others in the same subordinate category. In the first place, gender inequality, while present and doggedly persistent in some areas, is not as marked as racial inequality, and perception of inequality is more difficult when it is not extreme. . . . Second, the economic fates and the claims to prestige of men and women are inextricably intertwined. Both sexes jointly share their gains and losses as members of ethnic groups or economic classes. Third, they agree on many fundamental assumptions about life and society, not only because of their common fates as husbands and wives, but because of their early socialization as brothers and sisters. This does not negate the existence of gender differences in socialization. Both systematic research and personal accounts are replete with examples of the differing treatment of boys and girls in the family and in school. Still, both are given many of the same messages about basic societal values, including individualism and a theory of justice in which the distribution of rewards is to be expected from the distribution of individual talents. Cleavage and conflict rarely develop between groups that share such fundamental values.

Fourth, and probably the most profound inhibitor of gender consciousness among women, is the structure of their relations with other women and with men. Solidarity and recognition of group deprivation are fostered when category members interact most frequently with each other and only moderately with the outgroup; when intimate interaction is confined to those within the ingroup; when relations with the outgroup are predominantly competitive or, at the very least, not intimate. Women's relations with each other and with men could not be more different from this pattern. Their relations with each other, while frequent and intimate, are at times competitive. At the same time, nearly all women have, or have had, close emotional and familial ties to men. Further, some women derive their social status and prestige entirely from their roles as wives and homemakers, which provide protections, meet dependency needs, and even allow flexibility and control when traditional arrangements work out ideally. These traditional roles are not without rewards for women. As a consequence some women have a vested interest in the social unit that also strengthens their unequal status. Men, individually and collectively, also have had a stake in justifying and maintaining the inequality in the structure of male-female relations. Until recently they have controlled the legitimating mechanisms that justify male dominance, including the production of theories about gender differences. Moreover, for many women, associations outside the family involve cross-cutting ties, in part with men and in part with women of more privileged statuses, which mute their recognition of the deprived circumstances of women as a class.

These structural conditions in their own lives obstruct strong gender consciousness and ideological change among women, despite shifts in status and in general attitudes toward gender roles. For these reasons, this [article] examines gender consciousness in women, including trends over the 1970s into the more conservative years of the early 1980s. Comparisons are drawn with the race consciousness of blacks, the age consciousness of older people, and the class consciousness of people in working-class jobs.

[* * *]

Components of Groups Consciousness

The concept of group consciousness is complex, but four main components are suggested by two current theories of collective action: the relative deprivation and the solidarity/resource mobilization theories. Invoking different terms, each seeks to explain how and why change-oriented action emerges in a constituency.

The first component—*collective orientation*—assumes that the group desires change in rank or power because either it has been subordinated or its dominance has been challenged. We are interested here in comparing women's attitudes toward collective action with that of other subordinated groups. In our definition of group consciouness, collective action is geared to change, and in this sense gender consciousness is feminist.

The other three components are associated with individuals' feelings and perceptions about their membership in a social category. The second component—individuals' *discontent* about the power of their social category—reflects the central concern of relative deprivation theories. Group consciousness and the emergence of collective action relate to the intercategory or intergroup connections that people make with those of dissimilar status or between those in their category and an out-group. The critical question is what structural and psychological forces encourage individuals to draw these comparisons so as to become collectivley discontented.

One structural condition that encourages or blocks outward comparisons is the degree of legitimacy ascribed to the prevailing social structure. This suggests a third component: how category members appraise the *legitimacy of disparities*. Disparity will not be experienced as deprivation unless members believe it springs from illegitimate forces. Group disparities may be considered fair and just if they are believed to develop legitimately from the inadequacies of individual category members. The same disparities will be judged unjust if they are believed to result from structural barriers that hold back category members.

The fourth component—*identification*—reflects a recognition of shared values and interests that turns a category into a collectivity. Most relative deprivation the-ories do not explicitly address how the sense of collectivity strengthens recognition of shared deprivation or provides a political interpretation for deprivation. Solidar-ity theories, however, stress the motivational importance of members' awareness of common feelings, values, and interests. When members share a strong identity and have strong bonds to others in the category, recruitment, mobilization, and organi-zation are more easily achieved. In addition, identification has cognitive effects that are important for political consciousness. By sharpening the salience of groups and the likelihood of using an intergroup perspective for comparison, identification heightens recognition of collective deprivation and encourages withdrawal of legit-imacy because deprivation, when perceived as a common rather than individual con-dition, is more easily interpreted in structural and political terms.

[* * *]

Procedures

Samples

Three national probability samples of adults were surveyed by the Institute of Social Research. The 1972 national election study (NES) included 1537 women and 1168 men, the 1976 NES, 1662 women and 1208 men, all interviewed face-to-face; two waves of the monthly consumer surveys in 1983 included 730 women and 588 men interviewed by telephone. In addition, one panel of 742 women who participated in both election surveys is used for analyzing which subgroups changed most and least.

Measures

Collective orientation was measured from responses to forced-choice questions. These probed views about action stategies women should follow to improve their market statuses. One alternative advocated that women work together to change the laws and social processes that cause job and wage inequality; another advocated individ-ual effort by each woman to get ahead on her own. . . .

Discontent was measured from evaluations of the influence of various groups in American society. The interviewer stated that "some people think that certain groups have too much influence in American life and politics, while other people feel that certain groups don't have as much influence as they deserve. On this card are three statements (too much influence, just about the right amount, too little influence) about how much influence a group might have." Absolute discontent, represented by the statement that "women" have "too little influence" was assessed in all three surveys. Relative discontent, the discrepancy between evaluations of the power of "women" and the power of "men," was assessed beginning in 1976.

One measure of *withdrawal of legitimacy* was derived from responses in 1972 and 1976 to three forced-choice questions in which respondents were asked to identify the causes of gender differences in income, occupational status, and general position in American life. For each question, one alternative attributed these differentials to systemic obstacles and institutional arrangements such as market discrimination or poor schooling; the other to women's personal deficiencies such as lack of ambition or preferences and natural endowments antithetical to economic success. . . .

Gender identification/sense of collectivity was measured by asking respondents to look at a set of 16 category labels that included "women." The interviewer asked, "Which of these groups do you feel particularly close to—people who are most like you in their ideas and interests and feelings about things?" Respondents were then asked to look at the list again and choose the *one* to which they felt closest. Degree of identification was operationalized as: (1) *not identified,* women who did not pick the label "women" as a category to which they felt even close; (2) *identified,* women who said they felt close but not closest to "women;" (3) *closely identified,* women who said they felt closest to "women." This measure was not used in the 1983 telephone survey.

[* * *]

Strength of Gender Consciousness

Comparisons among Subordinate Categories

Questions similar to those representing the four components of gender consciousness were asked of people over 60 about "older people," of people in working class occupations about "workingmen," and of blacks about "blacks," to compare the strength of women's gender consciousness to the group consciousness of other subordinate categories.

Many of the structural conditions that constrain gender consciousness among women do not operate as strongly in other subordinate categories, especially among blacks. The amount of objective racial inequality and the reality of residential segregation help blacks recognize disparity. Relationships with the outgroup are more typically emotionally distant; and the black community has been organized for directed social change for a longer time. Prior organization and leadership are critical resources for developing and mobilizing group consciousness for collective action. Political scientists credit solidarity and organization as the resources that best explain political participation rates among blacks that exceed expectations based merely on their educational and economic characteristics.

FIGURE 15.1 Similarity in Men's and Women's Views, Compared to Differentiation in Whites' and Blacks' Views, 1976

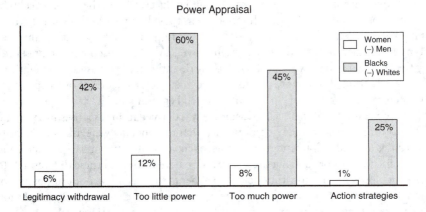

Power Appraisal

[I]t is not surprising that women were not as group-conscious as blacks in either 1972 or 1976 (see Figure 15.1). But it is surprising that most components of women's gender consciousness were weak compared with the class consciousness of people in blue-collar jobs and even the age consciousness of people over 60. . . .

Women's *identification* with other women was much less widespread. Compared to women, three times as many blacks and people 60 or older, and two-and-a-half times as many people with blue-collar jobs "closely identified" with their own groups. . . .

Identification can also be examined by looking at those women who closely identify as women when they objectively belong to at least one other subordinate category. Here the concern is with competing choices among subordinate memberships. Compared to such women in 1972, seven times as many blacks who belonged to at least one other subordinate category identified closely with "blacks." Five times as many older people and three times as many blue-collar workers did so. The comparisons in 1976 were approximately the same. . . .

Discontent and *collective orientations* were also weaker among women. For these dimensions, comparisons were made between members who closely identified with their subordinate categories. This provides comparisons of independent samples because respondents could choose only one category that they feel "closest to."

Compared to closely identified women in 1972, one-and-two-thirds as many closely identified older people and blacks were discontented with their category's power and influence. Discontent among closely identified blue-collar workers was not very strong and was approximately the same as among women. Closely identified members of the other subordinate categories were also stronger than women in their collective commitments. On a seven-point scale probing what members of their category should do "to have influence and get the things they want," the choices ranged from "organize as a group" to "work as individuals." Compared with closely identified women in 1972, two-and-a-half times as many blacks, nearly twice as many blue-collar workers, and one-and-a-half times as many older people selected the two most extreme collective positions on the scale. Women continued to show nearly the same relative weakness in the 1976 comparisons.

Legitimacy was the one aspect of gender consciousness about which closely identified women were politically conscious. They were as aware as closely identified
blacks of structural causes of their own group's disadvantage in the labor market. (The
legitimacy measure compared here does not include the item measuring women's attitudes toward gender roles, since blacks were not asked a comparable question.) In
both 1972 and 1976, women's average scores on an index measuring causal attribu-
tions for gender disparities were nearly identical to those of closely identified blacks.

[* * *]

The 1976 data in Figure 15.1 show impressive racial differentiation and impressive
gender consensus. (The 1972 data cannot be used because the survey did not ask
about the power of whites and men.) Differences between men and women and
between blacks and whites are shown for discontent, legitimacy, and collective orientations. For discontent, the data compare men's and women's evaluations of the
power each ought to have in life and politics; blacks and whites made the same kind
of evaluations for each of their groups. For legitimacy, causes men and women attributed to gender disparities were compared; similar comparisons were made for blacks
and whites of their explanations for racial disparities in wages and occupational status. Although the phrasing of the items on the gender and racial indexes is not identical, each had the same number of forced-choice items with one alternative blaming
structural forces and the other personal deficiencies. The same is true for collective
orientation indexes, with one alternative advocating collective action by women (or
by blacks), and the other favoring individual action.

[The 1976 data show] the only statistically significant difference between men and
women pertained to evaluations of power. And that lone difference is dwarfed by the
extremely large differences between blacks and whites. Sixty percent more blacks than
whites said blacks have "too little" power, and 45 percent more blacks said whites have
"too much" power. Blacks and whites also had highly discrepant views about the causes
of race disparities and blacks' strategies for reducing them. In contrast, men and women
held nearly identical opinions about the individual and structural forces that produce
gender disparities and strategies for women to improve their statuses.

TOWARD CRITICAL THINKING

1. Patricia Gurin argues that the structure of gender relations in American society has
   prevented women from developing a group consciousness as strong as have African
   Americans. What alternative explanations does Gurin not consider? Are African Americans and women reasonable groups to compare? Why or why not? What is the position of African American women within this theory?

2. What do you think of Gurin's decision to include "discontent" and "legitimacy of disparities" among the four components of gender consciousness? According to Gurin,
   why must women be discontented and think of their differences from men as illegitimate to be considered gender consciousness? What other measures of gender consciousness might be more useful?

READING 16

Feminists and the Gender Gap

(1988)

Pamela Johnston Conover

Political psychologist Pamela Johnston Conover expands Patricia Gurin's (Reading 15) work to explain the persistent "gender gap" in women's political attitudes and partisan identification. Conover's line of reasoning is, at first consideration, fairly direct. Some women, with a particularly strong or transformative kind of gender consciousness, which she calls "feminist consciousness," have clearly distinct preferences and goals in the political process that stem from their advanced group identification with other women. Conover believes that it is the behavior and attitudes of this subset of women that drives the gender gap. While other researchers had sought to identify some critical change in the party platforms or presentations in 1980—the election in which the gender gap first came to public attention—Conover's approach establishes itself more firmly in the principles of political psychology and traces a slow shift over time in women's political and social attitudes. This explanation of the gender gap is particularly exciting because it offers us a theoretical illumination of the phenomenon that also sets up a claim for representation within the government. It also helps answer the perennial question in research on women in American politics: does their difference make a difference? Conover's answer to this question in this article published in the *Journal of Politics* is clearly yes.

Pay special attention as you read, though, to the problems we discussed with Gurin's methods. As you will soon see, they come to the forefront in Conover's article—and in its critical reception in the readings that follow.

During the 1980s, the discovery of "the gender gap" drew attention to the women's movement and to the topic of sex differences in public opinion and participation. Now that a substantial body of research has accumulated, it is possible to assess what is known about this phenomenon. [This article] investigates the gender gap in basic values in order to explain the growing gender gap in public opinion. . . .

The Nature of the Gender Gap

The term "gender gap" is a catch-all phrase referring to a variety of phenomena. First, there may be gender gaps in levels of *mass participation;* however, recently these gaps have narrowed if not disappeared and consequently currently attract little attention. More interesting are the *electoral* and *partisan* gender gaps. The electoral gap refers to the differing vote choices of men and women. In recent years, women have been more likely than men to support Democratic candidates. Closely related to the electoral gap is the partisan gap which refers to the differences between men and women in their party identifications. During the eighties, women have increasingly given their allegiance to the Democratic party so that currently they comprise a majority of Democratic identifiers.

Both the electoral and partisan gaps have been the subjects of considerable research. Yet, although this research has clarified the extent of a gender gap in electoral results and partisan distributions, it has faltered in explaining *why* such gender gaps exist. Most studies point to the changing behavior of women though some argue that the changing behavior of men has produced the gaps. And most accounts hint that underlying these electoral and partisan gender gaps are sex differences in policy preferences and ideology.

That brings us to the fourth, and perhaps the most critical, variant of the gender gap: the growing disparity in the political attitudes of men and women. This gender gap in public opinion is important for several reasons. For one thing, to the extent that they are issue-based, the full explanation of the electoral and partisanship gaps becomes dependent upon understanding the gender gap in political preferences. More generally, the gender gap in public opinion may alter the salience of various political issues thus prompting changes in the political agenda. And, as the gender gap widens on particular issues there may be aggregate shifts in the public's preferences which in turn create pressure to change the direction of public policy. As [political scientists] Robert Shapiro and Harpreet Mahajan point out, women are such a large group that even the emergence of small sex differences in issue preferences can have substantial consequences on public policy.

Yet, despite the potential importance of the gender gap in public opinion, it has attracted less attention than the other three. Moreover, the research that has been done has concentrated on documenting the existence of this gap rather than on explaining it. In this vein, Shapiro and Mahajan's study is perhaps the most exhaustive. Their examination of public opinion data collected over the last twenty years reveals sizable and persistent gender differences in attitudes toward issues involving the use of force, and smaller, but growing sex differences toward other policies concerning regulation and public protection, social welfare, and traditional values. Shapiro and Mahajan go on to conclude that "the salience of issues has increased greatly for women, and as a result differences in preferences have increased in ways consistent with the interests of women and the intentions of the women's movement."

But what accounts for such changes? In addressing this question, two distinct bodies of literature will be brought together: feminist political theory and empirical research on the gender gap. Specifically, insights gleaned from feminist theorists advocating a "woman-centered perspective" will be integrated with empirical evidence on gender differences to produce a fuller interpretation of the origins of the gender gap in public opinion.

"A Woman's Perspective"

Most explanations of the gender gap in public opinion are based on the notion that men and women have different political values and priorities which stem from fundamental value differences. Such an explanation triggers three questions. First, how and why do women's values differ from those of men? Second, how do such value differences manifest themselves in political preferences? And finally, what is the empirical evidence pertaining to a gender gap in political values? . . .

The Nature and Origins of "A Woman's Perspective"

The question of whether men and women differ in their fundamental values has concerned feminist theorists for some time. Nineteenth century American feminists often entertained the idea that, compared to men, women naturally embrace morally superior values. Writing in the late 1960s and early 1970s, contemporary feminist theorists described basic differences between the sexes as social constructions emanating from the different roles that men and women play in a patriarchal society. More recently, in analyzing such male-female differences as a source of oppression, feminists began to return to the themes of the nineteenth century and to perceive women's differences from men not as a "form of inadequacy or as a source of inferiority," but instead as a matter of pride, confidence, hope, and superiority. And so there emerged in the mid-1970s a "woman-centered perspective" focusing on the female experience as an unique source of values for society.

Advocates of this woman-centered perspective stress the distinctive aspects of women's lives, the values fostered by such life experiences, and the positive contributions to society that such values can make. Moreover, in the course of these analyses some theorists have shifted away from a view of gender differences as socially constructed toward a perspective which stresses intrinsic, biological differences underlying femaleness and maleness. As [feminist theologian] Marilyn Chapin Massey explains, these radical feminists claim that "women speak a new truth arising from their unique physical experience . . . (a truth that) does not complement Western male moral discourse, but instead aims to subvert it."

What is this "new truth" that women speak? In "Maternal Thinking," [philosopher] Sara Ruddick suggests that women's interests in the preservation, growth, and acceptability of their children shape the way they look at the world. Some also argue that women approach ethical problems differently from men. Perhaps the most influential statement of this kind is [psychologist] Carol Gilligan's: she posits that women are more oriented toward interpersonal relationships, and that this results in a conception of morality that stresses caring and responsibility toward others. In contrast, men are more concerned with rights and rules, and thus they emphasize justice and fairness in their moral decisions.

It is argued, then, that a "woman's perspective" is responsive to growth and accepting of change, embodies compassion and caring for others, and manifests humility in its sensitivity to the realities of the environment. It is also a perspective with uncertain origins: it might be fostered by different social roles or it might be an intrinsic manifestation of the innate differences between men and women. But, regardless of its origins, the question must be asked: how does a woman's perspective come to influence politics?

Politics and "A Woman's Perspective"

Proponents of a woman-centered analysis argue that an infusion of women's values into the political arena will transform society in a positive fashion. But, as critics have pointed out, it is not altogether clear precisely how this injection of values and subsequent cultural transformation are to take place. If it is to be argued that a "woman's" values have the potential to transform politics, some mechanism of transformation must be identified.

From the perspective of some feminists, the most obvious mechanism to fill such a role is a *feminist identity and consciousness.* Specifically, it is argued that in the absence of a feminist identity a woman's values usually lie dormant beneath the male-oriented values of the dominant culture. But, in the process of becoming a feminist, women develop a sense of consciousness that enables them to discover their true values which may then serve as a basis for their politics. Thus, becoming a feminist helps women "recover" their basic values which, in turn, shape their sense of political consciousness, and ultimately their preferences on political issues.

Some would object, however, that a feminist *political* consciousness rooted solely in a woman's values is not enough to ensure either the infusion of those values into politics or the subsequent adoption of distinctive issue preferences. Instead, they argue that if the public world is to be transformed a woman's values must be coupled with, if not subordinated to, democratic political values. As [political theorist] Mary Dietz asserts "the only consciousness that can serve as a basis for this transformation . . . is a distinctly political consciousness steeped in a commitment to democratic values, participatory citizenship, and egalitarianism." In essence, such theorists posit that if women are going to alter the political agenda, a particular set of political values may be more crucial than a "woman's" values.

These theoretical arguments have several implications that are potentially testable. First, at the aggregate level, they suggest that the widening of the gender gap in the late 1970s may be linked to the growing strength of the women's movement. And indeed, this is an argument that a number of scholars have made though not empirically tested. Second, these theoretical arguments imply that a woman's values should be more readily expressed by feminists and more obviously reflected in their politics. Third, and finally, the injection of a woman's values into politics may be related to a commitment to democratic values. . . .

[* * *]

With that in mind, three questions will be addressed empirically in this [article]. First, is there a gender gap in political values and more basic value orientations? Second, do women's values differ according to the strength of their feminist identities? And third, if there are gender differences in values, to what extent are they attributable to feminists?

Data and Methods

In order to explore these questions, I shall use data collected in the 1985 National Election Study Pilot (NES). Three sets of measures are created from these data: a measure of feminist identity, measures of value orientations, and measures of issue preferences.

A Measure of Feminist Identity

In order to explore the above hypotheses, women with a feminist identity must be distinguished from those who lack such an identity. In approaching this measurement question, a feminist identity will be treated as a form of social identity, and as such it has two components: a sense of membership in the category or group and a sense of psychological attachment to the group. With that in mind, previous studies may be examined in order to determine possible measurement strategies.

One approach is to use objective indicators. But, this would require the questionable assumption that specific objective categories, such as work status or education, are reliably and highly correlated with a *feminist identity*. A second, more direct, approach to identifying feminist women is based on an assessment of beliefs. For instance, as [Patricia] Gurin [Reading 15] explains, a "collective orientation" and an awareness of gender inequities are beliefs which may be treated as indicators of a feminist consciousness and identity. Yet, a third, even more direct, approach is to focus on the extent to which women consciously identify themselves as feminists.

The third approach is the one adopted here. In so doing, it is assumed that how a woman thinks of herself is as important as her objective status and beliefs in determining her behavior. In effect whether a woman actually thinks of herself as a feminist is assumed to have a fundamental impact on how she looks at the world. . . .

[* * *]

But, as defined earlier, self-categorization is only one part of a social identity; psychological attachment is another component that must be measured. Accordingly, responses to the . . . question tapping "feminist" self-categorization were multiplied by the respondent's feeling thermometer rating of feminists. . . .

[* * *]

Measures of Value Orientations

As discussed by recent theorists, the central values in a woman's perspective are not hypothesized to be political in nature. Nonetheless, for two reasons it is important to investigate whether there is a gender gap in political values. For one thing, a gender gap in political values may help to explain the gender gap that we already know exists in specific policy preferences. More important, even though particular political values such as egalitarianism may not be central to a woman's perspective, they may be essential to the political expression of that perspective.

Therefore, three political value orientations and one measure of political identity are used in the analysis. . . . An "egalitarianism" scale measures attitudes toward equality of opportunity; high scores indicate a strong commitment to equality. An "individualism" measure taps attitudes towards the work ethic and individual effort; high scores signify a strong sense of individualism. The "symbolic racism" scale deals with a mixture of the protestant ethic and negative affect toward blacks; high scores represent a strong sense of symbolic racism. Finally, the traditional liberal-conservative identification measure is employed; high scores indicate "very conservative."

Four more basic value orientations that relate to a woman's perspective are also considered in the analysis. Two of these, moral traditionalism and religious fundamentalism, tap conceptions of morality. The third one, sex roles, while not central to a woman's perspective should provide insights into the nature of differences among women. And, the final one measures sympathy for the disadvantaged.

To explain further, the "moral traditionalism" measure taps a preference for traditional patterns of family and social organization that reflects an underlying reverence for the past and a resistance to change. High scores on this measure indicate a strong commitment to moral traditionalism. The "fundamentalism" scale measures a "born-again" religious orientation in which the Bible is interpreted literally and religion plays a guiding role in daily life; high scores signify a strong fundamentalist bent. The "sex role" measure taps the respondent's preference for traditional vs. "modern" conceptions of sex roles; high scores represent a preference for modern sex roles. Finally, because it is so central to a woman's perspective, it is essential to consider as well an "ethic of caring." Unfortunately, the NES Pilot Study does not include questions that directly tap sympathy and caring for others. Consequently, "sympathy for the disadvantaged," a measure that indirectly assesses an ethic of caring, must be relied upon. . . . While this measure does not directly assess the emotional responses of sympathy and caring, it does get at the general emotional reaction of the respondent to the disadvantaged and thus represents a reasonable approximation. . . .

Measures of Issue Preferences

Finally, in order to examine the extent to which value differences contribute to the gender gap in public opinion, it is necessary to measure issue preferences. Accordingly, a variety of domestic and foreign affairs issues were analyzed for gender differences. This examination uncovered gender differences on six of seven foreign policy issues; on three of ten racial issues; and on nine of fourteen economic and social issues. For further analysis, issues with significant gender differences were selected from each of these categories. In all instances, the relevant items have been recorded so that *low* scores indicate the issue preference most congruent with a liberal perspective. Specifically, in the foreign affairs arena low scores indicate a fear of war, a desire for peace and nonintervention in Central America, and less commitment to a strong national defense. In the domestic policy area, low scores represent support for social spending and abortion, and opposition to school prayer.

Findings

Value Differences between Men and Women

Do men and women differ in their political values? [The data] provide a clear answer to this question. . . . [T]here are no significant differences . . . between men and women on any of the three specific political value orientations—egalitarianism, individualism, and symbolic racism. . . . Moreover, and somewhat more surprisingly, although women tend to identify themselves as liberals more frequently than do men, the sex differences for this variable are not statistically significant. If there is a distinctive woman's perspective, it is not apparent in the political values of women as a whole.

Is there, then, anything at all that might meaningfully be called "a woman's perspective?" Men and women differ very little in their commitment to modern conceptions of sex roles. . . . Yet, in and of themselves these sex role orientations are not a crucial element in defining a woman's perspective. In the same vein, there is also a lack of significant sex differences on the moral traditionalism measure. . . . But, it is difficult to interpret the meaning of this finding. Some argue that a concern with the sanctity of the traditional family is an element of a woman's perspective, whereas others vigorously oppose the idea of linking the traditional family with an argument about women's values or democratic values in general. Thus, whether such a finding is supportive or contradictory to a woman's perspective argument is a matter of controversy. . . .

[* * *]

In summary, the evidence for a woman's perspective is mixed. Women do not seem to differ from men in political values. Thus, if there is a woman's perspective in terms of fundamental values, it has yet to emerge in the political values of the mass public. On the other hand, women do differ from men in religious fundamentalism and, most importantly, in their sympathy for the disadvantaged. Such findings lend preliminary support to the woman's perspective argument.

Value Differences among Women

Paradoxically, the lack of large sex differences in basic orientations and especially in political values can also be seen as consistent with that part of the woman's perspective argument which suggests that feminine values are typically overwhelmed by masculine values in a patriarchal society such as the United States. If a woman's perspective is to emerge, the argument goes, women must experience a sense of feminist identity and consciousness. Thus, it is misleading to consider women as an undifferentiated group. Women differ in how they think of themselves—in the strength of their feminist identity—and such differences may well be related to variations in values and issue preferences.

In more formal terms, the model suggested by this argument is one in which the development of a feminist identity and consciousness leads to the reshaping of values that were originally formed by early socialization experiences and by adult social location. The feminist's "reshaped" values then determine her more specific issue preferences both by creating preferences on issues that were formerly unimportant and by changing existing issue positions. In effect, the development of a feminist identity constitutes a resocialization experience for a woman; it directly influences her values, and through her values it indirectly affects her specific issue positions. For present purposes, however, we need not test the full-blown model but only the implications of this model that are central to understanding the gender gap. In particular, the model suggests that women should differ in their values and issue preferences according to the strength of their feminist identity. Is this the case?

[* * *]

... Women who strongly identify themselves as feminists tend to have distinctive political and basic value orientations: as compared to nonfeminist women, they are more liberal, less racist, more egalitarian, less traditional morally and with regard to sex roles, and more sympathetic to the disadvantaged. Furthermore, as suggested by the woman's perspective argument, a feminist identity is not only *related* to a distinctive pattern of values but it also helps to *produce* those values. In particular, though the strength of a woman's feminist identity is by no means the only determinant of her values, it is a *major* factor in shaping those values. Moreover, the values of feminists clearly manifest themselves in the issue preferences which they adopt. Women with a strong feminist identity do, indeed, embrace a set of policy preferences which if implemented would fundamentally alter the nature of public policy. In this regard, it is important to recognize that both political values and more basic value orientations (e.g., sympathy for the disadvantaged) shape the policy preferences of feminists. Thus, our findings tend to support the argument that a feminist consciousness must affirm not only a woman's perspective, but also democratic values if it is to be politically distinctive.

Are these findings surprising? No, not really. Certainly in the context of the woman's perspective argument, it would be surprising if we did *not* find that women with a strong feminist identity have distinctive values and issue preferences. More generally, the very nature of political ideologies and social identities suggests that people who identify with a particular movement should adopt those values and issue preferences associated with it. ... It *is* surprising, however, that previous researchers have not explored more fully the value orientations and issue preferences of feminists. This may reflect a more general tendency to give insufficient attention to the considerable variations among women. Yet, recognizing such variations may alter our interpretation of the gender gap. Thus, these findings about feminists are surprising in the sense that they suggest an unexplored explanation of the gender gap: the idea that perhaps only a subset of women, such as feminists, rather than women in general, differ from men. We explore that possibility now.

The Gender Gap and a Feminist Identity

Women differ in their political values depending on the degree to which they identify as feminists. Is it mainly feminists, then, whose views explain the gender gap in issue preferences? ...

[According to the data], nonfeminists, like women in general, do not differ from men in political values. The feminists, however, do differ from men significantly on three of the four political value orientations: egalitarianism, symbolic racism, and ideology. Specifically, feminists are more committed than men to the value of equality; they evidence less symbolic racism than men; and they are considerably more liberal than men.

With respect to the more basic value orientations, recall that our earlier analysis uncovered sex differences in religious fundamentalism and sympathy for the disadvantaged. When men are compared separately to feminist and nonfeminist women, the sex difference in religious fundamentalism persists in both cases. Feminists and nonfeminists alike tend to be more religious than men. For the remaining values, however, the pattern of sex differences changes when women are divided into feminist and nonfeminist groups. Specifically, nonfeminist women compared to men have a stronger sense of moral traditionalism; in contrast, feminists resemble men in their level of moral traditionalism.

But, most important are the findings with regard to sympathy for the disadvantaged. Nonfeminist women are similar to men in their degree of caring for the disadvantaged: the mean value for nonfeminist women is .68 on the disadvantaged scale as compared to .67 for men. By contrast, feminists differ greatly from men in the stronger sense of caring that they display; they average .74 on the sympathy scale. Thus, the gender gap in sympathy for the disadvantaged is due entirely to the more caring posture adopted by feminist women. This finding may be interpreted in several ways. On the one hand, it may indicate that a feminist identity is, indeed, necessary to express in politics a woman's natural tendency toward caring. Alternatively, the high degree of sympathy that feminist women display may be an outgrowth of their other political values (e.g, egalitarianism) and not their femaleness per se. Or, some combination of these two explanations may be at work.

One way of testing these alternative explanations is to compare feminist women to feminist men. If the differences in sympathy persist between these two groups, it would tend to support the argument that women are naturally more sympathetic and caring than men. On the other hand, if the sex differences in sympathy disappear when feminist women are compared to feminist men, it would suggest that the political values associated with feminism help to account for the greater sympathy of feminist women. Unfortunately, the 1985 NES Pilot Study does not include a comparable measure of feminist identity for men. Thus, at this time it is impossible to determine if feminist women are more sympathetic to the disadvantaged than men because of their femaleness or because of their political ideology.

Finally, we can turn to the question of the gender gap in issue preferences. Earlier it was discovered that a feminist identity is associated with a distinctive pattern of issue preferences. This raises the possibility that the gender gap in issue preferences may be mainly due to the liberal policy positions of feminist women. . . .

Previous research has demonstrated that consistently the largest gender gap is on foreign policy issues. With respect to such issues, nonfeminist women do not differ significantly from men with the exception of the issue of Central America. In contrast again, feminists differ significantly from men on every foreign policy issue. Thus, in most cases, the sizable gender gap on foreign policy issues appears to be due to the antiwar, anti-involvement positions adopted by feminists.

In the domestic policy realm, nonfeminist women differ significantly from men on issues affecting the old (e.g. medicare and spending on older people) as well as spending on unemployment. Beyond that, however, the nonfeminist women resemble men in their spending preferences. In contrast, on virtually every domestic policy issues feminists differ significantly from men, adopting on average more liberal positions than those of both men and nonfeminist women. Only on social policies such as abortion and school prayer do feminists resemble men in their issue preferences. Thus, both nonfeminist and feminist women contribute to the gender gap on domestic issues, but the contribution of the feminist women is by far the greater of the two. Taken together, these findings on domestic and foreign policy issues suggest that the gender gap in policy preferences is only rarely due to widespread differences between men and women as whole. Instead, on most issues the gender gap in public opinion is a function of the liberal positions that a subset of women—feminists—consistently adopt.

[* * *]

TOWARD CRITICAL THINKING

1. Are you surprised by Pamela Johnston Conover's finding that feminists differ from men in their basic value orientations? In her own words, these findings are "not particularly astonishing" but they point to the perhaps paradoxical importance of attending to differences among women to understand the gender gap. What other differences among women might Conover have profited from examining?

2. If Conover is right that a subset of women—feminists—drives the gender gap, what are the implications for the women's movement? Can feminist leaders claim to speak "for women," or can they speak only on behalf of their sister feminists?

READING 17

Feminism and the Gender Gap—
A Second Look

(1991)

Elizabeth Adell Cook and Clyde Wilcox

Taking a second look at Pamela Johnston Conover's study of feminists and the gender gap (Reading 16), Elizabeth Adell Cook and Clyde Wilcox make two counter-arguments. First, they challenge Conover's notion that feminists within the mass public can be identified as a subset of the category "women." Many men also are feminists, they argue, just as Conover concedes that many women are not. Furthermore, they show that feminism has a similar impact on the values and political preferences of feminist men and feminist women, undermining Conover's derivation of feminist consciousness from a special "woman's perspective" from which men were by definition barred. They also continue to find gender gaps when they compare Conover's own data on feminist men to feminist women, potentially feminist men to potentially feminist women, and nonfeminist men to nonfeminist women. This finding alone destabilizes Conover's case for a women's perspective activated by feminist awakening.

Basically, Cook and Wilcox—a wife and husband team of feminist political scientists—show that Conover did not fully explain the gender gap. Now we can see, from the vantage points of the analyses below, that feminism does not explain the outcomes of elections that have been labeled evidence of the gender gap. This article, published as a "Research Note" in the *Journal of Politics*, used data to examine contentions already developed by Conover rather than to develop new explanations.

The increasing gender gap in vote choice has prompted research into the sources of gender differences in political behavior and partisan attachments. Recent studies have reported a gender gap in political attitudes as well, particularly on the use of force, but on other issues as well.

Although the gender gap is by now well documented, there has been less effort to explain the gap. Some have suggested that the gender gap is due to the lower socioeconomic status [SES] of women, although research has found that SES differences account for only a small part of the gender gap. Recently, [Pamela Johnston] Conover [Reading 16] has provided evidence to support a "women's perspective" explanation of the gender gap.

Some feminist theorists have argued that women have different values than men. Some have attributed these differences to socialization, others to the distinctive aspects of women's experience, including motherhood. These values lead to less support for violence, and to an ethic of caring and nurturance that translates into sympathy for the disadvantaged. Conover suggested that the process of becoming a feminist may awaken these feminine values that may be dormant among nonfeminist women.

Using data from the 1985 National Election Study Pilot Survey (NES), Conover reported that although there were only modest differences between men and women on political values and attitudes, there were substantial differences between feminist women and all men. Moreover, feminism was a strong predictor of basic and political values and policy preferences among women. She interpreted this as evidence that "becoming feminist may be a catalyst that helps women recognize their underlying 'female' values . . . if there is an underlying women's perspective that encompasses an ethic of caring, its expression is facilitated by a feminist identity."

Conover's work provides the first empirical link between those scholars who have written on women's perspectives and those who have focused on the importance of feminist consciousness. As such, her work makes an important theoretical and empirical contribution to our understanding of gender differences. Such empirical work is long overdue. The link between feminist consciousness and the women's perspective position posited by Conover is intuitively plausible.

Conover's definition of feminist consciousness combined a feeling thermometer toward feminists with an item asking women how often they thought of themselves as feminists—most of the time, some of the time, occasionally, or never. The feminist identification item is a vast improvement over the closeness measure used in previous studies, and we think it a useful measure. It has one important limitation, however: it was only asked of women. Although many have argued that men cannot have a feminist consciousness, they can certainly hold feminist beliefs and have feminist sympathy. Though the sources of feminist sympathy may be different from those of feminist consciousness, it may have the same political consequences. If feminism is a strong predictor of values and attitudes of men as well as women, then feminism may lead to feminist, not feminine, values and policies.

Conover found that feminist women were significantly more liberal than all men. She suggests that this is due to the politicizing effects of feminist consciousness, which awakens women to their gender-specific values. It also might be an artifact of isolating a set of liberal feminist women without isolating a similar group of feminist men. To determine whether we are seeing the effects of feminist or women's values, we must compare the attitudes of feminist men and women, and nonfeminist men and women.

This note will further explore the relationship of feminism and the gender gap. Using data from the 1984 American National Election Study, we identify men and women who are feminists, potential feminists, and nonfeminists, and compare their political values and attitudes.

Data and Measures

Our data come from the 1984 American National Election Study. We have selected this survey instead of the more recent 1988 survey because the NES Pilot study used by Conover involved reinterviewing a subset of respondents from the 1984 study. Our measure of feminism was introduced by Cook. The measure combines the equal role scale used in a number of surveys by [Elizabeth Adell] Cook and an adjusted feeling thermometer toward the women's liberation movement.

Those respondents who do not strongly support an equal role for women are labeled as nonfeminists. Those respondents who believe in equal gender roles but do not support the women's liberation movement are termed potential feminists, and those respondents who support gender equality and the political movement that promotes that equality are termed feminists. Cook demonstrated that in the 1972 NES, her measure was strongly related to attitudes that other scholars have identified as components of a feminist consciousness: group identification, system blaming, power discontent, and support for collective action. Although the measure taps feminist consciousness among women, it might be labeled feminist sympathy among men. For the sake of simplicity, we will refer to it as a measure of feminism. Slightly more than a quarter of both men and women are classified as feminists, and slightly less than one-third of both sexes fall into the potential feminist category.

The 1984 survey did not contain all of the items in the 1985 Pilot survey. To measure political values and attitudes, therefore, we have created scales that are sometimes identical to, and sometimes merely similar to those used by Conover. We have duplicated her measure of fundamentalism and liberal-conservative identification, and constructed measures of egalitarianism, individualism, and gender equality that are very similar to hers. Our measure of sympathy for the disadvantaged is also similar, although we have adjusted the feeling thermometers as noted earlier. Instead of a symbolic racism scale, we have created a measure of relative minority affect from the adjusted feeling thermometers for blacks and Hispanics.

Our measures of issue preferences are also similar, though not identical. . . . We do not replicate Conover's analysis, but we use different measures and data to get a different focus on the relationship between feminism and the gender gap.

Gender Differences

We find limited gender differences in basic values. These values are: religious fundamentalism, gender-role equality, societal equality, individualism, minority affect, sympathy for the disadvantaged, liberal/conservative ID, policy preferences, government spending, guaranteed job, government medical insurance, spending (social security, food stamps, Medicare, government jobs for the unemployed, assistance to blacks), minority aid, civil rights too fast, bussing, defense spending, détente—USSR, involvement in Central America, isolationism, conventional war, nuclear war, government aid to women, abortion, and school prayer. There are no significant gender differences on minority affect, sympathy for the disadvantaged, or gender equality values, and modest, statistically significant differences on general equality, individualism, and liberal-conservative identification. The largest relationship is with fundamentalism. . . . Conover reported a significant gender difference in sympathy for the disadvantaged, but our adjusted-affect measure does not confirm this. Women do rate the poor, welfare recipients, and the elderly approximately 4° warmer than men, but women assign warmer feeling thermometer scores in general than men. Of the 21 groups in the 1984 NES, women rate all 21 warmer than do men, and this difference is statistically significant for 20 of 21 groups. The gender gap in affect for the disadvantaged is almost identical to the gender gap for all other groups. At the very least, women's sympathy for the disadvantaged is no greater than their sympathy for other groups. We prefer to argue that there are gender differences in response tendencies to feeling thermometer items.

On policy preferences, women are significantly more liberal than men on 15 of 20 issues considered, but these differences are small. Gender differences were largest on support for spending to aid the unemployed, and on war and peace issues, issues consistent with the women's perspective thesis.

Feminism, Values and Policies, and Gender

Conover argued that the lack of significant gender differences on basic and political values suggests that "feminine values are typically overwhelmed by masculine values in a patriarchal society such as the United States." A feminist consciousness is seen as necessary for the emergence of a women's perspective. She found that among women, a feminist consciousness was strongly correlated with liberal values and policy preferences.

Yet it is unclear from this evidence that a unique women's perspective is crystallized by an emerging feminist consciousness. One alternative explanation is that feminism is linked to *feminist* values and policy preferences among both men and women. [We calculated] bivariate and partial correlation coefficients for both men and women, with feminism as the independent variable and values and policy preferences as the dependent variables. In the partial correlations, we included the five control variables used by Conover: party identification, age, education, race, and income. The data suggest that feminism is indeed strongly correlated with liberal values and policy preferences, but that the correlations are significant for both men and women. The correlations are slightly higher for women than for men, but these differences are statistically significant for only two issues, and on one (assistance to blacks), feminism leads to a more liberal position among men than women.

What do these results indicate for the women's perspective argument? First, they suggest that feminist consciousness in women and feminist sympathy in men are both strong predictors of values and policy preferences. Clearly the values and policy preferences that are associated with feminism are not uniquely feminine. Others have suggested that women's values may be shared by men in some circumstances, and it could be argued that feminism sensitizes men to feminine values. Such an argument would suggest that the women's perspective derives from social and political, not biological sources. We prefer the more parsimonious argument that feminism is not associated with a "women's perspective," but rather with feminist values—liberal egalitarian values and policies.

One additional problem with the thesis that feminism awakens a "women's perspective" is the question of the direction of causality. It is possible that the development of a feminist consciousness leads to more feminine values and policy preferences, but it is also likely that those women and men who have liberal values and policy preferences are the most likely to develop feminist consciousness and sympathy. A preliminary analysis using the Cook feminism measure in the 1972–1976 NES panel study revealed that liberal women and men were significantly more likely than moderates and conservatives to increase their scores on our feminism scale, suggesting that part of the correlation is due to the successes of the feminist movement in recruiting liberals. These new feminists did not change their attitudes or basic values as they developed their feminist leanings during the four years of the panel study, though they may have done so later. A complete untangling of this reciprocal causality would require the estimation of a nonrecursive model.

Feminism and the Gender Gap

If feminism is not associated with uniquely feminine values or policy preferences, it is nonetheless possible that such values and attitudes distinguish men from women, regardless of their level of feminism. Although Conover reported that there were few significant gender differences among nonfeminist women and all men, we find significant gender differences between feminist men and women, potential feminist men and women, and nonfeminist men and women. . . . [A] statistically significant gender gap exists on different issues for all three groups. . . . The gender gap is again more substantial and consistent on policy preferences than on general values. The nature and size of the gender gap varies across issues for feminists, potential feminists, and nonfeminists. On abortion and gender-equality values, nonfeminist women are significantly more conservative than nonfeminist men, but the relationship is reversed among potential feminists and feminists. The gender gap on fundamentalism is confined to nonfeminists and potential feminists, and the gender gap on spending issues is largest among nonfeminists. Among feminists, the gender gap is largely confined to war and peace issues. Few of the differences in correlations are statistically significant, but they hint at the complexity of the relationship between gender, feminism, and policy attitudes.

Conclusions

We find that feminism is associated with distinctive values and policy preferences among both men and women, suggesting that feminism is not a catalyst for uniquely feminine values and policy preferences. It is possible to interpret from these data that feminism awakens in both men and women support for a woman's perspective, but we prefer to argue instead for the existence of a feminist perspective that consists of egalitarian values and generally liberal policies. We find that the relationship between feminism and values and policy preferences is reciprocal: developing a feminist consciousness may lead to more egalitarian values and policy preferences, but feminists are also recruited among more liberal and egalitarian women and men.

We also find a significant gender gap among nonfeminists, potential feminists, and feminists. This suggests that the gender gap is *not* due to increasing numbers of feminist women, who are offset by, yet different from, feminist men. The gender gap instead remains to be fully explained.

Our analysis is far from a definitive test of the women's perspective thesis. We know of no survey data designed to test the argument, as these data were not. Moreover, to the extent that some accounts of a woman's perspective have focused more on the *process* of political reasoning than on final political opinions, survey research may be unable to provide a definitive test. Our analysis does suggest, however, that feminism does not awaken uniquely feminine values, and that the gender gap exists among men and women with different levels of support for feminism. Feminism does not explain the gender gap.

TOWARD CRITICAL THINKING

1. In an omitted footnote to Reading 16, Pamela Johnston Conover entertains the possibility—seemingly reinforced by Elizabeth Adell Cook and Clyde Wilcox's findings—that what she approaches as a "women's perspective" is actually a feminist perspective, but she rejects that contention. Based on your reading of the two articles, who do you think is correct?

2. Conover and Cook and Wilcox have different ways of operationalizing feminism—that is, different ways of defining and measuring feminism as they analyze their data. What are these differences? Do they matter when it comes to their conclusions? Whose definition do you find more persuasive?

READING 18

The Independence Gap
and the Gender Gap

(1997)

Barbara Norrander

This article from *Public Opinion Quarterly* presents Barbara Norrander's unique perspective on the gender gap. She argues that the source of the gap is women's decreased likelihood of identifying as political independents—the independence gap. In this way, Norrander continues the critique of Pamela Johnston Conover's work (Reading 16) begun by Elizabeth Adell Cook and Clyde Wilcox (Reading 17). Rather than reversing Conover's basic assumptions about men and women as Cook and Wilcox do, Norrander attempts to rewrite the historical narrative of the gender gap. Because the phenomenon emerged to public discussion in 1980 as an apparent preference among women for Democrats, both Conover and Cook and Wilcox try to explain the gap in terms of why women might be more liberal. Approaching the question from the standpoint of political parties research, Norrander marshals considerable data showing that this way of asking the question is wrongheaded. Instead, she argues, scholars would do better to look not for party switchers (as the first classic article in the field, Daniel Wirls's "Reinterpreting the Gender Gap," published in 1986 does) or for attitudinal changes (as Conover does), but rather for the uneven rates at which men and women have simply disidentified from the party system altogether.

With this fresh perspective, Norrander does indeed reach different conclusions—but does she answer our basic questions about the gender gap? As you will see, Norrander presents some evidence to account for women's lower inclination to identify as Independents, but she is unable to find a definitive reason for this. In short, Norrander's new direction doesn't provide scholars with answers so much as it opens up for us a host of new questions.

Numerous scholarly studies and journalistic accounts focus on women's greater preference for the Democratic Party. These accounts pinpoint 1980 as the beginning of the gender gap. Yet, a longer standing difference between men's and women's partisan identities has been largely ignored. Since the 1950s, fewer women than men have called themselves independents. . . . [Researchers] found young women in the early

1970s were less likely to be independents than were young men but concluded it was an anomaly specific to that time. But the independence gap is not an anomaly; it has persisted for 40 years and thus warrants more extensive investigation. This article documents the independence gap from 1952 to 1994, demonstrates its persistence across a wide spectrum of subgroups, and investigates its consequences for the political behavior of men and women as well as its impact on the more familiar partisan gender gap.

How Large Is the Independence Gap?

The independence gap averaged 6 percentage points across the American National Election Studies (ANES) surveys from 1952 to 1994, and was statistically significant in 16 of the 22 years. The size of the gap varied inconsistently during the 1950s and 1960s, grew stronger in the 1970s and 1980s, diminished in the early 1990s, but rebounded in 1994.

The independence gap is also found in other surveys. . . . The gap averages 5.6 percentage points in the General Social Surveys (GSS) from 1972 to 1994 and is statistically significant in 13 of the 20 years. Furthermore, in most years when the independence gap does not attain significance in the GSS (1972, 1973, 1974, 1980, 1984, 1989, and 1993) it is significant in the ANES surveys. Thus, any comparison of the partisan preferences of men to women must account for gender variations in preferences for the independent label.

[* * *]

Do Demographic Traits Explain the Independence Gap?

One explanation for why men and women answer partisanship questions differently would be demographic dissimilarities between the sexes. Women tend to live longer than men, and thus surveys contain more elderly women than men. These more numerous older women may simply express the more partisan preferences of past eras and provide women as a whole with a more partisan complexion. Another possibility would be educational differences. The lower educational levels of women may explain their propensity to avoid the independent label, since college-educated citizens have increasingly become attracted to nonpartisanship. Conversely, the independence gap may disappear among racial or religious groups with strong identities with one party. The independence gap might also be more prevalent in the South. Southern women entered the electorate later than women in other parts of the country, with significant increases occurring in the 1960s. With less political tradition, Southern women may have been more willing to adopt the Republican label during the 1960s realignment than were their male counterparts who became independents instead. Finally, because a marital gap has existed since the 1970s with married individuals more likely to vote Republican, a check will be made for any link between marriage and the independence gap.

Table 18.1 presents the independence gap for different demographic groups by use of the combined 1952–94 ANES data. Contrary to the generational explanation, the independence gap is largest among the younger generation. Similarly, the independence

TABLE 18.1

Size of the Independence Gap among Different Demographic Groups, 1952–94

	Pure Independent	Leaning Independent	Weak Partisan	Strong Partisan	No. of Cases
Age:					
Born after 1942	2	6	−7	0	12,940
Born 1942 and before	−1	5	−4	0	28,410
Education:					
Grade school	−5	3	−3	5	7,789
High school	1	5	−6	0	20,138
College	3	7	−4	−5	13,440
Race:					
White	0	5	−5	0	36,380
Black	0	5	−7	3	4,389
Hispanic	0	4	−9	5	1,142
Region:					
East	2	7	−7	−1	8,589
Midwest	0	5	−4	−2	11,380
South	−1	4	−6	2	13,577
West	0	5	−4	−1	6,898
Marital Status:					
Married	−1	4	−6	2	26,367
Single	4	5	−5	−3	4,794
Divorced	0	6	−7	1	2,832
Separated	0	6	−6	0	1,173
Widowed	−1	1	−2	2	4,361
Living together	−2	14	−10	−2	416
Religion:					
Protestant	−1	5	−4	1	27,624
Catholic	1	5	−5	0	9,400
Jewish	1	13	−11	−3	1,036
Other	2	2	−5	1	3,165

Source.—ANES 1952–94.
Note.—The independence gap is measured such that a negative number indicates fewer men than women in a category. All patterns are statistically significant at .05 level.

gap remains after controls for education and is larger among the better educated. A similar pattern exists for income levels (not shown), with an independence gap in the highest three categories and a weak partisanship gap for the two lowest income groups. The gap appears among all occupations (not shown) except farmers. The joint working situation of farm couples may lead to more closely matched political identities, or a general creed of independence among farmers may extend to both sexes' political identities.

The gap also exists among all racial and religious groups, though it is largest among Jews, Hispanics, and African Americans despite the Democratic preferences of these groups. Region seems irrelevant, as is residence in cities versus suburbs versus rural areas (not shown). The gap is similar across categories of marital status except for the widowed (who show little gap) and those living together though not married (who show a larger gap). It is clear that the varying demographic traits of men and women do not explain the independence gap.

[* * *]

Gender Identities

Does the independence gap stem from a more general difference in the manner in which men and women view the political world? [Psychologist Carol] Gilligan suggests that socialization leads men to value separateness and women to value connections with others. Men's preference for separateness might be expressed in political independence, while women's sense of belonging might lead them to partisanship.

Only a few crude tests of this idea can be undertaken, since political surveys usually do not measure such psychological orientations. When given the option of selecting a number of groups to which they feel close, women do not choose more groups than men. In the 1988 ANES survey, both women and men on average felt close to 3.5 groups. When categories for "women" and "feminists" are added to the list of groups, women respondents select 4.0 groups and men choose 3.8.

While women may not indicate closeness to more groups, they rate a variety of groups in society higher than men. According to the 1952–94 ANES cumulative file, women rated 21 groups with an average feeling thermometer score of 63.7; men gave the cooler average rating of 60.8. Women rated 19 of the 21 groups higher than men, with the exceptions being big business and conservatives. These thermometer ratings provide some evidence that women feel more connected to a wider variety of groups than do men, which might help explain women's greater propensity to identify with a political party.

[* * *]

The Independence Gap and the Gender Gap

Does the independence gap play a role in the more traditional gender gap? Put differently, do the two different ways of coding leaning independents affect inferences about partisan differences between men and women?

[To answer these questions the data measure] the partisan gender gap when independent leaners are combined with pure independents and when they are combined with partisans. The [data] suggest a greater attachment of women for the Democratic Party, a pattern that first emerges significantly in 1960 and stabilizes after 1972. However, the distinctiveness of gender patterns in partisan preferences is muted during the earlier period because, until the 1980s, women were also generally more likely than men to identify themselves as Republicans. Indeed, it is not until 1990 that the pattern reverses and men are significantly more apt to identify themselves as Republicans.

When leaners are treated as partisans as opposed to independents, the patterns are somewhat different. On the basis of this fuller information, it is men who are more apt to identify with the Democrats in the 1950s and early 1960s, not women. Moreover, the greater propensity of men to identify as Republicans now becomes clearly established in the very early 1980s, not 1990. Thus, although more traditional treatments of the gender gap (which ignore leaning independents) mainly highlight women's greater concentration among Democrats, including the leaners reveals an equally great concentration of men among Republicans.

Conclusions

An independence gap, in which women are on average 6 percentage points less likely than men to view themselves as political independents, has existed in the United States for at least 40 years. Women opt for weak partisanship, while men choose the leaning-independent category. Demographic differences between men and women do not explain this gap. Indirect evidence indicates it may be due to men placing a greater value on separateness and women placing a greater value on connections with others. When leaning independents are ignored, the partisan gender gap appears to be due mainly to women's greater attraction to the Democratic Party, but taking them into account shows the gap is due equally to mens' greater attraction for the Republicans. Thus, the independence gap can affect our understanding of an important aspect of American politics.

TOWARD CRITICAL THINKING

1. Barbara Norrander makes a fresh contribution to research on the causes of the gender gap by changing the way the question is asked. Since that approach has proved fruitful here, it may be worth asking if a gender gap is what we should be explaining at all. What differences in political attitudes do you think might exist *among* women of different races, backgrounds, or ideologies? Based on what you've read so far, would that be consistent with the idea of a "gender consciousness"?

2. The number of independent voters—those who do not identify with Republicans or Democrats—continues to rise. Do you think this trend is the same as for women as for men? Do women have more to lose by disidentifying with the party system?

READING 19

The Changing Politics of American Men: Understanding the Sources of the Gender Gap

(1999)

Karen M. Kaufmann and John R. Petrocik

Perhaps spurred on by Barbara Norrander's (Reading 18) effort to approach the question of the gender gap from an innovative direction, Karen M. Kaufmann and John R. Petrocik take a look at a group of voters with whom scholars of women in American politics generally have not concerned themselves: men. In 1986, Daniel Wirls's "Reinterpreting the Gender Gap" first suggested that the gap might be explainable in terms of men's higher rates of defection from the Democratic to the Republican Party. Here, in an article published in the *American Journal of Political Science,* Kaufmann and Petrocik recover that basic idea but theorize a dramatic new addition. They hypothesize, based on earlier findings about the attitudinal differences among women and men toward politics, that men may just be more interested in some issues than women are, and vice versa. And, indeed, this hunch is borne out by the data.

But, the most interesting consequence of Kaufmann and Petrocik's research is not in the way it extends our earlier knowledge but in how it challenges it. Might we have been wrong all along to presume with Pamela Johnston Conover (Reading 16) that the gender gap and gender consciousness are related—that is, that one explains the other? The data shown here demonstrate that men (who are not able to *have* group consciousness under Patricia Gurin's (Reading 15) definition because of the "discontent" and "legitimacy of disparities" requirements in her definition) are the driving force of the phenomenon. What, then, explains this pattern? Why are men so much more interested in certain issues than are women? Can we explore this question by revising Gurin's original approach to group consciousness? Or, like Elizabeth Adell Cook and Clyde Wilcox (Reading 17), should we try to separate the effects of gender from the effects of particular kinds of consciousness or attitudes? These questions remain wide open within the literature, but Kaufmann and Petrocik's piece quickly has become the standard reference for all sides of the debate—an instant classic.

The gender gap (typically understood as the partisan difference in voting behavior between men and women) was not a feature of political commentary prior to Ronald Reagan's election in 1980. Conventional wisdom treated gender as a distinction without political importance and scholarship confirmed the conventional wisdom. By the middle 1980s, however, it had become an important electoral fact among academics and pundits. The gender gap became even more noteworthy during the 1996 presidential election because of its exceptional magnitude and political influence throughout the election year. The fourteen-point difference in the Democratic vote of men and women was an all-time post-war high. Equally impressive, this difference was a 40 percent increase over the male-female difference in the 1992 vote and twice as large as any change since observers began to pay attention to it in 1980.

Most research and virtually all public commentary on political differences between men and women have commonly viewed the gender gap as a function of changing *female* attitudes, their evolving objective circumstances, and their distinctive sensibilities. As such, American women have been the central feature of the gender gap story for the past twenty years, while men have most often been treated as the constant baseline against which the changing politics of women could be examined. This perspective, however, could not be further from the facts. *The continuous growth in the gender gap is largely a product of the changing politics of men.* Men have become increasingly Republican in their party identification and voting behavior since the mid-sixties while the partisanship and voting behavior of women has remained essentially constant. . . .

[* * *]

The Gender Gap in Voting
and Party Identification

Figure 19.1, which reports male and female party identification from 1952 to 1996, demonstrates that changes in male partisanship have been the driving force behind increases in the gender gap. For example, in 1952, 59 percent of men and 58 percent of women identified with the Democratic Party. While there was fluctuation in the party preference of women during the next forty years, their overall identification *did not change* during the period and the fraction preferring the Democratic Party did not drop below 50 percent after 1956. Democratic identification among men, by contrast, consistently declined after 1964 and has not been above 50 percent since 1980. Forty years ago men were Democratic by a margin in excess of twenty-five points; today they are Republican by a margin of about seven points. If men had been as stable in their party preference as women, the Democratic Party today would command the same national lead in partisanship over the Republicans—about twenty points— that they enjoyed during the period of mature Democratic dominance in the 1950s.

The partisan difference between men and women is paralleled by a difference in their presidential votes. Figure 19.2 plots the gender gap in party identification and voting behavior from 1952 to 1996 and [demonstrates] that the gender disparity in both is closely correlated. Changes in party identification somewhat lagged behind

FIGURE 19.1 The Party Identification of Men and Women: 1952–1996

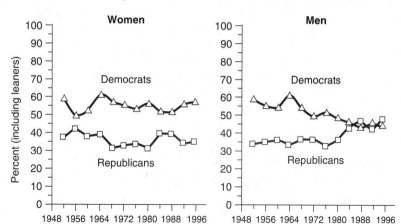

the gender gap in the vote in the 1960s and early 1970s. By 1980 they reached equivalent levels, and they continued to grow at roughly similar rates. The gender gap appears to have three distinct periods. It favored the GOP before 1964. After that, it surged in favor of the Democrats and, with the exception of 1976, held constant at a relatively modest five to seven percentage points from 1964 to 1988. In the 1990s, the size of the gender gap increased substantially in two successive presidential elections.

It is worth emphasizing that the gap did not, as conventional wisdom often assumes, begin in 1980; it preceded the Reagan era by at least sixteen years, and, if the smaller values before 1964 are to be credited, it extends back to the origins of the NES series. There was a relative Republican preference among women until 1960:

FIGURE 19.2 Gender Gap in Voting and Party Identification: 1952–1996

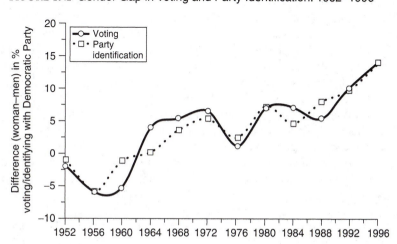

they preferred Dewey, Eisenhower, and Nixon slightly more than did the men in each of these elections. In 1964, however, men were decidedly more positive than women toward the [Barry] Goldwater candidacy, and the gender gap assumed its contemporary configuration of a Democratic tilt among women and a GOP tilt among men. The gap in voting behavior continued to grow in 1968 and 1972, virtually vanished in 1976 in the wake of Watergate and the Nixon pardon, only to reappear in 1980 at a slightly higher level than it was in 1972. It reached a full ten points by 1992 and a historic fourteen points by 1996.

Party Identification as the Source of the Gender Gap in the Vote

As a result of the changing party identification of men and women, the male-female vote difference in any given presidential election is partly specific to the forces of that election and partly a reflection of a more long-term "structural" feature of the party coalitions. [Our analysis] decomposes the vote difference into a long-term, structural component (party identification) and a second short-term component that reflects forces specific to each election. . . .

Four things stand out. . . . First, as others have noted, the gender gap in voting largely reflects the gender gap in party preference. In recent years, the observed difference in male-female voting would have been between one-half to two-thirds *less* if men and women had a more similar party preference. Second, the long-term component of the gap (the party identification component) has consistently grown over time; the only exceptions are years when the overall gender gap in the vote abruptly declined (in 1976 and 1988). Third, the voting gender gap had a proportionately small long-term component when it emerged in the early 1960s. In each successive election, however, party identification explained incrementally more of the gender difference in the vote. Moreover, it seems to do so in a way that has changes in party identification lagging behind voting behavior, a pattern suggesting that when candidates appeal differentially to men and women, these gender-specific preferences translate into greater partisan differences in the future. Fourth, the 1992 and 1996 elections represent a new escalation in the gap, causing it to reach levels significantly above those that attracted attention in the Reagan era. During the past two presidential elections, both the long-term party component and the short-term election component of the gender gap increased, presaging a larger structural (party identification) difference in the future—if the past is prologue.

A fifth observation should be added: the gender gap in party identification has assumed the dimensions of a major cleavage. Race, class, religion, union membership, and region have defined the social fault lines between the parties since the 1930s and, at one time, were all more powerful predictors of party identification than gender. In the last twenty years the relative importance of these social cleavages has undergone large changes. Regional differences have virtually disappeared; social class (represented by income) has increasingly shaped party preference; religiosity has also come to mark differences in party preference. Race has become particularly prominent. Most of this has been the subject of wide commentary and analysis. The prominence of gender has been less widely noted. As of 1996, gender predicted party identification better than some of the historically important social cleavages (region, for example) and as well as religiosity (which has received increasing attention). Also, like religiosity, gender is a division that cuts across every demographic characteristic except for race. Women in virtually every segment of the white electorate—whether defined by region, religiosity, class, religion, age, or marital status—are more Democratic because men of almost every type moved toward the GOP.

Focusing on Men

The previous data, which convincingly demonstrate the dramatic rise in the gender gap over the past two decades, has at least two interpretations. The one adopted here is that men have moved into GOP ranks as women have retained a traditional Democratic preference. But at least two studies interpret these changes in a different light and maintain that the growing political difference between men and women has resulted from the unwillingness of the latter to follow a secular trend toward greater conservatism and the Republicans. Daniel Wirls' account of the gender gap during the Reagan administration concluded with the observation that "both women and men are defecting from the Democratic Party and liberal values, and the gender gap has been the result of unequal rates of defection." [Political scientists] [Janet M.] Box-Steffensmeier, [Suzanna] DeBoef, and [Tse-Min] Lin echoed that conclusion when they hypothesized "that the rise of the gender gap is mainly a reaction of women to the national ideological swing to the right starting from the late seventies."

The perception that women resisted a trend justifies an analytical focus on women's distinctive characteristics as an explanation for the increasing gender gap. But there is no obvious reason for looking at the gap from the perspective of the women. It clearly offers no empirical leverage since the observed data and most relationships will be identical whether one observes a shift in male behavior or a refusal of women to follow men. More important, a focus on women seems less faithful to the most obvious trend in Figure 19.1: the changed partisanship of men and the stable party identification of women. Beyond that, there is no evidence to support the notion of a secular trend or that women are in fact resisting such a trend. For example, while Wirls and Box-Steffensmeier, DeBoef, and Lin argue for a conservative shift in the underlying political predisposition of the electorate, no such shift in ideology is demonstrated. Even Box-Steffensmeier and her colleagues' own data show an essentially flat "macro-ideology" from 1976 to 1994. Moreover, the slight movement by women to the Republican Party observed during the Reagan years (cited by Wirls as evidence that women were following men into the Republican Party), was short-lived. Women returned to the Democrats in 1988. In brief, the Republican conversion of men seems to be the fact in need of explanation, and it is the fact explored here.

Explaining the Gender Gap

[* * *]

. . . Much of the empirical analysis of voting and party differences between men and women as explanations has focused on attitude *differences*. . . . It expects gender differences in voting and party identification to result from underlying differences in political attitudes that are politicized in similar ways. It assumes that men and women have different attitudes, assign approximately equal importance to corresponding issues, and thus convert these attitude differences into a gender gap in voting and partisanship. Evidence in support of this perspective requires the gender gaps in partisanship and voting to become insignificantly small when issue and policy differences between men and women are held constant. This Attitude Hypothesis has considerable initial plausibility since there are consistent gender differences in attitudes across a wide range of issue dimensions.

The assumption that men and women equally weigh their dissimilar attitudes is, however, *not* an obvious a priori. Neither theoretical justifications nor empirical findings make it compelling. For example, self-interest and social identity considerations make it unlikely that female equality or abortion are as important to the political judgments of men as they are to women. Furthermore, if [sociologists] [Francis Fox] Piven, [Steven P.] Erie and [Martin] Rein, and [Ann Mari] May and [Kurt] Stephenson are correct, men and women are differentially sensitive to social welfare questions. Simply put, the presumption that men and women care equally about the same political issues as they make their political choices is an empirical question in need of further study.

The Salience Hypothesis explanation of the gender gap focuses on this prospective differential weighting of issues by men and women. It allows for attitude differences, but asserts that gender differences in voting and party identification are not solely the result of variance in political orientations but are importantly influenced by the different salience of issues between men and women. Thus, a matter on which they have virtually identical opinions might have quite different effects on their candidate evaluations or their feelings about the parties. Men and women might, for example, agree about the condition of the economy, but the opinion might do much more to shape the candidate choices of (let us say) men because the issue is more salient to them. Conversely, the political importance of an issue on which men and women hold very different opinions may be enlarged if the issue is disproportionately salient to either group or may be diminished if neither give substantial weight to it when making a political choice. The following analyses focus on the extent to which the gender gap is a product of attitude or issue salience differences between men and women. Using National Election Survey Data from 1992 and 1996 we employ a series of logistic regression analyses to test these hypotheses. . . .

[* * *]

The Results

[* * *]

The data . . . convincingly demonstrate that men and women do not always politicize issues to an identical degree. The analysis . . . attempts to sort out the relative influence of attitudes and salience with regard to the gender gap.

[* * *]

The results show large differences between the [1992 and 1996] elections. Attitude differences between men and women largely explain the gender gaps in party identification and the vote in 1992. The gender gap in party identification is reduced by only two points (7 percent remains) when controlling for salience differences in 1992, while the gender gap in the vote would have been even larger (at sixteen percentage points) if men had weighed the issues as women did. Controlling for differences in attitudes, by contrast, reduced the Republican advantage among men to zero. If men had been as liberal as women were in 1992, the weight they assigned to the issues would have produced a party identification and a vote that was *more* Democratic than that of women. In brief, a gender gap in policy attitudes appears to have shaped the gender gap in voting and party identification in 1992.

Issue salience was a substantially larger component of the gender gap in 1996. The gender gap in party identification is reduced some 70 percent—from over fourteen points to four points—when differences in the salience of issues is controlled. Controlling for the salience differences produced a virtually identical reduction in the gender gap in the vote in 1996. But attitude differences continued to be important. Gender gaps in the vote and partisanship are reduced every bit as much with attitudes controlled as when issue salience was controlled. The overlapping estimates thus indicate that the greater conservatism of men and the different weights they assigned to these attitudes made almost equal contributions to the gender gap in 1996.

The consistent importance of social welfare attitudes for the gender gap in the vote and party identification, the more conservative opinions of men, and the prominence of social welfare issues in creating and maintaining the New Deal party coalitions intuitively place social welfare opinions at the center of any explanation of the gender gap. Specifically, they suggest that their relative conservatism on social welfare questions played a role in creating the gender gap as we know it from the preceding data. Other issues as well almost certainly played a role, but the magnitude of the coefficients for these latter variables suggest that their influence is probably smaller than social welfare issues. On the other hand, the substantial effect of social welfare attitudes in 1992 and 1996 and the strong correlation between male-female differences in welfare attitudes and party identification represent plausible a priori evidence that gender differences on the "social safety net" may be a major cause of the gender gap. . . . [L]ongitudinal data on the gender gap in social welfare attitudes and party preference, confirms this expectation.

. . . [M]en were more conservative than women on social welfare questions during the entire 1952–1996 period. But their party preference began to conform to their social welfare attitudes between 1966 and 1978, when party disputes about "big government" and welfare spending became more salient with the arrival of militant Republicanism in the form of Goldwater and, later, Ronald Reagan. After 1964, the two trends change together. Overall, the pattern is consistent with the notion that the greater salience of social welfare spending for men may have been the source of their changes in party identification. Certainly the cross-sectional relationships between social welfare issues and the gender gap are not equivalent to demonstrated causal relationships, and, as noted above, the emergence of the gender gap in partisanship has not been compared with the emergence of any gender gaps in other attitudes. Nonetheless, the relationship . . . is consistent with the individual data presented above and is certainly suggestive that social welfare issues may be a principal force behind the gender gap.

[* * *]

Conclusion

. . . [T]entatively, there is no reason to think that gender differences will subside to any great degree in the near term. The contemporary debate over the suitable role of government and the indispensability of the social safety net is at the heart of current interparty policy battles. To a great degree, the future of American party coalitions and the future of the gender gap will depend on the evolution of these policy debates. While gender continues to be less influential than race and income, these data strongly suggest that gender may become an ever more politically influential social cleavage simply because differences tend to be self-reinforcing. Parties design agendas that respond to their constituencies, and as the Democrats and Republicans exploit social welfare issues to mobilize their familiar support they will be priming an issue that underpins the gender gap. Salience effects around the social welfare attitudes that distinguish men and women may ensure that the fourteen-point gender gap of 1996 will not be its high-water mark for the contemporary period.

TOWARD CRITICAL THINKING

1. Perhaps the most interesting finding of this study is the observation that men and women politicize issues such as social welfare to different degrees—that is, that there are variations in issue salience for which scholars have not previously accounted. What explanations could you offer for this pattern in the data?

2. Karen M. Kaufmann and John R. Petrocik conclude their study with the suggestion that the gender gap as motivated by salience differences will continue to grow in the future. Do you predict that the renewed focus on national security post-9/11 will reduce or heighten this difference? How could you test such a prediction?

READING 20

Injecting a Woman's Voice: Conservative Women's Organizations, Gender Consciousness, and the Expression of Women's Policy Preferences

(2002)

Ronnee Schreiber

What is the difference between gender consciousness and feminist consciousness? For Pamela Johnston Conover (Reading 16), it is a question of degree—feminists are *exceptionally* conscious of their gender. For Patricia Gurin (Reading 15), there may not even be a difference—gender-conscious women are discontented, consider their treatment wrong, and orient themselves toward collective action for change. But, for Ronnee Schreiber, the question may be more complicated. She begins by choosing two unusual places to look for gender consciousness: the staunchly conservative Independent Women's Forum and Concerned Women for America. The choice seems strange at first to a scholar trained in the Gurin tradition—where is the discontentment?—but Schreiber presents compelling evidence in this article published in *Sex Roles* that these groups are indeed the site of a kind of gender consciousness that we are not theoretically equipped to handle. They consist of and are led primarily by women; they identify themselves as women's organizations; and they consider it their work to advance a "woman's voice" on a wide variety of political issues—especially those in which feminist groups traditionally claimed to speak for women.

At the same time, though, these groups seem diametrically opposed—almost interest for interest and goal for goal. The virtue of Gurin's model is that it allows us to reason from gender identity to political action—that is, she gives us a way to turn our hypotheses about group consciousness into predictions about actual behavior. Gender-conscious women will prefer policies that benefit women, will vote for more feminist candidates, and so on. When Schreiber makes it clear that gender consciousness is a part of these conservative women's political outlooks, she implicitly asks us to reconsider this assumption. If gender consciousness does not lead in any particular direction, how can we say it is any *one* kind of consciousness present in a wide variety of women? Wouldn't it rather be something such as a personal consciousness of a gendered position? Clearly, we have much more theorizing and testing to do, but one thing remains clear: radical change in the way we think about these issues looms just over the horizon.

A question that has consistently motivated women and politics research is: which women support the "women's movement" and its policy goals?[1] Explorations of this question have come from scholars examining "gender consciousness." Their analyses suggest that gender conscious women, that is, those who identify with women as a group and feel affected by the social conditions under which that group lives, are the ones who support the women's movement and will express a "woman's perspective" on policy issues. This literature frequently conflates *women's* activism and policy issues with *feminism*: and it fails to explain the behavior of conservative women. As such, it not only forecloses understanding of conservative women's activism, but leads to mistaken conclusions and assumptions in feminist explanations of women's policy preferences and activism.

In this [chapter] I examine two national conservative women's organizations— the Concerned Women for America (CWA) and the Independent Women's Forum (IWF)—to show how conservative women leaders link gender identity and policy preferences. . . . Like feminists, these women, through their organizations, not only act collectively as women, but also bring a "woman's perspective" to policy issues. Although some scholars have not denied the impact of right-wing movements on feminist goals and activities, others have characterized conservative women as victims of false consciousness, pawns of conservative men or right-wing funders, or "women's auxillar[ies] of the conservative elite," thus diminishing the attention and serious consideration appropriate to such a political force. Although we get some sense of the relationships among gender identity, political activism, and policy preferences among feminist women from gender consciousness research, there is little beyond the small number of studies of women's activism on abortion and the Equal Rights Amendment (ERA) to explain the link between gender identity and policy preferences among conservative women. And, in studies of women's organizations and women's collective policy activism, almost no research exists on how conservative women's organizations act in the policymaking process. As the CWA and IWF are prominent national organizations, these omissions are significant ones.

[* * *]

The CWA and IWF are not "just" conservative organizations; they are national conservative *women's* organizations. Their status as such shapes policy debates and influences political outcomes. They are well positioned to exert influence as countermovement organizations—to take on the feminist movement, mobilize women, and vie for the right to make claims about women's policy preferences and goals. In

---

[1]Here I use the phrase "women's movement" to mean the *feminist* women's movement as it reflects how the gender consciousness scholars cited in this article have defined and measured the term.

the following section I discuss in more depth how the gender consciousness literature portrays the relationship between gender consciousness and policy preferences, and indicate how it fails to account for, or explain, the actions of conservative women leaders and organizations.

Gender Consciousness and Policy Preferences

Although a survey of the gender consciousness literature shows some lack of consistency across the studies, generally scholars argue that gender consciousness is an important link between gender identity and political action and policy preferences. . . .

To their credit, gender consciousness scholars do indicate that identifying with women as a group is not a sufficient condition for collective action among women. Ideological differences preclude such unity. It has been argued, however, that feminist consciousness and/or politicization can be a bridge between gender identity and collective action. And, in terms of collective policy preferences, feminist consciousness, coupled with liberal ideological values, has been found to create gender gaps between men and women. I do not dispute these findings. They come from the relatively few, but important, studies of the connections among gender identity, ideological perspectives, and policy preferences. As such, the data help explain why some women are more likely than others to support feminist policy goals. For feminist activists, this is a critical and often vexing question.

The link between identity and ideology, however, needs to be pursued even further. My concern with the gender consciousness literature is not only its lack of attention to conservative women but its conflation of feminist interests with women's interests. . . .

In these studies, gender consciousness research . . . is more revelatory of feminist beliefs than it is of women's self-awareness as a demographic cohort. The end result is a clustering of conservative women with men, erasing the potential for, and thus the understanding of, the distinctively gender conscious policy preferences among conservative women. And, even when scholars are attentive to the differences between feminist and nonfeminist women, conservative women are eventually left out of analyses because they are not feminist and presumably act like men. But conservative women are changing public discourse about women's interests; indeed one of the main goals of the IWF is to transform debates about "women's" issues by offering the viewpoints of conservative women. Similarly, the CWA refers to itself as the "nation's largest public policy women's organization." As these interest groups lay claim to representing women, they also have the potential to mobilize women and link them to conservative causes. In addition, when conservative women leaders act as women to make claims for women, they undermine feminist claims to knowing and representing women's interests.

My corrective to the omission of conservative women from the gender consciousness literature is to study conservative women collectively organized, that is, in women's organizations. Although the gender consciousness literature mostly focuses on women at the mass level, it can also be used to explain women active at the elite level and those organized into interest groups. . . .

The CWA and IWF are clearly gender conscious in one sense: they are women's organizations and identify themselves as such. But, without seeing or understanding the relationship between gender consciousness and policy preferences for conservative women, we cannot adequately explain the terrain of political debates on a range of important political issues. Thus, I ask if and how collectively organized conservative women are gender conscious in their expression of public policies. That is, do they, like feminist activists and organizations, articulate a "woman's perspective" on policy issues?

[* * *]

The Organizations

Both the CWA and IWF represent conservative women, though each speaks for a slightly different constituency. Like feminists, conservative women are not monolithic. [Sociologist] [Rebecca] Klatch categorized them as either social conservatives or laissez-faire conservatives, with each expressing a different worldview about gender, religion, economics, and the role of government. *Social conservatives* are deeply religious, see the traditional heterosexual family as the core of society, and root social problems in the moral realm. *Laissez-faire conservatives* point to the economic realm as the source of problems, and emphasize individuality and the desire for freedom from government intrusion. Klatch also argued that socially conservative women tend to be gender identified, whereas laissez-faire conservative women do not recognize their "collective interests as women" and are not necessarily antifeminist. Although the organizations I study generally conform to Klatch's distinctions, with the CWA being composed of socially conservative women and the IWF of laissez-faire conservatives, the laissez-faire conservatives of the IWF also express the need to act collectively as women and thus have formed into a women's organization. Unlike the laissez-faire women that in Klatch interviewed, this group of laissez-faire conservatives does believe that feminism is, at least partly, to blame for many social and economic problems. Thus, both organizations are explicitly antifeminist and both believe that feminists have undervalued the need for attention to gender differences between women and men. Despite these variations from Klatch's ideal types, these two organizations nicely represent the range of conservative women in the United States.

[* * *]

Concerned Women for America (CWA)

The CWA was founded in 1979 by Beverly La Haye. Its formation and subsequent growth coincided with the politicization of the Christian Right in the late 1970s and early 1980s. . . . [T]he CWA began with local prayer chapters that mobilized women around issues such as opposition to the equal rights amendment (ERA) and legalized abortion. . . . Today the CWA has a professionally staffed office in Washington, DC, and members in all 50 states, and claims to be the largest women's organization in the United States.[2] Through e-mail, a monthly magazine, a website, and phone calls, its national staff work closely with local members, updating them on legislative affairs and training them to be effective activists. . . . Its multi-issue policy agenda includes opposition to homosexuality, abortion, pornography, and funding the United Nations. . . .

Independent Women's Forum

In comparison to the CWA, the IWF is a much younger and smaller organization. . . . Established in 1992, it grew out of a group of women who worked for the George H. W. Bush administration and who met regularly to hear speakers and network. These conservative women leaders are well connected to, or are themselves, key policy and opinion makers. Resembling more of a think tank than a grassroots organization, the IWF was founded to take on the "old feminist establishment." . . . As a group of laissez-faire conservatives, it describes itself as an organization that promotes "common sense" and provides "a voice for American women who believe in individual freedom and personal responsibility . . . the voice of reasonable women with important ideas who embrace common sense over divisive ideology." . . . Unlike the CWA, it does not have a grassroots membership, but like the CWA, it employs professional staff.

The IWF delights in caricaturing feminists and "debunking" supposed myths about issues such as the need for an equal rights amendment and pay equity policies. . . .

The CWA and IWF as Gender Conscious Policy Advocates

The CWA's and IWF's expression of a "woman's perspective" on policy issues reflects a complex interplay between ideology and strategy. First, both groups believe that women bring gendered and unique perspectives to policy concerns. In this sense, their gender consciousness has ideological roots emanating from the belief systems of the women who lead the organizations. But, as countermovement organizations, vying with feminists over who legitimately represents women, the CWA and IWF also recognize the value of having conservative women as policy advocates. It is more difficult for conservatives to be attacked as "antiwoman" if conservative women are making political claims as and for women. Thus, the framing of policy goals from a "woman's perspective" both reflects their conservative ideology about gender differences and stems from a desire to establish credibility as women's organizations. In this latter sense, it is a strategic choice—one that exemplifies the power and salience of identity politics in the United States. The purpose of this study is not to disentangle the ideological effects from the strategic ones, but rather to show the results of both.

[* * *]

---

[2]On its website, www.now.org, the National Organization for Women (NOW) claims to have 500,000 members, but the CWA contends that NOW really has less than 100,000.

Just "Mainstream" Women Speaking Out

The CWA and IWF chastise feminists for making universalist claims on behalf of women. Nonetheless, both the CWA and IWF also make broad-based claims for women.

In much of its publicity information, the IWF proclaims itself to be the "voice of *reasonable* women with important ideas who embrace common sense over divisive ideology" (emphasis added). Here the word "reasonable" is loose and unspecific, suggesting that its constituency of women can be construed quite broadly. . . . The CWA offers analogous reasoning about its representation of women. Although the organization clearly talks about being composed of, and speaking for, "Christian" women, it also frequently asserts that it is "mainstream." Indeed, in speaking of which women the CWA's goals appeal to, group founder LaHaye claims that "the *vast majority* of women, thank God, want to raise children with integrity and strong character" (emphasis added).

Interviews with organizational leaders also produced narratives about the organizations' perception of the relationship between gender identity and policy preferences. Respondents expressed strong commitments to helping women and examining issues as they affect women. And, according to these organizations, women's interests are not just those associated with traditional women's issues, but also those that arise in the context of dealing with a range of public policies. Although IWF board member [former Secretary of Labor and economist] Wendy Gramm initially qualified that "the main mission [of IWF] is simply . . . to educate others about how *this* group of women thinks," she emphatically added that the IWF also seeks to show "how issues affect women, what is the impact on women of different policy issues. So it really is an educational role, injecting *a woman's* voice into the policy debate" (interview, emphasis added). Her colleague Kimberly Schuld also expressed how the organization is gender conscious in its expression of women's policy interests: "We talk about the impact on women, not women's issues. That is the way I see it. For instance, we could take a tax issue and say 'how does this impact women' and 'where are you missing that in your communications to women.' "

[* * *]

Similarly, the CWA's former President Carmen Pate noted how the organization seeks to speak for women.

> With every issue, we can bring in why it should be of concern to women, and that is what we try to do: why mom should be concerned, why wives should be concerned, why you should be concerned about your daughters. That is the connection that we try to make. How will this impact women long term? (interview)

[* * *]

Although these organizations formed because they were critical of feminists for claiming to represent the majority of women, both groups talk about their missions in ways similar to feminists. These conservative organizations speak on behalf of women, demonstrating that the expression of a woman's perspective with regard to public policies may not necessarily be feminist. In addition, the CWA and IWF have the potential to transform the meaning of women's interests to be more consistent with conservative values about gender roles and families. In so doing, they effectively compete with feminists over the construction of women's interests.

The CWA's Opposition to Abortion: It's a Woman Thing

The CWA challenges the feminist assertion that when it comes to abortion rights, it is in the interest of women to be pro-choice. For the socially conservative CWA, opposition to abortion and most forms of birth control is central to its agenda. The organization lobbies for legislation to limit and/or make abortion illegal and opposes federal funding of most domestic and international family planning programs. Although its position on reproductive health issues is consistent with many other socially conservative organizations that oppose abortion because of beliefs about the "sanctity of life" (e.g., the Christian Coalition, the National Right to Life Committee), the CWA also strongly holds that support for abortion and family planning programs hurts women. That is, they are gender conscious in their explication of why they oppose abortion. Women are, according to the CWA, "abortion's second victim." Talking as women, about women's interests in this case, not only reflects the CWA's gendered perspective on the issue, but also enables it to tackle pro-choice advocates who have long argued for attention to women's bodies and lives in reproductive health care debates.

Another example of how the CWA articulates a "woman's perspective" about abortion policy is found in its discussions about "Post Abortion Syndrome" (PAS). In effect, PAS is shorthand for what the organization believes are negative consequences women face after having abortions. The CWA argues,

> Post-abortive women may: require psychological treatment/therapy, suffer post-traumatic stress disorder, experience sexual dysfunction, engage in suicidal thoughts or attempt suicide, become heavy or habitual smokers, abuse alcohol and illegal drugs, acquire eating disorders, neglect or abuse other children, have relationship problems, have repeat abortions, re-experience the abortion through flashbacks, be preoccupied with becoming pregnant to replace the aborted child [and] experience anxiety and guilt.

In linking specific women's health concerns to its antiabortion platform, the CWA also claims that "abortion can significantly increase a woman's risk of getting breast cancer"; therefore, "abortion is deadly—not only for unborn children, but also for the women who abort them." . . .

The CWA also condemns international family planning programs that provide women with Norplant, a form of birth control that can have adverse side effects on women. It refers to women in the United States and abroad who use Norplant as "human guinea pigs" and worries that "today, the U.S. government is using our money to bruise and batter women and children around the world." Thus, the CWA lobbies for abolition of federal funds to support domestic and international family planning programs, especially those that counsel for or perform abortions, and those that provide Norplant and other abortifacients. Indeed, here the CWA's arguments, or at least its gender consciousness policy stance, is reminiscent of feminist critiques of sterilization abuse.

[* * *]

IWF on Title IX: Demeaning to Women

Through a program entitled Play Fair, the IWF takes on a prominent feminist policy achievement—Title IX. Title IX, part of a 1972 law that outlaws gender discrimination in federally funded educational institutions, has been used successfully to increase attention to, and funding for, women's sports in colleges and universities. The Office for Civil Rights (OCR), a division of the U.S. Department of Education, is the agency in charge of enforcing Title IX. To do so, the OCR developed a three-pronged test to determine if schools were in compliance. Schools could show that the ratio of male and female athletes closely parallels the ratio of male and female students—this is sometimes known as *proportionality*; a history of expanding opportunities for athletes of the underrepresented sex; or, that the interests of the underrepresented sex had been fully and effectively accommodated. A school only needs to meet one of these three criteria, but in 1996, the OCR issued a clarification stating that the first option, proportionality, was the surest way for schools to demonstrate that they were in compliance. The IWF likens this proportionality option to a quota system and is therefore highly critical of Title IX. It claims that too many schools opt for this test, thereby strangling men's sports and demeaning women's athletic accomplishments.

From the point of view of the IWF, Title IX regulations are akin to affirmative action, a policy the IWF opposes and contends hurts women. Speaking from a "woman's perspective," the organization argues that it is women's relative lack of interest in sports, not discrimination, that creates discrepancies in the numbers of female and male college athletes. The IWF charges that feminists have misinterpreted the meaning of gender differences and women's interests in this case, because feminists are prone to antimale biases. Feminists, it argues, are quick to blame men for women's relative lack of involvement in collegiate athletics and are eager to cut resources for men's sports. As IWF founder Anita Blair said about the enforcement of Title IX through proportionality. "This is mean-spirited, dog-in-the-manger feminism at its worst. Why deny men sports opportunities just because relatively fewer women are interested in athletics?"

Noting that women should be concerned about Title IX enforcement, and anticipating the queries about its position, the IWF published a document entitled "Why

Would a Women's Group Complain About Title IX?" In this text, the IWF declared that Title IX "demeans the legitimate athletic accomplishments of women." It also proclaims Title IX to be a woman's issue because, as the organization sees it, Title IX reinforces misguided ideas about the origins and meanings of gender differences. From the point of view of the IWF, "most women know that men and women are different, and that women are different from each other. Not all of us want to be scholars, not all of us want to be athletes. We look to ourselves, not the government to know the difference."

[* * *]

Title IX is one of the most profound legislative achievements of the feminist movement in the past three decades. Certainly it is a "women's issue" from the standpoint of those who fought for it and benefited from it. But the IWF, critical of how the law has been interpreted and enforced over the years, sees it as an affront to women's abilities to make decisions about their interests free of government involvement and ideological persuasion. And, like the CWA, the IWF articulates its concerns from a woman's perspective, indicating that these organizations are indeed gender conscious as they make policy claims.

Conclusion

My foray into conservative women's organizations' framing of policy goals does not only highlight the limitations of current research on gender consciousness. It also elucidates the very real and significant consequences of having conservative women's voices reverberating through legislatures and in the media. The presence of the CWA and IWF means clashes will occur among women about the meaning of women's status in politics and the family and about the nature and origins of gender differences and the role of government in women's lives. As gender conscious political institutions, feminist and conservative women's organizations battle over whose stories about women are most representative. And, given that their narratives about women's lives have concrete policy implications, this battle over authenticity is meaningful. [Political scientist] Shane Phelan suggested that "[r]ather than arguing with one another about which story is true, [we] must look instead at what is at stake in our different stories; we must examine the consequences of our stories in terms of power and change." Following this thinking, the next step in this line of inquiry would be to examine the relative impact feminist and conservative women have had on policy debates and outcomes. How have issue-based differences in the expression of "women's perspectives" influenced policymakers' ideas about women's interests? Which policies have been shaped by the public debates and lobbying efforts of conflicting groups of women? Is there any room for coalition or compromise among women on certain issues?

In terms of the gender consciousness literature specifically, I propose exploring the intersection of gender and ideology more closely. Gender consciousness can compel women to act as women, for women, across the political spectrum.

Through gender conscious arguments, conservative women's organizations articulate and legitimize their perspectives on a range of important public policies. Thus, understanding the actions and relevance of these ideologically conservative organizations requires using gender as an analytic category. In so doing, we also see how different women construct the meaning of gender roles and differences, and what gender identity means to different women in the context of political participation.

[* * *]

TOWARD CRITICAL THINKING

1. Compare and contrast Ronnee Schreiber's work with Elizabeth Adell Cook's and Clyde Wilcox's (Reading 17). Both articles underline the problems with the persistent conflation of "woman" with "feminist," but they are also quite different in terms of method and conclusions. How do you imagine they would criticize one another's research?

2. Gender consciousness is supposed to provide the theoretical bridge in our descriptions of women's political activism between their identities and their behavior. Gender identity is thought to structure women's material needs and political interests at the individual level, in turn providing for each individual woman a rough set of "women's goals" to structure her work. Are you convinced by Schreiber's argument that this theory is incorrect so long as it fails to account for the tremendous diversity among women's political goals? Could it account for such diversity without losing its ability to offer any particular predictions or conclusions?

WRAPPING UP

1. If Karen M. Kaufmann and John R. Petrocik are right that it is men's, not women's, differences that motivate the gender gap, what impact will this have on thinking about group consciousness? Men, as the usual beneficiaries of sex discrimination in America, have no interest in changing the gender hierarchy and, therefore, cannot have "group consciousness" under Patricia Gurin's theory. How might her theory have to be redrawn to account for men? Does Ronnee Schreiber's study of conservative women or Elizabeth Adell Cook's and Clyde Wilcox's attention to feminism irrespective of sex suggest any possible clues?

2. Gurin finds, ironically, that the deepness of the everyday experience of gender—the fact that it permeates our daily lives and, in so doing, structures our psychology—is part of what prevents women from developing group consciousness as strong as that developed by African Americans. Many theorists, however, would decry this statement. Gender and race, they often insist, can only be completely understood within a theory that accounts for their intersection in the lives of women of color, who experience gender and race not as separate constructs but as overlapping, inherently connected identities. How would Gurin's thinking about gender consciousness (and the literature on the gender gap it has inspired) have to change to account for this critique?

CHAPTER 6
Finding a Place in the Political Parties

READING 21

Women in Campaigns: From Lickin' and Stickin' to Strategy*

(1977)

Ellen Boneparth

On the national political stage, Mary Beth Cahill managed John Kerry's 2004 presidential campaign, Donna Brazile managed Al Gore's 2000 presidential campaign, and Susan Estrch managed Michael Dukakis's 1988 presidential campaign, but many more women work in local party politics. In the first national survey of citizen campaign activity beginning in 1952, Kristi Anderson reports in "Working Women and Political Participation, 1952–1972" that women consistently were less likely to be involved in campaigns than men. However, when she examines the differences between the participation of housewives and working women over this period, she finds that the participation of women working outside the home increased nearly three times that of homemakers over the twenty-year period.

Building on traditional gender-roles theory, Ellen Boneparth explores the backgrounds of women campaign workers and looks at the type of work women do on campaigns. Traditional gender-roles theory argues that political activity, whether it is for a campaign or for a political party, is not consistent with women's roles as wives and mothers. The traditional public/private split between men and women results in politics being viewed as a man's world and subsequently a pursuit that is not appropriate for or attractive to women. At the time Boneparth's article was published in *American Politics Quarterly* in the late 1970s, the women's movement was challenging this division of labor and dramatically changing opportunities for women to move into the public sphere.

Using data drawn from campaigns in Santa Clara County, California, which political scientist Janet Flammang once called a "feminist capital," Boneparth examines whether women's involvement in campaigns is limited to volunteer work and support services that would reinforce traditional gender roles or if women were challenging those roles by working full-time in jobs such as campaign manager. In addition, she compares men and women

*Note: the man quoted in the article who inspired the title for the piece is the father of current U.S. Senator Mary Landrieu (D–LA).

candidates' propensity to have women on their campaign teams. She was one of the first to explore the relationship between women working in politics and Boneparth's work set the stage for future research that examined women voters' likelihood to vote for women candidates, as discussed by R. Darcy and Sarah Slavin Schramm (Reading 25) and Kathleen Dolan (Reading 29).

[* * *]

The field of American politics has been a particularly rich one for research on women. However, the roles of women in political campaigns have been only casually examined. Women have been recognized as constituting the bulk of the volunteer workers, but their contributions are described as limited to envelope stuffing and doorbell ringing. Male biases are revealed in a study of attitudes toward women workers in the Daley machine in which party leaders [in Chicago] agreed that women make good canvassers for two reasons: pretty women can get their foot in the door, and all women appreciate opportunities to get out of the home. Or, as Mayor Moon Landrieu of New Orleans put it, "Women do the lickin' and stickin', while men plan the strategy." More serious discussions suggest various explanations for the restricted roles of women in campaigns: lack of interest and campaign experience among women, the professionalization of campaigns, limited resources among women for political activity, and discrimination by male political activists.

However, one would expect that, with rising levels of political participation, women are also advancing within the ranks of campaign workers. . . .

[* * *]

Socioeconomic and Political Backgrounds

Studies of female political participation consistently suggest that participation is strongly correlated with high socioeconomic status, particularly with respect to levels of education and income. High levels of education are seen as equipping women with the ability to replace themselves in the home by purchasing childcare and domestic help and with the financial resources to support political parties and candidates.

What types of women are likely to hold responsible positions in political campaigns? The functionaries were characterized, on the whole, by high socioeconomic status. As a group, they are far more privileged than the U.S. female population and reflect the general affluence of [Santa Clara County, California]. Some college training was reported by 94% of the functionaries; 60% had completed college; 17% had advanced degrees. Income levels were also high; only 16% had family incomes of under $10,000; 33% had incomes between $10,000 and $20,000; and 51% had family incomes over $20,000. Since only 30% of the functionaries were employed full-time, these high income levels reflect, for the most part, the high occupational levels of the respondents' husbands. Despite a 25% third world population in the county, 97% of the functionaries were white. Finally, the functionaries were, for California, long-time members of the community—almost half of the respondents had lived in the county for more than 15 years.

An important question concerning female political participation is how women combine political and family roles. Research on officeholding has shown that the great proportion of women who run for office do so only after they have passed the child-bearing and child-rearing stages of their lives. However, the responsibilities of family life do not seem to keep women from holding responsible positions in political campaigns. In this study, 75% of the functionaries were married or had been married and had children. In fact, those who had families had relatively large families—44% had three or more children. Moreover, while the largest proportion of the functionaries (39%) was over 44 years old, 27% were 35 to 44 years old, and 34% were under 35.

The typical female functionary, then, was a white, affluent, well-educated but nonemployed wife and mother. Clearly, family roles do not prevent women of high socioeconomic status from holding responsible positions on campaigns. This is not to suggest that the demands of campaign work pose no conflicts for family life, but, rather, that the limited time span of the political campaign may make it easier for women with families to devote time to campaigns as compared to holding office.

The political backgrounds of the functionaries provide additional insights about women campaign workers. Not only did almost all of the respondents identify with the major political parties, but . . . partisanship was strong. Sixty-nine percent of the functionaries (79% of the Democrats and 56% of the Republicans) identified themselves as strong partisans. In keeping with this pattern of strong partisanship was the finding that almost one-third of the functionaries were active in political party organizations: 11% had held leadership positions in regular party organizations, 11% had held leadership positions in political clubs, and 10% had been leaders in both types of organizations. These percentages are high, given the nonpartisan atmosphere of California politics.

An even more common background characteristic was participation in previous political campaigns. Almost all the functionaries (91%) had worked in previous campaigns; two-thirds had worked in three or more campaigns; one-fifth had worked in ten or more campaigns. Clearly, the functionaries were drawn from the ranks of experienced political activists. In fact, 23% of the functionaries had held elective or appointive office at the local level. Last, the functionaries were community as well as political activists. . . .

[* * *]

The implications of these findings are twofold. First, as increasing numbers of women move into the higher levels of education and as female career patterns shift to increasing activity outside the home, increasing numbers of women will play leadership roles in political campaigns. However, because political participation is so closely correlated with socioeconomic status, the changes will be gradual and the ranks of female political leaders will for some time continue to be drawn from the elite.

Campaign Activities

[* * *]

The functionaries in this study were not restricted to support roles in the campaign. Nearly half (46%) of the respondents worked on the campaign full-time; the part-time workers averaged around 20 hours a week. One quarter of the functionaries were paid for their efforts eight times the national average. . . . Most revealing were the types of positions the functionaries held: 9% were campaign managers, 11% were campaign officers, 16% were heads of precinct organizations, 10% headed other types of campaign activities (special events chairperson, publicity chairperson, and the like), 10% were office managers, and 20% were county or municipal campaign coordinators.

A comparison between functionaries working for male and female candidates revealed that functionaries working for female candidates were more likely to hold positions as campaign manager and office manager, while functionaries working for male candidates were more likely to serve as county or municipal coordinators. These findings suggest that women are somewhat more likely to hold top leadership positions in campaigns for female candidates. However, such a finding must be considered tentative because of the small number of campaigns for female candidates included in this study. Moreover, three-fourths of the male candidates made healthy use of women in responsible positions: when top positions were held by men, women were well utilized in "middle-management" campaign activities.

Despite the fact that most functionaries had defined areas of responsibility, a large proportion of the respondents indicated that they engaged in multiple campaign activities; one-fourth engaged in eight or more activities. The most common of these activities were volunteer recruitment (67%); headquarters work (63%); campaign strategy, special events, and getting out the vote (54%); and telephoning and fund-raising (50%). Interestingly, the sex of the candidate made some difference in terms of the number of activities engaged in by the functionaries. Women working for female candidates were more likely to engage in multiple activities from the top to the bottom of the campaign than women working for male candidates. Interviews with functionaries from one woman's campaign suggested explanations for this pattern. Two female campaign managers commented on their desire to "teach a lot of novices about politics" by bringing inexperienced women into major campaign decision-making. At the same time, however, these women sought to have all workers share in the more routine tasks in order to "divide up the drudgery" and lessen "divisions between the professionals and volunteers."

Not surprisingly, the volunteers were distinguished from the functionaries by their limited involvement with leadership activities (planning strategy, fund-raising, headquarters work, and special events) and their more extensive involvement in support activities (precinct walking, getting out the vote, and telephone canvassing). It is important to note, however, that almost one-fourth of the volunteers participated in leadership activities as well. Thus, for some volunteers the campaign provided them with the kind of learning experience that could enable them to move into leadership positions in the future.

The data suggest that women are doing a lot more in campaigns than "lickin' and stickin'." Women are moving into leadership roles and are gaining expertise in a number of areas such as planning strategy, fund-raising, precinct organizing, and management activities, in which they played quite limited roles in the past. Furthermore, it was suggested that campaign organizations may undergo some changes as a result of the inputs of women—that women may seek to "democratize" campaigns by enlarging the ranks of top decision-makers and by distributing both the challenging and routine campaign tasks in a more equitable fashion.

Sex Discrimination on the Campaign Trail

The last major concern of this study was to try to understand how women perceive their roles in campaigns, in particular, in relation to the roles played by men. Do women perceive sex discrimination in campaigns? In which areas of campaign work, if any, do they experience differential treatment?

. . . More than half of the functionaries perceived discrimination against women participating in political organizations and parties, two-thirds perceived discrimination against women in attaining public office, and three-quarters perceived discrimination against women in obtaining executive positions in business. In addition, over half of the functionaries had positive evaluations of the women's movement: 51% responded that the movement for women's rights and equality was progressing too slowly; and 55% responded that the impact of the women's movement on American society had, as a whole, been positive. Thus, as a group, the functionaries were cognizant of issues of sex discrimination and were either strongly or moderately supportive of efforts to change the status of women. . . .

[* * *]

The first type of sex discrimination examined concerned salaries for campaign workers. Responses on this subject were extremely ambivalent. Respondents commented that women should be paid equally to men and that, in some cases, they were not. However, three-fourths of the respondents also believed that they personally should not have been paid for their work. . . .

[* * *]

Sex discrimination was perceived to be a more serious issue in the area of decision-making. About half of the respondents interviewed pointed to the exclusion of women from the inner circle of decision-makers.

In addition, feelings ran high about the treatment of women by campaign workers. Descriptions of male attitudes ran the gamut from condescension to protectiveness, from not taking women seriously to being insensitive to their particular needs. . . .

The area in which the respondents perceived the least discrimination was the treatment of women by the candidates. The respondents felt that the candidates respected their efforts, took them seriously, and considered women equally with men in making job offers after the election. The male candidates were much more favorably evaluated than male campaign workers. This suggests that dealing with the public sensitizes men to the issue of sex discrimination better than work in other arenas such as business and the professions.

Finally, the respondents were asked whether they thought there would be any differences working for a female, rather than a male, candidate. Most replied that it was impossible to generalize on this question, either because they lacked experience working for female candidates or because they thought that the personality of the individual candidate was the key factor. However, a few respondents who had worked for women commented that female candidates attract more women workers who "seem to get more done" and who are more "sympathetic and aware of people" than men. Most noteworthy seemed to be the belief that women handle decision-making differently from men. . . .

[* * *]

Feminism on the Campaign Trail

The respondents were asked a number of questions concerning their attitudes toward the women's movement. These questions permitted a division of the respondents into two groups: women who were strongly supportive of the women's movement (here-after, referred to as "feminists") and women who were mildly supportive or, in a few cases, mildly critical of the women's movement (referred to here as "moderates"). The campaign experiences of these two groups were then compared.

The feminists were more likely than the moderates to be Democrats, working for female candidates, employed, and interested in running for office. These charac-teristics suggest that some feminists approach the political campaign as a vehicle for changing the status of women. Their involvement in campaigns for female candi-dates demonstrates their commitment to electing women to public office. Their efforts within these campaigns to bring inexperienced women into major decision-making reveals their interest in educating women for more influential political roles. Their desire to work for pay and run for office suggests that they enter campaigns not only to achieve general political goals, such as electing good candidates, but also to gain personally in terms of acquiring political expertise and economic rewards. Their levels of satisfaction with the campaign were lower than those of the moderates— suggesting that, despite good campaign positions, they were somewhat dissatisfied as women with their campaign roles.

However, one must not exaggerate these findings. Many feminists as well as moderates held campaign orientations (acceptance of sex discrimination, fear of office-holding, altruism) that will retard the movement of women into high-level politics. Moreover, a feminist strategy, conspicuous by its relative absence, was the attempt to use political campaigns to raise issues of special concern to women. While the pursuit of such a strategy is dangerous for female candidates who must face resis-tance to their candidacies based purely on their sex, male candidates can deal with a variety of women's issues without being labeled "libbers." However, with only two exceptions, none of the feminists in this study indicated any particular motivation or activity on behalf of specific women's issues.

Thus, despite impressive levels of participation in campaign activities, women have yet to utilize fully the opportunities presented by the political campaign. There was some evidence in this study of efforts by women to democratize the campaign structure, but there were no efforts made to combat sex discrimination in the campaign organization. While many respondents undeniably learned a great deal about the treatment of women in political campaigns and will perhaps "know better next time," the inequities they experienced may, for some, lessen their commitment in the future. Furthermore, while women became more visible in the community as a result of the victories of three out of four female candidates, their issue concerns remained relatively invisible. Last, the high socioeconomic status of the participants reminds us of the failure of the political elite, both men and women, to recruit women at the lower levels of the socioeconomic ladder, thereby expanding the participation of all women in politics.

The movement of women into responsible positions in campaigns reveals the desire of women to expand their participation in politics. Moreover, it is an essential step toward greater success in electing candidates, female and male, committed to the concerns of women. In the early days of the women's movement, activists stressed the need to recruit women to run for office. After suffering numerous electoral defeats, political activists realized that recruiting willing female candidates was only part of the problem. A second requirement was teaching women how to win elections by involving them in political campaigns. In addition to the immediate goal of winning elections, a further opportunity exists, namely, to utilize the political campaign, in and of itself, as a means of raising the status of women. Political campaigns provide opportunities to redistribute political resources, to educate the community, and to build political coalitions—opportunities which are sorely needed by women seeking greater influence within the political process.

TOWARD CRITICAL THINKING

1. This classic examination of the differences between men's and women's campaign activity has yet to be replicated. Do you think that the finding that men and women campaign workers do similar campaign work would be different today? How do you think the increased professionalization of campaigns, particularly for federal and statewide office, has affected the types of work women are doing on campaigns?

2. What do you think are the implications of the differences between the proportions of women in leadership positions on women candidates' campaigns compared to men candidates' campaigns?

Reading 22

Gender Roles and Party Roles

(1979)

Diane L. Fowlkes, Jerry Perkins, and Sue Tolleson Rinehart

In her book on the history of women party activists, *A Room at a Time*, Jo Freeman examines the different ways in which women worked for political parties from the 1880s to the 1960s. She characterizes the movement of women into party politics as gradual and prone to sudden increases followed by small declines in activity. Early in their history, the national party organizations established women's bureaus such as the National Federation of Republican Women—founded in the late 1930s and still active today.

Here, in an article published in the *American Political Science Review*, Diane L. Fowlkes, Jerry Perkins, and Sue Tolleson Rinehart examine similar questions and the different roles men and women play in the organization of the political parties at the local level. Using data drawn from surveys of men and women party activists from two counties in Georgia in 1977, the researchers ask if women's traditional roles of wives and mothers spill over into their political work. Comparing the political party as an organization to that of a family, their research examines the gender division of labor in the organization and maintenance of local political parties. The authors hypothesize that women disproportionately will be responsible for the work that supports the party within the organization, similar to women's responsibility for maintaining the home life of families. In contrast, men will be more likely to engage in work that promotes the party and its members, similar to men working outside the home to provide for the family.

Though an increasing number of women are active in party politics, their emergence into the ranks of the politically active does not appear to be totally unrestricted by traditional gender role expectations. Even where there is a conscious attempt to promote equality between the sexes, women still tend to perform routine tasks while men tend to dominate the functions surrounding organizational goals and political candidacy. This research examines gender roles and party roles in one southern party setting. . . . [T]he study moves away from a purely sociological perspective to a consideration of the effects of Republican or Democratic organizational context and asks, in effect, "What are the motivations, roles, activities and career aspirations that differentiate, respectively, Democratic and Republican men and women activists?"

The research perspective draws upon explanations of gender differences offered in previous studies of party activists [that] posit a parallel between the family and party organization. . . . To the extent that party activists receive and follow the gender role socialization traditionally prescribed for each sex, women would be expected to be more expressive and men more instrumental across four aspects of party organization: the pursuit of electoral careers, incentives for participation, party role definitions and performance of party duties.

The instrumental nature of political ambition is quite straightforward. As in the family, presumably some party members will spend a life of support within the organization (expressive roles) while others will venture forth in pursuit of career goals outside the basic unit (instrumental roles). The organizational "family" promotes the extra-organizational political careers of its ambitious members, who are expected to be men.

In a similar vein, the standard three-part division of incentives for participation can be divided into *instrumental/expressive* categories. Material motives involving the pursuit of individual monetary and career rewards would be instrumental, while solidary or social considerations would be expressive. Purposive incentives involving attempts to affect public policy by using the organization to alter the direction of government could be considered instrumental.

Role definitions and activities in party studies typically fall into an *organizational/electoral* dichotomy. This dichotomy closely parallels the expressive/instrumental breakdown, with electoral activities in effect representing instrumental efforts. A more fundamental dimension, however, may cut across organizational and electoral categories. Both organizing and electoral work involve perfunctory tasks as well as nonroutine activities. The rather routine task of attending meetings is to be contrasted with the more innovative work involved in recruiting new members and expanding the organization. Electorally, tasks such as putting out the mail must be contrasted with recruiting candidates and raising money. In this study, *routine* organizational or electoral roles and activities are considered expressive, while *nonroutine* organizational or electoral roles and activities are considered instrumental.

Because this study is concerned with building a political taxonomy of the sexes, we must also consider a second category, party membership. Much evidence illustrates the differences between the parties in recruiting and other activities, which depend upon majority-minority status, the social setting and the like. Although some of this evidence is contradictory and some difficult to compare, the important point from our perspective is that gender roles do not operate in a political vacuum. It is to be expected, for example, that one party's emphasis on organizational as opposed to electoral goals or varying emphasis between the parties on the cultivation of political careers could create more party than gender differences.

Methodology

The data for this study come from a survey of Democratic and Republican political party officials in Fulton and DeKalb Counties, Georgia, conducted from January to late April of 1977. The counties contain approximately two-thirds of metropolitan Atlanta's 1.5 million population. The Atlanta area supports viable Republican organizations that have emerged as successful competitors with the Democratic organizations, especially at the local level, although the Democrats remain the dominant party.

The study focused on the people at the base of the four organizations because of the comparability of positions across parties and because the greatest proportions of women are found at the lowest levels. . . . Respondents were provided with a series of reasons for their continuing involvement in party politics and were asked to rate the importance of each. We asked open-ended questions to tap role perceptions and administered a series of specific items on actual activities performed. As for political ambition, each respondent was asked if s/he were interested in running for office if the opportunity arose.

[* * *]

Findings

[* * *]

The findings suggest that party activists can be distinguished by party and by sex. But which party members exhibit the more instrumental or expressive incentives and role definitions? Which sex is more ambitious and more responsible for the instrumental or expressive activities? . . .

[* * *]

[The Democrats] score on the expressive ends of the incentive of enjoyment of politics and routine-nonroutine organizational roles but on the instrumental ends of the incentives of business contacts and future office-seeking. The Republicans are the reverse image of the Democrats on these party variables. . . . [T]he Democrats tend to have instrumental scores on the incentives of the chance to run for office and the chance to make business contacts. Democrats have expressive scores reflecting enjoyment of politics and expressive, that is, routine scores on organizational roles. Thus, the Democratic activists are more likely to emphasize material and solidary incentives than are the Republicans, while the Republicans adopt more nonroutine organizational roles than do the Democrats.

. . . [M]en score consistently on the instrumental ends of the party variables. Women score consistently on the expressive ends of the party variables. . . . [W]omen exhibit less electoral ambition than men, attend more meetings, do more telephoning and less canvassing. Women also are less motivated to work for the party because of the opportunity to make business contacts and are more likely to define their electoral roles as routine.

. . . [T]he expressive/instrumental concepts consistently distinguish between the sexes but not between the parties. The Democrats and the Republicans, when considered simply as party members, exhibit a combination of expressive and instrumental incentives and party role definitions.

. . . Democratic women and Republican men are at the extremes with the means of Democratic men and Republican women falling to the inside of the extreme positions. . . .

. . . Democratic women are more instrumental than Republican women, as are Democratic men in comparison to Republican men. . . . In other words, the level of instrumentality for both sexes is higher in the Democratic party, but the magnitude of differences between the sexes is similar in both parties. This pattern is especially marked for electoral ambition, the variable contributing most to distinguishing between the sexes. . . .

Discussion

As in other organizations, many aspects of life within the political party are gender-related in that men and women are differently employed. This study specifies and measures four aspects of party organization: party role definitions, party duties or activities, incentives for participation and electoral ambition. The evidence presented here suggests that in these party organizations gender distinctions are particularly evident in two areas: ambition and activities. Activities such as attending meetings and telephoning can be understood as fulfilling the expressive support function and more commonly as "women's work." More importantly, the party's major goal—that of recruiting candidates and capturing office—is also gender-related. According to our research, men are more ambitious than women, an expressive/instrumental differential that comports well with recent evidence that the under-representation of women in elective office is more the result of a paucity of women candidates than discrimination against them at the polls.

What are the sources of sex-typed behavior? What are the implications for the party organization of change in gender roles? Possible sources of gender discrimination are early socialization and adherence to stereotypes because of fear of sanctions against deviant behavior. And, of course, discrimination on the part of the party elite also is a possible source. However, as change occurs in society and challenges are carried out by women in party organization, one would expect that fewer women would be available for the routine functions they have performed in the past. Women may well be accommodated by being given a share of the more important positions, but will men begin to share in carrying out the very important expressive functions at the base of the party? As women adopt less traditional gender roles and become less responsible for performing their traditional party roles, and if men cannot be encouraged to do the same, the party organization, which is already weak because of other reasons, may become weaker.

The whole organizational life of the party, however, cannot be understood in terms of gender distinctions. The parties face common requirements in different ways, and the manner in which they meet common needs can be more a function of inter-party variation than of gender differences. In two of the areas investigated—party role definitions and incentives for participation—party rather than sex is the more important variable. With respect to party role perceptions, Republican men *and* women see their organizational work as innovative, while Democratic women *and* men see their organizational roles as routine. And, while it is true that within both parties women are somewhat more motivated than men to work because they enjoy politics, the larger distinction is between the parties; both Democratic women *and* men are more expressive than their Republican counterparts. Similarly, women have less motivation to work for material rewards than men, but the important distinction is between the parties, with the Democrats the more instrumental of the two groups of activists. Even on those matters that are primarily gender-related such as political ambition, the Democratic party contains higher levels of ambition than does the Republican party.

[* * *]

TOWARD CRITICAL THINKING

1. The researchers warned that as women became increasingly involved in the electoral roles of the party traditionally assumed by men, men would have to do more of the organizational or supportive work that has been women's traditional responsibility, or the party organization at the local level would be weakened. At this point, we have witnessed women's increasing level of activity in the electoral arena of party politics. Have men stepped in to assume the organizational responsibilities of the party? If not, have the parties become weaker as the authors predicted?

2. The differences in the party organizations were based on a time when the Democratic Party dominated southern politics. How would the change to Republican Party dominance of the South alter their conclusions? Are their conclusions unique to the political culture of the South? Why, or why not?

READING 23

The Political Culture of the Democratic and Republican Parties

(1986)

Jo Freeman

During the 1970s, the political parties underwent a great transformation in response to significant political and cultural changes occurring in the country. The political system was facing the challenges of the Watergate scandal and the aftermath of President Richard Nixon's resignation, in addition to new demands by historically out-of-power groups such as students against the Vietnam War, the civil rights movement, and the women's rights movement. While the focus of this article published in *Political Science Quarterly* detailing the different cultures of the Democratic and Republican parties is not specifically on women, women's activities in the political parties are used as examples to support Jo Freeman's broader theory of basic party difference.

Freeman pays particular attention to the different ways the two major parties responded to the demands of women in the 1970s to increase their numbers as national convention delegates and include support for the Equal Rights Amendment and abortion rights in the party platforms. Through attending the national party conventions of both parties from 1976 to 1984, Freeman notes that the divergence of the two parties on these issues was not necessarily a direct response to the differing political cultures. Subsequent research by scholars such as Christina Wolbrecht in *The Politics of Women's Rights: Parties, Positions, and Change* in 2000 and Kira Sanbonmatsu in *Democrats, Republicans, and the Politics of Women's Place* in 2002 suggest that the changes in the parties over their positions on women's issues were caused by the necessity to build winning electoral coalitions. However, the way in which the Democratic and Republican parties are organized and their different institutional norms of behavior facilitated the different responses of the parties to the demands of women at this critical time in the nation's history.

The two cultures of the parties have been used by scholars subsequently to explain the differences between the political activity of Republican and Democratic women. This work suggests that while women in both political parties have had shared experiences as outsiders to politics and faced similar challenges to increase their participation and political influence, the distinct cultures of the two parties result in variation in the experiences of Democratic and Republican women both working for the parties and in advocating for women's issues.

Although political parties have been a pervasive part of American politics, studies of their internal organization and style have not received a great deal of attention. . . . It is the contention of this [article] that despite the similarities in governing forms, and even policy outcomes, there is nonetheless a fundamental difference between the national Democratic and Republican parties. That difference can be seen not so much in outcomes, which must pass through the filter of political reality, as in the mode by which internal politics is conducted. The difference is not one of purpose, but of political culture.

I am relying on the definition of political culture in the *International Encyclopedia of the Social Sciences:*

> . . . the set of attitudes, beliefs and sentiments which give order and meaning to a political process and which provide the underlying assumptions and rules that govern behavior in the political system. It encompasses both the political ideals and operating norms of a polity. Political culture is thus the manifestation in aggregate form of the psychological and subjective dimensions of politics. A political culture is the product of both the collective history of a political system and the life histories of the members of the system and thus it is rooted equally in public events and private experience. . . .

This is a study of national party elites in the party system created by the New Deal realignment. The subjects include holders of public and party office and activists in national party affairs (party and presidential campaign staff, delegates to national conventions). The data for this article derive primarily from interviews with these officials and activists, from observations made by me at the 1976, 1980, and 1984 national conventions of the Republican party, and at every national nominating convention of the Democratic party since 1964. . . .

[* * *]

There are two fundamental differences between the parties in which all others are rooted. The first one is structural: in the Democratic party power flows upward and in the Republican party power flows downward. The second is attitudinal: Republicans perceive themselves as insiders even when they are out of power, and Democrats perceive themselves as outsiders even when they are in power. . . .

[* * *]

The different direction in the flow of power also creates different conceptions of legitimacy. In the Democratic party legitimacy is determined by who you represent, and in the Republican party by whom you know and who you are. It is this difference that makes the Democratic party so much more responsive to demands for reform within it and the Republican party so much more responsive to changes in leadership.

[* * *]

The operation of these different forms of legitimacy can readily be seen in the activities of feminists at the 1976 conventions. A group of women including [Democratic National Committee] DNC members, prominent feminists, and elected officials met with the Carter campaign to negotiate whether there would be a floor fight on the minority report to the Rules Committee that future conventions should require that half of all delegates be female. These women felt it necessary to call and report to meetings of women delegates (and whatever non-delegates cared to attend) on the progress of the negotiations every day. When they finished, all women attending, including non-delegates, took to the floor to express their own opinions on what should happen. After agreement was reached in the negotiations, the women's caucus leadership asked the participants to vote on the agreement. Since Jimmy Carter packed the meeting with delegates committed to him, the outcome was forseeable, but no one suggested that the process was irrelevant. The daily reports, debate, and ratification were all essential parts of the legitimation process. They gave the largely self-selected leadership of the women's caucus their claim to represent a key constituency.

At the Republican convention, four women with close personal ties to the Ford campaign, but operating as the Republican Women's Task Force (RWTF) of the National Women's Political Caucus, quietly lobbied to keep the Equal Rights Amendment (ERA) in the platform. They called one meeting, the Sunday before the convention, which was poorly attended. There they passed on information on what they intended to do and what kind of volunteer help they could use. There was no debate or discussion, no votes, and no further meetings. Furthermore, they focused strictly on the ERA, leaving abortion to others, because ERA was the only issue Ford supported. They said that reelecting Ford was the single most important thing they could do for women.

The 1980 GOP convention had few former Ford supporters. The women who represented the RWTF had no influence at the convention, which saw the ERA removed from the platform by an overwhelming vote, because they had no access to the Reagan campaign, which had complete control of the proceedings. Mary Louise Smith, former chair of the Republican National Committee (RNC), finally intervened with Reagan on their behalf. She was able to secure a meeting, but no influence, because she too had supported the wrong candidate.

[* * *]

Organizational Style

[* * *]

The Republican party sees itself as an organic whole whose parts are interdependent. Republican activists are expected to be good soldiers who respect leadership and whose only important political commitment is to the Republican party. Since direction comes from the top, the manner by which one effects policy is by quietly building a consensus among key individuals, and then pleading one's case to the leadership as furthering the basic values of the party. Maneuvering is acceptable. Challenging is not. This approach acknowledges the leadership's right to make final decisions and reassures them that those preferring different policies do not have competing allegiances. On the other hand, open challenges or admissions of fundamental disagreements indicate that one might be too independent to be a reliable soldier who will always put the interests of the party first. This cuts off access to the leadership and thus is quite risky—unless the leadership changes to people more amenable to the challengers. While not risky like an open challenge, quietly building an internal consensus is nonetheless costly of one's political resources. Activists learn early to conserve their resources by only contesting issues of great importance to them.

[* * *]

In the Democratic party, keeping quiet is the cause of atrophy and speaking out is a means of access. As the type and importance of powerful groups within it has changed over time, there has been a great deal of conflict. . . .

Since the purpose of most of the conflict is to achieve acceptance and eventually power, it does not matter whether the issues that are fought over are substantive or only symbolic. In the 1950s and 1960s these fights were usually over credentials as southern delegations were challenged because of their refusal to declare their loyalty to the national ticket and their inadequate representation of blacks. In the 1970s and 1980s, the fights have usually been over platform planks, but some have concerned rules changes or designations of status. In 1976 women's groups fought over the equal-division rule to require that half of all delegates be women. Although they lost, they had to find another issue in 1980 because the DNC decided to adopt "50–50" in 1978. That year they focused on minority planks on abortion and denying party support to opponents of the ERA. In 1984 the issue would have been a woman vice presidential candidate, but this was preempted by Walter Mondale's selection of Geraldine Ferraro as his running mate, so there was nothing to fight over.

[* * *]

Fights do not have to be won in order for those picking them to be successful. They are opportunities for demonstrating political skills and establishing territory. Feminist leaders didn't win the equal division fight in 1976, and everyone knew that had it gone to a floor vote, they would have lost. What they won was recognition. The Carter campaign negotiated with them, because they showed that there were a substantial number of women willing and able to fight on the issue. This established the right of women to be recognized as an important group within the party. However, Carter refused to negotiate with feminists in 1980, largely because he perceived them as surrogates for his rival, Ted Kennedy, and not important in and of themselves. This was changed by their success in getting the convention to adopt two minority planks that the Carter administration opposed. By showing that they were both politically skilled and persistent, feminists successfully claimed the right to represent women within the party.

[* * *]

The open confrontations that occur in the Democratic party do not take place within the Republican party, because it is a very different kind of organization. If one were to place the many different forms of collectivities on a spectrum, the Democratic and Republican parties would not occupy the same point. At one end would be groups exhibiting a great deal of spontaneity that are easy to join and have minimal structure, such as fads and crowds. At the other would be formal organizations that have well developed divisions of labor, hierarchical layers of authority, are selective in their membership, and are relatively impervious to spontaneous impulses, such as corporations or at the extreme end, military bodies. In the middle are most social movements, which, however diverse they may be, exhibit both noticeable spontaneity and a describable structure. Parties and campaigns lie on the more organized end of the spectrum, but because they must mobilize voters, raise money from contributors rather than by selling a product, and recruit volunteers to accomplish their goals, they exhibit many properties of social movements.

[* * *]

Dissent and Disloyalty

One of the most common observations of the Democratic party is how much more fractious it is than the Republican party. Although there are bounds on dissent, one can say things about the Democratic party leaders and candidates, publicly, that in the Republican party would be deemed disloyal. Only the Republican party has an eleventh commandment—thou shalt not criticize a fellow Republican. . . .

The difference in the bounds of dissent can be seen in the different ways the parties have treated those who had fundamental disagreements with their party's presidential candidates. In 1980 the National Organization for Women (NOW) voted not to endorse Jimmy Carter and at the convention led a floor fight for a minority plank strongly disliked by the candidate. Despite this opposition in an election year and the fact that no one thought NOW would possibly defect to the Republicans, NOW President Ellie Smeal was invited to meet with President Carter that fall and was subsequently (after Carter's defeat) hired as a consultant to the DNC. Indeed, refusal to toe the line and leadership of a successful floor fight strengthened NOW within the party because it had demonstrated clout.

In the Republican party many, though certainly not all, prominent Ford supporters, found themselves eased out after Reagan was elected, including ones who professed loyalty to the President but disagreed with some aspects of his program. Feminists who criticized Reagan for his opposition to the ERA have been virtually read out of the Republican party. Although George [H.W.] Bush was selected to be Reagan's running mate despite many well known disagreements, it was a practical decision that was not completely accepted by Reagan's own supporters. The opposition to Bush was much greater and runs much deeper than that of Democrats to Lyndon B. Johnson as John F. Kennedy's running mate or to Hubert Humphrey as Johnson's. Even after several years of total subservience to Reagan policies, Bush is still viewed with great suspicion by hard-core Reaganites.

[* * *]

. . . While many Democrats are party people first and foremost, many others are not. The idea that one should juggle competing loyalties is unexceptional, as is the possibility that one might seek to resolve conflicting agendas by getting the party to adopt the positions of nonparty groups. The Republican party frowns on multiple loyalties. Indeed it looks with great suspicion on anyone susceptible to conflicting agendas as potentially disloyal. A major reason Republican feminists have had so much more trouble rehabilitating themselves into the Reagan party than others who did not initially support him is because they are assumed to have a major or even primary loyalty to feminism and feminist organizations. Even in 1976, when Republican feminists were aligned with party leaders, one organizer commented that because the GOP is not "an interest group party . . . the RWTF is viewed with skepticism. Party regulars have a hard time adjusting to the presence of an organized interest." The current leadership views feminist organizations as Democratic party front groups. Thus it is virtually impossible to be both an accepted Republican activist and an outspoken supporter of feminist goals. Since the party discourages people from identifying themselves as members of a group with a group agenda, it minimizes the possibility of multiple loyalties. . . .

[* * *]

Does Difference Make Any Difference?

This article has argued that there are significant differences in the political culture of the major political parties—differences that manifest themselves in different organizations, styles, attitudes, and approaches. These differences have been commented on only in passing by students of political parties. Instead, the literature has viewed the parties as possessing the common goal of putting together a winning coalition by being "all things to all people." There has been an implicit assumption, untested by field studies, that this common goal requires similar political strategies by similar political organizations. Although it has never been explicitly stated, the model behind this assumption appears to be the Democratic party, because the descriptions in the literature of how a political party operates "fit" the Democratic party. Until the Republican party scored significant successes in the 1980 elections, it was assumed to be merely a pale imitation of the majority party, striving unsuccessfully to put together a winning coalition. Since then, there has been a tendency to view the operating style and approaches of the Republican party as "the party of the future."

I would argue that the Republican party is *not* a poor imitation of a normal coalition-building party, but a different type of political organization that does things in different ways. The differences in its political culture have put the Republican party at a disadvantage in its competition with the Democratic party for most of the New Deal era. However, the roads to political success have been changing rather rapidly in the last fifteen years, and the new roads are ones that the Republican party is well equipped to travel. Thus, their strategies are now becoming the new model, which is not necessarily an appropriate one for the Democratic party. . . .

[* * *]

TOWARD CRITICAL THINKING

1. Jo Freeman's contrast of the Democratic and Republican Party cultures suggests that women acting as a group would have more success at achieving their desired ends in the Democratic Party, which at that time was made up of members of several interest groups and in which power was based on whom you represented. Following Freeman's description of the culture of the Republican Party, how would Republican women successfully advance their concerns within the party? And, more importantly, do her observations hold true today?

2. This description of the differences between the two political parties was written long before the 1994 Republican Revolution that led to a change in party control of Congress. Has majority status for the Republican Party changed the political culture of the party, or has the Democratic Party become more like the Republican Party during the past twenty years? What effect do these changes have on women in the party organizations?

READING 24

Political Parties and the Recruitment of Women to State Legislatures

(2002)

Kira Sanbonmatsu

Early research on women and politics found that women were often recruited to run for office by their political parties as "sacrificial lambs" when there was little or no chance of winning the election. Similarly, the parties often recruited women to fill the vacancies when their husbands died in office to maintain control of the seat so that the party had time to vet and advance a new male candidate, as discussed by Barbara Palmer and Dennis Simon (Reading 14). As a result, in the past, the parties often have stood as institutional barriers for women who want to run for elected office.

In this research published in the *Journal of Politics*, Kira Sanbonmatsu examines the significance of political parties for the number of women serving in state legislatures. By studying the variation in the proportion of women elected to state legislatures, Sanbonmatsu explores the differences among the proportions of women in each party in state legislatures.

In addition, she explores demographic differences between Republican and Democratic potential women candidates and different structural variables that would affect the possible candidacies of women. These variables include measures such as the level of professionalization of the legislature and party control of the chamber that identify the level of desirability of the office. The effect of the level of the desirability of different offices is also explored by Palmer and Simon (Reading 14) and Charles S. Bullock III and Susan A. MacManus (Reading 26).

The percentage of women in state legislatures has increased dramatically since the early 1970s, from about 6% of all state legislators to about 22% today. Often overlooked in these averages is the significant variation across states in women's representation—from a low of 8% in Alabama to a high of about 40% in Washington. Past scholars who have sought to explain this puzzle of women's representation usually analyze women as a group, without making comparisons between Democratic and Republican women. Yet there are reasons to believe that women's path to office differs by political party. By disaggregating women by party, we can identify factors that influence women's recruitment and improve our understanding of women's political underrepresentation.

Previous explanations for the variation across states in women's representation have often focused on contextual factors such as social structure (e.g., ideology, political culture), electoral rules (e.g., multimember districts), and the institutional setting (e.g., the degree to which the legislature is professionalized). This study places the role of parties at the center of the analysis. . . .

I argue that the explanation for variation across states in women's representation differs by party. First, the state's social eligibility pool has a greater effect on Democratic women's representation than Republican women's representation. Second, party shapes the political opportunity structure facing women candidates. The effects of legislative professionalism and the partisan composition of the legislature differ for Democratic women compared to Republican women. This study suggests that aspects of the political opportunity structure facing women candidates are specific to each party.

[* * *]

Past Research on Political Parties and Women's Representation

Understanding why more women do not hold elective office is an important normative question with implications for the legitimacy of our democracy. There are policy implications as well, since women legislators are much more likely than men to articulate and support issues of interest to women as a group.

One scholarly approach to women's representation has entailed studies of individual women's races for the legislature. . . . Women continue to be underrepresented despite a significant body of research demonstrating that men and women fare similarly when they run for office; it is therefore necessary to look earlier in the recruitment process to understand women's continued underrepresentation. Indeed, understanding the factors that lead women to run for office and why women are discouraged from running is a neglected area of research. We miss half the story of women's representation if we only study women who run for office and ignore the women who do not run.

An inquiry focusing on the state as the unit of analysis is appropriate because the state legislatures are in fact 50 different institutions. The hypotheses investigated here concern factors that are likely to affect women candidates at the state level. State-level studies can complement individual-level studies of women candidates.

Renewed scholarly interest in political recruitment makes this research timely. Practitioners have recently focused their attention on recruitment as well. The pattern of women in the state legislatures has implications for women's election to statewide and federal offices since women state legislators may run for higher office.

The recent trend of greater devolution of federal power to the states also makes research on state legislatures increasingly important.

[* * *]

The Social Eligibility Pool

One way to conceptualize political parties is as a pool of potential candidates for office. . . . The theory of parties as office-seekers construes parties as solely concerning elites, neglecting the public altogether. . . .

This conceptualization means that each party's base of women adherents in the electorate is a source of candidates: the party can be thought of as a mechanism by which women can become political elites. This theory implies that if the parties' bases are comprised of different social groups, then the two parties' bases of women may differ as well. I therefore hypothesize that the effect of the state's social eligibility pool on women's representation differs by party.

The social eligibility pool is recognized as an important determinant of women's representation: states with more working women, women executives, and women law students and lawyers are likely to have more women in the legislature than other states. But scholars have neglected the possible interaction of party with the social eligibility pool. There are several reasons to believe that Democratic and Republican women may constitute two different candidate pools. The greater involvement of Republican women in electoral politics in the late 1800s and through much of the 1900s may have been a by-product of the class difference between the two parties since Republican women may have had more time and resources for politics. In the past, Democratic women elites have been less likely to be homemakers and more likely to be in the labor force. Today, Democratic and Republican women state legislators come to office through different networks and with different bases of organizational support. Yet there has been little research comparing the two groups of women.

Because Democratic and Republican women state legislators seem to have different backgrounds, the relevant eligibility pool for women candidates may be somewhat different for each party. If Republican women elites are more likely to be homemakers than Democratic women elites, then women's labor force participation in the state may have a greater impact on Democratic women's representation than Republican women's representation.

The Political Opportunity Structure

A second way to conceptualize the party is as a group of office-seeking individuals. In this view, parties consist of elites competing for electoral office. Parties develop organizations precisely to enhance their chances of winning office. This view calls our attention to the role of the party in shaping the political opportunity structure.

By political opportunity structure, I mean structural factors that shape candidate emergence. . . . I examine three ways that parties may shape the political opportunity structure facing women candidates: legislative professionalism, partisan composition of the legislature, and party influence over nominations.

I hypothesize that legislative professionalism has a stronger effect on Democratic women's representation. If the parties' eligible pools of women candidates are different, then party may interact with the negative effect of legislative professionalism. Past studies have found that women are less likely to hold office in the more professional legislatures and more likely to hold the office if it is less desirable—possibly because of increased competition among potential candidates for the office or the higher costs of campaigning in those states. Women's presence is negatively related to salary, length of session, and staff, and positively related to turnover and the ratio of seats to population.

More professional states are also thought to hold greater appeal for Democratic than Republican legislators. . . . [D]ifferences in the attitudes and demographic backgrounds of Democrats and Republicans are likely to affect their incentives to run for office. Republicans probably prefer legislatures that are less professional because they may be more likely to want the flexibility to pursue an occupation—perhaps law or business—in addition to serving in the legislature. Democrats, however, probably find professional legislatures more appealing; they may be more likely to want to serve as a full-time occupation, and they may find the salary in professional legislatures more attractive than Republicans do. The opportunity costs of serving in the legislature may simply be higher for Republican candidates since Democratic legislators are more likely to pursue politics as a career. . . .

If more professionalized legislatures are more attractive to Democratic than Republican candidates, then professionalism may create more competition among potential Democratic candidates. The impact of legislative professionalism on women's representation may therefore have a stronger effect on Democratic women than Republican women.

I also hypothesize that states with low pay and long sessions are positively related to Republican women's representation but have no effect on Democratic women's representation. I expect that there is an interactive effect for these two components of professionalism for Republican women, but not Democratic women. In some states, the legislature is in session much of the year, and yet the pay is not high enough for a breadwinner. If the legislative demands make it difficult to maintain a separate profession, then Republican men may be less interested in the office, creating opportunities for Republican women. The same opportunities may not exist for Democratic women. Democratic men's interest in serving may be less affected by the interaction of pay and session length than Republican men's interest because Democratic men may be less concerned about the opportunity costs. And Democratic women may be less likely than Republican women to be housewives. Thus legislatures with long sessions and low pay may create disproportionate opportunities for Republican women because of income and occupational differences between the two parties and differences in women's backgrounds.

I also test the hypothesis that being in the majority negatively affects both Republican and Democratic women's representation. Thus Democratic control of the chamber should negatively affect Democratic women but positively affect Republican women, and vice versa. Scholars have found a negative relationship between women's representation and Democratic party dominance and a positive relationship with Republican party dominance. Most women state legislators were also Republicans for most of the century. However, these past studies have not examined the effects of majority party status on women by party.

The traditionally negative impact of Democratic party dominance may reflect greater bias against women among Democratic than Republican elites—a possibility that is discussed further below. However, this relationship may simply reflect majority party status since Democrats tended to predominate in the state legislatures until recently. A legislative seat may be more desirable to someone in the majority party, so there may be more intraparty competition for nominations.

Finally, I test the hypothesis that traditional party organization states are negatively related to both Democratic and Republican women's representation. Greater party influence over nominations may benefit women because the parties may recruit women. However, the parties may serve as negative gatekeepers; they may not support women's candidacies or may not recruit women to run in the first place. A negative party effect may reflect the status of women as relative newcomers to politics. In areas with strong party influence over nominations, it may be hard for any group—including women—to gain access to the nomination. A negative effect may also reflect bias; for example, the negative effect of Democratic party dominance on women's representation may have resulted from the traditional gender role beliefs of Democratic party leaders, given their working class and ethnic backgrounds. The greater proportion of Republican women state legislators may indicate that party influence over nominations benefits Republican women but not Democratic women. However, [political scientist Albert] Nelson found a negative effect for traditional party organizations for both groups of women.

Data and Methodology

I collected data from 1971 to 1999 in order to analyze the effects of the social eligibility pool, legislative professionalism, partisan composition, and traditional party organization on women's representation. . . . My analysis seeks to explain why women's representation within each party varies across states. The dependent variable is the percentage of women out of all legislators in their party. There are two observations for each state for each year: one for Democratic women as a percentage of all Democrats in the lower house, and one for Republican women as a percentage of all Republicans in the lower house. The percentage of women state legislators is highly correlated with the percentage of women candidates. By comparing the representation of women within the two parties, I am assuming that certain districts are likely to elect either Democratic or Republican legislators.

[* * *]

Analyses

. . . [T]he social eligibility pool [of] working women is positively related to women's representation for both groups of women, but the effect is larger for Democratic women. . . .

Legislative compensation is not statistically significant for either group of women. However, length of session is negatively related to Democratic women's representation. . . .

. . . Perhaps because Republican women legislators are somewhat more likely to be housewives, legislatures with demanding schedules but low compensation provide a favorable context for Republican women.

The partisan composition of the legislature, measured by a lag of the Democratic margin in the lower house, is negatively related to Democratic women's representation but unrelated to Republican women's representation. Being in the majority does not have the negative effect on the recruitment of Republican women that it does on Democratic women.

Finally, traditional party organization is negatively related to women's representation for both groups as expected. . . . To the extent that traditional party organization seems to exert a more negative impact on Democratic women, this result is consistent with some previous scholars who have argued that Democratic party elites may have served as barriers to women's candidacies. . . .

. . . More liberal states and states with a greater percentage of multimember districts are positively related to women's representation, consistent with past research. Moralistic political culture, which is often cited as a key factor in shaping women's representation, does not achieve statistical significance. Region (south) does not have an independent effect.

[* * *]

. . . Democratic women face greater obstacles in their pursuit of office if they are seeking a seat in a Democratic-controlled legislature. There appears to be greater competition for seats within the Democratic party in Democratic majority legislatures, compared to competition within the Republican party in Republican majority legislatures. Democratic women may have trouble winning the backing of their party if the primary is competitive.

[* * *]

TOWARD CRITICAL THINKING

1. The author suggests that, to better understand the differences among the state party organizations' levels of recruitment of women candidates, we need to understand how men's interest in state offices affects women's opportunities. How could we measure men's interest in state office?

2. Based on the findings of how women in the social eligibility pools of the two political parties differ, how would the recruitment plan to increase the number of Democratic women candidates contrast with the recruitment plan to increase the number of Republican women candidates?

WRAPPING UP

1. The articles in Chapter 6 examined different questions about women in the political parties using data collected from the local, state, and national levels. What influence does the level of the party organization have on questions about women and the political parties? If similar questions were asked at all levels, would you expect to get the same results? Why, or why not?

2. Democratic and Republican women differ from each other in a number of ways. In addition, their respective parties differ in their positions on what have been traditionally defined as women's issues and subsequently their relationships with women's rights organizations. How are these differences significant for the study of women and political parties?

READING 25

When Women Run against Men

(1977)

R. Darcy and Sarah Slavin Schramm

In 2002, Senator Mary Landrieu (D–LA) ran against Republican State Commissioner of Elections Suzie Terrell in both the general election and a very competitive runoff election. Senator Susan Collins (R–ME) was challenged that same year by Democrat Chellie Pingree in her second reelection effort to the U.S. Senate. Before women ran against each other for office, particularly for seats in the U.S. House of Representatives, women candidates were most likely to face male opponents. This article, published in *Public Opinion Quarterly* by R. Darcy and Sarah Slavin Schramm, was one of the first to explore the dynamics of campaigns where women faced off against male candidates. This research set the stage for subsequent analysis of the electoral factors that affect the success rates of women candidates.

Darcy and Slavin Schramm examine men and women general-election candidates in three election years and analyze survey data on voter response to women candidates for the House of Representatives. Women candidates are differentiated from their male counterparts and each other on key variables that continue to be important in explaining the success of women candidates: seat status (challenger, open seat, or incumbent), party affiliation (Democrat or Republican), and type of district (urban or rural).

Darcy and Slavin Schramm are the first to explore questions further addressed in subsequent research on whether women voters are more likely than men voters to be interested in the candidacies of and to vote for women. Most importantly, Darcy and Slavin Schramm demonstrate that, just as there are factors that detract from women candidates' electoral success, there are also important variables that enhance the candidacies of women.

When a woman runs against a man, will she be helped or hurt by her sex? . . .

Scholars have posited party, incumbency, and "national tides" as important factors determining the outcome of congressional races. On the other hand, we have reason to suspect a gradual decline in these forces in the face of the increasing importance of idiosyncratic district factors in such races as well as for other contests.

[* * *]

Popular mythology and scholarly wisdom (however speculative) both point to sex as a candidate characteristic which could be of interest to voters. There are reasons for expecting women candidates to do worse than men, and there are reasons for expecting women candidates to do better than men. Among the theses given to support the latter position are the following:

1. Women candidates have an easier time gaining public recognition. They attract more attention and are remembered more easily than male candidates. Since candidate recognition is associated positively with votes cast for the recognized candidate, women candidates have an advantage over men with regard to the ease with which they gain recognition and votes.

2. Americans view their legislative bodies as representative of preponderant social groupings. A candidate from a group as vastly underrepresented as women are appeals to some voters' sense of fair play, and thus she has an advantage over a candidate from a group that has more than its fair share of representatives.

3. Women (especially housewives) often are unstimulated by politics and insensitive to the political information they incorporate. This may be due to the absence of female political leaders able to articulate a woman's political viewpoint. Candidates of their own sex might increase the "stake" of women in the election, activate their interest, and mobilize their vote.

4. Recently it has been suggested that voters, expressing renewed concern for morality in government, could be rejecting establishment-identified candidates. . . .

There are also reasons for expecting that being a woman will work against a candidate. Among them are the following:

1. A significant number of people (both men and women) still believe a woman's place is in the home rather than in the political arena. . . .

2. Most women move into occupations congruent with the roles traditionally assigned to them. Furthermore, the media perpetuate this tendency by reinforcing traditional images of women. By becoming a candidate for Congress—an occupation still relatively closed to them—a woman assumes an aggressive role which runs counter to this traditional image and the electorate's expectations about what is appropriate.

To determine exactly what voter response to women who are candidates for the U.S. House of Representatives has been recently, we examined all contested races in which the two major parties participated and drew a total of at least 90 percent of the vote. The elections studied were 1970, 1972, and 1974. There were 1,099 such races. Ninety-one of the candidates were women. They participated in 87 races.

As suggested above, two important vote sources are candidate party and incumbency. Democrats overall are likely to get more votes than Republicans; incumbents more than challengers. Two-thirds of the women candidates here were Democrats, but relatively few women were incumbents. In order to make a clear distinction among the variables sex, party, and incumbency, we chose to examine how well women and men candidates of the same party and incumbency status ran against several kinds of male opponents. The kinds of male opponents examined were:

1. Republican male incumbents
2. Republican male challengers (running against incumbents)
3. Republican male nonincumbents (running against other nonincumbents)
4. Democratic male incumbents
5. Democratic male challengers (running against incumbents)
6. Democratic male nonincumbents (running against other nonincumbents)

[Data show] women candidates do not run as well as men against male incumbents. The disadvantage women have in challenging incumbents is slight, however, and probably has little effect on the ultimate outcome of the race. Incumbents do well no matter what the sex of their opponents.

Differences are larger between the vote-getting ability of men and women candidates when the race is against a challenger or when there is no incumbent in the race. . . . While there is a great deal of overlap in the performance of men and women candidates in these races, on the average, Democratic women candidates do better than Democratic men. Republican women candidates, however, do worse, on the average, than Republican men. This difference in the performance of Republican and Democratic women candidates is largest in the case of women incumbents. . . . Democratic women incumbents average 75.1 percent of the vote while Republican women incumbents average only 54.5 percent—a 20.6 percent difference. Men incumbents of the two parties differ by an average of only 7.1 percent. When not challenging incumbents, women Democrats do somewhat better on the average than men Democrats. The reverse is true for Republican women.

When candidate party and incumbency status are controlled, candidate sex is found to have little explanatory power. Further, what differences there are between the vote-getting ability of men and women candidates are in opposite directions for the two parties. Thus, we find candidate sex has little or no effect on electoral outcomes. There is a difference between the vote-getting ability of women Republican and women Democratic candidates, however, which is larger than that between the men of the two parties. This unanticipated interaction between candidate sex and party leads us to look further into voters' reactions to women candidates.

The Voters: Survey Analysis

To better focus on responses to a candidate's sex we obtained the 1970, 1972, and 1974 Survey Research Center's Election Surveys. Information about candidate sex and incumbency was merged with survey responses to permit a further examination of voter behavior in this area.

A number of propositions are of interest to us here. First of all, it has been suggested the nomination of a woman candidate might facilitate the awareness of American women voters and even increase their participation rate. . . . [O]verall, men in the electorate recognize women candidates running in their districts more frequently than do women in the electorate. . . . [It] cannot be said that women candidates in and of themselves garner more recognition than men candidates, or that women in the electorate react to women candidates differently from men in the electorate. . . . There is no difference in the recognition of male and female incumbents overall or in each of the elections studied. Thirty-five percent of the electorate knew male incumbents, 35 percent knew female incumbents.

Secondly, it has been suggested that women candidates might politicize an allegedly politically passive female population. . . . The voting turnout of women in races in which there were women candidates was not significantly greater than their turnout in races in which there were no women candidates. The same holds true for men. . . .

It has been suggested that candidate recognition is associated with voting. This might account for the difference we observed between the vote-getting ability of Republican and Democratic women candidates. If women Democrats were better known than women Republicans, this could account for their differential vote-getting abilities. . . . Republican women have significantly *more* recognition than Democratic women, who, paradoxically, have the recognition gained by greater incumbency. Further, . . . Democratic candidates (of both sexes) have a higher proportion of their votes coming from those who do not know the name of the candidate for whom they voted. Once again, this was the case in each of the elections studied. However helpful recognition may be, it does not account for the advantage possessed by Democratic women candidates; nor does it account for the disadvantage possessed by Republican women candidates.

Patterns of Nomination

Women were nominated in fewer than 10 percent of the districts examined. Is there some pattern to the nominations which might produce the interaction between party and candidate sex observed above?

If women from both parties are more likely to be nominated in urban or otherwise Democratic districts, then Democratic women candidates would be helped and Republican women candidates would be hindered. Most voting in these districts would be party-line Democratic, and a large proportion of the voters might not be aware of the candidates. Under such conditions, whatever effects recognition may have on voter choice would be nullified by the large proportions of party-line voters. A Democratic woman candidate would get these votes whether she was recognized or not; a Republican woman would lose a good number even if she was recognized.

It has been shown that Democratic women tend to rely on extra-party organizations such as the [National] Women's Political Caucus to support their nominations, and these organizations tend to be more available and active in large metropolitan areas. Furthermore, urban organizations are likely to have a larger pool of activist women who are potential candidates. What about Republican women candidates? Republicans in an urban or otherwise hostile situation are faced with nominating candidates most of whom will stand small chance of election. There is little competition for a place on such a ticket. An opportunity for ticket balancing—that is, introducing population subgroups not typically represented on the party ticket—is too good to bypass in these situations. We know that Republican women are much lower in congressional ambition than their Democratic counterparts and hence may be more likely to wind up in noncompetitive districts as "throw-away" candidates. The result could be the nomination of Republican women in districts similar to those nominating Democratic women.

For evidence to support this reasoning, we begin by looking at district residential patterns as an index for constituency type. Using the urban portion of a district from a tripartite breakdown into urban, suburban, and nonmetropolitan (rather than the more usual but less comprehensive urban-rural dichotomy), . . . [the data show] districts that nominate women candidates are over 10 percent *more* urban than those which have confined their major party nominations to men. However, it is the districts nominating Democratic women candidates which are most urban. Districts nominating Republican women candidates are close to the average in their urbanness. . . .

[* * *]

These nominating patterns help to explain the interaction we have observed between candidate sex and party both in the election returns and in the survey data. In races against male opponents the average difference in vote between Democratic and Republican women candidates is 12.4 percent, while the difference between the men of the two parties is only 7.7 percent. . . . The electoral advantage enjoyed by Democratic women candidates and the disadvantage suffered by Republican women is due to the characteristics of the districts which nominate them. Democratic women are more likely to be nominated in helpful urban districts while women of both parties are being nominated in districts which are less friendly to Republicans than districts nominating only men.

[* * *]

TOWARD CRITICAL THINKING

1. The authors find differences between the success of Democratic and Republican women incumbents in the general election that is greater than the differences between Democratic and Republican men incumbents. What factors at the time of this research led to this difference? Do you think these differences exist today? Why, or why not?

2. The authors conclude that the electorate in general and women voters in particular are indifferent to the sex of the candidate. Do you believe this is true today? Why, or why not?

READING 26

Municipal Electoral Structure and the Election of Councilwomen

(1991)

Charles S. Bullock III and Susan A. MacManus

When research found that the electorate was not biased against women candidates, scholars turned to other explanations for the low number of women serving in elected office. One of the first areas of research compared different electoral structures to see if some methods of electing representatives gave rise to more women holding elected office. Research on the differences between the U.S. federal system, with single-member congressional districts, to other countries' parliaments, with multimember districts, found that the latter lead to more women serving in national legislatures. For example, in Sweden, Denmark, the Netherlands, Finland, and Norway, more than 35 percent of the members of parliament are women, whereas women constitute only 14 percent of the U.S. Congress in 2005.

To study the differences in electoral systems specifically in American politics, focus shifted from the federal to the state and local levels, where there was greater variation in the different types of election systems. In addition, more women had run and served in elected office at these levels of government than in the Congress at the time of this research. Charles S. Bullock III and Susan A. MacManus tested a number of variables that differentiate various city councils to see what factors were significant in predicting higher proportions of women in those bodies. Published in the *Journal of Politics*, this research on local city councilwomen set the stage for future exploration at the state level on how differences in electoral systems, political cultures in regions of the country, and characteristics of state legislatures, such as level of professionalization, affect the proportion of women serving in state legislatures.

[* * *]

Research on racial and ethnic minority representation has often found structure, especially the type of election system, to be related to variations in minority representational levels. In contrast, the limited research on the determinants of female representation has found little linkage with structural features.

Even when structure has been found to be related to female representation, relationships are often in the opposite direction than for minority representation. For example, several researchers have found single-member districts to be positively correlated with black representation, but studies of female representation suggest that women fare best when elections are at-large. Most data used to study female representation come from the 1970s and some structural variables included in more recent analyses of minority representation (e.g., presence of staggered terms or majority vote requirements) have not been tested in the context of female representation. Nor have region-by-region comparisons been made.

This [article] explores the impact of several structures on female city council representation using 1986 data collected from all U.S. cities with 1980 populations more than 25,000. The structures to be analyzed are: (1) type of election system (pure at-large, at-large from posts, at-large from residency districts, mixed, single-member district); (2) majority versus plurality vote requirements; (3) staggered versus simultaneous terms; (4) council size; (5) length of council terms; (6) incumbency return rate; and (7) city size. A region-by-region analysis is conducted to test whether political culture interacts with structure to produce different results. . . .

The Expected Effects of Structure

Previous research . . . leads us to expect that structure will explain little of the variation in female representation levels. However, individually some structures have been found to have a slight impact.

Type of Election System

. . . [W]omen probably encounter voters of both sexes who are reluctant to have a female act as their sole representative. In multimember districts, voters could select candidates of each sex, thus promoting the level of female representation.

[Data] confirmed that at-large elections were "kinder" to women than were single-member district elections. . . .

Majority versus Plurality Vote Requirements

Former NOW president Eleanor Smeal has alleged that the majority vote (runoff) requirement retards female representation since a woman who polled a plurality when facing multiple males in the primary could lose if sexist voters rallied to the surviving male in the runoff. The limited research to date has not supported Smeal. . . . Therefore, we doubt that runoffs will be associated with lower percentages of councilwomen.

Staggered versus Simultaneous Terms

This structure has been hypothesized to negatively impact racial and ethnic minorities especially in pure at-large systems. . . . [S]taggered terms could limit the effect of single-shot voting by a minority group by reducing the number of positions at stake. One could hypothesize that staggered terms reduce female city council representation and simultaneous elections would increase it. . . .

Council Size

Research has suggested that smaller councils have fewer women. . . . Competition is inferred to be lower when more council seats are available. Council size has also been used as a surrogate for the desirability and importance of the office. . . .

[* * *]

Length of Council Term

Like council size, length of a council term is typically regarded as a measure of the prestige or desirability of the office ("the longer the term the more attractive"). Fewer councilwomen are expected in cities with longer terms. The evidence on this proposition has not been supportive. . . .

Incumbency

Incumbency is widely recognized as a powerful "structure" in explaining municipal electoral outcomes, particularly in nonpartisan settings and where turnover is low. High incumbency return rates impede the entry of women and minorities into public office because the initial pool of incumbents is predominantly male.

City Size

Researchers have long expected size to be an important determinant. . . . [C]ampaigns may be more expensive in larger cities. If women are less able to raise campaign funds, this disadvantage will be more pronounced in big cities. . . .

[* * *]

The impact of city size may be affected by the council size. The desirability hypothesis suggests that women would less often serve when the ratio of population to council membership is high. . . .

Region

Several studies of female council representation have dichotomized the nation on the basis that the South is "the region most likely to manifest differences between males and females toward the role of women and politics." . . . Despite the image of a disproportionately sexist South, studies using region as a predictor found female representation levels to be only slightly lower in the South.

To date, there has been no region-by-region comparisons of female city council representational levels. There is, however, literature on women state legislators that offers hypotheses about what to expect from regions other than the South. . . . The suffrage movement originated in the Northeast, and its initial successes came in the West. . . .

[* * *]

Conclusions

There is little evidence that structural features influence the incidence of councilwomen, and this finding is not restricted to a single region. As anticipated, women are more likely to serve on western councils. The expectation derived from earlier work that the South would be particularly hostile to the election of women was not borne out since the proportion of councilwomen in the South is in line with that of the nation, exclusive of the West. Surprisingly, the Northeast was the least hospitable environment for women and in that region the incidence of women was only two-thirds as great as in the West. Staggering terms is not an impediment to the presence of councilwomen. Nor is the majority vote requirement an obstacle, save in Midwest. The Midwest is also the only region in which types of districting are related to female council membership where women did best in mixed formats.

Our findings do not support expectations that female successes are limited to less desirable positions. Contrary to the office desirability theory, women are not disadvantaged by council size, longer terms, or competing when more incumbents were reelected. Moreover, women serve at higher rates in larger cities. The only support at the regional level for the desirability hypothesis comes from the West where the percentage of women is greater in cities with larger councils.

The lack of linkage between structure and the presence of female councillors means that the proportion female among urban officeholders will not be easily increased through reforms. On the other hand, fears that efforts to increase black council membership through structural changes might raise barriers to the election of women are not supported.

The failure of structural features to explain variation in the incidence of councilwomen points to the likely significance of another factor—candidacy rates among women. Weakening of sexual stereotypes and growth in the numbers of female officeholders promotes the expectation that as larger numbers of women run, their presence at the council table will rise. Since the desirability explanation bears little fruit, it is likely that as the percentage of councilwomen rises, it will occur in a wide range of settings.

Our results prompt us to wonder about the genesis of the propositions tested here. The roots of some are in the civil rights literature. We suspect that there has been too great a tendency to assume that since women, like blacks, have traditionally been few in elective positions, the antecedents will be similar. The two groups differ on so many dimensions, such as geographic concentration and group identity, that it is not surprising when the correlates of their presence in elective office differ.

There is reason to believe that the problem may be more than simply generalizing to a dissimilar population. The lack of relationship between structure and the presence of female councillors fits a broader pattern uncovered by research using mid-1980s data. Research based on observations from the 1970s often suggested that certain municipal structures—particularly single-member districts—promoted the election of blacks. Scholars using more recent data have failed to find a statistically significant relationship between type of electoral system and the incidence of black councillors. Specifically, blacks are not more likely to be elected under single-member districts in cities at least 5% black having more than 100,000 people, cities with at least 50,000 people and 5%–50% black, or in cities having populations of at least 25,000. Nor are Hispanics advantaged by single-member districts in cities of 50,000, or from cities of at least 25,000. Nor is there strong evidence that other structural aspects promote black or Hispanic officeholding.

The driving force in models of black and Hispanic council membership is the ethnic composition of the population. The smaller variation across cities in the percentage of females than in the percentage of blacks or Hispanics and probably weaker gender than ethnic identity results in the absence of a variable strongly associated with female councillors. Our research on women conforms to recent work done on blacks and Hispanics in demonstrating the modest contribution of structure as an explanation of officeholding patterns.

TOWARD CRITICAL THINKING

1. The authors find little difference between the types of electoral systems in city councils and the proportion of women serving on those councils. This finding is inconsistent with the overwhelming evidence from research on women candidates in countries with parliaments elected through multimember districts. What accounts for the difference? Why doesn't the electoral system of city councils affect women's chances of winning, but the electoral system at the national level does?

2. The authors find some regional variation between the proportions of women serving on city councils. Do you believe that the political cultures in different regions of the country play a significant role in the electability of women candidates? Of African American or Hispanic candidates? Why, or why not?

READING 27

Gender Stereotypes and the Perception of Male and Female Candidates

(1993)

Leonie Huddy and Nayda Terkildsen

Despite the consistent finding by scholars that voters generally are not biased against women candidates, researchers have continued to probe how voters perceive and evaluate women candidates for elected office. An important line of this inquiry is research on the significance of gender stereotypes on voters' evaluations of candidates. Traditional gender stereotypes come from the same historical and cultural factors that underlie the traditional gender-roles theory. Gender-roles theory helps to explain the *behavior* of women in politics, whether it is running for office, as discussed by Susan J. Carroll (Reading 11) and Richard L. Fox and Jennifer L. Lawless (Reading 13), or work they do for campaigns or political parties, as explored by Ellen Boneparth (Reading 21) and Diane L. Fowlkes, Jerry Perkins, and Sue Tolleson Rinehart (Reading 22). In contrast, political gender stereotypes explain how women are evaluated, particularly in terms of their credentials or qualifications, by voters and also by the news media, examined by Kim Fridkin Kahn (Reading 28).

In this article published in the *American Journal of Political Science*, Leonie Huddy and Nayda Terkildsen conducted experimental research that tested whether men and women candidates are evaluated by voters based on political gender stereotypes. They distinguish between trait stereotypes and belief stereotypes. Trait stereotypes, for example, classify women as caring, compassionate, and passive and men as competitive, aggressive, and assertive. Belief stereotypes might result in the perception, for example, that women candidates are more liberal on policy issues than their male counterparts. The underlying dynamic that Huddy and Terkildsen are looking at is whether women are credible as candidates in terms of experience and character, and on political issues. Specifically, the researchers are interested in which stereotypes, trait or belief, voters are more likely to use when evaluating women and men candidates. Their conclusions provide practical information to women candidates about how to confront and overcome political gender stereotypes as well as how to use some gender stereotypes to enhance their candidacies.

As increasing numbers of women run for local, state, and national elected office, slowly eroding the male-dominated nature of election campaigns, there is growing research interest in voters' reactions to female candidates. Most of this recent research has focused on the electability of female candidates in an attempt to uncover voter bias that might explain women's generally lower levels of representation, particularly at the national level. In general, researchers have searched for evidence that voters are more reluctant to vote for female candidates. Such straightforward gender bias, however, has been difficult to uncover in a range of studies based on self-reported willingness to vote for generic, qualified female candidates, analyses of recent elections that included a female candidate, and experimental studies that pit hypothetical female and male candidates against each other. Based on present findings, voters cannot be blamed for current low levels of female political representation, though there is no shortage of alternative culprits.

It would be a mistake, however, to abandon research on the political impact of gender just as its prominence in candidates' campaign strategies is increasing. Female candidates who have run recently for highly visible state or national elected office have waged increasingly combative campaigns in which they have stressed their toughness and aggressiveness, typically masculine qualities. At the same time, their male counterparts have clamored to appear sympathetic, kind, and accessible, typically feminine traits. Apparently, both male and female political candidates feel compelled to adopt at least some positions or traits thought typical of the other gender.

This recent growth in the number of self-styled androgynous candidates is designed, in part, to overcome persistent gender stereotypes that portray female politicians as better able to handle . . . "compassion" issues—poverty, education, child-related, and health policy issues—but worse at dealing with big business, handling the military, or defense issues. . . . From even the most casual observation of recent political campaigns, it is clear that a candidate's gender is politically relevant, though not necessarily a harbinger of electoral success or defeat.

So far, these differing expectations among voters about the types of issues handled well by male and female politicians have proved the most consistent form of political gender stereotyping—the gender-based ascription of different traits, behaviors, or political beliefs to male and female politicians. While the existence of gender-based expectations about politicians' areas of issue expertise has been amply documented, its explanation has received considerably less attention. We argue that this stereotyping may have two quite different origins. According to the *trait* approach, voters' assumptions about a candidate's gender-linked personality traits drive expectations that women and men have different areas of issue expertise. Thus, female candidates are seen as better at dealing with the aged because women are stereotyped as more compassionate and gentle than men; male candidates are expected to handle a military crisis more competently because men are typically seen as tougher and more aggressive than women. The *belief* approach, on the other hand, stresses another, more political aspect of gender stereotypes—expectations that women are more liberal and Democratic than men. From this perspective, female candidates are stereotyped as more competent to deal with compassion issues, issues traditionally seen as best handled by liberals and Democrats, because of their more liberal political outlook.

Gender Stereotypes

Trait Stereotypes

There are pervasive and remarkably uniform differences in the personality traits ascribed to men and women. There is considerable agreement across a large number of psychological studies that a typical woman is seen as warm, gentle, kind, and passive, whereas a typical man is viewed as tough, aggressive, and assertive. . . .

Our first goal, then, is to examine the impact of stereotypic expectations about male and female candidates' personality traits on expectations about their respective areas of issue expertise. Are female political candidates simply subject to the same sex stereotypes as women in general? If so, the perception that women are more competent at resolving issues concerning poverty or education may well stem from expectations that they are more compassionate and nurturing. Expectations that men are more competent at managing international negotiations and the military may arise because they are seen as more aggressive and assertive. . . .

[* * *]

Belief Stereotypes

Alternatively, women may be seen as better at compassion and worse at military issues because they are stereotyped as more liberal and Democratic than men, not because they are seen to possess typical female traits. Our reasoning is twofold. First, there is some evidence to suggest that male and female politicians are stereotyped as holding different political views. . . .

Second, there is good reason to suspect that candidates perceived as liberal and Democratic, the stereotypic political outlook commonly ascribed to female politicians, are also seen as more competent to handle domestic and social welfare issues but less adept at dealing with economic and defense issues. . . .

We, thus, plan to examine the impact of gender-based belief stereotypes on the perceived issue competency of male and female politicians. Ascribing stronger liberal and Democratic leanings to female politicians could explain why they are seen as better at compassion issues: Democrats are simply thought to work harder on the unemployment issue or to care more about eradicating poverty than Republicans. On the other hand, viewing Republicans as better able to deal with the military and defense might explain why male politicians, who are more likely to be viewed as conservative and Republican, are thought to handle such issues more masterfully.

While the existence of both trait and belief stereotypes leads to predictions of greater perceived female competency on compassion issues and greater male competency on military and defense issues, the belief approach predicts more pervasive stereotyping of male and female political candidates than the trait approach. This arises because, in addition to greater perceived competence on compassion and lesser competence on military issues, Democrats are also seen as less able to deal with economic issues and better able to cope with race relations and women's issues, for example. Additionally, the belief approach might also predict greater perceived female competency on women's issues because female politicians are assumed to be stronger feminists, though this possibility remains untested as yet. Based on belief stereotypes, then, male candidates should be seen as more competent on economic issues but less competent on racial or women's issues than their female opponents. In contrast, the trait approach predicts that male and female politicians will be rated as equally competent on all three issues.

Traits versus Beliefs

In discussing whether perceived differences in male and female candidates' areas of issue expertise stem from stereotypic beliefs about their personality traits or political ideology, we enter an ongoing debate about the extent to which the different facets of gender stereotypes (or any other kind of stereotype for that matter) are linked. If gender stereotypes come as a tightly interconnected package of expectations about men's and women's traits, behaviors, and beliefs, our attempt to analyze their separate impact on assessments of political candidates is rendered futile. . . .

This debate has its parallel in discussions about the degree to which impressions of a candidate's personality traits and political outlook are associated. There is consensus that at least some information about presidents is stored as information about their personality traits. However, the link between candidates' perceived personality traits and their presumed political views is less clear. Borrowing from social psychological models of impression formation, a number of researchers implicitly assume that information about a candidate's issue positions directly shapes impressions of their personal qualities. . . .

Political Relevance

Are personality traits or political beliefs the most powerful source of political gender stereotyping? The answer to this question is of more than academic interest. It also has practical implications for political candidates who wish to overcome the possibly negative consequences of gender stereotypes that result in female candidates being viewed as less competent at handling typically male issues such as defense and the military. If such perceptions arise from stereotypic assumptions about male and female candidates' personality traits, they might be overcome by female candidates who downplay their soft compassionate qualities in favor of more tough masculine traits or male candidates who emphasize their compassionate and nurturing characteristics in addition to their assertiveness and self-confidence. Moreover, such a strategy should work even if candidates do not alter their positions on specifically "male" or "female" policy issues, or on any policy issue at all.

If, on the other hand, political gender stereotyping arises because women are seen as more liberal, the political solution may be more costly. To overcome gender stereotypes in this case, female candidates would need to adopt more conservative positions on at least some policy issues such as crime, defense, or the size of government, on which they are assumed to be less competent than their male colleagues; male candidates would need to adopt liberal positions on sexual harassment, health care, and other programs on which they may be at a disadvantage. . . .

[* * *]

Data and Methods

Our main objective is to explain why female candidates are stereotyped as better at compassion issues and males at military and defense-related issues—the most pervasive forms of political gender stereotyping. To examine this stereotyping, we rely on data from an experiment in which undergraduate participants were asked to infer the beliefs and traits and rate the issue competency of a male or female political candidate with typically masculine or feminine traits. Based on trait stereotypes, we expected candidates described as possessing typically masculine traits to be rated as more competent on military, crime, and defense issues regardless of their gender. Similarly, candidates described as having feminine traits should be rated as more competent on compassion issues. However, candidates' rated competency on economic or women's issues should not be affected by gender traits because their competency on these issues does not seem to require typical male or female personality traits.

In contrast, the belief approach generated the competing hypothesis that inferences about a candidate's political ideology were responsible for their perceived areas of issue competence. Based on this approach, we expected the female candidate to be seen as more liberal, Democratic, and feminist than her male counterpart, more competent on compassion and women's issues, and less competent on military and economic policy regardless of her gender-linked traits. We further expected these differing inferences about the political outlook of the male and female candidate to have greater impact on their rated issue competency than inferences about their personality traits.

[* * *]

Undergraduate participants were randomly assigned to hear about a woman or man with typically masculine or feminine traits who was running for national or local office. . . .

Respondents read a brief description of a candidate from a western Connecticut county . . . who was running for political office at either the federal or local level. Our hypothetical candidate was described to respondents as possessing typically masculine or typically feminine personality traits with his or her occupation, level of experience, and other personal information held constant. Elizabeth McGuire, the female candidate, was described in the following way when given feminine traits and running for local office:

> *Elizabeth McGuire*, a lawyer, has been described by legal colleagues as an intelligent, *compassionate, trustworthy,* and *family-oriented* opponent with proven leadership skills and strong *people* skills. Ms. McGuire, forty-two, is a life-long resident of Connecticut, a long-time political activist, and currently is seeking office at the local level.

Robert McGuire was described similarly in the male candidate–feminine trait condition. In the masculine trait condition, both Robert and Elizabeth McGuire were described as intelligent, *tough, articulate,* and *ambitious,* and as having strong leadership and *administrative* skills. All four conditions were repeated for hypothetical candidates who ran at the national level.

Results

[* * *]

. . . [G]ender trait stereotypes were largely responsible for the most pervasive forms of political stereotyping. Typical female traits such as warmth, sensitivity, and compassion were thought to qualify female candidates for dealing better with compassion issues, such as education, health care, and the problems of the poor and aged. Assertiveness, aggressiveness, and self-confidence, typical male traits, were thought to aid male candidates in coping better with military or police crises. Candidates with typical masculine traits were also viewed as more competent to handle economic issues. We found considerable evidence for the existence of gender-belief stereotypes, which portray a female politician as more liberal, Democratic, and feminist than a male politician. However, belief stereotypes had less influence than traits on expectations about both the male and female politicians' areas of political expertise. The female candidate was seen as more competent on compassion issues, in part because she was assumed to be Democratic and liberal. But beliefs did not explain the male candidate's advantage on military issues or the female candidate's greater expected competency on women's issues.

Discussion

[* * *]

Moreover of the traits investigated in this study, typical masculine traits proved more beneficial to the hypothetical candidate than typical feminine traits. The candidate seen as possessing the most instrumental personality traits was seen as more competent to handle military and economic issues. The female candidate rated as possessing the most instrumental personality traits was viewed as better equipped to handle women's issues. Apparently, instrumental personality traits were viewed as necessary to cope not only with typical "male" policy areas but also to further women's interests in the male-dominated world of politics. In contrast, warmth and expressiveness proved an asset to candidates only when dealing with compassion issues. . . .

[* * *]

Of course, the relative superiority of male traits does not necessarily mean that female politicians confront an insurmountable barrier in gaining voters' confidence. As seen in this study, a female candidate was able to successfully reverse gender-trait stereotypes by portraying herself as possessing typical masculine traits. This strategy is not fraudulent, given some evidence that female candidates perceive themselves as possessing masculine traits. Nor is it politically risky. A woman's image as more warm and caring is not jeopardized by emphasizing her masculine traits because masculine and feminine traits form relatively independent dimensions. . . . Moreover, the possession of instrumental traits did not lower a woman's rated competency in any of the four policy areas.

The real struggle faced by female candidates, then, is to convey successfully to voters that they possess masculine personality traits. . . . Perhaps female politicians are not penalized at the polls because they work hard to stress their masculine traits, a potentially fruitful strategy that might provide them with the double benefit of elevated competency ratings on typically "male" and "female" issues, including women's issues. Female politicians might gain credit on compassion issues because they are assumed to possess feminine traits and might benefit further from the possession of masculine traits on military, economic, and women's issues.

[* * *]

TOWARD CRITICAL THINKING

1. Are the traditional personality stereotypes that classify women as passive and compassionate and men as aggressive and tough still as operative today?

2. What are the implications of the findings from this research for women candidates running in a post-9/11 political climate? What do the conclusions reached by the authors suggest that women candidates do to enable voters to see them as tough and capable to deal with terrorism?

READING 28

The Distorted Mirror: Press Coverage of Women Candidates for Statewide Office

(1994)

Kim Fridkin Kahn

Building on the work of R. Darcy and Sarah Slavin Schramm (Reading 25) that found women can be equal to men in the eyes of the electorate when running for office, Kim Fridkin Kahn's work published in the *Journal of Politics* explores the differences in media coverage of men and women candidates. The media have increased in importance in electoral campaigns over the years, and differences in coverage given to men and women candidates could affect voter evaluations and support for these people. A recent study by The White House Project, an organization founded to advance the election of women to executive office, found that the media coverage of women candidates focuses on the three Hs, "Hair, Hemlines, and Husbands."

Fridkin Kahn examines whether there are differences in the quantity and type of coverage men and women candidates receive in U.S. Senate and state gubernatorial elections. Examining races with women candidates in the 1982 through the 1988 election years, Fridkin Kahn conducts a content analysis of newspapers to compare the coverage of men and women. She also analyzes the campaign commercials of men and women candidates to see how candidates' advertisements influence the media coverage of both sets of candidates.

Subsequent research on the differences between men and women candidates' paid TV ads has found that women use specific strategies to overcome voter stereotypes. For example, another study conducted for The White House Project found that women were more likely than their male counterparts to dress more professionally for their television commercials and to have a male voiceover to reinforce the credibility of their candidacies. Conversely, men were more likely to be pictured dressed casually and with their families in an attempt to soften their images and to make them more appealing to voters, particularly women voters. Taken together, this research demonstrates the significance of paid (television advertisements) and unpaid media in elections for voter evaluation of both men and women candidates.

Most people do not experience politics directly. Instead, their perceptions of the political world are shaped largely by the news media's representations. Yet because many significant events take place daily and news organizations cannot cover all of these events, newspeople must be selective. As a result of this selectivity, the news media shape, rather than mirror, the political landscape. The news media's ability to shape political reality is especially potent during electoral campaigns where citizens rely almost exclusively on the media for their political information. In this [article] I examine how accurately the news media represent the candidates they cover by looking at whether the news media treat male and female candidates differently. If the media differentiate between male and female candidates in their coverage of campaigns, this difference may influence the decisions of voters.

The media may cover male and female candidates differently for a number of reasons. First, gender differences in news coverage may reflect stereotypes newspeople hold about male and female candidates. . . . Second, differences in news coverage of male and female candidates may be driven by organizational incentives. . . . For instance, newspeople rely on "standards of newsworthiness" when selecting among various potential news items, and one of these standards is novelty. . . . Finally, gender differences in news coverage of male and female candidates may reflect differences in the campaign strategies of men and women. Men and women may conduct their campaigns differently, and gender differences in press coverage may simply mirror these differences. . . .

Relying on theories of voting, we can speculate about how gender differences in news presentations influence people's voting decisions. First, an important criteria for vote choice in electoral campaigns is recognition of the opposing candidates. Although candidate recognition is not an issue at the presidential level, it can be consequential in subpresidential contests where candidates are less widely known. . . .

After recognition has been achieved, a candidate still needs to be positively evaluated. Evaluations of candidates can be influenced by these four factors: (1) the voter's party identification; (2) evaluations of the candidates' issue stands; (3) evaluations of the candidates' personality; and (4) assessments of the candidates' viability. . . .

Gender differences in news coverage are unlikely to be equally consequential in all electoral contests. Instead, because the influence of the news media grows with the size of the constituency, gender differences in news coverage are potentially more important in national and statewide elections than in local contests. In particular, in statewide races for governor and U.S. Senate because of the good "media market fit," and the competitiveness of these contests, media coverage is more prevalent and gender differences in news attention may be important.

Although both gubernatorial and senatorial races are likely to generate more press coverage than local contests, the two offices differ in a number of important ways that may influence patterns of news coverage. First, press coverage may differ because the relevant issue domains for the two offices differ. While U.S. senators deal with foreign policy and national security issues along with other issues of national and international consequence, governors deal more extensively with statewide concerns such as education and health. These two alternative issue domains correspond to the stereotypical strengths of male and female candidates. Female candidates are viewed as more competent at dealing with education, health, and environmental issues, while men are considered better able to deal with foreign policy and defense issues. Given these alternative issue domains and corresponding stereotypes, news coverage patterns may be different for these two offices.

Similarly, differential rates of success for women candidates in U.S. Senate and gubernatorial campaigns may influence news coverage patterns. Women have been about four times as successful in winning governorships than winning seats in the U.S. Senate, and this significant difference in success rates for these two offices may influence press coverage of these statewide campaigns. Since women can stress their stereotypical strengths in races for governor, and because they are more successful at winning governorships, news coverage of female gubernatorial candidates may be more favorable than news coverage of female Senate candidates. Given the differences between these two statewide offices, I will examine gender differences in campaign coverage of both senatorial and gubernatorial elections. . . .

Data and Methods

[* * *]

The data reported here are drawn from a content analysis of newspaper coverage of 26 U.S. Senate races and 21 gubernatorial races between 1982 and 1988. The choice of these years maximizes the number of women candidates selected and avoids extending back so many years that coverage patterns no longer represent current practice. . . .

[* * *]

Newspapers were chosen for analysis for both substantive and practical reasons. On the substantive side, there is considerable evidence that newspapers carry more information about state-level campaigns than local television news, and that people receive more information about statewide races from newspapers than from television. . . .

[* * *]

In addition to the data on press coverage, I have also analyzed the candidates' own campaign advertisements. Because they are completely controlled by the candidate and the candidate's campaign, political advertisements represent the candidate's own "presentation of self." By examining the spot advertisements, we can look at what the candidates choose to emphasize in their campaigns. In addition, by comparing the candidates' television commercials with the press coverage of the campaign, we can look at the correspondence between the candidate's message and the news media's message. . . .

Results

Quantity of Campaign News

Media treatment of male and female candidates may differ in a number of important ways, but one potentially important difference is the sheer quantity of news coverage. . . .

The results of the content analysis of news coverage suggest that women candidates do receive less press attention, but only in races for the U.S. Senate. While more than 95 paragraphs about male U.S. Senate candidates are published each week, fewer than 79 paragraphs a week are written about the senatorial campaigns of women candidates. This gender difference in the amount of news coverage occurs in both competitive and noncompetitive races. Similarly, the gender difference in news attention is not a mere reflection of status differences for men and women; female Senate candidates continue to receive less coverage than their male counterparts, regardless of their status as incumbents, challengers, or candidates in open races. In contrast, women do not consistently receive less coverage in gubernatorial races than their male counterparts. Overall, 113 paragraphs a week are written about both male and female gubernatorial candidates.

These results suggest that voters may have a more difficult time acquiring information about female senatorial candidates as opposed to female gubernatorial candidates. This lack of available information may result in an electoral disadvantage for women candidates running for the U.S. Senate. Since the quantity of news coverage is positively related to voters' recognition of candidates, and since voters are unlikely to vote for a candidate whom they do not recognize, voters may be less willing to vote for women candidates in senate campaigns. . . .

[* * *]

Horserace Coverage in the News

Since assessments of a candidate's issue positions, traits, and viability all influence voting decisions, news information about these evaluation dimensions are likely to influence vote choice. . . .

The results of the content analysis shows that in U.S. Senate campaigns, the press does focus more extensively on the horserace when covering female candidates. Twenty-seven percent of all articles written about female U.S. Senate candidates discuss the horserace, while only 21% of the articles about male candidates mention horserace issues (see Table 28.1). While the magnitude of this gender difference is not great, these differences are remarkably consistent and occur for all types of senatorial candidates, women in competitive and noncompetitive races receive more horserace coverage than their male counterparts, as do female incumbents, challengers, and females running in open races.

As expected, gender differences in horserace coverage do not occur in gubernatorial contests. The print media do not differentiate between male and female candidates when discussing horserace issues in gubernatorial campaigns. Fifteen percent of all articles about gubernatorial candidates, regardless of the sex of the candidate, focus on the horserace.

Since voters are exposed to more horserace information for female U.S. Senate candidates, voters may weigh viability concerns more heavily when developing overall evaluations of these candidates. But the actual content of the horserace information is also consequential. . . .

TABLE 28.1
Percentage of Articles Devoted to the Horserace

	Senate Races		Gubernatorial Races	
All Candidates				
Male Candidates	21%	(5,708;40)	15%	(5,219;32)
Female Candidates	27%	(1,378;12)	15%	(1,561;10)
Competitive				
Male Candidates	22%	(4,271;26)	17%	(2,911;18)
Female Candidates	27%	(847;6)	15%	(1,427;8)
Noncompetitive				
Male Candidates	17%	(1,437;14)	13%	(2,308;14)
Female Candidates	27%	(531;6)	13%	(134;2)
Incumbents				
Male	21%	(1,954;15)	16%	(1,682;9)
Female	30%	(254;2)	10%	(324;2)
Challengers				
Male	19%	(1,606;11)	17%	(1,853;8)
Female	28%	(602;6)	16%	(879;3)
Open-Race Candidates				
Male	21%	(2,148;14)	13%	(1,684;15)
Female	24%	(522;4)	16%	(340;5)

Note: Horserace coverage includes any discussion of a candidate's chances of winning, including comparisons of the candidates' organizations, discussion of poll results, and discussion of the candidates' performance in campaign debates. Entries are the percentage of articles devoted to the horserace with the number of articles coded for each candidate type and the number of candidates in parentheses.

If reporters are informed by the historical experience of women candidates, then horserace coverage may be more negative for women candidates and especially for women candidates for U.S. Senate. The data ... show that women do receive more negative viability assessments than their male counterparts, but these differences are both substantively and statistically more impressive in senatorial elections. For example, in senatorial races women are more likely to be described as "somewhat competitive" in their bids for election while men are usually considered "competitive."

Although women candidates in U.S. Senate races generally receive less favorable press ratings, this pattern does not hold for open races. In these nonincumbent races, male and female U.S. Senate candidates receive approximately the same viability ratings, while women candidates in gubernatorial races are viewed as somewhat less viable than their male counterparts. ...

The news media differentiate between men and women in their reporting of the horserace. Perhaps because they are relying on the historical experience of women candidates, reporters focus on viability issues when covering female candidates. This is especially the case for female senatorial candidates, and the characterization of the horserace discussion is usually more negative for these female candidates. Given these patterns of findings, voters who look to the news media for information may come to believe that women candidates are less electable, and they may be less likely to vote for these candidates.

Press Coverage of Issues

Citizens think about policy considerations, in addition to the candidates' viability, when evaluating competing candidates for statewide office. . . . In both senatorial and gubernatorial races, women receive less issue coverage than their male counterparts, and in some instances the differences are quite significant, both statistically and substantively.

The tendency of the press to play down issue concerns for women candidates is remarkably consistent. In fact, the issue coverage of female candidates lags behind male candidates in seven of eight comparisons displayed in Table 28.2. There are at least three possible explanations for this pattern of findings, and they correspond to the three reasons offered at the start of this [article]. First, newspeople may believe that women are less competent at dealing with the major issues of the day, so their views on these issues are considered less newsworthy. Second, there is the practical consideration of how much space to allot for the discussion of issues since journalists may prefer to emphasize other sorts of campaign news when covering women. Finally, coverage of issues for women may be less extensive because women may talk about issues less frequently in their campaigns.

I explicitly test this third explanation by examining the candidates' own campaign communications. When we compare the amount of issue discussion in the candidate's own campaign communications with the amount of issue coverage in the news, we find that gender differences in issue coverage is *not* a reflection of the candidates' own campaign messages. Men do not spend more time describing their issue positions in their advertisements. In fact, women are more likely than men to talk about issues in their campaign advertisements; 65% of all advertisements by female candidates mention policy concerns, while only 58% of male candidates' advertisements do. This greater concern with issues for female candidates occurs in both senatorial and gubernatorial races.

Given the scarcity of issue coverage for women candidates, it is important to examine the types of issues that do receive media attention. Do reporters, for example, emphasize the same sorts of issues for all candidates, or are there predictable gender differences in the substance of issue coverage? Based on research on sex stereotypes, I categorize issues as "male" issues or "female" issues. "Male" issues are those issues where men are considered more competent (e.g., defense, foreign policy), while "female" issues are those issues where women are seen as superior (e.g., health, education policy). The discussion of issues will vary with the gender of the candidate if (1) reporters and editors hold the same stereotypes as their readers, or (2) if male and female candidates emphasize different issues in their electoral campaigns.

The discussion of issues by the media does vary with the sex of the candidate in senatorial races. In particular, "female" issues are discussed more extensively for

TABLE 28.2

Average Number of Paragraphs Published about Issues Each Week

	Senate Races		Gubernatorial Races	
	Mean (S.D.)[a]	N[b]	Mean (S.D.)[a]	N[b]
All Candidates				
Male Candidates	26.8 (15.1)	40	39.9 (20.0)	32
Female Candidates	21.9 (12.7)	12	34.1 (15.1)	10
Incumbents				
Male Candidates	26.7 (13.4)	15	47.0 (21.9)	10
Female Candidates	23.7 (24.2)	2	42.7 (8.6)	2
Challengers				
Male Candidates	23.6 (14.5)	11	43.7 (18.0)	9
Female Candidates	16.7 (8.1)	6	14.7 (4.4)	3
Open-Race Candidates				
Male Candidates	29.3 (17.7)	14	31.9 (18.3)	13
Female Candidates	28.8 (12.9)	4	42.1 (9.4)	5

[a]Entries are the mean number of paragraphs published about issues each week with the standard deviation in parentheses.
[b]Entries are the number of candidates included for each candidate type.

women who are running for the U.S. Senate. "Female" issues are mentioned 40% of the time for female candidates, but less than one-third of the time (30%) for male candidates. Overall, however, "female" issues receive relatively little attention (32%) when compared with the coverage of "male" issues (68%).

In gubernatorial races a different pattern emerges. Overall, "female" issues receive a great deal more news attention (51%), and these issues are *not* emphasized more for female candidates (45%) than for male candidates (53%). Differences in the offices of governor and U.S. senator are probably responsible for these differences in issue emphasis. Such "male" issues as foreign policy and defense are simply not relevant for gubernatorial candidates, while these issues are more critical for potential U.S. senators.

Are the gender differences in policy discussion a reflection of the candidates' own campaign messages? The data . . . suggest that the correspondence between the issues presented in the news and the issues highlighted in the candidate's advertisements is greater for male candidates in both senatorial and gubernatorial races. For example, in U.S. Senate races male candidates' advertisements mention "male" issues more than 70% of the time, and news coverage of their candidacies reflects this devotion to "male" issues. For female senatorial candidates, on the other hand, there is considerable incongruity between what the candidates are saying and what the newspapers are reporting.

The greater correspondence between the news media's agenda and the agenda of male candidates may reflect a bias of the news media, or it may reflect real differences in the campaigns of men and women candidates. On the one hand, if reporters hold stereotypes about men and women candidates, they may consider male candidates more "legitimate" and may listen and report their rhetoric more faithfully. On the other hand, differences in the correspondence between the press and the candidates' messages may reflect real differences in the campaigns of men and women candidates. Male candidates, for example, may be more effective campaigners than their female counterparts, which may account for differences in media coverage of their campaigns. . . .

[* * *]

Personality Traits in the News

Just as assessments of a candidate's viability and issue positions influence citizens vote choices, so do judgments about a candidate's character. . . .

Discussion of character traits for U.S. Senate candidates is sparse for both male and female candidates; fewer than 15% of all articles mention the candidate's personality traits. In races for governor, the attention given to personality traits is somewhat more common for female candidates (21%) than for male candidates (15%). This greater emphasis on personality for female gubernatorial candidates holds for all types of candidates: incumbents, challengers, and candidates running in open races.

This focus on personal characteristics for female gubernatorial candidates is echoed in the candidates' campaign communications. In their political advertisements, women candidates for governor talk about their personality traits (e.g., their leadership ability, their integrity) somewhat more often than their male counterparts. Women discuss their personal traits in 55% of their advertisements, while male candidates talk about traits in 49% of their advertisements. . . .

[* * *]

Even though the personality traits of competing candidates are not a major source of news in statewide campaigns, the substance of this trait discussion may vary with the gender of the candidate. If journalists hold stereotypes about men and women, the coverage of the candidates' personal qualities may reflect this bias. Or the candidates themselves may stress different traits in their campaign appeals. Male and female candidates may stress these alternative personality characteristics in their campaign messages if (1) they share the same sex stereotypes as the journalists and voters, or (2) if they believe it will be effective strategically to stress alternative trait dimensions.

To examine the substance of trait coverage by the press, we can divide traits into two categories based on the sex stereotyping literature. "Male" traits are those traits that are seen as characteristic of men (e.g., strong leader, knowledgeable, intelligent) while "female" traits are those traits which are consistently associated with women (e.g., warm, compassionate, honest). Using this categorization, we find no differences in trait coverage for male and female gubernatorial candidates. In the senatorial cases, however, there is somewhat more discussion of "male" traits for men (62% versus 55%).

In general, reporters discuss "male" traits more frequently than "female" traits, perhaps because they consider these traits more relevant for statewide office. They may think, for instance, that questions about a candidate's leadership are more important than questions about a candidate's compassion. Yet by emphasizing these "male" traits and by making them salient to the public, reporters may encourage voters to develop more favorable impressions of male candidates.

Women may be able to alter voters' stereotypes by emphasizing "male" traits in their own campaign communications. If, for example, women act "unstereotypically" and demonstrate their leadership ability and their strength, then voters may revise their views of "typical" male and female candidates. According to their campaign advertisements, women do act "unstereotypically," stressing "male" traits far more frequently than "female" traits. In fact, in both senatorial and gubernatorial races, women are more likely than their male counterparts to stress "male" traits. Yet . . . news coverage more faithfully represents the campaign messages presented by male candidates. The correspondence between the message presented in the advertisements and the coverage provided in the news is clearly higher for male candidates— in both senatorial and gubernatorial races. Again, this may be because male candidates are more effective campaigners, *or* it may be that reporters pay more attention to what male candidates are saying.

By stressing their stereotypical weaknesses and talking almost exclusively about "male" traits, women may be trying to dispel voters' preconceptions about the "typical" female candidate (e.g., women are weak leaders). Yet this strategy can have only limited success because reporters are less responsive to the messages presented by women candidates.

[* * *]

TOWARD CRITICAL THINKING

1. Kim Fridkin Kahn uses newspapers to measure the amount and type of coverage of men and women candidates. In today's media environment with cable television and the Internet, is newspaper coverage still an adequate measure to assess candidate coverage? Moreover, her content analysis was conducted by counting the number of news articles, columns, and editorials pertaining to men and women candidates. How would you quantify coverage on the Internet? What challenges do the new media pose for future research?

2. The author notes that women have been more successful in gubernatorial than U.S. Senate elections in part because governors deal more with domestic and social issues, whereas Senators are more involved in foreign affairs. Recent elections have brought more women to the Senate, and the current political climate has forced governors to be more involved with homeland security. How do you see these changes impacting women's chances of success in subsequent elections? What effect will these changes have on the type of media coverage men and women candidates receive?

Reading 29

Electoral Context, Issues,
and Voting for Women in the 1990s

(2001)

Kathleen Dolan

Kathleen Dolan builds on early research by R. Darcy and Sarah Slavin Schramm (Reading 25) to examine more closely the potential advantages women candidates have when running for office. Dolan pays particular attention to the electoral environment asking how differences in issue salience across elections affect voters' propensity to support women candidates. Specifically, she contrasts voters' support for women candidates in three electoral cycles: (1) 1992, the "Year of the Woman"; (2) 1994, the "Year of the Angry White Man"; and, (3) 1996. She examines how the gender consideration in the electoral environment of each election affected women's candidacies in this article published in *Women & Politics*.

In addition, Dolan is one of the first to measure differences in the issue priorities of men and women voters and how those differences contribute to their evaluations of men and women candidates. Research on the differences between men and women voters has found that men and women have different levels of support for Democratic and Republican candidates (see Chapter 5 for further discussion on the gender gap). In addition, men and women voters have different issue priorities, so while they may not disagree on a particular issue, they differ in the level of priority they give that issue.

[* * *]

Considering the context of a particular election, or series of elections, is an important element of understanding the gender dynamic in elections. We must recognize that each election environment is shaped by unique candidate, party, and political influences, and that these factors can have an impact on whether gender and gender-related issues will have a significant role in shaping behaviors. The research reported here attempts to examine how the environment in which elections are conducted influences gender considerations in vote choice in congressional elections in the 1990s. Specifically, it examines whether the amount of gender information in the electoral environment has an impact on the public's vote choice considerations when faced with a woman candidate in 1992, 1994, and 1996.

213

Much of the recent work on gender in American elections has focused on 1992. This "Year of the Woman" was one of tremendous success for women candidates, particularly at the congressional level. A record number of women ran for Congress that year, capitalizing on an increase in open seats following the 1990 redistricting, on increased sources of campaign financing and support from political parties and women's PACs such as EMILY's List, and on significant public attention to gender issues such as abortion and sexual harassment, as well as on the under-representation of women in office. Perhaps the most indelible image from this election is the dramatic increase in women elected to Congress—from 31 to 53 after the 1992 election. Several factors—the presence of numerous women candidates, issues, structural considerations, and electoral context among others—joined to make 1992 an election year in which gender considerations played an important role.

Congressional elections since 1992 have been different. If one focuses only on outcomes, 1992 appears to be something of an anomaly. The dramatic increase in women elected to Congress has not been repeated in subsequent elections. Indeed, women's representation has increased incrementally. This has occurred despite a steadily increasing number of women candidates. Recent work suggests that neither the number and quality of candidates nor bias on the part of parties, financial contributors, or voters can easily explain the differing outcomes of the elections of the 1990s for women candidates. While the success of women candidates in 1992 can be partially explained by the number of open seat opportunities in that election, this is not the only explanation. At the same time, a decrease in open seat opportunities since 1992 is not the sole explanation for the results.

Perhaps the most obvious difference between 1992 and subsequent elections was what I term the "electoral environment." The environment of the 1992 election was one with a heavy focus on gender issues: women candidates received large amounts of attention, as did so-called "women's issues" such as abortion, family leave, and sexual harassment. Many of the women candidates for Congress ran "as women" and as outsiders of a corrupt institution. An argument for the influence of the electoral environment would suggest that the presence of these women candidates and the focus on them and the gender issues they articulated created a unique dynamic that had an impact on voters. . . .

[* * *]

Since the environment of 1992 provided a great deal of information about women candidates and gender-related issues, I would expect that these considerations would be significant in structuring people's vote choice. At the same time, since 1994 and 1996 were comparatively "gender-free," I would expect that gender-related issues are less likely to be related to vote choice in those years. Of course, the gender-rich electoral environment of 1992, or any other election, is only meaningful as an influence if voters are aware of it. If candidate sex and gender-related issues are pieces of information that exist in the environment and voters use this information to inform their vote choice, then I would expect gender-related variables to be more important to those voters who were more aware of the environment. Voters who take in more of this gender information during an election campaign will obviously have more of it at their disposal when evaluating candidates and framing a vote choice, making it more likely that a gendered environment will shape their voting behavior than that of people who are relatively oblivious to the messages of the environment.

Methodology

To test the hypotheses under consideration here, I examine the individual-level sources of support for women candidates for the House of Representatives in 1992, 1994, and 1996 using National Election Study (NES) data. Since the NES does not interview respondents in every state or congressional district, not every race with a woman candidate is included in the sample. However, for each of the years under analysis, the districts included in the NES sample that have women candidates for the House are representative of all districts with women candidates from the perspective of seat status. . . .

The analysis conducted seeks to determine whether electoral environment has an impact on the considerations that shape vote choice; specifically, does the presence or absence of information about candidate sex and gender-related issues have an influence on the determinants of support for women candidates? The dependent variable is vote choice, coded to reflect whether respondents voted for the woman candidate (1) or her male opponent (0). The models estimating support for women candidates include a number of variables considered to be relevant to vote choice and variables intended to measure the influence of the electoral environment. Control variables include respondent party identification, ideology, sex, race, and age. I also include a measure of the incumbency status of the woman candidate and a variable that accounts for the degree of correspondence between the party identification of the respondent and the woman candidate ("party correspondence" in the model). This variable allows for an examination of whether Democrats are more likely to vote for women candidates than are Republicans after controlling for the expected influence of party identification, namely that people tend to vote for the candidate of their party.

The remaining variables in the model account for general and gender-related issues that are likely to shape respondent vote choice, particularly when there are women candidates in the race. Previous work has indicated that voters often hold stereotyped views of the competencies of women and men candidates and may use these in formulating their vote choice. Included here are measures of respondents' positions on evaluating Congress, defense spending, social welfare spending, abortion, government spending on child care, and attitudes towards feminists/the women's movement. . . .

Analysis

Since the argument being advanced here is that the gender-related information in the environment of an election can influence the considerations voters use in formulating their vote choice, we would expect to find that voters in 1992 were more likely to employ gender issues in deciding to vote for a woman candidate than voters in 1994 or 1996. . . . Beginning with 1992, we can see the influence of the electoral environment on voters in that year. . . . Clearly, important long-term influences such as incumbency and shared party affiliation provide the same benefits for women candidates as they do for men. However, party identification and political ideology do not demonstrate a consistent influence on voting for a woman across the three elections. Therefore, Democrats are not consistently more likely to vote for women than Republicans, controlling for the "same party" effect, and liberals are not necessarily more likely to do so than conservatives. Instead, incumbency and shared party affiliation are much more likely to motivate vote choice in these elections.

Beyond these controls, there are a number of variables significantly related to voting for women House candidates in 1992. Voter sex, age, and race are all significant, as women, older people, and minorities are all more likely to choose the woman candidate. Several issue concerns are also significant. Negative evaluations of Congress, positive attitudes towards feminists, and a desire to see the federal government increase spending on social welfare programs are all important to respondents choosing women candidates. Each of these findings supports an argument for the importance of the electoral environment: there were gender gaps in support for women candidates in many races; the election of 1992 was strongly anti-incumbent; several candidates, including Bill Clinton, campaigned for a renewed focus on domestic issues; and many women candidates ran "as women," focusing on their sex and their different approaches to many issues. This evidence is especially compelling because none of these variables is significantly related to vote choice in the analysis of 1994 or 1996.

This argument is further strengthened by the significant relationship between voting for women candidates and the . . . three issues in the model. Here the effect of these issues on vote choice is strongest among those with the most information. Those respondents who were most aware of the electoral environment and its heavy focus on gender-related issues are the most likely to employ these issues in choosing a woman candidate. This is evidence of the ability of information in the electoral environment to activate personal and attitudinal attributes in evaluating women candidates: the environmental connection influenced voting behavior.

If 1992 was an election with a strong presence for women candidates and gender-related issues, 1994 was the mirror opposite. Despite another record number of women candidates for the House, the electoral environment of 1994 was almost entirely without emphasis on candidate sex or gender-related issues. . . . The only significant influence beyond the control variables (incumbency and party) is race, with minorities being more likely to support women candidates. But there is no gender gap in support for these women, no influence of issues thought to be important to women candidates, no evidence that the most informed people focused on these issues. The considerations relevant to voting for women in 1992 were not significant in 1994: voters relied not on gender-related information, but instead on the more traditional influences of incumbency and party. In short, this suggests that the electoral environment of 1994 did not provide a specific focus on women candidates and gender-related issues, which may have resulted in people finding it difficult to make the connection between these candidates or issues and their own political interests.

[The 1996 election] was more like 1994 than 1992. Beyond the control variables, there is limited evidence of respondent demographics or gender-related issues being related to voting for women. However, the one significant variable, the interaction of position on defense spending and respondent awareness, does support the hypothesis about the influence of the electoral environment. Here, people who supported lower levels of defense spending were more likely to support women candidates. The impact of this attitude was strongest among those respondents with the most information. While 1996 was not an election year with a strong focus on women candidates per se, this finding might indicate that people who were more aware of the information that *was* in the environment were able to identify the greater focus on domestic issues advanced by many woman candidates. But, again, the lack of significance of most of the gender-related variables and interaction terms to voting in 1996 is an indication of the lack of prominence of these issues in the campaign. Instead, the focus in the congressional campaigns was more partisan in nature, centering on whether the Republicans could retain their majority status. This focus is borne out in the analysis: the decision to vote for a woman or not is primarily driven by traditional factors like party, incumbency, and ideology.

Discussion

One of the limitations on our ability to fully understand the election of 1992 is the fact that much of the work to date has treated this election in isolation. This project attempts to analyze the unique features of 1992 by comparing it to other years. The analysis presented here demonstrates that voters approached women candidates for Congress differently in 1992 than they did in subsequent elections. Voters that year experienced a relatively unique electoral environment, one in which there was a tremendous amount of attention to, and information about, candidate sex and gender-related issues. This research suggests that voters used a unique set of personal and issue considerations as a basis for their vote choice exactly because the information that helped them make the link between these concerns and the woman candidate for whom they voted was available. In contrast, in the relatively "gender-free" settings of the 1994 and 1996 elections, personal or attitudinal attributes that might have been related to voting behavior in races involving a woman were not, because people were not stimulated by the electoral environment to make the necessary connections. Instead, people relied more heavily on traditional determinants of the vote like party identification and incumbency.

[* * *]

The research reported here finds that gender-related vote considerations were more important to voters choosing women candidates in 1992 than in subsequent elections and that the gendered information was most important to those people who were more aware of the electoral environment. This work, along with the work cited above, indirectly supports the assumption that electoral context is an important part of the relationship between women candidates and the public. A focus on gender and gender-related issues may make it easier for some voters to identify correspondence between their interests and particular women candidates. Without this focus, it may be that women candidates are simply candidates in the minds of many voters. For women candidates and those who support their election, such a conclusion is a double-edged sword. On the one hand, it may signal a true diminishing of voter bias against women candidates. On the other, it may indicate that, barring particularly advantageous electoral environments in the future, women's increased presence in Congress may be incremental. But understanding the impact that electoral environment and context can have on the fortunes of women candidates helps us draw a more complete picture of recent congressional elections. The Year of the Woman was a unique election, not just in the sense that more women were elected, but in the sense that the gendered context of the election stimulated a different pattern of voting behavior than has occurred in later years. In short, the context of the election of 1992 influenced the behavior of the electorate.

TOWARD CRITICAL THINKING

1. Why do you think it is that, while previous research found no support for the hypothesis that women voters will be more supportive of women candidates (such as R. Darcy and Sarah Slavin Schramm [Reading 25]), Kathleen Dolan *did* find such support in 1992?

2. Dolan examines the differences between the influence of men and women voters' issue concerns on their vote choice. How does she think the varying salience of issues affects men and women voters' assessments of candidates?

WRAPPING UP

1. Most of the research discussed in Chapter 7, while noting gender differences in media coverage and in the effect of electoral context, found that women candidates for legislatures are not hindered by their gender in the eyes of voters. Do you think this is true for all levels of office? What about executive or judicial elections as opposed to candidates for legislatures?

2. What factors can you identify that are not discussed in the above literature but you think would affect women candidates' chances of electoral success?

READING 30

Women in Congress: 1917–1964

(1966)

Emmy E. Werner

In 1950, political scientist Louise M. Young surveyed the involvement of women in state-houses and Congress, noting a very slow upward trend in women's election to office at both levels. In her book *Understanding Politics*, she noted that the number of women in statehouses was increasing at a much faster rate than that of women in the U.S. Congress. In 1964, Emmy E. Werner built on this work in a study reviewing trends in women's representation and party affiliation in both the statehouses and Congress.

In the ten year period of the 1960s, fewer total women had served in Congress than served in the two years of the 108th Congress (2003–2005). This article on women in Congress thus is fascinating not only for the rich detail it provides on the first women who served in that body but also for comparison to the women who currently serve in the U.S. House and Senate. With this research, Werner became the first social scientist to examine systematically the backgrounds and career paths of women members of Congress. Writing at the dawn of the women's rights movement, with its push for the greater inclusion of women in the political process, she notes that when she began her research, there were no biographical collections about the women who served in Congress. Werner also notes the paucity of many references in the psychological literature to the concept of women as leaders.

Because there were so few women in Congress, and few male political scientists who viewed the issue of gender as worthy of examination, it is not surprising that it took until 1966 to see a piece published on this topic in a political science journal, the *Western Political Quarterly*. Here, Werner provides a thoughtful and detailed analysis of who these women pioneers were, as well as how they got to their positions in the House or the Senate. She notes that few women actually sought elective office; instead, as political scientist Diane Kincaid (Blair) later was to analyze in much greater detail, they got to office over their husband's "dead body." In fact, Kincaid hypothesizes that because so many women were not elected directly to their positions, political scientists did not find them sufficiently interesting to study.

Data contained in this article underscore why only recently have more sophisticated analyses of women in the state or national legislatures been conducted. In 1920, the year in which women were granted the right to vote by the Nineteenth Amendment, only 29 women served in statehouses nationwide. Thus, Werner's work is important not only because she was the first to collect this kind of data, but also because she provided an important benchmark for future researchers.

This report is the first in a series on American women in political leadership positions on the national and state level. Biographical information available on U.S. congresswomen will be examined in order to answer the following questions: 1. What experience did they bring to their offices in Congress? 2. How did they win their seats in Congress? 3. How satisfied was the electorate with them? 4. What happened to them after completion of their terms in Congress? 5. What are the trends in and prospects for women's representation in the U.S. legislature? The present report deals with the seventy women who have served in the twenty-four Congresses between 1916 and 1964—from Jeanette Rankin, who was the first woman to be elected to the House of Representatives to the thirteen who have served in the 88th Congress.[1]

[* * *]

The major reference for this report is the *Biographical Directory of the American Congress* (1776–1961). For the three congresswomen who were elected after the *Directory* was published biographical information was sought in the *Congressional Directory*. . . .

Discussion of Results

In Table 30.1 are shown, grouped in five regions, the states which have sent women to the U.S. Congress during the past forty-seven years. Thirty-six states out of the fifty, or about three-fourths of all the states of the Union, are represented. . . . Interestingly enough, Wyoming, which was the first in the Union to give women the right to vote (in 1896, when still a territory and twenty-four years before adoption of the Nineteenth Amendment) has never sent a woman to Congress. Relative to their proportion of the population, the Western states (Rocky Mountain and Pacific area) have contributed a significantly larger percentage of women to Congress than any other region. . . .

[* * *]

---

[1]To the writer's knowledge there has been no published analysis of biographical data which includes all the women who have served in the U.S. Congress.

TABLE 30.1
States Represented by Women in U.S. Congress (65th–88th)*

State	Number	State	Number
North Atlantic		*North Central*	
Maine	1	Ohio	1
New Hampshire	—	Indiana	2
Vermont	—	Illinois	7
Massachusetts	1	Michigan	2
Rhode Island	—	Wisconsin	—
Connecticut	2	Minnesota	1
New York	7	Iowa	—
New Jersey	2	Missouri	1
Pennsylvania	3	North Dakota	—
	16	South Dakota	2
South Atlantic		Nebraska	2
Delaware	—	Kansas	1
Maryland	1		20
Virginia	—	*Western*	
West Virginia	1	Montana	1
North Carolina	1	Wyoming	—
South Carolina	3	Colorado	—
Georgia	4	New Mexico	1
Florida	1	Arizona	1
	11	Utah	1
South Central		Nevada	—
Kentucky	1	Idaho	1
Tennessee	2	Washington	2
Alabama	1	Oregon	3
Mississippi	—	California	3
Louisiana	1	Hawaii	1
Texas	—	Alaska	—
Oklahoma	1		14
Arkansas	4		
	10		

*Editor's note: Werner's data does not add up to numbers presented in text.

Party Affiliation

Forty of the women who have served in Congress have been Democrats, thirty have been Republicans. The proportion of congresswomen in each of the major parties reflects roughly the division of the electorate. . . .

Relatives Who Served in Congress

During the first two decades after women won the right to vote, the majority of congresswomen gained their seats not by their own efforts, by running as candidates and depending upon the popular vote, but via the road of "widow's succession." They were appointed by the governors of their states to their husband's seat after his death. Seldom did they seek re-election. This picture began to change during and after World War II when more women began to seek and win congressional seats by their own efforts.

Of the women who served in Congress between 1916 and 1963 about one-half have had relatives in Congress; slightly over one-third had husbands who were congressmen before them or, in some cases, served simultaneously with them (e.g., Senator P. H. Douglas and his wife, Representative Emily Douglas from Illinois).

Ten percent of the congresswomen came from families in which members of two generations served in the U.S. Congress. Two congresswomen can look back on an even prouder tradition—members of three generations of their families are listed in the Biographical Directory of the American Congress. . . .

Marital Status

Contrary to the popular stereotype of the suffrag[ist] spinster, 90 percent of the congresswomen have been married. This corresponds roughly to the percentage of married women, age thirty and over, in the U.S. population. The marriage rate for congresswomen is definitely higher than those for women in the professions (much higher, for instance, than that of women listed among the *American Men of Science*). There is no appreciable difference in the ratio of married to single congresswomen when we compare those born *before* 1900 with those born *after* 1900. . . .

[* * *]

Age at Which Congresswomen First Entered the House or Senate

There is a range of more than forty years between the youngest woman who obtained a seat in Congress and the oldest: Miss Winifred Stanley was elected to the House of Representatives at the age of 33. Mrs. Rebecca Felton was appointed to the Senate at the age of 77. The *modal* age at which congresswomen first obtain their seats on Capitol Hill is 52.

The tendency for women to enter Congress after their child-bearing and child-raising years are over is well illustrated by the age distribution of the women in the 88th Congress—the youngest was 49 years old, the oldest 78. The age-group which is most intimately involved in the upbringing of a new generation is not very well represented among congresswomen.

Educational Background

Congresswomen, as a whole, are a highly educated group. Four-fifths obtained training beyond high school; more than half graduated from college. The majority of the college graduates attended state universities or large "private" universities. . . . Relatively few graduated from women's colleges. Two-fifths of the college graduates took postgraduate work at a university: eight obtained a postgraduate degree. . . .

Major Political Activities Prior to Service in the House or Senate

Three-fourths of the congresswomen engaged in one or more major political activities prior to service in the House or Senate. . . . Ranking first is service in the state government. Roughly 20 percent of all congresswomen have served in the legislatures of the states they later represented in Congress. Others held important positions in the executive or judiciary branch of their home state's government.

[* * *]

Twelve percent gained their political experience directly on Capitol Hill as secretary or assistant to husbands who were congressmen. At least 10 percent served in city or town government before going on to Congress and an equal number held positions in county government. Others were active as chairwomen of their state party organization or the county party committee. . . .

[* * *]

Length of Service

Louise M. Young, writing in 1950, reports a high turnover rate for congresswomen. This situation has improved in the last decade and a half. Only between one-fifth and one-sixth of the women who served in the last seven Congresses have been affected by turnover. More than half of all congresswomen were re-elected for a full second term and a little over a third were twice re-elected and served six years or more.

After that, the ranks begin to thin rapidly. There have been all together ten congresswomen who were re-elected five times or more, who have served in the Congress over a decade and have obtained positions of seniority on important committees. . . .

[* * *]

TABLE 30.2

American Women in State and National Legislatures—
Trends 1920–1963

Year	Women in State Legislatures		Women in U.S. Congress	
	Number	Increase	Number	Increase
1920	29	—	—	—
1921	31	+2	4	+4
1923	84	+53	1	−3
1925	126	+42	3	+2
1927	124	−2	5	+2
1929	149	+25	9	+4
1931	146	−3	8	−1
1933	132	−14	8	−
1935	129	−3	8	−
1937	140	+11	9	+1
1939	130	−10	9	—
1941	140	+10	10	+1
1943	162	+22	9	−1
1945	234	+72	11	+2
1947	211	−23	8	−3
1949	217	+6	10	+2
1951	235	+18	11	+1
1953	289	+54	15	+4
1955	308	+19	18	+3
1957	321	+13	16	−2
1959	341	+20	17	+1
1961	no data available		19	+2
1963	351	+10	13	−6

Women as Legislators on the State
and National Level

The data in Table 30.2 allow a comparison between the number of women in the
U.S. Congress and those in the state legislatures from the adoption of the Nineteenth
Amendment till the present. The number of women in both the state and national
legislatures tends to increase during the years of presidential elections (with the
exception of the 1960 election which resulted in an increase on the state level, but
a sharp decrease in Congress), and during World War II. It tends to decrease during
years of unemployment and economic and social unrest (depression, several small

recessions in the 1950's and early 1960's) and at the end of a war, whenever there is sharper competition for jobs. The *gain* in the number of women in both the state and national legislatures is less pronounced during the off-years when there is no presidential election to capture the interest of the voter. . . .

[* * *]

Summary

[* * *]

. . . At present, there exists somewhat of a paradox in women's participation in the American legislative process. After an all-time high in the 87th Congress their number has dropped to less than there were a decade ago. In the meantime, the number of women in the state legislatures continues to increase steadily, as does the number of eligible female voters which now exceeds that of eligible male voters.

Factors which may contribute to an understanding of this situation are the lag between the laws establishing civic equality and the customs of society, the vestigial sex roles carried over from the nineteenth century, women's own anti-feminine tradition, and the fluctuation of woman's political leadership opportunities in times of social and economic unrest.

TOWARD CRITICAL THINKING

1. Emmy E. Werner found that the then less populous western states sent a disproportionate number of women to Congress. Today, California and Washington are each represented in Congress by two women senators, and the California House delegation includes the largest percentage of women in any State House delegation with more than one woman and the House woman Democratic Leader, Nancy Pelosi. Is there something different about western political culture that could account for these differences from the rest of the nation? What other elements might be a factor?

2. How many women members of Congress are from your state? How does this compare to the data presented by Werner?

READING 31

The Impact of Women on State Legislative Policies

(1991)

Sue Thomas

The National Organization for Women (NOW) was founded in 1966, the same year that Emmy E. Werner's "Women in Congress: 1917–1964" (Reading 30) was published. Soon, the fledgling women's movement was to receive more and more publicity as a new generation of women began to demand equal rights, equal pay, and an end to all forms of discrimination. Writing in 1977, in her pathbreaking book *Sex Roles in the State House*, political scientist Irene Diamond, found that in 1971 the percentage of women in state legislatures ranged from 0.7 percent in Texas and Minnesota, to a high of 17.2 percent in New Hampshire. Information such as this, as well as general observations, led to the founding of the National Women's Political Caucus (NWPC) in 1972 by many NOW members and other activists who believed that it was important to get more women elected to public office. They wanted more women elected because they thought that women legislators would have different policy priorities and simply because they thought it was wrong for women to be underrepresented in a democratic society.

The NWPC conducted trainings around the country to encourage women to run for local and state office. And, as more women ran for and were elected to state legislative office, a burgeoning number of political scientists, many of them female, turned their attention to the study of women in local and state legislatures. Several studies conducted in the late 1970s showed a gender gap in ideology of women office holders as well as differences in their voting behavior. But, one small study of women city council members conducted by political scientist Susan Gluck Mezey showed no evidence of differences in policy priorities.

By the late 1980s, there were enough women in state legislatures to allow political scientists to study the impact of women in statehouses in a comprehensive manner. In this article published in the *Journal of Politics*, Sue Thomas was among the first to use sophisticated quantitative analysis techniques to examine the impact of women on women's issues in the statehouse. Thomas offered preliminary answers to the question "Do women in public office make a difference?" and inquired about the kind of difference women made and under what conditions they had an impact on the policy outputs of legislative bodies.

[* * *]

The fundamental expectations of this study are that increased representation of women in state legislatures will provide increased support for women. This will, in turn, result in the emergence of distinctive gender-based political priorities. Most important, these distinctive priorities will be most evident and most successful in states with the highest proportion of female representatives. Five primary hypotheses concerning the relationship between the percentage of women in state legislature and actions of both women and men within them are offered. These include:

1. In the states with the highest level of female representation, women legislators will exhibit higher levels of policy priority differences from men. . . .

2. Although women's and men's differing priorities on issues of women, children, and the family are expected to be enhanced in those states with higher proportion of women legislators, any other issue priority differences are *not* expected to be related to relative proportions of women in the statehouses. It is possible, for example, that women may place higher priority than men on education and medical issues (historically, an area of concern and expertise), however, no patterns related to the proportion of women in the legislature are expected. This is because issues apart from those dealing with women, children, and the family have long been included in mainstream legislative agendas. . . .

3. Not only will the proportion of women in the state legislature affect the introduction of legislation concerning women, children, and the family, it will also affect passage rates of such legislation. . . .

[* * *]

4. The higher the proportion of women in office, the more likely it will be that the ethic of the legislative chamber itself will shift toward higher introduction rates of bills dealing with women, children, and the family. . . .

5. . . . [T]he highest overall passage rates of legislation concerning women, children, and the family will be achieved in states with the highest proportions of women in the statehouses. . . .

[* * *]

Data and Methods

[* * *]

Data were gathered from a 1988 survey of members of the lower houses of the state legislatures in 12 states. . . . These states were chosen primarily because they represent the full range of proportions of women in state legislatures from barely 3% in Mississippi to 30% in Washington (see Table 31.1). Diversity in geographical region

TABLE 31.1
Women in State Legislatures*

State	Total Women/Lower House	% of Women
Washington	30/ 98	30.6
Vermont	41/150	27.3
Arizona	15/ 60	25.0
South Dakota	13/ 70	18.6
Nebraska**	9/ 49	18.4
Iowa	18/100	18.0
Illinois	20/118	16.9
North Carolina	20/120	16.7
California	12/ 80	15.0
Georgia	24/180	13.3
Pennsylvania	14/203	6.9
Mississippi	4/122	3.3

Total number of female legislators at the time of this measure = 220.
*This information provided by the Center for the American Woman and Politics, Eagleton Institute of Politics at Rutgers University and reflects figures for 1987 as that was the year the study was begun.
**Nebraska is a unicameral legislature so calculations were based on one chamber.

and political culture were additional criteria for selection, with chosen states representing the three major political cultures and all regions. All women legislators . . . were surveyed along with 30 male legislators in each state (except in Vermont where 41 males were sampled to match the 41 female legislators). The response rate was 54%, ranging from 78% in Washington to 22% in Mississippi. . . . [T]he total number of responses was 322.

[* * *]

Findings

Gender and Inter-Legislative Differences in Types of Priority Bills

One way to investigate whether bringing more women into legislatures affects policy is to measure gender-based differences in priority legislation. . . .

Answers to a mail survey question illuminate hypotheses 1 and 2. Legislators were asked to list their top five priority bills of the last complete legislative session. Eight coding categories differentiate bills dealing with women's issues, children's and family issues, budget and tax issues, crime, education and medical issues, business and economic issues, energy, environment, and public land use issues, and welfare issues.

... Dealing first with issues of women, children, and the family, ... female members in the states within the high and low categories conform to the expectation quite nicely. In Arizona, Vermont, and Washington, the states with more than 20% women legislators, women gave priority to bills dealing with these issues more often than men did. In the states with under 10% women, a very different result exists. In Mississippi, women and men appear equally uninterested in legislation in these two categories as neither introduced any such bills. In Pennsylvania, with slightly higher representation of women than Mississippi, women and men are tied, with no bills on issues relating to women. However, female legislators made priorities of bills dealing with children and the family more often than did men. ...

[* * *]

... [Moreover,] political culture is not a credible predictor of whether women will place priority on bills dealing with women or children and families more often than men.

Two categories encompassing areas traditionally of interest to women are education and medical issues and welfare. Dealing first with education and medical issues, women in nine of the 12 states had more priority bills in this area than the men in their states. However, no patterns relating to percentage of women exist. Nor are gender differences related to political culture or region. The only three states in which women's mean level of priority bills did not exceed men's were California, Washington, and North Carolina, two western and one southern state. ... For this issue area, then, traditional expectations for women's involvement in educational and medical issues are confirmed, but no link exists between the percentage of women in the legislature and the extent to which women legislators place priority on these types of legislation.

Welfare bills also exhibit no pattern based on percentage of women in the legislature. ...

Gender differences in prioritizing business bills also do not vary by level of women's representation. ...

As anticipated, the last three sets of issues, crime, budget, and environment/energy/public land use, display no particular patterns. ...

[* * *]

Inter-Legislative Differences in Priority Bill Introductions

[* * *]

... To determine whether the states with the highest percentages of women in the legislature also had the highest level of bills concerning women, children, and the family overall, comparisons were made of the mean number of instances legislators named all types of bills among their top five priorities. Only in the case of bills dealing with either women or children and the family did any remotely relevant finding emerge. Mississippi and Pennsylvania, the states with the lowest percentage of women, scored eleventh and twelfth on both these measures. In no other instance did any pattern based on percentage of women (or, for that matter, region or political culture) emerge.

Based on the discussion above, 25%–30% female membership in legislative chambers does not constitute a critical mass able to affect overall policies and priorities. . . . On the other hand, it appears that at least 10% female representation is necessary for women's distinctive interests to appear. . . .

Gender and Inter-Legislative Differences in Success of Selected Legislative Priorities

. . . [T]he next logical questions are whether women are successful in passage of their priorities, specifically those dealing with issues of women, children, and the family, and to what extent success is related to the proportion of women in the legislature (hypothesis 3). The operationalization for this measure is the passage rate of those bills introduced by each legislator in his or her top five priorities for the last legislative session that deal with women's, children's, and family issues. . . .

[* * *]

There is substantial gender-based difference in mean level of success of all respondents. Almost 13% of men's priority bills dealing with women, children, and families passed while almost 29% (more than double) of comparable bills introduced by women passed. Turning to the patterns among the states, in the low category, women in Mississippi tied with men in that state by having none of their bills in these issue areas pass, the worst absolute record in all 12 states. Interestingly, women in Pennsylvania were more successful than men in passing priority bills concerning women, children, and families (hypothesis 4).

A somewhat mixed picture is displayed by the states in the high category. In Washington and Vermont, the states with the two highest percentages of women in the legislature, women officeholders far surpassed men in passing priority bills dealing with women, children, and families. However, in Arizona, the men were more successful in passing their priority bills in this area. In fact, only in Arizona and California, the two states out of 12 in which women were not more liberal than their male counterparts, the women did not exceed the men in passage of this type of priority bill. Since these bills are generally categorized as liberal measures, the result is not so surprising. In short, women in all but three of 12 states were more successful than men in passing priority bills dealing with women, children, and families. . . .

[* * *]

Inter-Legislative Differences in Priority Bill Passage

Is the percentage of women in legislatures positively related to the likelihood that the legislature will pass a bill concerning women or children and families (hypothesis 5)? The answer appears to be "no." Washington, Arizona, and Vermont, for example, were fourth, seventh, and tenth on a scale measuring the ratio of bills passed to those introduced dealing with women, children, and family legislation. In other words, we can be fairly confident that slightly less than one-third women within a legislative chamber does not constitute a critical threshold for relatively assured diffusion of policy priorities. . . .

[* * *]

Speculation about explanatory variables related to passage of legislation of priority to women may include political, social, and economic factors. One political variable testable here is the presence or absence of a formal women's legislative caucus within the state legislatures. While investigation of the relationship of this variable and the first measure of the dependent variable produces little of significance, examination of states with caucuses produces an interesting finding. The top five states in the passage of such legislation are, in order, California, Iowa, Illinois, Washington, and North Carolina. Except for Washington, these are the only states of all 12 that have formal women's legislative caucuses. Further, Washington is the state with the highest percentage of women in the lower house. This suggests that visibility either in the form of the presence of a formal women's caucus or relatively high percentages of women, is necessary for the passage, on a general basis, of legislation dealing with women, children, and the family. . . .

[* * *]

Implications

The results of this study offer several important insights into a much echoed question among scholars of gender politics. Do women in office make a difference, and if so, under what circumstances? It appears that women do indeed make a difference. First, they are more likely than men to introduce and successfully steer legislation through the political process that addresses issues of women, children, and the family.

Second, we can also identify at least one of the circumstances under which that difference is enhanced. That is, women appear to be more likely to introduce and pass distinctive legislation in situations in which they may find support—in this case, circumstances of increased numbers, of support from the creation of women's legislative caucuses. While theories have predicted that the behavior of minorities changes as their status is altered, the findings here present evidence that this may be the case for women in politics, at least for women in statehouses.

Relatedly, the results of this study also suggest that general theories of the behavior of officeholders do not sufficiently account for the actions of women in office. While increased exposure to and success within a political system may generally result in a convergence toward existing norms, there appear to be circumstances under which members of the system, while moving toward the norm in some respects, may also develop their own norms or goals. The situation of emerging political minorities, in this case, women, may be one of these exceptions. Women (as well as black representatives) . . . do reflect the norms concerning legislative tactics, but both have pursued alternative policies.

[* * *]

TOWARD CRITICAL THINKING

1. Sue Thomas notes that where women are less than 10 percent of a legislative body, they don't appear to make a difference. Why would that be? With only 14 percent of the U.S. Congress being female, do you think that women in the national legislature are more apt to make a difference than those in statehouses? Why or why not?

2. The United States lags far behind much of the world in the number of women in elected bodies. For example, today Scandinavian countries as well as Rwanda and Argentina vastly surpass the U.S. in the proportion of women in elected positions. In fact, the U.S. ranks sixty-first out of 185 nations. Why is this so?

READING 32

Power and Influence in State Legislative Policy Making: The Interaction of Gender and Position in Committee Hearing Debates

(1994)

Lyn Kathlene

Sue Thomas's work (Reading 31) analyzed the policy impact of women in state legislatures once they were found in sufficient numbers. Lyn Kathlene's work was made possible as the increasing numbers of women in statehouses led to women's substantial presence on a host of legislative committees around the United States.

Future President Woodrow Wilson once wrote that "Congress in session is Congress on public exhibition, whilst Congress in its committee rooms is Congress at work." Committees in the statehouse as well as in the U.S. Congress are where bills originate and where most bills die. Committee service also allows members to learn more about potential legislation as experts come before them in public hearings to testify for or against laws under consideration. Committee hearings also give members an opportunity to perform in public and to establish their personalities for the press as well as the public and other committee members. They are especially important to legislators who are the sponsors of particular pieces of legislation. Hearings give the sponsors the opportunity to try to convince other legislators about the pros of the proposed bills under consideration. Moreover, in a study of Santa Clara County commissioners, political scientist Janet Flammang found that supportive female colleagues encouraged women to speak out more. Most other early work that examined legislative bodies where there were few women, however, found that women were likely to be more reticent than their more vociferous male colleagues.

In this article published in the *American Political Science Review,* Kathlene uses an exhaustive study of committee hearings in the 1989 Colorado State House to ask important questions about how women legislators speak out during committee hearings. She also examines how women's presence on a committee affects the behavior of men on the committee. Legislative bodies long have been known as "boys' clubs," and Kathlene seeks to determine how the presence of women breaking into their exclusive club causes men to react. Thus, she seeks to assess whether men and women exhibit different behaviors or styles during these public events. Looking at the behaviors of committee chairs, bill sponsors, and other committee members, she examines whether males and females act differently in any of those capacities during committee hearings. Building on work that found women legislators made a difference in the types of legislation that gets considered, here Kathlene tries to take our understanding of women and politics further by analyzing member behaviors in a key step of the legislative process.

[* * *]

While structural and personal characteristics of an individual (e.g., leadership position, party affiliation, terms in the legislative chamber, policy goals, constituency concerns, desire to make good policy, and expertise or interest in a particular bill) have been considered important determinants of participation in committee hearings, the effect of a committee member's sex has been completely ignored. . . .

[* * *]

In the legislative setting, individuals (and therefore groups) obtain influence primarily through two methods: (1) appointments to powerful positions and (2) assignments to and participation in committees. . . .

[* * *]

This research attempts to discover where the barriers—and when the imbalances—occur in one important decision-making setting: the committee hearing. While it is possible that men always dominate verbal interactions in mixed-sex groups, other research indicates that the dynamics of dominance are more complex. Such factors as the positional power of speakers plays an important role in gendered verbal behavior, and it appears that there may be important power and influence differences depending on the topic (or issue) being discussed. Documenting precisely whether and when women are effectively kept out of committee hearing debates and under what circumstances women are successful is important for understanding how the status quo resists change despite numerical gains in elected women representatives.

[* * *]

Sample Selection of Hearings

Twelve committee hearings were selected from the 68 taped and transcribed hearings gathered. I was interested in selecting a group of bills that were likely to bring out women's voices. All eight family/children bills that were sampled during the 1989 session were selected for this analysis based on the presumption that women were likely to engage in discussions about family and children issues since other research has found that women are more likely to prioritize and sponsor these issues. Four other

nonfamily bills selected on the basis of hearing and sponsor characteristics comparable to the family/children bills (i.e., sponsor's sex, chair's sex, the proportion of
women on the committee, and the first committee assigned to the bill) provide for a
comparison between family and nonfamily bills.

Half of the bills were sponsored by a female; 5 of the 12 hearings were chaired
by a female. It was not unusual for the vice-chair to direct the hearing or to cochair
the hearing. Four of the selected hearings were chaired by more than one person. In
these hearings, it was the male chair (rather than the female vice-chair) who predominated over most of the hearing (80% or more); therefore, these hearings are
coded as male-chaired. The percentage of female legislators at the hearing, including the chair and the sponsor, ranged from 12% to 64%. Eight of the 12 bills passed
out of their first committee (the hearing under study in this analysis). Ultimately 5
of the 12 bills became law. . . .

[* * *]

Dependent Variables

To determine "who holds the floor" in legislative committee hearings, five dependent
variables were tested. The first measure, *percent* TIME ELAPSED, is the percentage of
the hearing that has elapsed when the speaker first talks, calculated by dividing the number of words spoken at the hearing prior to a speaker's first utterance by the total number of words spoken at the hearing. The point in the hearing when a speaker enters the
committee discussion may be an important measure of influence. . . .

The second two dependent variables, WORDS SPOKEN and TURNS TAKEN,
are discrepancy score measures that subtract the expected frequency (the sum of the
speaking behavior divided by the number of people present at the hearing) from the
actual frequency of a particular speaking behavior. The discrepancy score standard-
izes for differences in the length of the hearing time to make interhearing speaking
behavior comparable. WORDS SPOKEN measures the time a speaker holds the floor.
This is an indicator of how vocal a person was during the hearing. Research outside
of political settings has found that men talk more than women, whether in mixed-
or same-sex groups. Other studies have documented that males are the more talka-
tive in mixed-sex conversations in the workplace, classroom, and in couple situations, and that males talk longer in monologue-type situations. TURNS TAKEN
measures how often speakers initiated and engaged in discussion. This is an indicator of how actively involved a person was in the hearing. . . .

The final two dependent variables, *percent* INTERRUPTIONS MADE and
percent INTERRUPTIONS RECEIVED measure the different ways committee members gain and lose their speaking turns. Most turns, even in less formal settings than
a committee hearing, are gained through "smooth speaker switches," where a person
waits until the speaker has completed their utterance. How a person gains their speaking turn is an important indicator of both social norms (i.e., politeness) and power
or dominance. Numerous linguistic and sociological studies of mixed-sex group
dynamics document the male's verbal aggressiveness. For example, one study found

that males interrupting females accounted for 96% of all interruptions. Another study found that men were more likely to talk while a woman was speaking than while a man was speaking, though the context and situation of the verbal interaction are important determinants that can reverse the pattern. Interrupting another person reflects the speaker's position of power and dominance, whether it be social or institutionally derived. In committee hearings, there are potentially two conflicting conditions regarding power and dominance. Research on sex differences suggests that men will do a disproportionate amount of interrupting and that women will be interrupted more often than men. But positional power (e.g., chairing the hearing) should mitigate the socially constructed power differences between the sexes. Women chairing committees should not act differently from their male counterparts—or at least, they should be more dominant (i.e., do more interrupting) than either rank-and-file committee members or witnesses.

[* * *]

Results

Descriptive Statistics

A total of 116,051 words were spoken with a mean of 9,671 words per hearing. Across all 12 hearings there were 1,747 smooth speaker switches and 195 interruptions. Total interruptions ranged between 4.0% to 26.0% of all speaker switches, with an average of 11.2%. The interruption rate is low in comparison to research findings in conversational dynamics. No doubt this was due to the formality of the setting. Parliamentary procedures both produce more speaker switches (the chair constantly acknowledges each speaker—55.1 percent of all turns were taken by chairs) and lessen the likelihood of interruptions (speakers generally wait to be acknowledged by the chair). Similar to findings in conversational analysis, most interruptions during the hearings resulted in a successful turn (86.2%) for the person who did the interrupting, further validating the importance of studying who interrupts whom.

Positional Role

Position at the hearing is an important determinate of speaking behavior. . . . [C]hairs, committee members, and witnesses all differed significantly from sponsors. . . . Chairs took the most turns speaking, while sponsors dominated hearings in speaking time. Sponsors and chairs both made and received more interruptions than committee members or witnesses. The significant differences in elapsed time among the roles are an institutional artifact: sponsors always had the opportunity to summarize their bill verbally at the start of committee hearings; chairs spoke next by virtue of their role as moderator of the hearing; witnesses and committee members were the last to enter into the committee discussion.

[When sex is added to the question,] the positional patterns found in the first model remain essentially the same. In addition, except for interruptions received, men and women at the hearing also differed significantly from one another. Women entered the discussion later, spoke less, took fewer turns, and made fewer interruptions than men.

[When sex and position are considered,] position continues to distinguish among different speaking behaviors, and female chairs are significantly different than male chairs. Women chairing committees spoke less, took fewer turns, and made fewer interruptions than their male counterparts, suggesting that men and women have different leadership styles. The same gendered pattern holds for female committee members and female witnesses in comparison to their male counterparts, although these differences are not statistically significant.

Since positional role is highly significant, in statistical terms as well as substantive terms, the analysis will compare speaking behavior *within* each positional role across all 12 hearings.

Committee Members

[* * *]

. . . Unlike an informal conversation among friends, there are several political and institutional factors that could produce differentiated patterns beyond or instead of gender. Partisan differences seem very likely. We might expect that the minority party (in this case, the Democrats) to be less vocal than the majority Republican party. Or minority party members may be particularly active in committee hearings in order to vocalize their objections to or imprint their concerns on the bill before it reaches the highly partisan dynamics of the House floor debates. Or there may be no discernible party differences since committees are viewed by the legislators themselves as one of the least partisan arenas in the legislature.

Other factors could also be important. . . . Having a personal interest or expertise in the issue area of the bill could explain differences in verbal behavior. . . .

Finally, legislative expertise may account for greater participation. The number of terms served in the legislature can be used as a general measure of legislative expertise. We would expect newly elected legislators to be inexperienced in state legislative policymaking at a number of different levels (e.g., parliamentary procedures, historical detailed knowledge about failed bills in previous years, and general insider politics) and lack the clout to be included in important off-the-record dealings with legislative leaders, state bureaucrats, and lobbyists. . . .

Results of Personal and Institutional Models

. . . [S]ex is highly significant on all five measures of speaking behavior. Women, on average, waited until more than two-thirds of the hearing was over before they uttered their first words, while men engaged halfway through the hearing. Men spoke longer and took more turns, and men made and received more interruptions than women committee members. The first multivariate model results indicate that sex continues to be significant across the five measures even after accounting for committee members' interest in the bill, their party affiliation, and their freshman status. In each of the measures, it was the male committee members who dominated the committee hearings.

Other variables are also important in understanding verbal behavior. As predicted, committee members who had an interest in the bill spoke longer and engaged in discussion more frequently. They were also interrupted more often, which follows from their greater verbal activity. Except for making fewer interruptions, minority party status did not affect speaking behavior in committee hearings. . . . [F]reshman status did not lessen their participation in the hearings. . . .

Additional Committee Hearing Factors and Interactions

. . . If women have a special interest in certain types of legislation, due to their personal experience or belief that they can represent women's interests better than men, then female committee members should be more vocal in hearings on family issues.

The sex of the sponsor may have an effect on the committee members' speaking behavior. If women are bringing different views and values to policymaking based on a more needs-based, rather than individual-rights, orientation toward society, then the bills that women sponsor, regardless of issue area, may embody this difference and perhaps strike a responsive cord among the other women committee members.

Chairing a committee is an important position of power because the chair can control much of the hearing dynamics, including in what order committee members will be recognized to speak, which committee members' ideas will be encouraged or cut off, and whether the bill will receive a final committee vote or be tabled (usually resulting in the death of the bill). Given findings in all-female groups that women engage in supportive and cooperative, rather than competitive, linguistic strategies, female committee members may be more at ease or more inclined to speak when the chair of the committee is also female. However, other research indicates that even when a token male (or female) is present, the group dynamics change toward a less supportive interaction style. Therefore, the presence of a female chair may not be enough to bring out female voices. Yet the more democratic leadership style of women—as opposed to men's more autocratic style—may provide the opportunity for more women to participate. But being democratic implies an inclusive style that should facilitate all voices, not just women's voices. Thus, men's more aggressive verbal behavior may be even more pronounced under a female chair. Based on these conflicting propositions, female committee members may participate more or less than men when the chair is female.

It may not be enough that the chair or the sponsor is female if the rest of the committee is comprised of mostly males. In order for women to be heard, they may need to comprise some minimal percentage in a committee hearing. Conversely, the increased presence of women may result in more verbal activity by men reacting to women's intrusion in the legislative setting. The 12 hearings were divided into three groups based on the percentage of women legislators at the hearing (including all the committee members, the sponsor, and the chair). Three bills comprise the *female tokenism* category, in which less than 30% of the legislators were women. Five bills are in the *female critical mass*, where 30% to 50% of the committee is comprised of women. Finally, four bills fall into the category of *female majority*, where, by definition, over 50% are women. If [business professor Rosabeth Moss] Kanter's proposition holds, female committee members will become more verbally active when more women are present. If [psychologist

Janice] Yoder is correct, female committee members will be less active due to men's stepped-up participation to counter the increased proportions of women at the hearing.

Results of Additional Considerations

. . . [A]fter controlling for situational factors related to the hearing, the same pattern of male domination . . . remains. Regardless of whether the chair or the sponsor is a man or a woman or the hearing is on a family issue, female committee members engage later, speak significantly fewer words, take significantly fewer turns, and make and receive fewer interruptions than their male counterparts. However, committee members speak significantly earlier as the proportion of women on the committee increases.

. . . It is the men, rather than the women, who become significantly more vocal when women comprise greater proportions of the committee. . . . Similarly, male committee members engaged earlier—and female committee members, later—when the sponsor of the bill was a woman. An examination of the transcript reveals that male committee members asked questions of female sponsors immediately after their introduction and more male committee members engaged early in questioning witnesses that testified for a female-sponsored bill, regardless of the proportion of women at the hearing. Both behaviors tended not to be present when a man sponsored a bill, suggesting that females (but not males) in positions of importance have their ideas scrutinized by rank-and-file men.

While the male committee members engage significantly earlier, they are not speaking or taking more turns under the different situational characteristics of the hearing. The same cannot be said for female committee members. Women not only engage later when there are more women at the hearing, but they also speak fewer words. And women, contrary to the expectation, speak significantly less than men at hearings addressing a family issue, even after controlling for interest in the issue area (which remains significant). . . .

[* * *]

Chairs

In the first analysis of positional roles, we saw that men and women chairing hearings had different speaking behaviors, with female chairs participating less—and interrupting less—than male chairs. In the analysis of witnesses and committee members' speaking behavior, we saw that under a male chair, the chair and his male colleagues on the committee questioned female sponsors early in the hearing. A slightly different approach to examining chair behavior can illuminate what these differences mean to committee members and witnesses. Since chairs play a central role in directing committee discussion, the *type of turns* taken by chairs were coded into one of three categories: *Parliamentary turns* were procedural turns, as when the chair calls a witness or recognizes a committee member who wanted to speak; *clarifying turns* request an affirmation from a previous speaker about the content or meaning of a statement; *question/opinion turns* interject a new idea into the discussion. Beyond taking the floor away from speakers, male chairs also influenced and controlled committee hearing discussions through engaging in substantive comments more than female chairs did. Table 32.1 examines the sex differences by type of turn.

Men and women chairs did not differ in their use of clarification questions. However, women were more likely to act as facilitators of the hearing, as evidenced through their almost exclusive use of procedural turns. And while men, too, used mostly procedural turns, in one out of six turns (on average), men interjected personal opinions or guided the committee members and witnesses to a topic of their interest. Men used their position of power to control hearings in ways that we commonly associate with the notion of positional power and leadership. Indeed, the earlier gendered patterns among committee members may be the interaction of women chairs acknowledging all voices (to be more inclusive) in conjunction with male committee members' more assertive verbal behavior (as evidenced in their interruption and speaking patterns) when there is a woman sponsor, a feminized hearing, or a family issue being considered. In other words, while the conversational terms of the game had been changed through different chair styles, the more dominant verbal behavior of men as committee members became accentuated in a hearing where the chair used a more democratic, less autocratic style.

Discussion

Although it is commonly believed that women's increased presence in state legislatures will lead to their greater power and influence in policymaking, this assertion has never been tested through observation. As an initial step toward empirically documenting these changes in women's political access to power, I examined their speaking behavior in legislative committee hearings. The findings reported here suggest that women legislators, despite their numerical and positional gains, may be seriously disadvantaged in committee hearings and unable to participate equally in legislative committee hearings. . . .

TABLE 32.1
Type of Chair Turn Taken by Sex

	Mean Percent	
Type of Turn	Male	Female
Procedural	78.6	94.4
Clarification	4.7	2.2
Question/opinion	16.7	3.4
Total %	100.0	100.0

Note: The percentages shown are the mean percentages for the chairs of each gender, based on 8 male chairs (who collectively took 391 turns) and 9 female chairs (who collectively took 338 turns).

[* * *]

Ultimately, to understand gender-power differentials, we need to examine how the content of a bill changes as it passes through the process and look closely at who is influencing the changes. Is male verbal aggression directed at women-sponsored bills or women's issues resulting in a transformation of their bills that is disproportionately influenced by male voices? Or do women as chairs or committee members have ways (other than verbal participation in committees) to imprint their concerns on legislation as it moves through the process? For example, whether women's ideas raised in committee hearings are reflected in amendments sponsored by men become an important indirect measure to consider in future analyses.

Examining the speaking behaviors of legislators during committee hearings provides us with yet another view of how powerful gender is in our culture. Bringing more women into politics will not translate directly into a proportionate amount of female power and influence. In fact, there may be a powerful backlash present when women exceed a certain critical mass in a highly masculinized institution such as legislative politics. Yet it is clear that the presence of more women legislators will lead to more women sponsoring bills and chairing committees. When women chaired committees the dynamics of the hearing changed for witnesses and female sponsors in complex ways, some of which may provide for more democratic policy making, particularly if the negative effects of increased verbal aggressiveness by men can be countered. This examination of speaking behavior only begins to tap into gender differences that may have profound substantive implications for legislative decision making.

TOWARD CRITICAL THINKING

1. Lyn Kathlene finds that men's behavior changes significantly as the number of women increase in a legislative committee. How different do you think the U.S. Congress would be if women were 50 percent of congressional committees? What differences would you expect to see?

2. What factors does Kathlene find are the most important in understanding women's behavior in committee meetings? What roles do you think personality traits and individualism play?

READING 33

Gender Styles in State Legislative Committees: Raising Their Voices in Resolving Conflict

(2000)

Cindy Simon Rosenthal

The works of Sue Thomas (Reading 31) and others, including Beth Reingold on women in the California and Arizona state legislatures and Edith J. Barrett on policy priorities of African American women in state legislatures, continued to find that women's presence in the legislature made a difference in the type of legislation considered. Later, Lyn Kathlene (Reading 32) found that male committee chairs spoke more than their female counterparts. Here, Cindy Simon Rosenthal takes these works and those of others to their logical extension to examine the differences between male and female leadership styles. 1992's "Year of the Woman" (see Reading 29), when record numbers of women were elected at the state and national level, drove home the fact that women were transforming politics. But, due to the seniority systems used in most legislatures, women were slow to rise to positions of power. As they did, though, many scholars and practitioners began to observe what Simon Rosenthal calls the "feminization of leadership," which transformed a "male model of competitive gamesmanship into a shared, inclusive style."

In this article from *Women & Politics,* Simon Rosenthal looks at how women and men committee chairs exercise their leadership. By using survey data, focus groups, and in-depth interviews, she analyzes the motivations, traits, and behaviors of women in these leadership roles to see if they have any association with gender. In advancing the notion of integrative leadership, she finds that women committee chairs in statehouses are more inclusive, collaborative, and policy-oriented. In an era of intense partisanship, her work holds out hope that the election and retention of women (allowing them to garner sufficient seniority or prestige within a legislative body) will provide one solution to end the problem of partisan stalemate.

Gender Styles

[* * *]

This research focuses on the gendered nature of legislative institutions by examining the conflict resolution styles of state legislative committee chairs. . . . Studying state legislative committee chairs offers a sizeable cohort of men and women engaged in fundamentally similar leadership tasks but under varying institutional circumstances and in more than a single state. Specifically, this research asks whether women committee chairs raise their voices to resolve conflicts in a different way from their male colleagues? If so, how do institutional variables—the gender composition of the membership, the distribution of gender power, and the extent of professionalization—influence conflict resolution style? Finally, the results of the analysis allow discussion of a more fundamental question: does an organizational analysis of gender in legislatures reveal that political science has conflated masculine behavior to stand for legislative norms? . . .

[* * *]

First, as the research on leadership and women's socialization suggests, women committee chairs are expected to be more inclined toward cooperative conflict resolution behavior. The primary rationale for hypothesizing gender differences in legislative leadership comes from our understanding of social roles and socialization, and the gender dimensions of the world of work generally. The cooperative style is not inherently feminine; but through socialization and traditional conceptions of social, family, and work roles, women are more likely to have learned and practiced skills high in cooperative behavior—accommodation and collaboration—and men are more likely to have developed skills emphasizing personal assertiveness and competition. . . .

Closely related to the first hypothesis but drawing on the seminal work of Rosabeth Moss Kanter [published in] 1977, I predict little difference between men and women in terms of competitive conflict resolution behavior. Because of their token status, minorities or socially different subgroups within an organization face pressures to conform to norms established by the dominant group; thus "tokens" often invest extra effort "required for a satisfactory public appearance, sometimes accompanied by distortions of private inclinations." . . . Since legislatures have largely been peopled by men and featured competitive male behavior, there is no reason to expect women to be markedly different from institutional norms. Only when subgroups become "balanced" with minority individuals constituting at least 35% does Kanter suggest that constraints of tokenism disappear. Since only three legislatures currently have that proportion of women, no significant decline in competitive behavior is expected to be associated with increases in the female membership.

Third, men's and women's conflict resolution behavior is expected to vary in relationship to gender power in a legislature. [Georgia] Duerst-Lahti and [Rita Mae] Kelly suggest that gender power, not numbers alone, is the variable of interest in understanding leadership and governance. . . . In this research specifically, increases in women's institutional power in a legislature are expected to correspond with less cooperative conflict resolution styles among men and more cooperative conflict resolution styles among women.

Finally, theorists on leadership, gender, and organizations suggest that there is an implied bias for masculine behavior in bureaucracies and organizations perpetuate masculinity by promoting and "cloning" like-minded middle and upper-level managers. . . . Following [Camilla] Stivers' logic, it is hypothesized that the more professionalized institutions will be associated with the more masculine conflict resolution style (i.e., competing). Conversely, collaboration and accommodation (the more culturally feminine styles) are expected to be inversely related to legislative professionalism.

[* * *]

The multivariate analysis of conflict resolution styles provides support for the four hypotheses noted earlier. . . .

As expected for the first hypothesis, controlling for personal and organizational factors, women are significantly more likely to embrace the more cooperative conflict resolution styles of collaboration and accommodation. As predicted by socialization theory, women differ significantly from men in their likelihood to embrace conflict resolution styles that are more oriented toward cooperation with others (i.e., accommodation and collaboration).

The second hypothesis is confirmed. While controlling for other factors, women and men do not differ significantly on the competing style of conflict resolution. This pattern of results is consistent with the expectation that women will conform to the dominant norm of more competitive behavior. Neither percentage of women nor women's power have a significant or differential impact on competitive behavior, suggesting deeply embedded institutional norms. At the same time, both men's and women's scores on the competing style decline slightly as the percentage of female legislators increases. Kanter's prediction about norms changing as more balanced groups emerge is not supported by these data; however, it is worth recalling that only three legislatures surpass the threshold of 35% female members that Kanter uses to define "balanced" groups.

The third set of hypotheses involves the reaction of both men's and women's behaviors to increases in women's power. The pattern of results for collaborating and accommodating styles when controlling for interactions between sex and women's power are the same. The [indicator] for women's power . . . conveys that as women's power increases, men's conflict resolution behavior on both styles trends downward. In other words, men's cooperative behavior declines as women's power increases. . . . The pattern of results on accommodation and collaboration also seems to support the prediction that with more institutional power women will experience a lessening of tokenism pressures to conform to majority norms and pursue more cooperative alliances.

Legislative professionalization, as expected by the fourth hypothesis, is positively and significantly associated with competitive behavior and negatively and significantly associated with accommodative conflict resolution behavior when controlling for other variables. These results are consistent with the hypothesis that professionalization will be positively associated with the highly assertive competitive behavior and negatively associated with highly cooperative accommodative style. Professionalization is not significantly associated with collaborative style, which is high in both assertive and cooperative behavior.

[* * *]

Focus Group and Field Interview Data

While survey research provides insights about women in legislatures, more ethnographic methods reveal subtleties about conflict resolution behavior in gendered institutions. In the three field states, women chairs were noted for embracing formal or informal methods of collaboration, for example, using task forces and subcommittees extensively, hiring a professional mediator or facilitator, devoting extra personal efforts to accommodating others and resolving differences on issues that defy "divide-the-dollar" compromise. Irrespective of differences in their states, women were reported to pursue collaborative decision-making even on the most contentious bills—the kind of divisive issues that could "start a fight in an empty room." Consider the preferred strategies of two Ohio chairs, a woman who articulates a collaborative win-win orientation and a man who prefers a more competitive style:

> Women want to make everybody a winner. If a bill comes and there are people in support of it, and groups opposed to it, I think we [women] are more apt to try to get everybody to sit down around a table or put it in a subcommittee and try to work out the differences. . . . Women go in with that win-win, keep-the-peace kind of attitude.

> There are basically two methods to approach a controversial bill. Sometimes I develop the Senate Finance Committee solution, have it drafted, drop it in the hopper, and watch everyone scream. Then I try to get folks together to work out the differences and reach consensus. The other way is to start by trying to find consensus first and then draft a bill. . . . I think that the first way is more effective. You've got their attention and they know you're serious.

While the woman embraces collaborative principles of open discussion, concern for the goals of others and win-win outcomes, the man articulates a more personally assertive approach to controlling the terms of the debate, forcing conflict, and then negotiating an outcome.

In the focus groups, female and male chairs emphasized different aspects of conflict resolution. The women expressed more concern for accommodating the wishes of others or collaborating with colleagues; the men talked about instrumental distributive tactics often in competitive terms. In three focus groups—one entirely of women, a second including both women and men, and the third entirely composed of men—chairs engaged in extended discussions of different meanings of consensus and different approaches to decision-making. Summarizing the thoughts of the other participants in the all-female group, a Wisconsin woman chair stated a classic accommodative orientation:

> We're willing to share more of the decision making, more of the power. We let go a piece at a time. First one piece and then another piece. We can share in the decision making in the interest of getting things done. Some times we luck out and we share a piece that we didn't care if we let go in the first place. (Laughs)

[* * *]

In the mixed group of committee chairs, the discussion followed along two distinctive tracks, the women focusing on the satisfaction of others and the men emphasizing tactics of securing winning coalitions. For example, a Maryland woman chair started the discussion of consensus with this thought: "I think ideally that consensus is a process, but also the product of a process in which all the members feel they have a stake in the outcome." A Missouri woman followed up, saying, "It's not unanimity, but it's a feeling of enough comfort [with the decision] that it's not going to be contentious or war." As the men joined in the discussion, the conversation turned to consensus as a tactical problem of counting votes (e.g., "you have to have enough [people support you] so you don't have to worry about a close vote").

In three focus groups, the participants were asked to define consensus and describe the conduct of committee business. The comments were coded as either distributive (i.e., framed in terms of winning and losing, interest group competition, bargaining, and majority votes) or integrative (i.e., framed in terms of deliberation, discussion and overall participant satisfaction in the outcome). In the group of only men, distributive comments outnumbered integrative comments by two to one (21 to 9), while the opposite pattern was the case in the all-female group (13 integrative, 6 distributive). The mixed group had roughly equal comments (12 integrative, 9 distributive).

In the focus group of only men, when asked if they observed differences between men and women chairs, the men discussed at length whether or not women are as adept as men at quid pro quo trades and compromises that go into legislative bargaining. On most matters of leadership style, the men saw few differences between chairs but a Connecticut chair complained that his female colleagues were not able to engage in expediencies as a favor to other committee chairs:

> The women chairs are less willing to work to the compromise and work out the details. There are committee chairs who come to you and ask: "You want a bill through my committee, you better take care of mine." That kind of thing. I found the women less willing to do that. [They say] "Oh no, I can't. You've got to get my bill out because it's good, but I don't really like your bill."

Several of the men rejected the assertion that women were by nature less willing to compromise; however, the group as a whole seemed willing to accept the idea that women chairs because of age, background or numbers were less skilled at the tactical strategies of compromise. Importantly, the conversation focused almost exclusively on the instrumental tactics of zero-sum decisions that are consistent with the distributive dimension of conflict resolution. Where the women committee chairs were caught up in a discussion about the integrative dimension of conflicts (e.g., the feelings of participants and the group's sense of ownership of a decision), the men were talking about the strategic calculations of trades and bargaining.

[* * *]

TOWARD CRITICAL THINKING

1. What are some of the reasons offered by Cindy Simon Rosenthal that underlie the expectations that women political leaders will have orientations different from those of their male counterparts? Would you expect women of color to have different orientations and leadership styles from those of white women?

2. What are some of the different leadership traits exhibited by women and men committee chairs? Would you expect women members of Congress who chair committees to exhibit similar traits? Why or why not?

READING 34

Are Women More Likely to Vote for Women's Issue Bills than Their Male Colleagues?

(1998)

Michele L. Swers

In 1992, as a record number of women were elected to the U.S. Congress, the number of women nearly doubled in each house. The growth in the number of women in the House of Representatives quickly made it an attractive target of study for political scientists. The Center for American Women in Politics (CAWP) at Rutgers University, for example, secured funding to begin to interview women members of Congress (see Reading 35). At the same time, CAWP also began to study the voting patterns of women in the House.

In this article first published in *Legislative Studies Quarterly*, Michele L. Swers around the same time also began to track the voting patterns of these women newly elected to the 103rd Congress, especially on bills of interest to women. Long ago, British political philosopher and member of Parliament, Edmund Burke, was one of the first to write about the roles of representatives in a democracy. Were representatives to vote their consciences? Or, were they to vote as they believed their constituents wished them to vote? Later, as we have seen in several of the entries in this volume, political scientists began to question whether women's interests could be represented by men. Other scholars looking at state legislatures concluded that women did indeed "represent women" and were more inclined to advocate for women's policy issues than were men. The question then remained, were women in the U.S. Congress similarly representing women's interests?

Swers became one the first political scientists to examine whether Democratic and Republican women in the House of Representatives voted differently than their male colleagues. Here, she uses roll-call voting to determine if gender has an effect on issue positions. She controls for a host of other factors that might explain differences, including party, ideology, region, and the composition of a congressional district. This work ushered in a new wave of research on women in legislative bodies.

Many scholars who study the influence of women in politics claim that the election of more women to the U.S. Congress is not simply an issue of equity, but will make a substantive policy making process span a wide range. Some feminist scholars believe that the presence of more women in legislatures will change the political process itself and the nature of bargaining. Congressional scholars who emphasize the primacy of the electoral connection maintain that representatives will respond to the same constituency interests regardless of gender. Yet, the primacy of electoral concerns does not negate the assertion that the election of women will have a substantive policy impact. Research suggests that the same geographical constituency can support many different reelection constituencies. Thus, a female candidate may be more likely to attract supporters who are concerned with women's issues. . . .

Previous Research

Political scientists have conducted extensive research to discern the determinants of congressional roll-call voting behavior. Much of this research points to the overwhelming influence of ideology, partisanship, and constituency factors as the determinants of representatives' voting decisions. However, none of these studies considers how personal characteristics of the representative, such as gender or race, may affect the pattern of a representative's voting record. . . .

This study seeks to determine the impact of gender on women's issue bills both as a group and on specific types of legislation within that category. The premise is that the more directly an issue affects women, the more likely it will be that women will vote together across party lines. For example, a representative's gender may have a more substantial effect on voting for bills that deal with women's health issues than on bills that deal with education.

Data and Methodology

[* * *]

. . . For each legislator, I developed a composite score of support for women's issues by summing the representative's votes over the fourteen [selected women's bills involving women's] issues and averaging them. . . .

I have hypothesized that gender will have its most significant impact on votes that deal most directly with women's health and reproductive issues, such as breast cancer research and abortion. Therefore, a separate composite score including the five votes that deal most directly with women's reproductive and other women's health issues was also analyzed. These bills include the Freedom of Access to Clinic Entrances Act, the Hyde Amendment, the Family Planning Amendments Act, the NIH (National Institutes of Health) Revitalization Act, and the Unsoeld Amendment to the (Elementary and Secondary Education Act) ESEA. . . .

[Other factors included in this analysis by Swers were:]

Personal Characteristics

Religion: . . . The religion variable is expected to have a negative effect only on those votes dealing with abortion and other reproductive issues.

African American: . . . African Americans are among the most liberal representatives. . . .

Southern: [Being] Southern is expected to [have a] negative [effect].

Freshman: . . . One might anticipate that freshmen will be more likely to be faithful to their constituency's interests as they are working to build a reelection constituency. . . .

Partisan Factors

Party: . . . Party is expected to have a positive effect on women's issue voting since women's issues tend to be supported by Democrats.

Ideology: . . . The scores range on a left-right continuum from -1 indicating most liberal to $+1$ indicating most conservative. . . . The score is expected to be negatively related to voting on women's issues. The inclusion of this measure makes the test of the influence of gender even more strict because [Keith] Poole and [Cindy Simon] Rosenthal report that this first dimension explains 80% of the variance in roll-call voting.

District Characteristics

Census data measuring the percentage of the district that is urban, the median household income, and the percentage of the district that is black are generally used to represent constituency characteristics in roll-call vote studies. These factors have an added significance in this analysis because many scholars maintain that differences attributed to gender can be entirely explained by the tendency of women to be elected in districts that are more urban, have a higher percentage of African Americans, and have a lower median household income. Additional variables measuring the percentage of the district that voted for President Clinton and Ross Perot in the 1992 election are also included.

Analysis and Discussion

. . . [G]ender exerts a substantial influence, though secondary to ideology, on legislators' votes on women's issues as a whole, and an even more important effect on votes concerning reproductive issues. For example, . . . a female representative is approximately 8% more likely to vote in support of a women's issue than a male representative. The comparable figure for reproductive issues is 11%. . . . [G]ender plays a much more significant role in the voting of Republican women. Knowing that a representative is a Republican woman increases the probability of voting for the set of women's issues by 23%, while the probability of voting for the subset of reproductive issues is increased by 29%. The importance of Republican women is attributable to the association of many women's issues with liberal voting and the Democratic party. Thus, while Democratic women are voting for these issues more often than men, Democratic men are also voting for them in large numbers. This pattern does not hold true for Republicans. Republican women are defecting from their party's standard, conservative position to vote for these women's issues.

The findings . . . also refute the assertion that differences attributed to gender can be entirely explained by the tendency of districts that elect women to be more urban, non-Southern, have a higher percentage of African Americans, and have a lower median household income. Among the district factors, representation of a Southern district borders on [statistical] significance in the expected direction. Only median household income is a significant predictor of women's issue voting and its impact is in the opposite direction. Districts with higher median household income are more supportive of women's issues. This finding may be explained by the fact that women's issues often encompass social issues, such as abortion, that cut across traditional class-based partisan cleavages.

An analysis of voting on each individual women's issue provides a more comprehensive picture of the influence of gender on the different types of women's issues and the relative importance of other personal, district, and partisan characteristics. . . .

The . . . analyses demonstrate that the significance of gender in voting on women's issues is largely derived from its impact on votes that concern women's health and reproductive issues including FACE, the Hyde Amendment (which places restrictions on access to abortion), the Family Planning Amendments, and the NIH Revitalization Act (which includes provisions of the Women's Health Equity Act). Gender also has a significant and positive effect on voting for the Omnibus Crime Bill, which contains the Violence Against Women Act and other provisions relating to domestic violence and sexual offenses.

Yet, the impact of . . . gender . . . was overwhelmed by ideological, partisan, and district factors on votes dealing with education and family issues such as the Elementary and Secondary Education Reauthorization Act, the Family and Medical Leave Act, and the School to Work Opportunities Act. . . . Interestingly, when the individual votes are subject to . . . analysis, the party variable indicating Democratic men . . . becomes negative and significant at the .01 level for all the votes except the Crime Bill and the National Service Program. This finding indicates that once the ideological component is removed from the party label, the Democratic men are less likely to vote for women's issue bills than Republicans or Democratic women. Thus, the model is picking up Democratic defectors and may be proxying for more traditional constituent concerns.

The significance of gender is magnified when one considers that the bills on which gender has its most significant impact, reproductive issues, constitute the women's issue legislation that is most salient to political activists. Highly contested bills relating to abortion and family planning continuously come to the floor for a vote in every legislative session. Pro-choice and pro-life groups actively monitor representatives' voting

TABLE 34.1
Probability That a Republican Legislator with a Given Gender, Ideology, and Constituency Will Vote for a Women's Issue Bill

Women's Issue Bills	Moderately Conservative		Conservative	
	Male	Female	Male	Female
FACE*	24%	71%	4%	22%
Against Hyde Amendment	9%	47%	2%	12%
Family Planning	44%	91%	7%	46%
NIH Revitalization**	50%	89%	10%	47%
Crime Bill	27%	48%	11%	23%

* Freedom of Access to Clinic Entrances Act
** National Institutes of Health Revitalization Act

records and distribute voter's guides during election campaigns. Thus, the prudent legislator who is concerned with "traceability" and "blame avoidance" should avoid taking a controversial stand that can be used by an opponent in the next campaign. This is particularly true of Republican women who are defecting from their party's traditional, conservative position to vote in favor of the women's issue bills.

Beyond the 103rd Congress: Generalizing from the Model

The . . . models indicate that gender had its most significant impact on the voting of Republican women. Given the pivotal role of these legislators, the Republican takeover of Congress in 1994 makes the position of Republican women even more significant in determining outcomes on women's issue voting. Yet the newly elected Republican women of the 104th Congress were ideologically more conservative than were the Republican congresswomen of the 103rd Congress. To determine how likely it is that a representative of a given ideology and gender will vote in favor of a women's issue bill, I used the model to predict probable votes on the five bills on which gender had a significant impact. The results in Table 34.1 indicate that moderately conservative Republican women are far more likely to vote in favor of the women's issue bills than are moderately conservative Republican men. Thus, moderately conservative Republican women are 47% more likely to vote for FACE, 38% more likely to vote against the Hyde Amendment, 47% more likely to vote for the Family Planning Amendments Act, 39% more likely to vote for the NIH Revitalization Act, and 21% more likely to vote for the Crime Bill than are their moderately conservative male counterparts. Similarly, the models predict that even highly conservative Republican women will be more likely to vote for the five women's issue bills than will highly conservative Republican men. However, the probability that they will vote for these bills approaches 50% in only two cases. Thus, the influence of gender on women's issue voting may be overwhelmed by ideology if the overall ideological makeup of Congress continues to diverge.

Conclusion

The findings of this study clearly indicate that while ideology is the strongest predictor of voting on women's issues, congresswomen are more likely to vote for women's issue bills than are their male colleagues even when one controls for ideological, partisan, and district factors. . . . [T]he more directly an issue affects women, such as votes concerning abortion and other reproductive issues, women's health concerns, and the protection of women against violent crime, the more likely it is that gender will play a role in determining a representative's vote. Gender plays a most significant role in the voting of Republican representatives. While many women's issues are supported by all Democrats, Republican women are defecting from their party's traditional position to vote in favor of these issues. The presence of these Republican women could determine the future of legislation on reproduction and other gender-related issues. The calculation of predicted probabilities for Republican women of a given ideology indicates that both moderately conservative and highly conservative women are more likely to vote for women's issues than are male colleagues with the same ideology. However, the impact of gender may be reduced if more highly conservative women are elected to Congress. In the final analysis, the results of the current study indicate that given two candidates of equivalent ideology, the Republican primary voter who subscribes to a more liberal position on women's issues may be better served by choosing the female candidate.

TOWARD CRITICAL THINKING

1. Michele L. Swers finds considerable differences between men and women legislators on what she terms "women's issues." Can you think of other areas where there might also be differences?

2. Swers notes that increasing numbers of conservative women in Congress might "pull" moderate Republican women to the right—away from traditionally "female" patterns of voting. Do you see any evidence that this has happened since the period she studied?

READING 35

Congressional Enactments of Race-Gender: Toward a Theory of Raced-Gendered Institutions

(2003)

Mary Hawkesworth

Quantitative work such as that conducted by Michele L. Swers (Reading 34) was based on an analysis of roll-call voting on women's issues in the U.S. House of Representatives. Her work is similar to that of scholars who examined women's voting patterns in various state legislatures. Many of the works on state legislators, including those of Sue Thomas (Reading 31), additionally incorporated interviews with women legislators to add richness to their quantitative findings. In this work published in the *American Political Science Review*, Mary Hawkesworth attempts to push the women and politics field, as well as political science, in general, to adopt a more comprehensive way to examine the complicated issues of gender and race. More specifically, she cautions that the complex intersection of race and gender produces unique pressures on African American women legislators not experienced by others. These pressures, she argues, cannot be appreciated from reliance on conventional forms of political science analysis, which often neglect issues of marginalization.

An examination of simple voting patterns of women in Congress, she argues, would fail to expose what she views as the pervasive discrimination that African Americans experience in the system, whether or not they appear to outsiders to have clout within the institution.

Hawkesworth uses interview data compiled by the Center for American Women in Politics to unearth the hardships that women of color have experienced in a variety of ways as they have attempted to represent the unrepresented and underrepresented. Here, she uses welfare reform efforts in the 103rd and 104th Congresses to show how the action of African American women legislators flies in the face of conventional political science wisdom. This race-gendering acts to exclude women's voices while subjecting them to overt discrimination and insensitivity.

In their path-breaking work, A *Portrait of Marginality*, Marianne Githens and Jewel Prestage . . . sought to illuminate . . . the pervasive and persistent underrepresentation of women of color in elective offices. In 1977, . . . women of color held 3% of the elected offices in the United States and five seats in the U.S. Congress. A quarter century later, women of color hold 3.7% of the seats in the U.S. Congress, 3.6% of the seats in state legislatures, and 3.09% of the mayoral and council offices at the municipal level. In addition to underrepresentation, studies of elected women of color consistently document forms of marginalization including stereotyping complemented by a policy of invisibility, exclusion of women of color from leadership positions within legislatures, and lack of institutional responsiveness to the policies women of color champion.

[Politital scientists] [David] Hedge, [James] Button, and [Mary] Spear found in 1996 that black women are more likely to experience discrimination within state legislatures than are their male counterparts: 76% of the African American women legislators reported encountering discrimination, compared to 60% of African American male legislators. In a recent study of African American women state legislators, [Politital scientist Wendy] Smooth has demonstrated that experiences of marginalization are not mitigated by seniority or leadership positions. On the contrary, the longer black women have served in office and the more powerful the positions they hold within legislative institutions, the stronger are their feelings of exclusion. . . .

[* * *]

When women legislators of color report persistent marginalization within legislative institutions despite years of seniority and impressive legislative accomplishments, they offer political scientists a clue that there is more going on in legislative institutions than has yet been captured in the literature. This article explores the experiences of marginalization reported by congresswomen of color in the 103rd and 104th Congresses in an effort to make visible power relations that have profound effects, constructing raced and gendered hierarchies that structure interactions among members as well as institutional practices, while also shaping public policies. . . .

[* * *]

From Race and Sex to Racing-Gendering

Political scientists have tended to treat race and sex as biological or physical characteristics rather than as political constructs. According to this "primordial view," race and sex precede politics. As part of the "natural" or "given" aspects of human existence, race and sex are apolitical, unless intentionally mobilized for political purposes. The effects of race or sex upon politics, then, are matters for empirical investigation but there is no reason to believe that politics plays any role in shaping the physical characteristics of individuals or the demographic characteristics of populations.

Within the past few decades, critical race theorists and feminist theorists have challenged the primordial view of race and sex, calling attention to processes of racialization and gendering through which relations of power and forms of inequality are constructed, shaping the identities of individuals. Through detailed studies of laws, norms, and organizational practices that enforced racial segregation and separate spheres for men and women, scholars have excavated the political processes through which hierarchies of difference have been produced and maintained. . . .

Developing a "theory of gendered institutions," feminist scholars have begun to map the manifold ways in which gender power and disadvantage are created and maintained not only through law but also through institutional processes, practices, images, ideologies, and distributional mechanisms. . . .

Feminist scholars of color have coined the term, *intersectionality*, to capture the intricate interplay of social forces that produce particular women and men as members of particular races, classes, ethnicities and nationalities. . . .

The term, *racing-gendering*, attempts to foreground the intricate interactions of racialization and gendering in the political production of distinctive groups of men and women. . . . The processes that produce a white male, for example, will differ from, while being fully implicated in, the processes that produce a black man, a Latino, a Native American man, a white woman, a black woman, a Latina, an Asian American woman, or a Native American woman. . . .

[* * *]

Racing-gendering can also involve certain "Catch 22s:" Women of color are simultaneously pressured to assimilate to the dominant norms of the institution and denied the possibility of assimilation. . . . Whether deployed intentionally or unwittingly, racing-gendering practices produce relations of power that alter the conditions of work and the conditions of life for women of color in subtle and not so subtle ways. They ensure that the playing field is not equal.

In addition to a variety of direct effects, racing-gendering practices also produce unintended consequences: anger and resistance. In [Aida] Hurtado's words, "To be a woman of color is to live with fury." In response to racing-gendering, women of color mobilize anger for purposes of social change. . . . In exploring the dynamics of racing-gendering in the U.S. Congress, it is important to consider that the identities of congresswomen of color may be constituted not only through the racing-gendering practices that silence, marginalize, and constrain but also through resistance and the political mobilization of anger that racing-gendering engenders. Indeed, I argue that the anger and resistance engendered by congresswomen of color's experiences of racing-gendering in the halls of Congress help explain certain of their policy preferences and the intensity with which they pursue legislation that they know to be doomed.

[* * *]

Racing-Gendering Enactments in Congress

[* * *]

. . . [Evelynn] Hammonds has suggested that for African American women, intersectionality is often manifested in invisibility, otherness, and stigma produced and reproduced on black women's bodies. Accounts black congresswomen provide about their daily experiences in Congress corroborate Hammonds's view. Consider, for example, the report of Congresswoman Cynthia McKinney [D–GA] that she routinely encounters difficulty getting into the House of Representatives. Security guards, it seems, "just don't think about people of color as members of Congress."

While routine demands for proof of her congressional membership credentials may seem a small matter, it is the kind of daily nuisance that marks a black congresswoman as "other," as a perpetual outsider.

[* * *]

Explanatory Possibilities of a Theory of Racing-Gendering

. . . To support . . . the claim that racing-gendering is distinctive from partisan maneuvers, I want to . . . compare instances of racing-gendering in the Democratically controlled 103rd Congress with those in the Republican-controlled 104th Congress in one policy area, welfare reform. . . .

[* * *]

. . . I will argue that the theory of racing-gendering provides a better explanation of the motivations and intensity of involvement of congresswomen of color in welfare reform legislation than other accounts of congressional behavior. According to studies of constituency influence in Congress, welfare recipients are not a constituency likely to receive strong representation in the halls of Congress. . . . Why then did congresswomen of color devote such time and energy to the representation of an unorganized majority-white underclass?

According to the view of legislators as rational optimizers, it would have been rational for congresswomen of color to "abdicate," i.e., to refrain from investing substantial time, energy, and legislative capital in welfare reform legislation. For the most part they lacked positions on key subcommittees, committees, and task forces shaping the legislation. Drafting alternative legislation involved high information costs. Their intensive efforts behind the scenes and on the floor involved exceptionally high transaction costs. In the 103rd Congress, their advocacy of an alternative approach to welfare reform pitted them against the president and the leadership of the Democratic majority in the House. In the 104th Congress, with the exception of Republican Ileana Ros-Lehtinen[R-FL], the congresswomen of color were members of the minority party. Working against the Republican majority and in opposition to the wishes of the Democratic president for a cause they knew was doomed makes little sense in terms of rational actor accounts of Congress. For those who construe legislators as "rational calculators of advantage" or "strategic politicians," congresswomen of color's opposition to the welfare reform legislation must be characterized as either too risky, providing insufficient benefits given the costs, or irrational. . . .

[* * *]

A Case Study of Welfare Reform

In the 103rd Congress when welfare reform was placed on the political agenda by President Bill Clinton and by the Republican minority, congresswomen of color were fully supportive of the prospect of reforming the welfare system. The reforms they sought, however, placed them at odds with dominant forces in the Democratic and Republican parties. The congresswomen of color sought a welfare reform that would eliminate poverty. Thus, they sought legislation that would address the structural causes of poverty, such as low wages and unemployment. They also sought strategies to address the needs of welfare recipients, such as lack of training, lack of transportation, and lack of child care, which constituted major barriers to workforce participation.

In 1993 President Clinton appointed a multiagency task force to hold hearings and develop a welfare reform strategy for the White House. Congresswomen of color tried to work within the task force and from outside the task force to influence the proposed welfare legislation. Representative Patsy Mink [D–HI] served on the Democratic task force and worked tirelessly to represent the interests of "poor women who have no representation in Congress . . . and who are left out in much of this debate." By her own account, she was largely unsuccessful. . . .

[* * *]

Mink's experience stands in marked contrast to [claims] that among policy insiders, participation in shaping policy is largely a matter of self-selection. . . . As a member of the President's task force, Mink was an insider. And although she supplemented her staff resources with research provided by the Institute for Women's Policy Research, the NOW Legal Defense Fund, the National Women's Law Center, MANA (a national LATINA organization), Wider Opportunities for Women, and the Coalition of Presidents (a coalition of presidents of 100 women's organizations), she was not able move the draft legislation in a more progressive direction.

Congresswomen of color who tried to influence the Democratic task force from the outside reported similar frustration. In the words of Representative Barbara Rose Collins [D-MI], "I felt very ineffective. I had my own ideas about welfare reform and nobody was interested in listening to what I had to say." . . .

Central to the concerns of congresswomen of color was the circulation of racialized stereotypes about welfare recipients, particularly the construction of welfare recipients as women of color—too lazy to work—who sought to cheat the system. To counteract the "stereotypes that were alive and well," congresswomen of color tried to inject social science research into the debate [by co-sponsoring] a conference on Women and Welfare Reform. . . . The elements of progressive welfare reform outlined at this conference became the basis for the alternative welfare reform legislation introduced by Patsy Mink and supported by all the congresswomen of color. . . . The congresswomen of color supported enhanced entitlements to eradicate poverty, but their policy recommendations remained far more progressive than the proposals endorsed by the Democratic task force, which were announced by President Clinton in June 1994. Introduced immediately prior to Congress' summer recess and the fall congressional elections, the Clinton proposal to "end welfare as we know it" died with the 103rd Congress.

The experiences of the Democratic women of color in the 103rd Congress as the Democratic majority crafted welfare legislation exemplify marginalization. Many reported that they could not gain access to key white male decision makers and, as such, could not influence the shape of the legislation. Despite repeated efforts to shift the terms of debate away from erroneous perceptions of welfare cheats and cycles of dependency, neither the social science knowledge they circulated nor the personal experiences they related were taken as authoritative or compelling. Even Representative Patsy Mink's substitute proposal, which garnered 90 Democrats' votes in the House, was dismissed rather than selectively incorporated into the president's plan.

Welfare Reform in the 104th Congress

In contrast to the concern with structural causes of poverty, which lay at the heart of the approach to welfare reform taken by congresswomen of color, the Republican proposals for welfare reform framed poverty as a matter of personal responsibility, particularly in relation to marriage and responsible fatherhood and motherhood. . . . In the words of Dick Armey [R–TX], "We need to understand . . . that it is illegitimacy and child-birth, fatherless children, that is so much at the heart of the distress that seems to be unending and growing worse and larger each year. So we insist that we must have a new approach that brings down illegitimacy, and quite rightly so many of us say, yes, bring down illegitimacy, but not through increased abortions."

Both H.R.4, The Personal Reponsibility Act, which was passed by the 104th Congress and vetoed by President Clinton, and H.R. 3734, which was enacted as The Personal Responsibility and Work Opportunity Reconciliation Act of 1996, denied welfare benefits to unwed teenaged mothers, allowed states to impose a benefits cap to encourage limits on recipients' family size, and required that paternity be established as a condition of welfare eligibility. The Republican-sponsored welfare reform also eliminated the federal entitlement program, Aid to Families with Dependent Children (AFDC), and replaced it with a block grant for Temporary Assistance for Needy Families, which required work as a condition for receipt of benefits and set a lifetime limit of five years for welfare eligibility. . . .

Congresswomen of color perceived the attack on single mothers at the heart of welfare reform proposals as an attack on the black family. . . . To counter Republican claims about the causes of poverty, congresswomen of color turned to social science. . . .

[* * *]

Despite Representative Mink's attempt to invoke the authority of the social science community and the U.S. Census Bureau to shift the terms of the welfare debate, the empirical evidence did nothing to dispel the correlation mistaken for causation at the heart of [welfare reform].

Congresswomen of color were deeply concerned that the Republican focus on out-of-wedlock births, unwed mothers, and single-women heads-of-household was a thinly veiled attack upon poor women of color. During a number of increasingly vitriolic floor debates the legitimacy of their concern became apparent as even the pretense of using race-neutral language to characterize the poor disappeared and Republican legislators denounced illegitimacy in the black community. For example, in his floor speech Representative [Randy] Cunningham [R–CA] linked illegitimacy in the black community not only with welfare, but with crime and drug addiction. Representatives Patsy Mink [D–HI], Sheila Jackson Lee [D–TX], Maxine Waters [D–CA], Eva Clayton [D–NC], and Nydia Velazquez [D–NY] repeatedly emphasized in floor debate that the majority of welfare recipients were white, but their factual claims failed to dispel racialized welfare myths. . . .

As a white women and the only member of Congress to have once been a welfare recipient, Representative Lynn Woolsey [D–CA] also took to the House floor to tell her colleagues that most welfare recipients were white. . . . The racialization of the poor had conflated welfare recipient and black women so powerfully in the minds of some members of the House that they refused to accept that the typical welfare recipient is a white woman who resorts to welfare for a short time after a divorce in order to support her kids while she gets back on her feet. Facts that did not conform to raced-gendered stereotypes about welfare recipients were simply dismissed. . . .

. . . In contrast to this image of perpetual dependency, Patsy Mink repeatedly emphasized that the majority of welfare recipients resort to welfare when beset by crises such as illness, unemployment, domestic violence, and divorce and remain on welfare for less than a year; indeed 80% of recipients rely on welfare for less than 2 years. Representative Lucille Roybal-Allard [D–CA] emphasized domestic violence as the reason that many women resort to welfare for short periods of time. . . . Reflecting upon these frustrating floor debates, Representative Eva Clayton [D–NC] said, "I was trying to speak out for reason. I'm not sure I succeeded in that. . . . I would like to think that my role was to present common sense. Again I don't think I succeeded in that."

In addition to empirical arguments based upon social science research, congresswomen of color raised constitutional arguments about the permissibility of discriminating against legal immigrants, punishing children for actions of their parents, and violating the rights of poor women to privacy in reproductive decision making. . . . Representative Sheila Jackson Lee asserted unequivocally on the basis of her own interactions with welfare recipients and on the basis of social science evidence that "women do not get pregnant to get welfare." . . .

[* * *]

Providing information about benefit levels in their states, congresswomen of color asked their colleagues to try to imagine raising a child on $184/month, the prevailing rate for a mother with one child in Texas in 1995. . . .

Congresswomen of color were among the most outspoken opponents of welfare reform in congressional debates. Like her Democratic counterparts in the House, Senator Carol Moseley Braun [D–IL], the only woman of color in the Senate, was an outspoken critic of the welfare reform bills in the Senate. She too tried to persuade her fellow senators that the legislation under consideration would not address the underlying problem of welfare: poverty. . . .

[* * *]

In the House and in the Senate, women of color worked arduously to air an alternative vision of welfare recipients and to advance an alternative version of welfare reform. According to one congressional staffer, "They spoke disproportionate to their seniority" on welfare reform. Yet their words seemed to have no effect. . . . [Philosopher] Gayatri Spivak has suggested that the refusal of the dominant to hear the voices of and for the oppressed is a perennial tactic in technologies of race-gender. It is a form of racing-gendering that permeated welfare reform debates in the 103rd and the

104th Congresses, ensnaring congresswomen of color in a prolonged and painful *pendejo* game.

As the majority in the 104th Congress insisted upon circulating misrepresentations of the poor in the context of welfare reform, congresswomen of color felt themselves increasingly marginalized. . . .

[* * *]

The perception of hostility toward African Americans was heightened by several episodes involving congresswomen of color. In the midst of her floor speech addressing H.R. 4, The Personal Responsibility Act, congressional veteran Cardiss Collins [D–IL] was interrupted by laughter from the Republican side of the aisle. Having characterized the Act as a "callous, cold-hearted, and mean-spirited attack on this country's children" that "punishes Americans for being poor" at the same time Congress was considering tax cuts for the rich, Representative Collins was dismayed by the laughter and all that it betokened. Interrupting her prepared comments, she addressed her colleagues directly.

> I see some of the Members on the other side of the aisle laughing. I ask this question: How many of them have ever been hungry. How many of them have ever known what it was not to have a meal? How many of them have known what it was not to have decent shoes, decent clothing, a nice place to live. . . . They do not know about poverty. So I challenge them to come to the Seventh Congressional District of Illinois, my district, and walk in the path of these children that they are cutting off from welfare. Walk in the path of the truly needy people who live by welfare because they have no other means by which to live.

At this point, Representative Scott McInnis [R–CO], who was presiding over the floor debate, recognized himself on a point of personal privilege. He rebuked Representative Collins for noting the laughter. But in doing so, he made a telling error. "Mr. Speaker, as to the gentlewoman's comments from the *State of Florida* [emphasis added], I take strong exception to her comments that there is laughter on this side of the aisle. While we may disagree with her point, her comments are taken with respect. I rather suspect that her comment about laughter was probably written into her speech." In rising to challenge Representative Collins's perceptions of floor activity, impugn her credibility, and accuse her of intentional deceit, even as he insisted that she was being respectfully heard, Representative McInnis demonstrated just how little attention he had been paying to her words: He confused 22-year congressional veteran Cardiss Collins from Illinois with Florida Congresswoman Carrie Meek, who was just beginning her second term. That the two congresswomen look nothing alike raises interesting questions about how seriously congresswomen of color are taken. That the very words she was being chastised for uttering included a reference to her home district in Illinois only intensifies the insult to Representative Collins. Feeling no obligation to know who she was or to hear what she was saying, Representative McInnis nonetheless felt at liberty to instruct her about what she may or may not say on the House floor.

[* * *]

On several occasions, events outside of the halls of Congress spilled over onto floor debates. Representative Cynthia McKinney reported a painful incident that she considered emblematic of the racing-gendering practices of her colleagues in the 104th Congress.

> I was trying to be bipartisan in my approach, so I was working with Nancy Johnson [R–CT] on a teenage pregnancy bill. Jim Greenwood [R–PA] had invited us to go on his cable television show, so we could talk about what we were doing, which was good I thought. So [during the show] he and Nancy have this entire conversation about teenage pregnancy and the legislation, and he doesn't direct a single question to me until he decides that he wants to ask "why is it that women have babies so they can get extra money?" That was the question that was directed at me.

The racing-gendering in this episode manifests the same epistemic configuration witnessed in floor debates. A white congressman refuses to accredit a congresswoman of color as an authoritative source of knowledge, even about the legislation she had written. A white congresswomen is complicit in this discrediting by failing to turn some of the questions over to Representative McKinney as a means of inviting her into the conversation. Then, having discounted her as a source of sociological and legislative knowledge, Representative Greenwood turns to a congresswoman of color for a corroboration of racist stereotypes. She is positioned as the voice of the scheming welfare recipient who is trying to cheat the system.

[* * *]

Representative Maxine Waters [D–CA] also took exception to the way that certain members of Congress were constructing welfare recipients during their television appearances, suggesting that their gross misrepresentation of welfare recipients was nothing short of irresponsible:

> Mr. Speaker, this morning a Republican member of this body, the gentleman from Florida, Clay Shaw, was shown on national TV making a most irresponsible and outrageous statement disparaging welfare mothers by saying, and I quote: "You wouldn't leave your cat with them for the weekend." . . .

Despite Representative Waters's call for an apology, none was forthcoming. Instead, the distorted racialized stereotypes of welfare recipients continued to circulate in discussions of welfare reform on the floor and in committees of the House and Senate until the Congress passed The Personal Responsibility and Work Opportunity Reconciliation Act in August 1996. Representative Waters, like many of the congresswomen of color, transformed her anger at the calumnies against the poor into efforts to mobilize public opposition to welfare reform.

Mobilization of anger is a tactic that several congresswomen of color reported deploying in response to the welfare reform legislation. Representative Corrine Brown [D–FL], for example, said that she felt it was her responsibility "to educate my constituents as to what was going on so they could be enraged and call their senators. . . . In August I conducted 50 town meetings [to which] anybody could come and listen." In response to the proposal to drastically cut the school lunch program, Representative Eva Clayton organized Forums called 'Feed the Folks' down in our district, and we must have received about 1300 different petitions to save the school lunch program."

[* * *]

In their efforts to legislate against the grain, congresswomen of color deployed the full repertoire of strategies available to legislators. In the 103rd Congress, they used their power within the Democratic Party to try to shape the content of President Clinton's welfare reform proposal. They cochaired scholarly conferences to try to shape public perceptions of the poor, as well as the content of welfare legislation. They used their power in committees to try to amend Republican sponsored legislation in the 104th Congress. They drafted one of two Democratic alternative bills to H.R. 4 considered in the House, as well as one of the Democratic alternative bills considered in the Senate during the first session of the 104th Congress. They secured a special order to allow a floor debate of the welfare legislation in the House of Representatives. They used their intellectual and rhetorical power in floor debates to try to alter congressional understandings of poverty. They scheduled press conferences featuring welfare recipients to try to get alternative images of the poor before the Congress and the public. They wrote "Dear Colleague" letters and circulated them with comprehensive social scientific studies in an effort to break the hold of pernicious stereotypes of the poor. They held town meetings across their constituencies to mobilize voters against the pending legislation. Even in the final hours they joined with a bipartisan group of 26 women members from both houses in sending a letter to the Conference Committee to try to shape the compromise bill that would eventually become law. But ultimately they failed to convince their colleagues to move beyond what they perceived to be racist stereotypes and policies that punished the poor. In the end, they used the power of their votes in Congress to oppose both versions of the welfare reform legislation. All 15 congresswomen of color—14 Democrats and one Republican—voted against The Personal Responsibility Act and The Personal Responsibility and Work Opportunity Reconciliation Act. Their opposition was intense and consistent across two Congresses, but there is no indication that in airing their minority view, they accorded legitimacy to the process or to the bill that resulted from it. On the contrary, their stories of marginalization and thwarted effort, of the silencing of reason and evidence, and of the pervasive racing-gendering of welfare recipients and congresswomen of color provide a resounding indictment of this form of majority rule.

Conclusion

[* * *]

Over a four-year period that spanned two dramatically different Congresses, the congresswomen of color came to task force and committee meetings, as well as floor debates, armed with social science studies, Census Bureau data, and Health and Human Services Department statistics to counter the emotional diatribes of some of their male Democratic and Republican counterparts. In their tactics and their demeanor, congresswomen of color embodied the norm of rational, comprehensive decision makers, while many men in Congress gloried in emotional, racially charged displays. The nature of the racing-gendering to which congresswomen of color were subjected—being ignored by their colleagues, experiencing others' willed refusal to hear their views, having their epistemic authority challenged, having their amendments blocked in committee and on the floor, having their positions misrepresented in floor debates, being chastised on the floor of the House, being invited to participate in TV debate only to be systematically ignored, being constructed as the voice of pernicious stereotypes of welfare recipients—pushed them from reason to anger. The emotion alleged to be their "natural" gendered disposition was instead the effect of racing-gendering in the institution of Congress. In this sense, racing-gendering in the Congress has palpable effects on individual congresswomen of color as well as upon public policies.

[* * *]

TOWARD CRITICAL THINKING

1. Does the frustration felt by African American women lawmakers over the portrayal of welfare mothers have analogies to other issue areas? What do the experiences of these African American women tell us about the intersectionality of race and gender as well as the nature of legislative politics? Is it still an old (white) boy's game?

2. Mary Hawkesworth's approach tells us a lot about life inside the House of Representatives. What other types of discrimination do you think women members might experience and how does this affect their work?

WRAPPING UP

1. Quantitative work of Sue Thomas (Reading 31) and Michele L. Swers (Reading 34) offer all sorts of reasons to expect women legislators, as well as women political leaders, to represent their constituents differently from men. Mary Hawkesworth's qualitative work (Reading 35) echoes their findings, but by focusing on the experiences of women of color. Which approach do you believe will be most fruitful in advancing the study of women legislators or their impact on legislative bodies? Why?

2. House Democratic Leader Nancy Pelosi recently proposed a Congressional Bill of Rights for the minority party that would insure that those in the political minority have a greater say in the drafting of bills, as well as the timing at which they come to the floor. Is this the kind of action that you might expect more from a woman leader in a legislative body than from a man? Why?

READING 36

Women as Policymakers: The Case of Trial Judges

(1981)

John Gruhl, Cassia Spohn, and Susan Welch

Through the 1980s, there simply weren't enough women judges on any American courts to allow for any kind of systematic quantitative analysis of their decision-making behavior. Women first began to enter the legal profession in record numbers in the early 1970s. Many of these women had graduated from college several years before entering law school, and soon, some of these women were appointed or even elected to local trial courts in states throughout America providing, finally, the opportunity for study.

When this article originally was published in the *American Journal of Political Science*, few research projects had yet to be conducted about the impact that women in elected positions had on policy making. Those studies that had been conducted, however, found that women tended to be slightly more liberal on several issues. Thus, these authors approach the study of women judges with the expectation that women judges might be more liberal than their male counterparts. Most studies of judicial behaviors to that time had focused on appellate court judges and had looked at a variety of possible reasons judges voted as they did, such as political party, family background, or other personal characteristics. None, however, had included gender. This study was among the first to try to determine if women judges approached sentencing defendants differently than did their brethren. It also looked at the behavior of local trial court judges.

To determine if there were any meaningful differences in the policy outcomes of decisions made by women and men judges, the authors sampled the sentences handed down in felony cases by male judges from 1971 to 1979 in a major metropolitan city in the Northeast and compared them to all of the felony cases decided by female judges. They include cases settled by a guilty plea, as well as those where verdicts were rendered by a judge or jury. When defendants were convicted the authors also record if the defendants were sent to prison, and if so, for how long.

Although studies of female policymakers have been increasing rapidly, almost no systematic work has been done to assess the degree, if any, to which female decision-making differs from that of males once females achieve policymaking positions. . . . We focus on the convicting and sentencing behavior of male and female trial judges to see if there are systematic differences in their treatment of defendants generally and in their treatment of women defendants specifically. . . .

[* * *]

. . . [It] is difficult to draw conclusions about whether women judges would make different decisions than men. It is possible that contrasts in the pre-officeholding attitudes of the judges might succumb to the powerful influences of socialization to the legal profession and to the judicial role. It is also possible that gender contrasts might be mitigated by the further influences of the courtroom "workgroups," in which judges must interact with prosecutors and defense attorneys. On the other hand, it may also be that these attitudinal differences between men and women might carry over and affect judges' decision-making behavior, especially when issues closely related to sex roles are concerned.

[* * *]

Hypotheses

Because studies have shown that women are slightly more liberal than men on a variety of issues, including those related to crime control, we expected to find that women judges would be slightly more lenient than men judges. Although there may not necessarily be a link between being liberal and being lenient, there might be such a relationship. . . . [J]udges who are liberal presumably are more receptive to the interests of lower-class groups, which comprise the bulk of criminal defendants, and consequently might be more lenient in convicting and sentencing. Accordingly, and in the absence of more conclusive studies, we hypothesized that women judges would be less likely to convict defendants, less likely to incarcerate defendants when they did convict them, and less likely to incarcerate defendants for a long time when they did incarcerate them. We expected to find exceptions to this for some types of crimes, such as rape. However, because other studies have suggested that men judges have protective or paternalistic attitudes toward female defendants, we also hypothesized that female defendants would be treated more leniently by men judges than by women judges. . . .

[* * *]

Findings

We expected female judges to be more lenient than male judges in determining guilt and assigning sentences. Examination of the decisions handed down in over 30,000 felony cases, however, reveals that our hypothesis is not confirmed. Though there are some differences in the convicting and sentencing behavior of male and female judges, these differences are not large and are not always in the predicted direction.

TABLE 36.1

Convicting and Sentencing Behavior of Male and Female Judges

	% Convicted		% Sentenced to Prison		Mean Sentence Given	
	Male Judges	Female Judges	Male Judges	Female Judges	Male Judges	Female Judges
Not Controlling for Type of Crime	55	50**	23	27**	31.26	32.34**
Controlling for Type of Crime	55	51**	23	25**	31.22	31.68
By Type of Crime						
Murder	57	56	95	96	74.97	65.31**
Manslaughter	82	86	65	66	43.10	39.56*
Rape	38	45	58	48*	45.73	41.51
Robbery	51	37**	48	50	38.36	40.60**
Assault	54	49**	16	20*	28.67	29.07
Minor Assault	55	57	3	8**	22.27	23.89
Burglary	44	45	11	16**	26.44	28.68**
Auto Theft	65	79*	4	1	23.46	23.51
Embezzlement	34	36	7	9	25.34	26.12
Stolen Property	83	80	8	9	25.23	25.28
Forgery	68	57	6	22**	26.46	30.39**
Sex Offenses	65	48*	36	38	37.94	36.65
Drug Possession	59	57	9	12*	26.17	25.92
Driving while Intoxicated	42	42	<1	0	22.57	25.79**

* $p < .05$.
** $p < .01$.

. . . Only the difference in percent of defendants convicted at bench trials . . . follows the predicted pattern: female judges are less likely than male judges to find defendants guilty. On the other hand, they are more likely than male judges to sentence convicted defendants to prison, and they tend to give slightly stiffer sentences than their male counterparts.

These differences, of course, may be due to differences in the types of cases decided by judges of each sex. One group of judges, for example, may have decided more serious cases than the other group. The data presented Table 36.1, however, indicate that the differences cannot be totally explained away in this manner. After controlling for type of crime, the difference in mean sentence given by male and female judges nearly disappears, but statistically significant differences in both percent convicted and percent incarcerated remain. Though the differences are not large, female judges are less likely than male judges to convict defendants, but are more likely than male judges to sentence convicted defendants to prison. Women, then, are slightly more lenient than men at one stage in the process (deciding whether or not to find the defendant guilty), somewhat less lenient than men at a second stage (deciding whether or not to sentence the defendant to prison), and neither more nor less lenient at a third (determining the severity of the defendant's sentence).

We should emphasize, however, that what differences there are are not large. Because of the large sample size, they are statistically significant, but they do not seem substantively significant.

These rather small overall differences may be masking more significant differences between male and female judges on particular crimes. To see if this was the case, we examined the convicting and sentencing behavior of male and female judges for . . . 14 felonies. . . . The results of our analysis are mixed. While the differences between men and women judges do vary by crime, there appear to be no consistent patterns in either the degree or the direction of these differences.

Examination of the differences which are statistically significant, for example, reveals inconsistencies for each of the three dependent variables. Women are less likely than men to convict defendants charged with robbery, assault, or sex offenses other than rape, but are more likely to convict defendants charged with auto theft. Similarly, women are less likely than men to sentence defendants to prison for rape, but are more likely to sentence them to prison for assault, minor assault, burglary, forgery, and possession of drugs. Finally, women are more lenient than men in sentencing defendants convicted of murder or manslaughter, but are less lenient in sentencing those convicted of robbery, burglary, forgery, and driving while intoxicated.

Similar inconsistencies appear when all of the differences, including those which are not statistically significant, are examined. Especially interesting is the pattern for rape. For this crime, female judges are more likely than male judges to convict, but are less likely to sentence to prison or to give a harsh sentence. Thus, even for a crime where we expected to find consistent differences, we found none.

These findings negate our initial hypothesis that female judges would be more lenient than male judges. Careful scrutiny of the behavioral differences between men and women judges for each of the crimes, in fact, leads us to conclude that there are no patterns in the data; we cannot, for instance, even conclude that the differences are consistent for crimes against persons or crimes against property, or for more or less serious crimes. Coupled with the fact that the overall differences between male and female judges are not large, these inconsistencies cast doubt on the substantive significance of the differences. In determining guilt and assigning punishments, male and female judges do behave somewhat differently, but the differences are so idiosyncratic as to be almost meaningless.

Much more consistent and meaningful differences appeared when we tested our second hypothesis. . . . [T]here are clear and unambiguous differences in the behavior of male and female judges toward male and female defendants. The most significant difference between male and female judges is in their treatment of female defendants. Female judges tend to treat male and female defendants more similarly than do male judges. While men and women judges convict female defendants at nearly the same rate, men judges are much less likely to sentence convicted females to prison. Men gave prison terms to only 12 percent of the convicted females, but women gave prison terms to 20 percent. Men judges apparently have paternalistic attitudes toward female defendants. They are almost as willing as women judges to convict female defendants but are much more reluctant to sentence females to prison. Female judges also give female defendants slightly longer prison terms than male judges do, though the differences are not great.

Male defendants are treated about the same by male and female judges. Female judges, for example, are slightly less likely than male judges to find male defendants guilty; they convicted 52 percent of these defendants, compared to 55 percent for male judges. In assigning sentences, on the other hand, women judges are somewhat harsher than men judges; they sentenced 26 percent of the male defendants to prison, compared to 23 percent for the men, and gave fractionally longer sentences to males than did male judges. Unlike the findings for female defendants, then, differences in treatment of male defendants are small, inconsistent, and probably not substantively significant. In their treatment of male defendants, men and women judges are more alike than different.

[* * *]

. . . [T]he presence of women judges has a twofold impact on women's equality—the obvious one of including women in the politically powerful roles of judges and the less obvious one of reducing the favored treatment which women defendants received in the past. This, in turn, may have broader policy implications for corrections institutions—with more women judges, these institutions may have to absorb more women offenders.

Because this is an exploratory, one-city study comparing male and female judicial behavior, we cannot claim that our findings can be generalized to other jurisdictions or that they will hold up over time. But our findings do suggest the importance of examining the behavior of female political elites. As demonstrated here, female political elites may stimulate equality in more than the obvious ways.

TOWARD CRITICAL THINKING

1. The authors conclude that there were few sentencing behavior differences between men and women judges. Why might that be the case? Keep in mind that this study does not control for a host of factors, work that political scientists have yet to undertake for a variety of methodological reasons as well as local court rules that restrict access to jurors.

2. The authors did find that women judges gave women defendants harsher sentences than did men judges. Is this an example of male paternalism, as the authors suggest? What other factors could explain these findings?

READING 37

A Reappraisal of Diversification in the Federal Courts: Gender Effects in the Courts of Appeals

(1994)

Donald R. Songer, Sue Davis, and Susan Haire

The work of John Gruhl, Cassia Spohn, and Susan Welch (Reading 36), as well as other research conducted around the same time, found little difference in male and female judges' actual behaviors. While other work showed that women who came to the bench, particularly the federal bench, had different career patterns than their appointed male counterparts, research continued to reveal little difference in the way that men and women treated defendants in their courtrooms. Still, feminist legal scholars continued to insist that women judges were different in important ways from their male counterparts.

In 1977, President Jimmy Carter pledged to appoint more women and minorities to the federal bench. Only eight women had served as federal judges prior to Carter's election. His plan to add more women soon resulted in the appointment of nine women to the U.S. Courts of Appeals (including future U.S. Supreme Court Justice Ruth Bader Ginsburg) and twenty-nine to the federal district courts—still only a small fraction of those jurists. Later, Presidents Ronald Reagan and George H.W. Bush were to add six additional women to the appellate courts.

In this article, published in the *Journal of Politics*, Donald R. Songer, Sue Davis, and Susan Haire revisit the issue of the voting behavior of women in the judiciary. This work, unlike that of Gruhl, Spohn, and Welch (Reading 36), looks at appointed appellate judges on the U.S. Courts of Appeals, which are collegial courts where three judges usually sit together to hear appeals of decisions from lower federal district courts. Here, they examine the voting patterns of all judges of the U.S. Courts of Appeals from 1981 to 1990 in three issue areas of the law to determine if differences in voting behavior can be attributed to the gender of the judge. They construct separate models, or ways to examine each issue area, to facilitate analysis. The authors are particularly concerned with whether or not women judges appear to speak in the "feminist voice" predicted by feminist legal scholars.

[* * *]

Feminist Legal Theory

. . . Feminist legal scholars argue that women lawyers and judges will bring a different perspective to the law, employ a different set of methods, and seek different results than the (male) legal tradition would seem to mandate. The well-known work of psychologist [Carol] Gilligan provides some empirical support for the claims that feminist legal theory makes. Gilligan discovered differences in the ways that males and females understand themselves and their environment, and the way they resolve moral problems. She found that males tend to define themselves through separation, measure themselves against an abstract ideal of perfection, and equate adulthood with autonomy and individual achievement; they conceive morality in hierarchical terms—a ladder. In contrast, females often define themselves through connection with others and activities of care, and perceive morality in terms of a web.

How might the differences that Gilligan found manifest themselves in judging? . . . [Law professor Suzanna] Sherry also drew on Gilligan's work to identify characteristics of what she referred to as a feminine jurisprudence. A jurisprudence that emphasizes connection (in contrast to autonomy), context (as opposed to fixed rules), and responsibility (in contrast to rights) would be feminine but, she pointed out, not necessarily feminist. Nor would it necessarily be liberal but would "encompass aspects of personality and relationship to the world that have nothing to do with one's political preferences." According to Sherry, Justice Sandra Day O'Connor's decision making manifests a jurisprudence that differs clearly from that of her male colleagues. O'Connor, in Sherry's assessment, has not been as willing as the other conservatives on the Court to permit violations of the right to full membership in the community. Moreover, she has tended to support individual rights only when they implicate membership in the community. O'Connor's decision making also has reflected a view that shaping the values of the community through governmental processes is an important function of community members.

It is important to note that feminist legal theory makes no claim that the differences between men and women judges will emerge simply as liberal or conservative voting patterns across the board. The theory suggests that women judges will be liberal insofar as they will vote to support claimants who allege discrimination that has resulted in exclusion from full participation in the community. In contrast, women judges would be categorized as conservative on the basis of their votes in cases in which individual rights conflict with community interests.

Methodology and Framework

We have formulated three alternative sets of hypotheses based on the predictions of supporters of diversification on the federal bench and social scientists, empirical analyses of voting behavior, and feminist legal theory. First, the initial predictions about women judges led us to hypothesize that they will be more liberal than their male counterparts across the three issue areas that we have included in our analysis: search and seizure, obscenity, and employment discrimination. Women, the early predictions implied, would be more protective of civil liberties because they are likely to have particular empathy for individuals who are disadvantaged (as women themselves have been) in American society.

In contrast, the empirical studies of voting behavior led us to our second hypothesis: female judges will not be more liberal than their male counterparts in any of the three issues areas. Regardless of the extent to which their early socialization differed from that of their male colleagues, their common socialization into the legal subculture and the partisan and contextual pressures from the democratic subculture which cut across gender lines tend to cancel out any gender-based differences.

Feminist legal theory provides the basis for our third set of hypotheses. Women judges will be more conservative in obscenity cases than their male counterparts—explicit sexual materials may be viewed as perpetuating the oppression of women and as damaging to the moral fiber of the community. They will be no more likely than their male counterparts to support the liberal position in search and seizure cases—to support the claim of a criminal defendant would conflict with the interests of the community. Finally, women will be more liberal than men in employment discrimination cases as women tend to emphasize rights that are interdependent, such as full membership in the community. Discrimination may be viewed as a problem of exclusion.

[* * *]

. . . [E]ach of the three models [constructed to test our hypotheses] includes identical measures of region, the appointing president of each judge who participated on the panel, and the gender of each judge. The models also contain variables which attempt to tap the most relevant case characteristics for each of the three areas of law investigated. Since statutes and precedents in these three areas are different, the case characteristics included in the three models are necessarily different. As a result, the models are not identical. Due to this use of partially different models for the three issue areas, some caution is necessary when interpreting the relative impact of gender in the three areas. Unfortunately, there appears to be no way around this dilemma. If case facts were omitted from the models in order to produce identical models for each issue area, the models would be seriously underspecified and any relationships discovered between gender and judicial voting decisions might be spurious.

Results

We examined the impact of gender on judges' behavior separately in each of three categories of cases with controls for case facts as well as region and presidential appointment. . . .

The model does a very good job of predicting the votes of the judges. Overall, the model correctly predicts 86.2% of the judges' votes in the universe of published obscenity decisions that we examined, a reduction in error of 53.2%. Both the presidential appointment variable and region were significant predictors of judges' votes. Additionally, the type of litigant and various case facts proved to be important. However, . . . the gender of the judge appears to have no effect on the likelihood of a liberal vote when other factors are taken into account. . . . Moreover, the addition of gender to the model adds nothing to the predictive power of the model. . . .

[* * *]

[The judge's gender in search and seizure cases] has no discernible effect. . . . Moreover, when the model was re-run without a variable for the gender of the judges, there was no reduction in the predictive accuracy of the model. Thus, it appears that the gender of a judge is unrelated to voting behavior in search and seizure cases.

[The model] of the effects of gender on employment discrimination . . . is successful in predicting 70.9% of the votes and produces a reduction in error of 40.7%. . . .

. . . [I]n sharp contrast to the results in obscenity and search and seizure cases, . . . the gender of the judge is strongly related to the probability of a liberal vote in job discrimination cases.

Having established that judges' gender has a statistically significant impact on their votes, we now ask, . . . what is the magnitude of this effect after the model has controlled for the effects of case facts, litigant characteristics, and presidential appointment? To answer this question, we computed the estimated probability of a liberal vote for male judges and for female judges. . . . When the values of all the other independent variables are set at their mean, the probability that a male judge will cast a liberal vote is 38% while the estimated probability of a liberal vote by a female judge is 75%. Thus, the impact of gender appears to be quite substantial.

Finally, we sought to determine whether the greater propensity of female judges to cast liberal votes was due to greater sympathy for the victims of gender discrimination (as expected by political activists) or whether it reflected a more general orientation toward equal protection. To obtain a rough answer to this question, we conducted two supplemental analyses. First, we re-ran the model for the subset of cases that did not raise any gender discrimination claims (e.g., race discrimination cases). The results suggest that gender-based differences among judges persist even in cases involving allegations of employment discrimination not related to sex. Overall, the model for nongender cases is very similar to that for the larger sample of all employment discrimination cases. The model predicts 71.8% of the votes correctly, with a reduction in error of 36.9%, nearly identical to the results for the full sample of discrimination cases. More importantly, gender of the judge continued to be strongly related to judicial votes, . . . and only slightly smaller in magnitude than the coefficient for gender in the model for all discrimination cases.

As a second test of whether the greater liberalism of female judges was primarily due to sympathy for the victims of gender discrimination . . . both the gender of the judge and type of case (sex discrimination or other types of discrimination) remained statistically significant and of approximately the same magnitude. . . . But the interaction between the two variables is very small and statistically insignificant. This suggests that whether the case involves gender discrimination or some other type of discrimination does not affect the greater propensity of female than male judges to cast a liberal vote.

The results of our analysis of obscenity and search and seizure cases suggest that there are no differences in the voting behavior of male and female judges. In employment discrimination cases, however, our results were quite different. Female judges were more likely than their male colleagues to support the alleged victim of discrimination. In sum, our analysis indicates that the introduction of women judges to the federal appellate bench has had a substantial impact on decision making in employment discrimination cases but no measurable effect on search and seizure and obscenity cases. Clearly, the effect of gender on judicial behavior varies with the context of the decision-making process. This finding does not support the sets of hypotheses derived either from the expectations of the activists or from earlier empirical analyses.

Among the alternative sets of hypotheses, only feminist legal theory recognizes that the behavior of women judges would not be confined to a single liberal-conservative dimension across issue areas. Although the results did not completely support the theoretical expectations associated with feminist jurisprudence, the analysis suggests that women judges will speak in a "different voice" when dealing with claims of discrimination. It is possible that the socialization of women who attend law school and pursue legal careers that culminate in federal judicial appointments subverts tendencies to express concerns for relationships and communities who have been targets of discrimination when their claims raise the interdependent right to full membership in the community.

Alternatively, it is possible that women judges do not bring a distinct perspective to judging. If so, the differences we found in voting patterns between women and men in employment discrimination cases may simply be a result of women judges' identification with other victims of discrimination. Thus, women judges' support for claimants in employment discrimination cases may simply reflect a concern for protecting individual rights in an area of particular salience to them, rather than a concern for connection, context, and responsibility.

The results of our analysis should be interpreted with caution. This study was confined to three narrowly defined issue areas. Moreover, the need to control explicitly for case content led us to develop models that contain different variables associated with the specific policy areas. Nevertheless, the results of this study, and other empirical analyses, represent a starting point for research on women judges. Women judges in significant numbers are so new to the legal system that, although it is now possible to begin to study their decision making, it is not yet within our reach to assess the extent of their impact with certainty. In time, as more women assume positions on the federal courts and as the decisions of women who are currently serving continue to accumulate, further research that reaches firm conclusions will become feasible. Such research must include analysis of voting behavior and judicial reasoning as well as the career patterns and socialization of women judges.

TOWARD CRITICAL THINKING

1. Donald R. Songer, Sue Davis, and Susan Haire suggest that, at least in the area of employment discrimination, women judges, as feminist legal theorists suggest, seem to speak "in a different voice." In what other issue areas might this also be true?

2. Why do you think that women legislators appear to speak more "for women" than their judicial counterparts? Could it be the socialization process that all lawyers experience? What else could account for any differences you perceive?

READING 38

Gender and Judicial Decisions: Do Female Judges Decide Cases Differently than Male Judges?

(2000)

Phyllis Coontz

After Donald R. Songer, Sue Davis, and Susan Haire (Reading 37) suggested that, at least in some areas, women judges might speak in a different voice, political scientists continued to look for the kind of differences that research on women in other areas, including voting and legislating, seemed to imply. In this innovative piece that incorporates aspects of both the John Gruhl, Cassia Spohn, and Susan Welch work (Reading 36) as well as that of Songer, Davis, and Haire (Reading 37), here Phyllis Coontz surveys 366 trial court judges across the state of Pennsylvania. Writing in *Gender Issues,* she presents both male and female judges with two hypothetical cases in which the personal and demographic characteristics of plaintiffs were mixed while the facts were held constant.

While research to this point had continued to show little difference in the voting behavior of male and female judges, some feminist scholars continued to advance their belief that women do bring different perspectives to the law. These views were buttressed by a 5–4 decision of the U.S. Supreme Court involving sexual harassment of students in public schools. Although Justice Sandra Day O'Connor often sides with other members of the Court to rule in favor of states' rights over federal law, she was the deciding vote in this case that made public schools liable for student-on-student sexual harassment. The dissenters argued that the outcome would "teach little Johnny a perverse lesson in federalism." O'Connor countered by noting that the decision would assure "that little Mary may attend class" (free from harassment).

Isolated opinions such as O'Connor's cannot be taken to *prove* that women "speak in a different voice" as Suzanna Sherry's work on feminist jurisprudence suggests. But, this article's innovative presentation of judges with hypothetical situations provides findings sufficiently suggestive to keep alive the debate about whether the gender of the judge and the plaintiff or defendant makes a difference.

[* * *]

Women in the Legal Profession

We know from statewide task force reports on gender bias in the [legal] profession from every state and a growing body of empirical evidence that women's experiences in the legal profession have been different. The most transparent example of this is the historical exclusion of women in the legal profession. Until the passage of Title VII [in 1964], women's representation in the legal profession never exceeded 3 percent. Today women make up approximately 28 percent of those in the legal profession and comprise over half of all law students. . . .

Despite gains in the number of women in the profession, the empirical evidence shows that they lag behind their male colleagues on every indicator of success. Not only is there a gap in the career trajectories of women and men, but it also appears that the gap widens as more women enter the profession. In fact the career gap is greater between women and men in the legal profession than it is between women and men in the general labor force. . . .

. . . [T]he number of women on the bench has not kept pace with the number of women in the profession. This suggests that the barriers that have worked to exclude women from the legal profession may be greater for women trying to enter the judiciary. Looking at the historical record, we see that although women were appointed to limited jurisdiction courts in the nineteenth century, it was not until 1921 that the first woman judge was elected to a general jurisdiction court. By 1940, only twenty-one states had women judges and by 1980 sixteen states had no female judges on courts of general jurisdiction. Today every state has women on state courts, but women make up a paltry 7.2 percent (873) of the 12,093 law-trained judges on full time state courts. If we examine women's presence on state-by-state basis, we see that some states have more women judges than others. For example, Alaska leads all fifty states with women accounting for 21.1 percent of their judges while Virginia falls at the bottom with women accounting for a meager 2.3 percent of their judges. There are still twenty-five states with no women on the State Courts of Last Resort (State Supreme Courts), twenty-two states have just one woman serving at this level, and three have women on their highest court for a national average of 8.3 percent. At the federal level, we see that women comprise only 7.4 percent of the 753 full-time federal judges, 9.5 percent of the 168 U.S. Circuit Court of Appeals justices and 6.9 percent of the 576 U.S. District Court judges. Of the nine United States Supreme Court justices, two are female. These statistics underscore a history of exclusion of women from the profession and the judiciary. . . .

[* * *]

[For this study, which c]ompare[s] female and male judges, the average responding female judge was white, 46 years old, married with minor children, and had been a judge for less than 6 years. The average responding male judge was white, 54 years old, married, with no minor children living at home, and had been a judge for more than 10 years.

For the litigant analyses, Version 1 and Version 2 of the survey were compared. For the judge's analysis, female and male judges were grouped and compared. Below is a brief description of the 4 vignettes.

Situation 1—Self Defense/Homicide

This vignette presented an abuse/self-defense claim in a homicide case. The defendant had previously obtained a temporary protection from abuse order from her boyfriend. One Saturday, the boyfriend followed her to a bar and threatened to kill her. The boyfriend left then broke into the defendant's apartment, frightening the baby-sitter and the defendant's children. He told the baby-sitter to tell the defendant that he would be back later. When the defendant returned and learned of the incident, she reported it immediately to the police. Approximately five hours later, the boyfriend returned and assaulted the defendant. She then stabbed and killed the boyfriend. In Version 1, the defendant was named Patricia Lawson and in Version 2 the defendant was named Shanika Washington. Judges were asked whether the defendant had grounds for self-defense, whether a judge and whether a jury would find the defendant guilty of homicide, and if so, what the length of sentence would be (assuming a standard sentencing range from 60 to 120 months per mandatory sentencing guidelines).

The only statistically significant difference (though small) was for length of sentence and here we see that the range is wider for Patricia Lawson (46 to 180 months) than Shanika Washington (45 to 120 months). The only apparent explanation is that race (albeit implied) figured in the decision-making process. While not statistically significant, it is nevertheless interesting to note that on the question regarding whether a jury would find the defendant guilty, more judges reported Patricia Lawson would more likely be found guilty by a jury than Shanika Washington.

[* * *]

Situation 2—Personal Injury Case

This vignette presents a personal injury case where an automobile accident left the plaintiff paralyzed from the waist down and unable to return to work or perform routing domestic/family activities. The plaintiff sued seeking a higher award than what a jury had given (seeking $2.2 million—$650,000 for pain and suffering and $1,550,000 for loss of earnings and medical expenses). In this case the gender was varied—in Version 1 the plaintiff was named Bob Kramer and in Version 2 the plaintiff was named Pam Foster.

There was a $45,258.22 difference in the mean amount of lost earnings awards between vignettes. While this difference is sizable, . . . the difference is not statistically significant.

Situation 3—Alimony Case

In this vignette a husband files for divorce from his wife. In Version 1 the couple is named Sheila and Michael Arnold and in Version 2 the couple is named Jose and Maria Garcia. The wife is seeking alimony. She is 56 years old, overweight, and was forced to stop working the previous year in the family owned hardware due to high blood pressure and hypertension. Judges were asked whether they would award alimony and if so, the amount and the length of the award. None of the differences between versions for this case were significant.

Situation 4—Simple Assault

Vignette 4 deals with a civil and criminal assault case. . . . [I]n Version 1 the defendant was named Sally Squires while the victim was named Joe DeLuca and in Version 2 the defendant was named Joe Lanza and the victim was named Sally Squires. The defendant and victim had a physical altercation following a dispute over a basketball game bet. The defendant won the bet, but refused to pay. The victim demanded payment and threw a beer in the defendant's face. The defendant got angry and retaliated by throwing a beer glass at the victim. A scuffle ensued wherein the defendant and victim sustained injury. . . .

Here we see that gender appears to make a difference. Judges would be less likely to find Sally Squires guilty of assault than they would Joe Lanza. Similarly, judges would impose a higher civil damage award for a male defendant.

The earlier analyses show that nonlegal factors entered into the decisions of some judges in vignettes one and four.

Does the gender of the judge make a difference in the outcome of a case? [The] results show that the judge's gender was a significant factor in at least one of the decision points in each of the four vignettes.

. . . [W]hen the gender of the judge is considered, . . . in almost half of the decisions (7 out of 15) statistically significant differences were found. Briefly these differences were:

- Female judges were more likely than male judges to find a male defendant guilty of assault than a female defendant, under the same factual circumstances.
- Male judges were half as likely as female judges to find a female defendant claiming self-defense guilty of homicide than female judges, under the same factual circumstances.
- Male judges' personal injury awards were over twice as large as female judges', under the same factual circumstances.
- Male judges were almost half as likely as female judges to believe a jury would find a female defendant claiming self-defense guilty of homicide, under the same factual circumstances.

- Male judges were not unanimous, as were women judges, in awarding alimony, under the same factual circumstances.

- Male judges imposed shorter sentences for simple assault than female judges, under the same factual circumstances.

- Male judges were more likely to award civil damages for simple assault, under the same factual circumstances.

- Male judges awarded one-third the damages awarded by female judges for simple assault, under the same factual circumstances.

[* * *]

Discussion

[* * *]

. . . [T]he analyses reveal two interesting patterns. The first pattern relates to litigant characteristics and the finding that litigant characteristics did not influence judges' decisions as a whole. This is reassuring. One possible explanation for the congruence among judges has to do with the effectiveness of legal training in preparing judges for the bench. A legal education emphasizes legal principles and focuses on the factual matters of a case.

The second pattern, showing differences between female and male judges, is more difficult to explain because this pattern reflects differences in judges' interpretations and may reflect the relevance that judges' lived experiences have on their interpretations of factual information. The survey did not ask judges to identify the legal principles they applied, but rather presented judges with concrete situations and asked them to indicate how they would decide. The application of legal principles to concrete situations is always interpretive, and while legal education can train judges to focus on the factual matters of cases, the meaning that factual matters have for judges is an interpretive social process and this is precisely where a judge's experiences could have bearing on the decision-making process. We, of course, expect judges to set aside personal viewpoints when deciding cases, yet beneath the robe of justice is an individual whose perceptions of the world have been influenced by their experiences in it.

The second pattern provides some support for Carol Gilligan's research, particularly with respect to her views about justice and fairness. Since gender, race, ethnicity, and socioeconomic status affect people's perceptions of fairness and justice, it is conceivable that female and male judges attach different weights to the factual aspects of identical situations. Until we explore what these differences are and acknowledge that they exist, we cannot begin to discuss what these differences may mean in terms of the behavior of judges.

[* * *]

TOWARD CRITICAL THINKING

1. This survey was administered as part of a statewide study by the Pennsylvania Bar Association to assess gender discrimination in the courts. Do you think that the official sanction of the bar association could affect these results in any way? Would they make men and women more sensitive to the kind of responses they would give?

2. Given the fairly large list of differences found by the author, which strike you as most surprising? Do any patterns emerge about women jurists?

Reading 39

Justice Sandra Day O'Connor and the Supreme Court's Reaction to Its First Female Member

(1990)

Karen O'Connor and Jeffrey A. Segal

President Ronald Reagan fulfilled a campaign promise when he nominated Sandra Day O'Connor to the Supreme Court in 1981. Although women's groups nearly universally hailed her appointment as the first woman on the Court, most early commentators and scholars of the Court concluded that she fit the conservative mold of other Reagan nominees. But as time has passed, several scholars have concluded that O'Connor does indeed speak (at times) "in a woman's voice." Often, she has been the swing (or deciding) vote in sex discrimination cases as well as often being the critical fifth vote to uphold the constitutionality of *Roe* v. *Wade*, which prohibits states from banning abortion in some phases of pregnancy.

Most of the research on women judges had examined whether men and women on the bench decide cases differently. What was new and innovative about this piece, first published in *Women & Politics*, was its attempt to measure the effect of a woman jurist's presence on the behavior of the other justices.

Lyn Kathlene (Reading 32) found that men in state legislatures appeared to become more hostile toward women the more women that there were in their legislatures. In contrast, the justices of the U.S. Supreme Court appeared to acknowledge the inevitability of a female member. In fact, just a few years before O'Connor's nomination, they changed the practice of calling each justice "Mr. Justice" to simply "Justice," in anticipation of a woman eventually being appointed to the Court. It took a suggestion from the second female justice on the Court, Ruth Bader Ginsburg, to change the name of the "Ladies Dining Room" to the "Natalie Rehnquist Dining Room" in honor of Chief Justice William H. Rehnquist's deceased wife, but no other outright "Men Only" signs greeted Justice O'Connor. This article, however, attempts to measure whether having a woman in the room when sex discrimination cases are discussed and votes cast has any impact on the patterns that individual justices had evidenced in prior sex discrimination cases. The authors examine the actions of the justices before and after O'Connor joined the Court to determine how her addition appears to affect the other justices. They also examine whether O'Connor follows the lead of other conservative justices in sex discrimination cases or if she votes instead "in a woman's voice."

The 55 cases selected for analysis include all cases decided by the Burger Court based on the Fourteenth or Fifteenth Amendment to the U.S. Constitution, Title VII or Title IX of the Civil Rights and Education Amendments respectively, or the Equal Pay Act in which a state, federal, or private action was challenged as sexually discriminatory. Voting patterns of the justices are identified by the use of cumulative scaling of all nonunanimous decisions. We then use simple crosstabulation in a preliminary effort to assess the effect of the addition of Justice O'Connor to the bench.

Little research has been done by scholars of the judicial process to determine the effect of a single Justice on the Court. In particular, no studies exist concerning the possible impact that the appointment of Justice [Thurgood] Marshall had on the other Justices in terms of their sensitivity to the issue of race discrimination. His appointment, however, occurred during the so-called heyday of the Court's liberal approach to race discrimination claims, and it is unlikely that any immediately discernable impact took place. In contrast, Justice Sandra Day O'Connor was appointed to a Court which, while generally supportive of sex discrimination complaints, had yet to apply the strict scrutiny standard used to resolve racial complaints to claims involving gender bias. . . .

. . . [W]e hypothesize:

1. The Court as a whole will become more supportive of sex discrimination complaints after the addition of Justice O'Connor.

Traditionalists and behavioralists long have noted the effects of additions to the Court. One aspect of personnel change involves the so-called "freshman effect" . . . [whereby] with the notable exception of Justice [John Paul] Stevens, new Justices tend to vote with ideological blocs. Other scholars have concluded that Justice O'Connor has aligned herself with the conservative bloc on the Court. Thus we hypothesize:

2. Justice O'Connor will vote with the conservative bloc of the Court in sex discrimination cases.

Findings

In 1983, political scientists [Karen] O'Connor and [Lee] Epstein found that the U.S. Supreme Court supported sex discrimination claims in 58.8% of the 68 cases they examined for the 1969 to 1981 terms. [T]he Burger Court adopted a pro-equality position in

63% of the cases it decided. Additionally, . . . four Justices routinely evidenced support for the pro-equality position substantially above the Court mean—[William J.] Brennan (90%), Marshall (83%), O'Connor (75%), and [Byron] White (74%). Justices Stevens and [Harry A.] Blackmun emerged as the centrist members of the Court, while Justices [Warren E.] Burger, [William H.] Rehnquist, and [Lewis] Powell were the most consistently negative with regard to sex discrimination claims.

An examination of the Court's support for sex discrimination claims *after* the appointment of Justice O'Connor, however, reveals a slightly different pattern. In fact, an overall rise in the Court's support for these cases occurred—75% vs. 63%—a finding consistent with Hypothesis 1. Indeed, Justices O'Connor and Blackmun are the "swing" Justices on this Court. . . .

[* * *]

When we focus our attention on the individual Justices' support for sex discrimination complaints after Justice O'Connor's appointment, several interesting changes can be observed. [As observed in Table 39.1,] the rank order and degree of support changed markedly. In general, while the support of Justice Brennan—the Justice whom [Saul] Brenner and [Harold] Spaeth found to be the sole issue specialist on gender discrimination—dipped a bit (83.3% vs. 92.7%), and that of Justice Powell stayed about the same (41.7% vs. 42.5%), all of the other Justices' support for these claims increased when Justice O'Connor was added to the Court. Justice White's support increased by more than 20% (91.7% vs. 69.8%), Justice Stevens rose from 57.1% to 83.3%, and even Chief Justice Burger's support rose considerably (32.1% to 50%). Even more remarkable was the increase in Justice Rehnquist's support: His support actually doubled!

The reasons for these changes may go beyond the addition of Justice O'Connor. Cases, however, did not get easier during this period. Thus it is clear that our findings support Hypothesis 1: The Court clearly became more receptive to sex discrimination claims after the appointment of Justice O'Connor.

Our second hypothesis posited that Justice O'Connor's behavior would follow that of others who experienced the freshman effect—namely, that she would vote with the ideologically conservative bloc. . . . [T]his did *not* occur. Clearly, Justice O'Connor's voting behavior on sex discrimination claims makes her a "centrist" Justice. Others, however, have found that O'Connor indeed voted with the conservative bloc on most issues. Thus, in cases involving issues of sex discrimination, Justice O'Connor often parts company with her conservative allies. While she is not in the liberal vanguard, she clearly moves to the center when cases involving gender are decided by the Court. We must, therefore, reject our second hypothesis, while noting that the addition of Justice O'Connor did not install a Justice as favorably disposed to sex discrimination complaints as four of her Brethren. Feminist hopes clearly cannot be staked on Justice O'Connor, although the addition of Justices [Antonin] Scalia and [Anthony Kennedy] may force her further to the left in these kinds of cases.

TABLE 39.1

Rank Order of Justices' Support for Sex Discrimination Claims, Pre- and Post-O'Connor Appointment

Pre-O'Connor Appointment		Post-O'Connor Appointment	
Brennan	92.7%	Marshall	91.7%
Marshall	81.4%	White	91.7%
White	69.8%	Brennan	83.3%
Stevens	57.1%	Stevens	83.3%
Blackmun	50%	O'Connor	75%
Powell	42.5%	Blackmun	63.6%
Burger	32.1%	Burger	50%
Rehnquist	25%	Rehnquist	50%
		Powell	41.7%
n = 55		n = 12	

Conclusion

. . . [P]rior to the appointment of Justice O'Connor to the Court, unanimous decisions concerning sex discrimination were rare; since her appointment, however, numerous cases involving a variety of different allegedly discriminatory practices or laws have been decided unanimously. Cases involving Title VII, the Social Security Act, sexual harassment, retirement benefits, and women's exclusion from private clubs have been decided in favor of the victims of sex discrimination.

This pattern leads directly to one of our most important findings, the dramatic rise in Chief Justice Rehnquist's support for sex discrimination complaints. While his overall support clearly lags behind the Court as a whole, he has supported the party charging sex discrimination 50% of the time. Given his prior record and his elevation to the position of Chief Justice, this change is likely to bode well for the future resolution of sex discrimination cases. As the Chief Justice, he is in the position to mold the Court to some extent. Clearly, he is not as conservative as some of his most vocal critics have charged—at least in terms of sex discrimination cases. Whether the change in his stance or in that of the rest of the Justices is due to the appointment of Justice O'Connor and directly attributable to her presence on the bench is impossible to determine with total accuracy. Nevertheless, a noticeable change occurred on the Court toward sex discrimination complaints when she took her place.

[* * *]

We also found that, contrary to the predictions of feminists or of "freshman effect" scholars, Justice O'Connor turned out to be a key swing Justice on issues of sex discrimination. Moreover, with the recent additions of conservative Justices Scalia and Kennedy, her presence on the Court could take on greater importance. Clearly, . . . her vote was pivotal in several cases. Most notably, in *Mississippi University for Women* v. *Hogan* (1982), Justice O'Connor, writing for the 5–4 majority, stressed her belief that the exclusion of men from state-supported nursing schools perpetuated sex role stereotypes and further depressed women's wages by keeping nursing a female-dominated profession. Prior to her appointment, the Court had split 4–4 in *Vorchheimer v. School District of Philadelphia* (1977), letting stand a lower court ruling allowing sex-segregated high schools. However, in *Ohio Civil Rights Commission v. Dayton Christian Schools, Inc.* (1986), another 5–4 decision, Justice O'Connor sided with the conservative bloc to cast the deciding vote in a pregnancy discrimination case. According to the narrow majority, the nonrenewal of a pregnant teacher's contract was justified by the school's religious doctrine, which held that women should stay at home with their children. In *Dayton*, when faced with competing First Amendment and equal protection views, the rights entitled to strict scrutiny (free exercise of religion) won out with Justice O'Connor over the lower, intermediate standard of review used in gender cases. When competing constitutional claims have not been present in other pregnancy cases, such as *Newport News Shipbuilding and Dry Dock Co. v. EEOC* (1983) and, more recently, *California Federal Savings and Loan Association v. Guerra* (1987), Justice O'Connor has voted against discrimination against pregnant workers.

The addition of the new Justices and the potential for the Court to swing further to the right leave Justice O'Connor in an especially important position. She now has the opportunity to take a more vocal role, should she so desire, to maintain the status quo or to set the Court on a more liberal path in this area of the law. . . . Feminists can only hope that Justice O'Connor, as someone who has faced discrimination, will come to view her role as a spokesperson on the Court for an underrepresented group . . . when issues of gender discrimination are at stake.

TOWARD CRITICAL THINKING

1. What reasons do the authors give to explain why Justice O'Connor might be more responsive to complaints of sex discrimination than other Justices? What about the dramatic effect that her appointment to the Court had on the other justices?

2. In the context of expectations that jurists be fair and impartial, does this mean that O'Connor is biased in sex discrimination cases? Would you expect her to find a strong ally in the second woman justice, Ruth Bader Ginsburg?

WRAPPING UP

1. Law professor Suzanna Sherry believes that Justice Sandra Day O'Connor's jurisprudence differs significantly from that of the men on the Supreme Court. Having read these articles, do you believe that women judges decide cases differently from men judges? Given the key role that Justice O'Connor often plays as a "swing Justice" on the Court, does this mean that a woman's voice often wins the day?

2. How would you design a research project to try to determine if women judges in your local trial court decided cases differently from men judges?

READING 40

A Woman for President? Changing Responses: 1958–1972

(1974)

Myra Marx Ferree

In 1872, Victoria Woodhull became the first woman to run for president of the United States although she was unable to vote for herself. Woodhull ran as the candidate of the Equal Rights Party. And, over time, more women were to run for president as minor-party candidates. This *Public Opinion Quarterly* article by social psychologist Myra Marx Ferree underscores the difficulties that would have been encountered by any woman running for president through the 1970s. Not only was the American public unaccustomed to women elected officials at almost any level, but to many Americans, voting for a woman for president simply wasn't an acceptable option. There only had been a handful of women governors, and as pointed out by Emmy E. Werner (Reading 30), social scientists had barely even begun to consider the concept of women as leaders.

In this early analysis of the discrimination potentially faced by any "well-qualified woman candidate," Ferree shows the dramatic increase in support for women candidates that appeared between 1969 and 1972, the year that Shirley Chisholm, an African American member of Congress from New York City, sought the presidential nomination of the Democratic Party. Chisholm did not gain the nomination, but she won 150 delegates to the party's national convention.

In the period from 1958 to 1969, the American Institute of Public Opinion (the Gallup Poll) surveyed the American public five times on its willingness to vote for "a well-qualified woman of your own party" for President of the United States. In the spring of 1972, the National Opinion Research Center, in its "General Social Survey," asked the same question.

Before looking at the answers, it is necessary to examine some of the limitations and strengths of the question. Questions vary in their specificity and this often has dramatic effects on the distribution of answers obtained. . . . Compare the responses to these two questions:

"Do women in the United States get as good a break as men?"

	Yes	No
Women	65%	35%
Men	72	28

"If a woman has the same ability as a man, does she have as good a chance to become the executive of a company, or not?"

	Yes	No
Women	39%	54%
Men	39	56

Clearly, people are more willing to agree with the broader generality than with the specific example. The question to be examined here is fairly specific, yet it might be argued that it is still so hypothetical that it is an "easy" question. Nonetheless, while it is debatable how well this opinion-voting actually measures the influence on the vote, a similar question on voting for a Catholic for President proved quite effective in an assessment of the anti-Catholic vote in 1960.

[* * *]

The hypothetical case presented in the question is in some respects more strongly compelling toward an affirmative answer than any actual woman candidate could be. In the first place, a candidate would be of only one party, and therefore likely to "lose" nearly half of her potential support. Moreover, how "well-qualified" she was would probably be debated rather than given.

The questions specifically addressed by this article are critical. Is there less prejudice now than in the past? . . .

The question, "And if your party nominated a woman for President, would you vote for her if she seemed qualified for the job?" was asked by Gallup of 7,578 respondents, roughly 1,500 in each of five separate surveys done in 1958, 1959, 1963, 1967, 1969, and by NORC of 1,613 respondents in 1972. One of the most striking things about the results obtained is the lack of any significant decrease in prejudice over time until 1972, when the drop was suddenly 13 percent (Table 40.1). Obviously, there has been considerable change in the past few years when compared to the previous decade. . . .

Why such a sudden change for women? I hope to demonstrate that one major factor involved was the emergence of the Women's Movement and the consequent

TABLE 40.1

**Change over Time in Percentage
of Respondents Willing to Vote for
[Women] Candidates for President**

| Year of Survey | Woman | |
	Percent "Yes"	Percent "No"
1958	55%	39%
1959	58	38
1963	56	40
1967	57	38
1969	55	38
1972	70	25

recognition on the part of many people that women, too, are a disadvantaged "minority." The simple abruptness of the change rules out most demographic explanations, since these changes occur more slowly and gradually. Hence, one must look for the causes of the change in the transient events of the time; here the Woman's Movement stands out.

Although the National Organization for Women (NOW) was founded in 1966, it did not garner much media attention at that time; more radical and media-conscious groups came into being in 1968 and 1969, but did not get nationwide publicity until late 1969 and early 1970. But by 1971 "women's lib" was an easily recognized term to the general population, and by 1972 there was considerable change in the willingness, especially of women, to vote for a woman for President. Before ascribing too much power to the Movement on such circumstantial evidence, we need to see what sort of changes have combined to produce the short-term shift.

One notable change is the disappearance of the sex difference. While from 1958 to 1969 men were somewhat more willing to vote for a woman than were women, in 1972 both sexes were equally willing. As Table 40.2 indicates, there was no intimation of growing parity in previous surveys. If anything, the gap in the 1960s was slightly wider than in the 1950s. While it is clear that both men and women changed considerably, it is equally clear that women changed much more. . . .

[* * *]

To summarize, the sudden change in attitudes toward women seems, first, to have come from both men and women, but from women much more dramatically than men. Where men had gradually been becoming more favorable over time, women had remained stable until recently and then changed abruptly. Second, it

TABLE 40.2

Differences Between Men and Women in Willingness to Vote for a Woman over Time[a]

Year of Survey	Percent Agreeing		Difference
	Men	Women	
1958	55%	53%	−2%
1959	60	55	−5
1963	59	51	−8
1967	62	53	−9
1969	58	50	−8
1972	69	69	0

[a]In this table, all percentages are based on white respondents only.

comes from younger and better educated women. Women who are both older and less well-educated are perhaps more "set in their ways" for they scarcely change at all. Alternatively, it may simply reflect the focus of efforts of the Women's Movement thus far. Third, and this is the point we now turn to, the change comes largely from those who are already tolerant of other minorities. My contention is that this is because women are now more likely to be seen as another minority, and consistency between items considered in the same class is greater than consistency between seemingly unrelated items.

[* * *]

TOWARD CRITICAL THINKING

1. In 2002, The White House Project found that twelve percent of the public still was unwilling to vote for a qualified woman for president. Why do you think this kind of discrimination still persists? Can you think of any women who might make a successful bid for the presidency?

2. Given the discrimination that continues to exist against potential female candidates for the presidency, is it rational for political parties not to seek out qualified women to run?

Reading 41

The Ferraro Factor

(1988)

Kathleen A. Frankovic

By 1983, the Gallup Organization was reporting that 80 percent of those polled would vote for a qualified woman of their own party for president. Many women's rights activists in the Democratic Party saw this as an opportunity to press for a woman vice presidential candidate. Polls about incumbent President Ronald Reagan's job performance showed his evaluations were at new lows, and many women saw the inclusion of a woman on the ticket as a way to capitalize on the gender gap (see Readings 16–19), invigorate the campaign, and inspire more women to go to the polls. As momentum for a woman candidate for vice president began to build, a group of women, called Team A, already were at work behind the scenes. According to Eleanor Clift and Tom Brazaitis's book, *Madam President: Shattering the Last Glass Ceiling,* as early as 1982, a group of women political activists had been meeting, often along with some women members of Congress, to come up with names of women to be forwarded to Walter Mondale, the likely Democratic nominee.

Kathleen Frankovic's work, published as a chapter in *The Politics of the Gender Gap,* edited by Carol M. Mueller, asks what impact the Ferraro candidacy had on the national election outcome. The question is important for several reasons. Frankovic's analysis underscores the pitfalls of public opinion polls when individuals are asked questions that could reveal their biases about women, as was noted by Myra Marx Ferree (Reading 40). (Other studies have shown the same problems when respondents are asked questions about race.) It also underscores the role that women's organizations played in getting the selection of a woman vice presidential candidate on the public agenda.

[* * *]

In July 1983, the National Women's Political Caucus met in San Antonio and questioned five Democratic candidates for the [presidential] nomination about their attitudes on women's rights, the feminization of poverty, and military spending. All the candidates except Senator John Glenn [D-OH] claimed they would appoint more women than ever to high-level posts in their administrations. While the question of a woman vice presidential nominee was raised informally at that meeting, it was not directly addressed in the questioning of the candidates. Women activists were discussing the idea, but there was no clear consensus that it was a realistic goal or that it was the right thing to do.

Three months later, at the meeting of the National Organization for Women [NOW], the candidates appeared again. This time, there was an additional question for them—would the candidates pledge to name a woman running mate?

[* * *]

In their public statements, the leaders of NOW justified the interest in a woman vice presidential nominee with reminders of the gender gap and the potential level of excitement that a woman's candidacy might create. Another goal of NOW was to place women at the core of party decision making. When the candidates met with NOW, they all passed the test, all agreeing to give serious consideration to a woman nominee. Mondale called himself a "feminist," and promised to take NOW's recommendation "very, very seriously." George McGovern described picking a woman as a "very likely prospect." Gary Hart indicated he would be proud to serve on a ticket with a woman "at either end." All of the announced candidates who were present promised to support the women's agenda.

The *Los Angeles Times* viewed the NOW convention as a turning point in the relationship of feminist organizations to mainstream party politics. Women were being addressed as a *constituency*, in the tradition of a pressure group in American party politics. Leaders talked about their "political credibility," and the potential value of the women's vote to the prospective Democratic nominee.

It is possible to view the October NOW meeting as the point at which the politics of choosing a woman candidate became the politics of a pressure group. . . .

. . . Senator Edward Kennedy noted the possibility [of a women vice presidential candidate] in a speech to the Women's Democratic Club; Gary Hart, in addressing the Americans for Democratic Action, announced that a woman, Representative Patricia Schroeder of Colorado, would be co-chair of his campaign. In early December, the Women's Presidential Project, organized by former Representative Bella Abzug, and including many women's organizations and activists, sent a questionnaire to all the candidates, seeking out their positions on relevant issues. This technique is typical for constituent groups within a political party.

The recognition of NOW as a legitimate interest group within the Democratic Party is demonstrated by press reaction to NOW's December 1983 endorsement of Walter Mondale. Front page stories in the elite press noted that the organization, in making its first endorsement in its 17-year history, was following on the heels of the AFL-CIO and NEA endorsements of Mondale, and making its endorsement at the same time that Alabama Black Democrats agreed to endorse Mondale for president and Jesse Jackson for vice president. Throughout the campaign, whenever Mondale's list of endorsements would be mentioned, NOW would be included along with the two labor groups. . . .

[* * *]

1983: The Early Data

The naming of a woman vice presidential candidate became a major goal of NOW and many other women's organizations in 1984. . . .

[* * *]

[Public opinion] polls highlighted a potential positive effect that a woman on the ticket might produce for the Democrats. A Gallup poll in October 1983 discovered that 26% of the public said they would be more likely to vote Democratic if a woman were nominated for vice president, while only 16% said that would make them less likely to vote Democratic. Men Republicans, who most polls showed solidly behind the reelection of Ronald Reagan, were only marginally more likely to say a woman on the ticket would turn them away from the Democrats than to say the candidacy would make them more supportive of the Democratic ticket. This particular Gallup Poll result would be widely cited by supporters of a woman vice presidential nominee throughout the 1984 campaign.

But all the above data should have been subject to more thorough interpretation than they received at the time. Were 80% of Americans actually inclined to vote for a woman candidate, or were they simply giving the socially acceptable response to what was very likely a female interviewer? The question that asked specifically about the impact of a woman running for vice president on the Democratic ticket lacked a middle alternative. Indeed, half of those questioned supplied their own response, that a woman on the ticket would have no effect on them. The absence of a middle alternative in the question itself may have artificially inflated the proportion of the electorate likely to be affected in either direction, leading to a conclusion that a woman vice presidential nominee could affect the direction of the vote cast by over 40% of the voters. . . .

Despite the poll questions' defects, by February 1984 many party activists believed them. In response to a special Gallup survey, party leaders said overwhelmingly that a woman on the ticket would help the party's chances in November. Two-thirds of the party leaders believed a woman vice presidential nominee would help the party. The 1983 evidence on the potential electability of a woman vice president and the possible gains for the Democrats in nominating a woman had been accepted by the party's leaders who would eventually have to support her candidacy.

[* * *]

The Development of the Idea: Spring 1984

By the beginning of 1984, the prospects of a Democratic nominee defeating Ronald Reagan were much less bright than they had been in mid-1983. The president's approval ratings, which had been in the mid-40s in the summer of 1983, had improved along with the economy throughout the fall, and jumped into the low to mid-50s after the invasion of Grenada in October. The gender gap in presidential approval was still sizable, but instead of a situation where a majority of woman disapproved of the president, by January 1984 as many women approved as disapproved of the president's performance.

. . . Early in March, when Gary Hart became the most popular contender for the Democratic nomination, he became the election choice of more registered voters than the president. While Hart's hypothetical victories against the president were short-lived, the support for him suggested a generalized willingness on the part of the public to consider and accept alternatives to the Reagan-Bush ticket.

NOW, having endorsed Walter Mondale, assumed a role in the Mondale campaign that required activity on their part. Several hundred NOW members would become delegates to the July Democratic convention. According to the *New York Times*, NOW chapters in Florida were especially active, providing 20% of the Mondale delegate slates and many of the activists in the primary fight. One regional director claimed, "We grew and we learned in two bloody battles for the ERA, and we have volunteers, lists of thousands of Democrats and ERA supporters, and a network already set up." For the first time, the capability developed to try and ratify the ERA would be used to support a presidential candidate. . . .

[* * *]

While NOW had committed itself to supporting the candidacy of Walter Mondale, there was evidence that the women voting in the early primaries were not necessarily following NOW's lead. . . . [B]y the time momentum had switched back toward Mondale in late March, women were more likely to vote for him than were men.

Amid the disarray created by the contest among the Democratic contenders, there was relatively little coverage of the movement for a woman vice presidential candidate. Until May, press reports of the possibility of a woman vice presidential candidate were limited to occasional interviews with party leaders and pollsters, and to the publication of a few quantitative analyses that cast some doubt on the prospects for the electoral power of a woman candidate.

In February 1984, a study done for the National Women's Political Caucus, funded by the American Council of Life Insurance, hinted at the remaining level of prejudice against a woman candidate. The study, an experiment involving the showing of commercials featuring men and women candidates to 200 voters, indicated that voters responded to the candidates in stereotypical terms, with men being seen as better in crises, and better at making tough decisions. Women were judged better at organization, understanding, and dealing with new ideas. The study also noted that, while three-quarters of both men and women claimed that the sex of a candidate wouldn't matter in their decision making, those responses were not necessarily related to the holding of stereotypical views. The conclusion was that in order to draw votes effectively, any woman running for vice president would have to be "better than any of the males" contending for the spot. Florence Skelly, who conducted the study, stated, "Even with sisterhood and the gender gap, you can't automatically attract women's votes with a woman candidate."

A second study, done in April by CBS News and the *New York Times*, suggested that there would be equal gains and losses for the Democrats should they choose to put a woman on the ticket [Table 41.1]. That study was done using a split-half design, with half the respondents being asked their preference between Reagan and Mondale alone, and then, later in the survey, being asked their preference with a woman added to the Democratic slate and George Bush added to the Republican ticket. The other half of the sample was asked the same Reagan-Mondale horse race question, and then asked a question that paired Reagan and Bush against Mondale and a male candidate, who was matched to the woman in the other half in terms of name recognition, experience, current position, region, and ethnicity. Movements toward the Mondale-woman ticket occurred among women, especially young, independent, and western ones; movements away from that pairing occurred among men, especially older, southern, and Democratic ones. In sum, the net impact was close to zero.

A separate analysis of the April CBS News/*New York Times* poll also suggested that many of those who said in response to a direct question that a woman on the ticket would influence them were already committed to a candidate. Using a variation of the

TABLE 41.1

Selected National Poll Questions on a Woman Candidate

		Totals (%)	Dem.	Rep.	Ind.
Gallup (4/29–5/2/83; N = 1517)					
If your party nominated a woman for president, would you vote for her if she were qualified for the job?	yes	80			
	no	16			
Gallup (9/7–10/83; N = 1513)					
If a Democratic presidential nominee in 1984 selected	more likely	26	33	17	24
a woman to be his vice presidential running mate,	less likely	16	13	23	16
would this make you more or less likely to vote for the	no difference	52	49	54	56
Democratic ticket?					
NBC News (1/22–23/84; N = 883)					
If the Democrats nominate a woman as their vice	more likely	8			
presidential candidate this year, would that make	less likely	10			
you more likely to vote for the Democratic	no difference	79			
presidential candidate, less likely, or would a	not sure	3			
woman vice presidential candidate make no					
difference in your presidential vote choice?					
Harris (3/8–20/84; N = 1506)					
Would you favor or oppose having a woman run	favor	71			
for vice president in 1984?	oppose	21			
CBS News/*New York Times* (4/23–26/84; N = 990)					
If the Democratic presidential candidate chooses a	yes	21			
woman for vice president, would it make a difference	no	74			
in whether or not you vote for the Democrat					
in November?					
If yes to above: Would a woman on the ticket	more likely	8			
more likely or less likely to vote for	less likely	10			
the Democratic candidate?	not sure	3			
ABC News/*Washington Post* (5/16–22/84; N = 1511)					
Do you think it would be a good idea or a bad	good idea	53			
idea for the Democrats to pick a woman as	bad idea	38			
their vice presidential candidate?					
Gallup (6/6–8/84; N = 741)					
If the Democratic presidential nominee selected	more likely		32		27
a woman to be his vice presidential running mate,	less likely		18		24
would this make you more or less likely to vote for	no difference		41		43
the Democratic ticket?	(vol.)				
ABC News/*Washington Post* (7/5–8/84; N = 1005)					
And suppose a woman runs for vice president with	more likely	16			
Mondale, will that make you more or less likely to	less likely	14			
vote for Mondale, or won't that make any difference	no difference	68			
one way or the other?					
CBS News/*New York Times* (7/12/84; N = 747)					
Mondale has named Geraldine Ferraro to be his vice	yes	17			
presidential running mate. Does that make a difference	no	80			
in whether or not you vote for Mondale in November?					
If yes to above: Does having Geraldine Ferraro	more likely	6			
on the ticket make you more likely or less likely	less likely	8			
to vote for Walter Mondale?	not sure	3			

more likely/less likely question (with a middle option provided), the survey discovered that 8% of those interviewed say they would be more likely to vote Democratic if a woman were on the ticket, while 10% said they would be less likely. However, half of those who reported being more likely to vote Democratic were already supporting Mondale; half of those who reported a woman would make them less likely to vote Democratic were already supporting Reagan. Excluding these respondents suggested the possibility of a four-point gain by Mondale and a concurrent five-point loss. This second analysis of the April CBS News/*New York Times* poll supplements the first and also indicates an extremely small net impact. . . .

[* * *]

Making a case for the selection of a woman as the Democrats' vice presidential nominee became easier as the press chose the data it would report on the question. The media's need for straightforward information made certain data sets inappropriate for its use. The press's reliance on interviews with feminist activists for much of its reporting also strengthened the activists' hand. In interviews, activists supplied the data and could selectively pass on what they considered to be useful information to reporters. . . . By June, the contrary pieces of information were essentially forgotten. In fact, in late May, Ferraro herself demonstrated the effectiveness of this strategy in her response to a direct question about the CBS News/*New York Times* poll by referring to other evidence. "Every other poll that I have seen shows a woman would help the ticket, and I believe those polls are accurate. There are a lot of voters who would vote for a woman," she stated.

Throughout the spring, numerous male party leaders seemed to agree. . . . Others suggested that a woman on the ticket would be most likely in a situation where the Democratic nominee was perceived as increasingly far behind the incumbent (the situation as it was in spring 1984). . . .

The argument that began with the notion that a woman could make a difference in a close election was being turned into an argument that made a woman on the ticket the Democrats' last chance in the face of a potential Reagan landslide. While that argument took account of the high level of Reagan's popularity, it was also an argument that promised substantial (or at least unanticipated) gains for the Democrats by placing a woman on the ticket. The data, however, were far from supportive on that point. Yet, by focusing on "unanticipated" gains resulting from the candidacy of a woman, feminists could turn aside the survey evidence that suggested no benefit. The nomination of a woman as a last-gasp effort of a Democratic nominee expecting to lose a general election against Ronald Reagan might be perceived as so dramatic that prior poll results could become irrelevant.

[* * *]

The Culmination of the Idea: Summer 1984

Once it appeared that Walter Mondale had won the Democratic nomination, Democratic leaders and the press once again became interested in the question of who would be Mondale's running mate. . . .

While Walter Mondale was interviewing candidates for the vice presidential nomination, elected officials who supported a woman on the ticket were recasting their arguments, stating their case as one that would help a weak nominee, just as Eleanor Smeal had in March. A woman would add excitement to the ticket, according to Governor Richard Celeste of Ohio, who said, "One of the things we need to do is generate fresh excitement coming out of the convention." A woman, he added, might be better able to articulate what was wrong with Reagan's economic policy.

For public officials, the debate focused on pragmatic considerations. The question more often asked was not whether a woman should be on the ticket, but *how* to get the Democratic nominee to accept a woman. The public debate, at least, had turned to the question of tactics. Representative Patricia Schroeder believed the idea was "dynamite, but you don't want to make it look like another special interest." Support for the idea came not only from individuals but from state delegations to the convention. State parties in Washington, Louisiana, Vermont, Idaho, and New York indicated their support for a woman on the ticket.

Feminist leaders, however, still argued that a woman would help the ticket. The only feminist leader who seemed at all skeptical of the electability of a woman vice president was Betty Friedan, who noted, "A lot of women won't vote for a woman just because she's a woman."

That hesitancy put Friedan in a distinct minority. Others claimed that putting a woman on the ticket would mean women would vote Democratic in the fall. That argument was made even though polls indicated that women were not at that time supportive of the Mondale candidacy; in fact, polls conducted in late June showed a majority of women favoring the election of Ronald Reagan, although to a lesser degree than did men.

What is more intriguing than the women leaders' support for the nomination of a woman was the ease with which the idea was being embraced by male politicians, and the ease at which the movement for a woman nominee coalesced behind the candidacy of Geraldine Ferraro. It did not come as a surprise in July when most other Democratic congresswomen endorsed Ferraro. Ferraro also had received early support from individual male politicians to whom she had special ties. In early May, Tip O'Neill endorsed the idea of woman vice presidential candidate, and named Geraldine Ferraro as his candidate for the job. New York City Mayor Ed Koch also endorsed Ferraro early. But it was surprising when Mayor Koch and Representative O'Neill's early endorsements were joined by endorsements from Governors Celeste (Ohio), Earl (Wisconsin), Cuomo (New York), Graham (Florida), Anaya (New Mexico), and Dukakis (Massachusetts), and the president of the United Food and Commercial Workers Union. On June 10, the Wisconsin delegation to the Democratic Convention endorsed Ferraro. Ferraro and San Francisco Mayor Dianne Feinstein were the subjects of a June 4 *Time* magazine cover story on the chances of a woman being nominated.

Support for a woman on the ticket existed among a broad spectrum of delegates to the convention. . . . The National Women's Political Caucus asked a closed-ended [poll] question on whether or not delegates favored nominating a woman for vice president. Three-quarters of all the delegates said they favored a woman vice presidential nominee. Only 10% opposed the idea.

. . . Data would continue to be used as a political tool. A July 1 *New York Times* advertisement, paid for by the Gender Gap Action Committee, which urged the naming of a woman vice presidential candidate, made its case principally on the basis of polls. The advertisement highlighted three distinct poll items, including the more likely/less likely Gallup question (asked again in June with the same wording as in October 1983), a Harris Poll question that asked if voters favored having a woman run for vice president in 1984, and an ABC News/*Washington Post* poll question that asked whether people thought it was a good idea for the Democrats to nominate a woman for the vice presidency. Reported by the Gender Gap Action Committee [GGAC], the Harris Poll found 71% favoring having a woman run for vice president; the ABC News/*Washington Post* poll showed 54% believing it was a good idea for the Democrats to nominate a woman. The advertisement also contained the June Gallup poll more likely/less likely percentages for Democrats and Independents only, which were the only figures reported by the Gallup Organization in its own release of those data. In addition, while the wording was exactly the same as it had been in October, the GGAC and Gallup did not provide comparable figures from the earlier poll. Yet for both Democrats and Independents, the margin of favorable over unfavorable reactions to the nomination of a woman was lower in June than it had been in October.

[* * *]

The data that were available in early July, both those cited by the Gender Gap Action Committee as well at those it chose not to cite, could be used to support the belief that majorities *liked* the idea of naming a woman, just as majorities had, in the past, expressed their willingness to vote for a qualified woman of their own party. Whether or not that meant a woman on the ticket would gain or lose votes for the Democrats was much less certain. . . .

On the same day as the appearance of the Gender Gap Action Committee advertisement, the Miami Beach NOW convention adopted a resolution, originally proposed by Eleanor Smeal, that if Mondale did not select a woman the name of a woman be proposed from the floor. Both Smeal and Judy Goldsmith, the president of NOW, claimed that the resolution was not a ploy to gain other commitments from the expected nominee, and that there was no other list of demands. In essence, the demand for a woman on the ticket was not negotiable.

Within a day individual women began backstepping from what was perceived as a political threat to the unity of the Democratic Party. Geraldine Ferraro said she would not allow her name to be placed in nomination from the floor as a challenge to Mondale's choice. . . . Barbara Mikulski indicated her commitment to Mondale and noted the difference between women elected officials and the leaders of a political movement. "We're used to working inside an institutional framework, while political activists move their agenda outside," she said.

But Goldsmith and other former activists were moving inside the system, and were no longer outsiders. Goldsmith traveled with the campaign for the last weeks of the primary season. She had met with Mondale two weeks before the NOW convention to discuss the vice presidential choices. Afterwards, at the NOW convention, she said that she had assumed an "insider's role" within the Mondale operation.

On July 12, Mondale made his announcement, hailed as one that would "redouble interest in the campaign," as a "dramatic move," and as a "high risk-high gain" strategy. But despite the enthusiasm with which many people greeted the ticket, there were some politicians who had been silent before but now expressed concern that the ticket might not be the best possible. That feeling was particularly prevalent among Democrats in the South and the West, who claimed that they were concerned about the liberal ideologies of both the presidential and vice presidential nominees.

The first polls conducted after the naming of Ferraro did not indicate any definite movement toward the Democrats. . . .

Additionally, throughout the fall, Geraldine Ferraro would be perceived in the same stereotypical terms as the women candidates studied by Florence Skelly in February. In Ferraro's case, the public saw a weakness in her ability to handle crises. From the time she was nominated, she was viewed as less capable than George Bush at handling foreign policy.

The Ferraro Nomination

On election day, the massive vote for Ferraro that the supporters of a woman vice presidential nominee had expected or hoped for did not come to pass. Relatively few voters indicated that the vice presidential candidates had an impact on the way they voted; of those, there was, at best, a tiny net gain for the Democrats.

[* * *]

Examining the first three years of the Reagan administration suggests another reason for the lack of any sizable Ferraro effect. The Reagan administration took a number of symbolic actions attempting to reduce the gender gap, including the appointment of Cabinet Secretaries Elizabeth Dole and Margaret Heckler, the nomination of Sandra Day O'Connor to the Supreme Court, and several expressions of concern about education (seen as a women's issue). None of those acts had any measurable impact on the direction and the size of the gap. Gender differences in approval of Reagan were the result of policy differences, and were never affected during his first term by these symbolic actions.

The nomination of Geraldine Ferraro can be viewed from the same perspective. Her nomination was not a change in policy direction for the Democratic ticket, but was primarily a symbolic action indicating an awareness of women's goals. Symbolic actions in one direction had no effect; therefore, symbolic actions in the other direction should produce no effect, either. The gender gap that did exist in the 1984 election should not be interpreted as a reflection of the Ferraro factor, but should be looked on as an extension of the earlier gender differences.

The Polls and the Press

The use of public opinion polls during the preconvention period raised expectations for the success of the Ferraro nomination. Published poll analyses suffered from the usual problems typical to journalistic use of data, and the search for simple conclusions. In addition, except for the NWPC study, no data were collected that directly examined the impact of women running for office.

[* * *]

Another difficulty with the polls conducted before the nomination can be seen in the understandable desire of both pollsters and press to have a simple and easily reportable measure of the potential impact of a female candidate. This desire resulted in the reporting of data that unintentionally aided the activists lobbying for the nomination of a woman. More complex analyses, and those that relied on experimental design, tended to be reported once, and then ignored. The more likely/less likely question, first asked by Gallup, was ideal in its simplicity, was used in one form or another by nearly every public polling organization, and became the perfect question for conveying what was thought to be the "bottom line" impact of a woman on the ticket. Throughout the prenomination period (and even during the fall campaign) overall results on that question, without controls for original preference, were reported. Party identification was sometimes used as a surrogate for original preference; but by March, substantial numbers of identified Democrats (often a third or more) were reporting their intention to vote for the Republican candidate. Selective reporting of results for Democrats only strengthened the activists' case and resulted in data being presented in the most favorable light.

In the search for the answer to the question of whether a woman would help or hurt the Democrats, pollsters and the press understandably looked for the most straightforward measurement possible. While pollsters may have conducted more extensive analyses, their press reports highlighted the most readily accessible findings. Overall results were the ones that would make headlines, and that meant relying on simple questions as much as possible. It also meant that pollsters frequently presented their data with more assurance than the data required—making the rather hopeful assumption that a simple question was measuring a more complex attitude. In that sense, they unintentionally helped those making the claim that a woman on the ticket would benefit the Democrats in the fall campaign and raised expectations to an unrealistic level. Feminists were sophisticated enough to exploit the weaknesses of both the pollsters and the press, and in the process, strengthened both their case for a woman on the ticket and their overall political impact.

[* * *]

TOWARD CRITICAL THINKING

1. In the 2004 presidential elections, there was little mention of any woman as a possible running mate for Democratic candidate John Kerry. Were women's groups derelict in their efforts? Or did the limited response to former Senator and Ambassador Carol Moseley Braun's efforts to secure the Democratic nomination for president (which was supported by NOW) serve as a lesson that women still have a long way to go before being considered serious candidates for the presidency?

2. In 2000, Elizabeth Dole made a run for the Republican presidential nomination but dropped out after she failed to attract the kind of financial support that George W. Bush was able to amass. Given current speculation that Senator Hillary Rodham Clinton (D–NY) may be eyeing a future run for the presidency, what are her chances given these scholarly assessments?

Reading 42

Reconceiving Theories of Power: Consequences of Masculinism in the Executive Branch

(1997)

Georgia Duerst-Lahti

The absence of a female president in the United States and the difficulties encountered by Elizabeth Dole and Carol Moseley Braun in their respective runs to be their party's nominee underscore the continued reluctance of some Americans to vote for a qualified woman for president. Georgia Duerst-Lahti, in this provocative chapter published in a path-breaking collection of essays, *The Other Elites: Women, Politics, and Power in the Executive Branch*, edited by political scientists MaryAnne Borrelli and Janet M. Martin, explores the dominant masculine conception of politics and the consequences of that conceptualization on women's participation in the executive branch. She underscores the fact that gender is relational and challenges her readers to reconceptualize the frameworks they use to evaluate all political participation. She examines as well the relationships between gender and power, especially in the executive branch in the Office of the President and the president's Cabinet.

Duerst-Lahti begins with the assumption that the identity of politics is masculine in nature, and that the executive branch, with its emphasis on military might, is especially masculine. She notes the paucity of women as governors and even as chief executive officers (CEOs) to bolster her case that our traditional ways of viewing politics must be expanded if we are to understand not only how the executive branch works, but the challenges that women face to reach parity there. And, just as importantly, she offers several distressing consequences of the masculinism in executive power.

[* * *]

Explanations for the relative paucity of women in executive positions are plentiful. The most common one—the "pipeline effect"—combines time and credentials: Women have had too little time since the societal changes wrought by the women's movement for large numbers of them to develop the needed credentials. This explanation clearly has merit, as two of the three cabinet secretaries in the first term of the Clinton administration served in lesser posts during the Carter administration. Still, one should not ignore centuries of women's exclusion through law, custom, and other social regulations—the vestiges of which make women's full inclusion so difficult today. . . .

[* * *]

Gender: A Primer

In the past two decades gender analysis has developed into a sophisticated subfield, with gender emerging as a pivotal social concept. Within gender analysis . . . is the seemingly new awareness that men have gender, too. As a category for analysis, gender is not interchangeable with sex despite the rampant misuse of both terms, especially in quantitative analysis. For categories of analysis, sex denotes the limited knowledge of a respondent as a physiological male or female who presents himself or herself as a man or a woman. Gender, in contrast, is *relational:* To understand feminine requires understanding masculine.

. . . Understanding the implications of gender is essential for understanding executive power because gender reveals that a female cannot enter a post previously held by a male and be entirely interchangeable with him—in meaning at least. Whereas job performance might be equally meritorious and the tasks performed the same, *gender shapes interpretation*. To acknowledge this fact does not diminish current "receptivity" toward women in positions of executive power. Rather, it accounts for the fact that as individuals shaped by society we still must contend with stored knowledge about "men" and about "women."

Much of gender analysis has focused on behaviors, roles, or traits and their appropriateness for males or females. This analysis grows out of structural-functional frameworks and, especially, strictly demarcated sex roles seen as complementary. In this framework culture imposes "appropriate" behavior or conduct. To act outside of prescribed norms is to deviate from cultural standards and to "cross over" sex-role boundaries. Much of feminist activism has been directed toward opening options to women under a system that has dramatically constrained women's "proper" conduct. Although enormous societal change has occurred since 1970 in terms of gender prescriptions, gender dualism remains deeply embedded in cultural expectations.

All of this suggests that political science must reconsider the use of the concept "gender neutral" in research findings and in thinking generally. The term "gender neutral" is usually used to indicate that men and women report the same answer on a survey or achieve no statistical difference on some quantitative measure. But neutrality implies that gender has no effect, that it is indifferent or takes no part in interpretations of the behavior. . . .

[* * *]

The concept of *transgendered* captures the dynamic of interpretation far better than does gender neutrality. The term implies that a biological male or female can cross past gender constructions and still be seen as appropriate, but it also implies that gender simultaneously continues to shape interpretations. Few doubt today, for example, that women and men can both serve well on school boards, although we might still expect men to gravitate toward the mechanics of building projects and women toward curricular matters. This distinction is crucial for understanding masculinism in executive power and for explaining why males and females are not fully interchangeable, in meaning at least.

Another closely related concept is *regendering,* or the reinscription of gender dualism in circumstances in which gender roles have broadened, weakened, or otherwise changed. With regendering, when a male has crossed into an occupation previously gendered as feminine or a female into a once-masculine occupation, conditions that were once strictly same sex no longer apply, and the practice of the occupation has gender reimposed upon it. This occurs even though no physiological reason exists to do so. Elaine Hall has written of the practice of requiring female Marine officers to undergo training in proper makeup while in dress uniform as an example of regendering a practice that no longer has a same-sex population. In this case, femininity is reimposed upon women who cross into masculine practice, and female Marines become regendered. These women are not Marines but female Marines, with gender dualism reimposed by rules and practices.

[* * *]

Posts in the executive branch are also gendered and can become regendered with changes in cultural interpretations. As long as the practice of being a public executive is gendered masculine, masculine privileges accompany the practice even as it is modified by transgendering and regendering processes. Whether these posts will become revalued remains to be seen.

Finally, much has been written about the relationship between gender and power. Often such writing suggests that men have the latitude to couple difference with dominance and to structure societal norms and belief systems to male advantage. Although this may be accurate, it is simplistic. Challenges to this characterization are easy to find and are often raised by the men's rights movement. Child custody awards in divorces, in which the mother has power superior to that of the father, or women's latitude to not be employed while also not being seen as failures provide examples. If women have power advantages in these circumstances, then they likely do in others as well; and if gender provides women with more power than men in some circumstances, then the larger claim of men's superior power can be refuted. Thus, if men's power is not absolute, then women can enter various power arenas by matching the positional demands. Executive power is such an arena. Clearly, analysis of gender and power is complex.

The concept of gender power provides a more potent analytic tool than sexism or male dominance—commonly used analytic concepts—as it captures varied and fluid situational power. *Gender power* results from our (e)valuations of things and behaviors, of ways of being, behaving, and structuring social relations. Gender power permeates and follows from all facets of human interaction, operating at interpersonal levels and within institutions and social categories. Normative gender power shapes normative assessments as well. Gender power varies in every situation but can be identified and analyzed in any particular setting.

[* * *]

Masculinism: Gender as Ideology

[* * *]

The ideological concomitant to feminism is masculinism. Masculinism operates as the guiding ideology of political life today and is difficult to deny once the possibility of its existence has been given any thought. An understanding of masculinism will help us understand the politics it shapes. Because of the nature of executive power, . . . masculinism is particularly important, as it places men at the center of executing the form of public power that carries the most discretion, much as it did with warrior kings of old.

Both masculinism and feminism fit within gender as an ideological structure. Feminists have long identified arrangements in which men (pre)dominate power resources and control power positions as ideological. For several decades, feminists have labeled the extant arrangements as patriarchy. These arrangements can be seen as the practices or actions that extend from decisions about who is suited to exercise political power, structure, and apparatus in the form of institutions and constitutions that shape the authority, laws, and rules that follow from those decisions. Under patriarchy, or the rule of fathers, men made decisions about the best way to structure power, who was suited to exercise that power, and the conditions under which it would be exercised.

Masculinism is a better name than patriarchy for the political ideology that structures current arrangements. . . .

Masculinism as an ideology has been largely invisible, masking itself well, as any successful dominant ideology does. . . .

Further, the clear conceptualization of masculinism as political ideology has been thwarted by the way political science has treated feminism as ideology. . . .

Feminism might more aptly be thought of as an overarching political meta-ideology that has approached political ideology from a gynocentric (women-centered) perspective rather than from the androcentric (man-centered) starting point of masculinism. . . .

Gender, then, is simultaneously ideology, categories of analysis, roles, a set of practices, and a source of power in its own right. With this tentative beginning, I now turn to an analysis of the executive branch and power.

The Executive Branch and Aspects of Power

When political scientists think about power in the executive branch, they usually focus on the president; the Executive Office of the President and its hub, the White House staff; and executive departments and agencies; and in passing they acknowledge a "kitchen cabinet." Power, however, is not uniform across various parts of the executive branch.

Each part of the executive branch has its own source of legitimate power, and the quality of that power varies greatly across parts. The president, or chief executive, holds the authority vested in an institution as well as in a person. The president is seen as the most powerful person in the world, at least in the textbook presidency. . . . The paucity of precise constitutional limits on presidential power is consistent with the discretion often vested in executives. Discretion, coupled with structural resources, provides a tremendous capacity to reward or coerce.

Important in presidential power are administrative units of the executive branch, most notably departments and agencies. These units have little constitutional basis; they derive their status by necessity and tradition from the single clause that the president "shall execute" laws. . . . In 1937 the Brownlow Committee issued its call that "the president needs help," and the staff posts of the Executive Office of the President (EOP) were born. . . . And with the increased size and power of the EOP came the need to manage it—hence, the development of the White House staff and the conversion of personal roles into institutional roles. To manage an entire set of close advisers, the chief of staff was established, and the position's powers then expanded greatly. . . .

Some power dynamics are especially important within this enormous framework. Access to the president remains a source of power across all parts of the executive branch, with greater access providing more power. Differences among the power of cabinet departments are well-known, with State, Treasury, Defense, and Justice constituting the more powerful inner cabinet and all other departments relegated to the less prominent outer cabinet. Considerable EOP power flows from high levels of information, expertise, and access.

[* * *]

Women as the "Other" in Executive Power

[* * *]

The executive branch's power structure tends to be organized in a centralized, functionally distributed, and hierarchical arrangement. Certain behaviors accompany that structure. Consistent with this structure, the presidency operates on the great man model of leadership. Concomitant to both is the pervasive but elusive spirit of *comitatus*, a camaraderie that creates particular demands.

Much of executive power is derived from what we want from executives. In contrast, legislatures are fragmented, decentralized, laterally arranged, and intentionally slow because they are intended to be deliberative. Executive power is characterized by unity of command, hierarchical arrangements, and—with centralized control—a capacity to act quickly and decisively when circumstances dictate.

These factors create circumstances in which women are understood as "other" in contrast to a masculine norm, and they do so in a way that is predictable inside gender ideology. In a system constructed under masculinism, one would predict that the greater the power available in any particular part of the executive branch, the fewer women we will find. We would also expect women to emerge first and most often in functional areas associated with women and second in less powerful outer cabinets. Because gender is constructed, however, it is fluid and subject to transgendering, regendering, and revaluation. As should become evident, particular factors produce gendered obstacles for women and opportunities for men.

Executive Branch Structure and Gender Power

Two aspects of the structural arrangements of the executive branch are most important for considerations of women's penetration of executive power: the regard for hierarchy and the functional distribution of agency work. . . . [H]ierarchical modes of organizing accord more closely with masculinity than with femininity. Women are less likely to be seen by others as appropriate for top posts, at least in part because they are less likely than men to be present in the hierarchical chain of command.

But even more important than hierarchy is functional distribution. Women populate administrative agencies; often, nearly half of employees are female. However, women are not commonly found in command positions (e.g., administrators) within the executive branch. . . . Women are much more likely to be found in staff units or staff positions . . . within line units. As such, they have little access to structural power resources—for example, authority to make critical decisions, to manage budgets, or to supervise personnel.

Critically, function is highly gendered. Gender influences what is seen as most valuable and hence as most powerful, as well as where women are most likely to enter executive power. . . . Under masculinism, one would expect women's entrance to occur first in the least powerful parts of the executive agencies.

The inner cabinet departments related to the functions of State, Defense, Treasury, and Justice are considered the most important and most powerful. For this reason, the appointment of Janet Reno as attorney general had particular significance—she was the first woman to head an inner cabinet department. Because of gender power under masculinism, one would predict women's gains would occur largely in the outer cabinet.

However big in budget and personnel and however crucial to the lives of most Americans, the Department of Health and Human Services is frequently and narrowly characterized as the overseer of welfare and faces popular disfavor and congressional attacks as a result. Several women have headed the department, thus gaining access to the power of size but operating within the confines of an unpopular mission. Similarly, women have a history of heading the Department of Labor, but labor is less prominent in a system that favors capital. . . .

Any appointment of a woman to a top post is important for changing gender power in the executive branch because each appointment contributes to changes in gender expectations and offers the opportunity to transform gender power. With a woman's appointment, the barrier of men's exclusive hold on the top executive posts is broken, and because of transgendering or regendering processes the office becomes less masculinized. . . .

Given all this, women's presence in top posts that have never been held by a woman and in agencies consistent with masculine expectations count as the most important gains. Because practices themselves are gendered, the possibility of achieving transgendered understandings is greatest with the first female appointment to a highly masculinized policy area. . . .

[* * *]

The Chief Chief

A major arena of inquiry into the problems women experience in penetrating the executive branch focuses on the ultimate head of the executive branch as a single leader. [Political scientist] Clinton Rossiter's classic list of presidential duties serves as a useful illustration: Chief of State, Chief Executive, Chief Diplomat, Commander-in-Chief, Chief Legislator, Chief of the Party, Voice of the People, Protector of the Peace, Manager of Prosperity, Leader of the Free World. Whereas Rossiter, like many who have built on him, acknowledges the distance between constitutional and statutory powers and actual responsibilities, the titles themselves reveal the masculine assumption.

The term *chief* is seldom associated with traditional women's work, and women as commanders are even more rare. The "protector" role has been almost exclusively a masculine endeavor, beyond the image of a mother protecting her children. "Voice" is only recently something women have been known to have, although surely women have always spoken, often in very public ways. As advertising agencies and female candidates are well aware, authoritative voices are still ceded far more readily to men. This factor also figures centrally into a president's prime power: the power to persuade. The elements that assist persuasion—such as a professional reputation, being seen as a commanding presence, and associated elements of public prestige—are also attributed more readily to men.

[* * *]

In terms of our thinking about leadership, this singularity accords with the "great man" model. In this gendered construction of a singular leader, cause and effect are blurred and reinforcing; nevertheless, cultural constructions much more readily accord the possibility of individual accomplishment deserving of greatness—accomplishments earned in one's own right, without regard to connections or support—to men. Gender power gives the advantage to men in terms of the "great man" model of the lone leader at the top. In contrast, women are challenged in at least two ways: in the belief that a woman is or can be singular and in the possibility of be(com)ing "great."

[* * *]

One critical area in which women are not yet found in significant numbers is the military, particularly in combat roles, and this has ramifications for being perceived as "executive material." Important in presidential considerations is the value placed on military service in creating the image of presidential merit. . . .

Perhaps the most striking contrast of divergent gender interpretation can be found in the importance of connections or, said another way, in the myth that "great men" act alone. The problem for women, however, is that men are assumed to be entitled to a helpmate wife who seldom threatens his stature, whereas a woman can have a helpmate only under unusual circumstances and in most cases will not be seen as uninfluenced by him. This might be thought of as the assumption of autonomy for men and of heteronomy for women. For example, 1984 Democratic vice-presidential candidate Geraldine Ferraro received severe scrutiny in her own right and emerged relatively unscathed. But her husband had some questionable dealings, and his actions were easily turned into an inordinately poor reflection of her. Clearly, with Hillary Rodham Clinton, attempts are under way to make the spousal reflection a transgendered reality. Paradoxically, however, to do so would mean acknowledging the power of presidential wives, which is itself upsetting.

[* * *]

Consequences of Masculinism in Executive Power

Whereas ideally gender ideology will cease to dictate social constructs and hence social and political practices, the present imbalance between masculinism and feminism as determinants of gender power in politics creates immediate consequences. In more concrete terms, the consequences of masculinism in executive power include the following:

- *Loss of talent as the pool of those who aspire to work in positions that carry executive power is greatly diminished. . . .*
- *A constrained worldview that limits the framing of problems and their possible solutions to a narrow set of experiences. . . .*
- *The legitimacy of the government itself. . . .*
- *The future of gender relations, power relations, and the possibilities for transforming human interaction.* Minimally, women in visible positions of executive power provide role models for girls and boys alike. More immediately, the absence of women in such positions perpetuates the belief that women are not qualified simply because male decisionmakers are not associated with them as collegial equals. . . .

[* * *]

TOWARD CRITICAL THINKING

1. Do you agree with Georgia Duerst-Lahti that the executive branch "is arguably the most masculine branch of government?" If it is, what does that say about women's abilities to be viewed as successful inhabitants of that world?

2. What challenges would any woman candidate for the White House face, given Duerst-Lahti's analysis? Does the fact that American society generally fails to see women as potentially great leaders affect those challenges? Have the two female secretaries of state in the last two decades affected our perception of women as leaders?

READING 43

Gender, Credibility, and Politics: The Senate Nomination Hearings of Cabinet Secretaries-Designate, 1975–1993

(1997)

MaryAnne Borrelli

Until the presidency of Jimmy Carter in 1976, few women served in high-ranking government positions. But Carter, and presidents after him, began to see appointing women as "good politics," although it wasn't until the presidency of Bill Clinton that women actually were nominated for, and some even eventually confirmed, as Cabinet secretaries in non-traditional women's spots. The confirmation of Janet Reno as U.S. attorney general and later Madeleine Albright as secretary of state truly were breakthroughs for women. But, the nomination of more women brought with it charges that women nominees were subject to different kinds of senatorial investigations. As historical "outsiders" in the political process, would they face distinctive challenges in establishing their credibility—credibility that their male counterparts simply were assumed to have?

As Georgia Duerst-Lahti notes (Reading 42), masculinism pervades the executive branch. At the apex of each executive branch department sits a Cabinet secretary (or an attorney general at the Department of Justice), and most people who have held those positions have been male.

As presidents increased the number of women appointed to their Cabinets, analysis of these women and how they were treated during their confirmation hearings became possible. MaryAnne Borrelli's comparison of men and women secretary-designates published in *Political Research Quarterly* reveals startling differences in the way that male senators treat men and women, regardless of the similarities in their governmental experience. This article also harkens back to the findings many congressional scholars. The women studied by Borrelli faced challenges to their "right" to be in positions of power that are similar to the challenges faced by the African American women in Mary Hawkesworth's study (Reading 35). And, again, these challenges come from the largely male U.S. Senate. Borrelli's findings also provide quantitative support for many of Duerst-Lahti's assertions (Reading 42).

The constitutional requirement that presidential appointments be approved by the Senate was intended to ensure the good character and competence of executive officers. Senators have duly questioned nominees regarding potential conflicts of interest and have assessed their policy expertise. Senators have also used the confirmation process, and most especially the confirmation hearings, to oversee the departments and to advance their constituents' interests.

Socializing the presidential appointee to legislative-presidential politics is, however, the most significant confirmation task. Typically conducted by a nominee's Senate authorization committee, confirmation hearings are the public inauguration of an important and on-going relationship. This is the nominee's formal introduction to the network in which he or she will mediate conflicting pressures for increasingly scarce resources. It is therefore entirely comprehensible that senators would be attentive to appointees' professional credentials, programmatic priorities, and partisan ideology. But senators are also and even more fundamentally concerned with each nominee's acceptance and practice of existent political folkways. In every hearing, senators carefully establish that the new policymaker shares their understanding of how decisions are to be made and implemented.

Confirmation hearings could therefore be expected to progress differently for nominees with and without experience in Washington politics. A Cabinet secretary-designate with service in the Congress or in the executive branch would presumably be viewed by Senate committee members as well-versed in Washington's political norms. The "rules of the game" having been mutually acknowledged, this hearing would progress rapidly to a discussion of policies and programs. A secretary-designate untried in national office, however, would be more cautiously received by Senate committee members. These nominees would need to be legitimized before the committee, whose members would also be more concerned to examine and instruct the "outsider." The first hypothesis, then, is that senators place greater confidence in presidential appointees who are Washington "insiders" and less confidence in presidential appointees who are Washington "outsiders."

Yet there is also a literature which indicates that men and women, independent of their professional qualifications, are routinely accorded differing degrees of credibility. Scholars have, in fact, shown that judgments of character and performance are often affected by gender stereotypes. An experimental study, for example, demonstrated that women attorneys were granted less credibility than were men attorneys. An ethnographic study found that women victims of crime were seldom judged believable witnesses. In these instances, as in various others, the observer's gender role socialization caused him or her to discount the woman's qualifications: A woman could not be reliable because women were presumptively passive, dependent, sexually unpredictable, and emotional. Reviewing this research, one scholar concluded that "whereas men, regardless of role or rule, are assumed to *possess* credibility, women must *earn* credibility." These findings oblige one to ask whether women are also disadvantaged in confirmation hearings, a query that becomes only more pressing when one considers the environment and the mores which confront women presidential appointees at these events.

The national executive branch is highly masculine in its personnel and in its ideology. . . . With specific regard to presidential appointees, therefore, the confirmation process has been designed by men senators to evaluate men secretaries-designate. . . .

[* * *]

This [essay] tests these . . . two hypotheses, one suggesting that the credibility of presidential appointees in confirmation hearings is a function of their status as Washington insiders or outsiders; and the other proposing that gender biases cause Senate committee members to treat women presidential appointees as less credible than men appointees. . . .

Research Design

This study focuses upon confirmation hearings for Cabinet secretaries-designate. . . . [E]very hearing for a confirmed woman secretary designate was examined, from 1975 to 1993, in order to see how women successfully navigated these events. . . . Also analyzed were the confirmation hearings of the men who were the women's predecessors in the Cabinet.

The first two women to serve in the Cabinet did not have confirmation hearings. Labor Secretary Frances Perkins was a member of Franklin D. Roosevelt's first Cabinet, whose secretaries were approved without hearings or floor debates. Health, Education, and Welfare (HEW) Secretary Oveta Culp Hobby joined Eisenhower's Cabinet in 1953. Having confirmed Hobby's appointment as the Administrator of the Federal Security Administration earlier that same year, the Senate deemed a second hearing unnecessary and approved her Cabinet appointment by voice vote. The women's confirmation hearing record therefore began with Carla Anderson Hills, nominated Secretary of Housing and Urban Development in 1975. It continued through the first term of the Clinton administration, encompassing seventeen confirmation hearings for fourteen successful secretarial appointments. The twelve confirmation hearings for their men predecessors were also studied. . . . [F]ive women secretaries either served in a newly founded department (and thus had no predecessor) or had another woman as their predecessor.

Given that the first hypothesis postulates that Senate committee members will grant the secretary-designate more or less credibility in accord with the appointee's status as a Washington insider or outsider, the biographical profile of each nominee merits consideration. The men and women nominees were similar in regard to age (men average 51.5 years at appointment, women 51.6), race (majority white; [Louis] W. Sullivan, [Patricia Roberts] Harris, and [Hazel R.] O'Leary are African American), and marital status (married; [Donna E.] Shalala and [Janet] Reno are single). Cabinet appointees have been an increasingly well-educated group, and all but four of the nominees have professional or postgraduate degrees. Thus, sampled nominees are representative of the larger population of Cabinet appointees. Some evidence of disparate personal lives for the men and women is found in their contrasting numbers of children (men average 3.8, ranging from 3 to 6 children; married women average 1.6, ranging from none to 4 children).

The secretaries-designate are varied in regard to their governmental service. At one extreme is Elliot Richardson, whose appointment as Commerce secretary-designate was his third to the Cabinet. At the other extreme are the three men ([Andrew L.] Lewis

[Jr.], [Robert A.] Mosbacher, and Sullivan) who had no governmental credentials at the time of their nomination. Though no woman had achieved Richardson's status, every woman secretary-designate had been an elected or appointed political figure. Thus, the range of the women's political experience was similar to that of the men, albeit without the insider/outsider extremes. Differences in their confirmation hearings, therefore, could not be attributed to patterned differences in their career paths.

In classifying the appointees, insiders were those who satisfied at least one of the following criteria: Either their primary profession was in the national government, or they entered the Cabinet directly from a subcabinet post, or they were transferring from one secretarial post to another. Those who did not satisfy any of these criteria were deemed outsiders. . . .

Discourse analysis was utilized to study the hearings. . . . Of interest were the speeches which described the Secretary-designate and thus revealed Senate assessments of his/her credibility. These speeches were of two kinds. "Opening statements" were delivered by confirmation committee members, and literally opened the hearings. These were followed by "introductions," delivered by the secretary-designate's home-state senators (and others), which formally presented the appointee. Both sets of speeches focused upon the ability of the secretary-designate to succeed in executive politics. . . .

. . . If the hypotheses advanced above are accurate, one would expect that insiders would encounter more supportive opening statements (committee members expressing confidence in these appointees' abilities) and that outsiders would require strong introductions to convince the committee of their abilities. Further, if women do have less credibility than men, one could anticipate that men would receive more favorable endorsements from the committee members and from the senators providing their introductions.

A thematic discourse analysis of the opening statements and introductions was conducted. Utilizing well-tested classifications of "masculine" and "feminine" established by gender power scholars, the speeches were systematically examined in order to determine which traits the senators (a) believed the secretaries-designate possessed and (b) expected the secretaries-designate to manifest during their Cabinet tenures. The congruence between the senators' assessments of the secretaries-designate, the sex and gender of the secretaries-designate, and the requirement of masculinist behaviors could then be charted.

[* * *]

Gendered Institutions:
(Re)Inscripting the Masculinist Norms of Politics

Arguably, the fact that men have predominated in both the Senate and the executive branch has caused the confirmation process to be an institution designed by men for the evaluation of men. Therefore, this discussion begins with the hearings of the men secretaries-designate. These offer considerable support for the contention that senators differentiate between Washington insiders and outsiders. [Table 43.1] Insiders find

TABLE 43.1

Men and Women Cabinet Secretaries, Classified as Washington Insiders or Outsiders

Insiders	Outsiders
Men Cabinet Secretaries:	
James T. Lynn	Andrew L. Lewis, Jr.
Elliot L. Richardson	Robert A. Mosbacher
Joseph A. Califano, Jr.	Louis W. Sullivan
Richard S. Schweiker	James D. Watkins
William E. Brock	
William P. Barr	
Women Cabinet Secretaries:	
Carla Anderson Hills	Patricia Roberts Harris (1977)[a]
Patricia Roberts Harris (1979)[a]	Juanita M. Kreps
Elizabeth Hanford Dole (1983, 1989)[a]	Shirley M. Hufstedler
Margaret M. Heckler	Hazel R. O'Leary
Lynn Martin	Janet Reno
Ann Dore McLaughlin	Donna E. Shalala
Barbara H. Franklin	

[a]Patricia Roberts Harris and Elizabeth Hanford Dole each held two Cabinet posts. The years of their confirmations are consequently appended to their names, so the reader can determine their status at the time of each Senate confirmation hearing.

their professional qualifications and political behaviors celebrated in committee members' opening statements. In these statements, committee members describe the nominee as a successful political actor, with whom they have well-established relationships. The introductions are reduced to formalities and sometimes eliminated. Outsiders, however, do not initially receive the committee's confidence or support. In their hearings, it is left to the senators performing the introductions to identify the nominees' qualifications. In fact, the committee members' opening statements for insiders and the senators' introductions for outsiders are virtually interchangeable. This points to the consistency of senatorial standards for Cabinet service and highlights the insider's advantaged position.

[* * *]

. . . [I]ntroductions were made by legislators from different parties, chambers, generations, and races; the nominees are from different administrations, appointed to various departments and therefore appearing before different Senate committees. Still, the same traits are highlighted in each introduction—toughness, unflinching decisiveness, strength, intelligence, dedication, and energy. . . . The consequent image of unremitting discipline, with its overtones of aggression and compelling confidence, is in keeping with traditional definitions of masculinity and is congruent with masculinist ideology. The credibility of the insider and the outsider men, therefore, rests upon their political service being identified and perceived as definitively masculine.

[* * *]

There are significant differences in the confirmation hearings of insider and outsider men secretaries-designate. *Insiders* find their qualifications listed and celebrated by the *committee members*; the insiders' Washington experience is taken as evidence of their ability to succeed in Cabinet service by masculinist practices. *Outsiders*, however, are legitimized before the committee by their *home-state senators* and others. These referees interpret the outsiders' professional accomplishments as evidence of the nominees' willingness to accept and practice such masculinist values as competitiveness, toughness, and aggressiveness. Thus, the study of men secretaries-designate indicates that there is indeed a different response accorded to Washington insiders and outsiders, such that insiders are welcomed by their authorization committee while outsiders must rely upon their home-state senators (and other sponsors) for legitimation. How the workings of such enduring senate norms as reciprocity and courtesy—to former colleagues-now-appointees, and to present colleagues recommending outsiders for executive service—condition committee members' responses merits further consideration. For now, in regard to the gendered character of these exchanges, it seems that the masculinity of men secretaries-designate is "re-inscripted" through senators' opening statements and introductions, which is to say that the appointees are reminded of masculinist norms. The fact that males are more readily identified with traditionally masculine behaviors doubtless facilitates the acceptance of men outsiders as credible Cabinet secretaries.

Institutionalized Gender:
(Re) Establishing the Feminine as Other

An analysis of the confirmation hearings for women secretaries-designate reveals that these appointees were commonly received as outsiders by the Senate committee members, even when their professional qualifications otherwise indicated they were Washington insiders. Four women insiders did find their achievements recognized in committee members' opening statements: Margaret M. Heckler, Lynn Martin (both former Representatives), and Patricia Roberts Harris and Elizabeth Dole (though only in their second Cabinet confirmation hearings, in 1979 and 1989 respectively). The women insiders who were received as outsiders were Carla Anderson Hills (then an Assistant Attorney General), Patricia Roberts Harris (1977; formerly the Ambassador to Luxembourg), Elizabeth Hanford Dole (1983; White House aide and former Federal Trade Commissioner), Ann Dore McLaughlin (then Interior Under-Secretary and a former Treasury Assistant Secretary), and Barbara H. Franklin (former White House aide and Consumer Product Safety Commissioner). Note that each of these women had previously held a Senate-confirmed presidential appointment. The differential treatment of men and women insiders is, this analysis suggests, the result of women nominees being perceived in traditionally feminine terms and thus being delegitimized by masculinist standards. Outsider women are also perceived and presented as feminine. Women secretaries-designate therefore encounter greater difficulty than do men secretaries-designate in establishing their credibility with the Senate committees.

. . . [C]ommittee members' opening statements for insiders Heckler, Martin, and Dole (1989) parallel those extended to the men insiders.

[* * *]

Though these confirmation hearings were conducted by the same committee, the speakers are from different parties and generations; the partisan majorities of the Senate also shifted between these hearings, changing the committee leadership. These variations, however, do not alter the assessment of insider status. These women have proven themselves within or to the Congress, in a manner that committee members cannot contest.

The other insider women—Hills, Harris (1977), Dole (1983), McLaughlin, and Franklin—encountered the opening statements that greeted outsider women and men. These speeches stressed the policy and departmental difficulties that the secretary-designate would encounter upon entering office, and expressed the hope that the nominee would prove equal to the challenges. The committee members' references to the nominees' executive experience were exceptionally brief or nonexistent. Consequently, the introductions performed by home-state senators were as crucial for these five women insiders as for the women and men outsiders.

The introductions of the five insider and six outsider women concluded with assessments of the nominees' credentials that subtly differed from those accorded the men outsiders.

[* * *]

. . . Surveying these speeches more widely, one finds attention is given to Hills' policy skills, Harris' political acumen, [Juanita M.] Kreps' administrative background, Dole's government service, Franklin's business career, and Reno's legal career. With the exception of the Reno introductions, however, these speeches do not go so far as to assert that the women secretaries-designate are competitive, aggressive, or tough—masculinist behaviors that are repeatedly attributed to the men outsiders. Instead, senators from different parties and generations describe the women as practicing feminine behaviors. The women secretaries-designate are introduced as intelligent, committed, flexible, youthful, and honorable, as evidencing fortitude, discipline, sensitivity, and sagacity; as able, conscientious, and dedicated; as dedicated, cheerful, and spiritual; as calming, enthusiastic, and attentive; and as respectful, open, and responsive. These qualities are in keeping with traditional conceptions of feminine leadership, which stress motivating others through persuasion, inspiration, and nurturance. Though this transformational leadership may be effective, it is not congruent with the masculinist ideology. Thus, the senators' introductions effectively delegitimize the woman, secretary-designate before her confirmation committee.

Note that this differential treatment of the men and women secretaries-designate cannot be attributed to differences in their career paths. As noted above, the men and women demonstrate similar patterns of professional development, though women did not exhibit the insider/outsider extremes evidenced among the men. The senators upheld a constant masculinist standard for judgment during these years, removing the possibility that legislative-executive tensions or partisan disagreements affected the hearings. The patterned variation among these confirmation hearings instead seems rooted in the senators' determination to establish the appointees' socialization to Washington folkways: Every hearing considered the appointees' conformity with traditional gender roles and with the precepts of a masculinist political ideology. For the men secretaries-designate, proving their masculinity provided evidence of their masculinist political intent. For the women secretaries-designate, it seemed that proving their femininity contradicted masculinist theories of leadership, potentially creating an image of professional incompetence. Though the introductions attempt to link feminine traits with successful leadership, they provide weaker endorsements of the women secretaries-designate and may thereby contribute to lowering the credibility of these political executives. These eventualities merit further investigation.

[* * *]

TOWARD CRITICAL THINKING

1. How do the masculinist norms discussed by Georgia Duerst-Lahti (Reading 42) evidence themselves in MaryAnne Borrelli's research? Does Borrelli give any indication that as more women participate in these hearings as legislators, women nominees will be treated more equitably?

2. What actions could women secretary-designates take to facilitate a fair hearing before the Senate? Does the kind of treatment reported by Borrelli result in discrimination against these women if they ultimately are confirmed?

Reading 44

Wives in the White House: The Political Influence of First Ladies

(1996)

Karen O'Connor, Bernadette Nye, and Laura van Assendelft

As more and more women join the ranks of Cabinet secretaries, few women find themselves in the inner circle of any presidents. Presidents Bill Clinton and George W. Bush have been welcome exceptions to that rule. It is clear, for example, that adviser Karen Hughes and Secretary of State Condoleezza Rice are part of President Bush's trusted inner circle. Still, historically, with few women in the Cabinet and even fewer as trusted advisers, many presidents looked to their wives not only for political support but advice. Often, first ladies were the only ones around a president who could provide candid advice without risking banishment from the inner circle. They don't have to be confirmed, as Georgia Duerst-Lahti's (Reading 42) work underscores. They don't challenge conventional masculinist notions. In fact, only when first ladies venture into unconventional roles do they appear to suffer for their role as a critical adviser to the president.

In this work first published in the journal *Presidential Studies Quarterly*, Karen O'Connor, Bernadette Nye, and Laura van Assendelft note that many first ladies have enjoyed considerable access to power as wives of sitting presidents. They point out that, historically, many women played important behind-the-scenes roles in policy making, whether it was recognized at the time or not. This article was not only one of the first to identify the varied roles played by first ladies historically, but it also became the basis of a host of conferences and other studies on first ladies. The unique role adopted by Hillary Rodham Clinton also fostered this interest in first ladies. When Bill Clinton ran for office, he often quipped that you got two for the price of one. Once elected, he proceeded to appoint his wife to head his controversial Commission on Health Care Reform, and criticism of Hillary Rodham Clinton skyrocketed. Yet, eventually, she was able to turn those troubles, as well as her husband's infidelities, into positives as she became the first first lady to seek—and win—election to public office. While several women held congressional office over "their husbands' dead bodies," it was unprecedented for a first lady to seek an independent political career. Thus, this article is important as it focuses attention on what may in the future become a base from which women could run for office.

After he left the White House, Harry S Truman appealed for greater American acknowledgment of the role of first ladies, wishing "I hope some day someone will take time to evaluate the true role of wife of a president, and to assess the many burdens she has to bear and the contributions she makes." Despite Truman's urging, the role of first ladies in political decision-making has gone largely unreported. Interestingly, even Truman biographers have failed to note the importance of Bess Truman to her husband. It was not, in fact, until Margaret Truman more recently penned *First Ladies* that the recognition due her mother's "behind the scenes political partnership . . . [a] closely held secret" became more widely recognized.

In light of recent discussions and interest in the role of first ladies, this is a systematic examination of their political influence. We begin with an overview of the political activities and backgrounds of first ladies by presenting quantitative comparative data on the thirty-eight women who have been married to sitting presidents. Next, we explore the various roles first ladies have played and trace the evolution of the role and duties of first ladies as their influence on politics and public policy has grown. . . . And, after discussing the evolution of the position of first lady as a policy influencer or maker, [we] offer conclusions and suggestions for further research on this important contemporary topic.

[* * *]

Data Collection and Methods

Measuring actual political influence—is not easy because it involves a problem that has confounded political scientists and historians for years. . . .

[* * *]

Confounding any systematic examination of first ladies are two factors: (1) the inherent difficulties in determining, measuring or attributing influence, and; (2) societal norms that continue to make it unattractive for most first ladies to give even the appearance of wielding influence. Most have been quick to recognize that once they appeared to act beyond the scope of traditional duties associated with their position, they and their spouse may be in for considerable negative publicity. No matter what motivations for exercising power were in play, it is unlikely that traditional political "credit taking" will occur. Time after time, public opinion polls reveal that a traditional role continues to be the one more accepted for first ladies to play.

Our appraisals of many first ladies, although gleaned from numerous secondary sources, may not reflect their true influence. Because of the nature of our subject, we attempted to examine untraditional methods of political influence such as their use of entertaining for political purposes. We were particularly interested in the roles that first ladies adopted while in the White House. Some, for example, pleaded invalidism and made no public appearances, some fulfilled minimal social obligations, and others could be characterized as active hostesses who used that role to improve their husband's political fortunes. We also looked to see to what degree could first ladies be characterized as helpmates or partners, therefore allowing us to imply some level of political influence. For example, did the president and the first lady discuss politics, did she serve as an informal confidant or adviser, write speeches, or actually travel on fact-finding missions for the president? We also identified another role for first ladies, that of policy advocate or policy maker who attempted to influence the president or others in his administration privately or publicly on policy preferences. From 1799, when Abigail Adams lobbied her husband concerning a treaty with the Dutch, first ladies have attempted to influence political decision-making. Here we operationalize first lady influence as any attempts to affect public policy, executive decision-making, or the course of a political career as evidenced in diaries, biographies, White House insider accounts, newspaper articles or other public records.

[* * *]

First Ladies: A Profile

A statistical overview of the background characteristics of the thirty-eight first ladies reveals the following.

Education. Most first ladies had less formal education than the men who they married. More presidents than first ladies graduated from college or earned an advanced degree (26 vs. 15). Only four first ladies had more formal education than their husbands—Mary Todd Lincoln, Eliza Johnson, Frances Folsom Cleveland, and Florence Harding.

Thirteen couples had similar educational experiences. Hillary Clinton, who shares a similar educational background with her husband, is the first first lady to hold an advanced degree. Lou Hoover, interestingly, was the first woman in the United States to be awarded an undergraduate degree in geology.

[* * *]

Employment. Very few early first ladies were employed outside of the home before marriage. Abigail Fillmore, a schoolteacher, was not only the first to work for wages, she was also the first first lady to continue to be employed after her marriage. Teaching was the most common profession. Eight first ladies, including Clinton's stint as a law professor, taught before their marriages. Few worked steadily after their marriages; most devoted themselves to their husbands and/or growing families. . . .

Interestingly, some first ladies worked for their husbands—either in remunerative or nonremunerative positions. Sarah Polk served as her husband's secretary from 1845–1849, and Florence Harding, Lady Bird Johnson and Bess Truman, were actually on the payrolls in their husband's congressional offices. . . .

No first ladies have actually been employed once their husbands became president. What is known as the "Bobby Kennedy law," which was passed by Congress in 1978 to prevent future presidents from hiring members of their families into governmental service, now prevents first ladies from having *salaried* positions in the federal government. A 1993 U.S. Court of Appeals decision, however, actually concluded that First Lady Clinton was a "full-time employee of the government" in spite of that law. In *Association of American Physicians and Surgeons* v. *Hillary Rodham Clinton*, the court addressed the legal status of the first lady in the course of its answering the question whether or not the President's Task Force on National Health Care Reform was an advisory committee for the purpose of federal law. The U.S. government claimed that Clinton *was* an employee because the "traditional, if informal, status and 'duties' of the president's wife as 'first lady' gives her *de facto* officer or employee status." In support of the position ultimately adopted by the Court, the government noted the "longstanding tradition of public service by first ladies" since Sarah Polk "who have acted (albeit in the background) as advisers and personal representatives of their husbands." Nevertheless, by law, a first lady cannot have a renumerative position within the federal government.

[* * *]

Political Ambition. Of the thirty-eight "first ladies," thirty-five married men who would later become president; three actually married men who were president at the time of their marriage. Forty percent of the first ladies had relatives who were involved in politics. Although many wives were thus somewhat familiar with politics, few of them probably ever envisioned that their husbands would become president.

First Ladies Mary Todd Lincoln and Florence Harding were among the few who professed their desire to become the nation's first lady from early childhood. Both women set out to marry men who might someday become president. . . . [S]eventeen of the thirty-eight wives married men who were involved in politics at the time of their marriages. Significantly, all fifteen who had relatives involved in politics married men who had some political experience. Thus, many wives may have had an idea that higher office for their husband was a distinct possibility. And, at least one tried to assure it. Sarah Polk accepted her husband's proposal of marriage on the condition that he first run for the state legislature.

Marriage Age. Most first ladies lived in eras when women married in their teens. Nevertheless, many of these women were older than the norm when they wed. The average age of first ladies at marriage was 24 years. The youngest was 17-year-old Eliza Johnson; the oldest was Woodrow Wilson's second wife, 43-year-old Edith Bolling Gault Wilson. The average age at marriage of the thirty-eight presidents included in this study was thirty years; the youngest and oldest first ladies married the youngest and oldest presidents, Andrew Johnson (18 years) and Woodrow Wilson (59), respectively. . . .

Children. Only two first ladies were childless—Sarah Polk and Florence Harding. Martha Custis Washington, Dolley Madison, and Edith Wilson did not bear any children during their marriage to the president but had children from earlier marriages. The thirty-eight first ladies had an average of 3.6 children. . . . Actually, we were somewhat surprised by the relatively low average number of children given the large number of children (an average of eight) most American women had until the last quarter of the nineteenth century. . . .

For whatever reason, this relatively low number of children per first lady, may be an important factor in some first ladies' political involvement and interest. In fact, some of the most involved presidential wives had few or no children . . . .

[* * *]

The Evolving Role of First Ladies as Policy Makers

The lives, histories and perceptions of the role played by women married to presidents reflect the changes that have occurred in women's status over time. Fairly clear patterns can be observed in the development of the office of first lady. . . . [I]ncreased demands on the presidency itself and changes in women's social roles have expanded both the need and ability of first ladies to act as political functionaries.

[* * *]

The Ceremonial First Lady. All presidents, as well as their wives (or some surrogate) have spent a considerable amount of time dealing with the social side of the presidency. Not only have presidents' wives been responsible for the day-to-day operation of the White House, they have also been expected to be the president's official hostess. So ingrained is that role, that in an effort to deprofessionalize Hillary Clinton, the White House made sure that early "news" stories about the first lady showed her in a Donna Karan dress selecting china for her first formal White House dinner. It wasn't a cookie bake off but it was close.

From the beginning, the first lady has had important ceremonial duties, often making her more critical to the political fortunes of the president than the vice president. Hosting teas and formal dinners, greeting foreign visitors, making social calls and otherwise entertaining the president's friends and enemies are duties that have been engaged in by most first ladies or delegated by them to surrogates. Although Martha Washington had no model, she quickly moved to host parties to assist her husband in achieving his political goals. There is evidence that when she became concerned about the cost of entertaining, the Washingtons opened their personal purse strings to assure that the new nation did not seem impoverished to foreign diplomats and other senior statesmen.

Dolley Madison set a standard for White House entertaining that was unrivaled in her lifetime. Madison first served as a surrogate first lady for the widowed Thomas Jefferson, and then earned her reputation as outstanding hostess as first lady during her husband's administration. First Lady Madison used what we term "entertaining for political purposes." So skilled was she at influencing her husband's political opponents that "it was no mistake that at formal dinners President Madison placed her, and not himself, at the head of the table next to key statesmen." . . .

Although there is strong evidence that many of the women who followed Dolley Madison privately influenced their husbands in a variety of ways . . . many of the first ladies who followed Madison preferred to plead invalidism and delegate their social duties to a daughter, daughter-in-law or other often younger family member. Whether these women were invalids or not is open to question since many who pleaded illness lived to ripe old ages. Nevertheless, for a long period of time, the nation's image of first lady was one of a woman out of sight. Over half of those women who occupied the office before 1900 delegated their role in whole or in part. Only one invalid, Florence Harding, who suffered a debilitating stroke shortly after working so hard for her husband's election, recovered and went on to become what we term an active hostess on behalf of her husband's political interests.

For the most part, healthy first ladies saw the efficacy of entertaining and fulfilling their ceremonial role to advance their husband's position. Only one of those delegated her social responsibilities. Of the twenty-two first ladies who did not plead ill health at some time during their term in office, sixteen qualify as active hostesses who viewed fulfilling their ceremonial roles as an opportunity to advance their husband's (and often their own) political and policy agendas.

[* * *]

The Political/Representative First Lady. Over the years, first ladies have often stood in for their husbands as well as traveled with them or on their behalf. . . . Wives have not only stood in for presidents since the beginning—Martha Washington set a tradition by filling in for her husband at a church service when he was ill—they have also traveled on their husbands' behalf. Given societal conventions, however, that frowned on women traveling alone, it was not until the 1960s that a first lady traveled long distances independently of her husband for political purposes. Still, Edith Roosevelt traveled abroad with her husband and soon thereafter Edith Bolling Gault Wilson traveled with her husband to witness the signing of the Treaty of Versailles.

Eleanor Roosevelt shattered all conventions by traveling widely on her own. Her husband's inability to travel and the public's acceptance of his staying in the White House to monitor the progress of the New Deal and then World War II, probably made her uncharacteristic travel acceptable in the eyes of many who might otherwise have criticized the first lady for her actions. . . .

[* * *]

Travel now not only is accepted but expected for first ladies. The American people want the president's wife to get out among them and for many presidents, a traveling first lady can shore up popular support for programs, bring positive attention to the administration—so long as the first lady is involved in activities that are considered within the traditional woman's realm.

[* * *]

The Policy First Lady. Over the years, . . . the entertaining/ceremonial role of the first lady expanded into a political role for many. Many first ladies play an important role in formulating policy, especially as a senior adviser to the president. . . .

To examine the evolution of the first lady in politics, we differentiate eleven types of private and public political activities ranging from discussing politics to influencing public policy, realizing that first ladies' political activity and influence are almost assuredly underestimated here. As [political scientist] Richard Neustadt has noted, influence is a nebulous concept that has plagued his own research as well as that of many who study the presidency.

Despite the reluctance of first ladies to appear to influence political decisions and the hesitancy of historians and political scientists to examine these women's political activities, first ladies have long been politically interested and influential. Informal policy adviser, for example, is clearly a role adopted by many first ladies. As such, first ladies are the only women to date who clearly have reached the president's inner circle of advisers. As revealed in Table 44.1, we were able to find evidence that at least thirty-one first ladies discussed politics with their husbands; twenty-six could be considered confidants or advisers. That role often included not only discussing politics, but also screening correspondence, highlighting news articles, and editing speeches. . . . [M]any first ladies have played informal policy roles and those who have done so go back to the early period. Abigail Adams, for example, was regarded by her husband as "his intellectual peer" and he "depended a great deal on her counsel."

TABLE 44.1
Measures of First Lady Influence

	First Lady Exhibited	
Type of Activity	Yes	No
Discussed Politics	31	7
Was Confidante/Adviser	26	12
Stated Private Policy Preferences	15	23
Influenced Appointments/Nominations	14	24
Traveled on Husband's Behalf	9	29
Stated Public Policy Preferences	8	30
Attended Policy Meetings	7	31
Influenced Public Policy	5	33
Personal Issue		
Had an Identifiable Issue	17	21
Lobbied President	17	21
Lobbied Congress	3	35

There is also evidence that Andrew Johnson "consulted his wife and daughter more than he did any fellow statesmen" in spite of the fact that his wife was an invalid who rarely left their private quarters.

A much smaller number of first ladies, fifteen, made their policy preferences clear to their husbands, and fourteen actually played an important role in influencing appointments or nominations. For some first ladies such as Mary [Todd] Lincoln, this kind of input was only sporadic and not necessarily effective. For others, such as Helen Taft, it was an everyday occurrence. Nancy Reagan was not the first to play a key role in how the White House and the administration was staffed. In contrast to Nancy Reagan, however, most first ladies kept their influences and preferences private, thus avoiding public criticism for their actions.

Seventeen first ladies, and all who have held the position recently, have become identified with issues of personal concern to them. Through these issues, first ladies rise from the surrogate position to speaking in their own right. Some, like Rosalyn Carter, had a long-standing interest in the particular issue. Others like Nancy Reagan appeared to search for an issue until launching her "Just Say No" campaign against drug use. Yet, all eventually worked hard on their particular project whether it was White House beautification, highway beautification, or health care.

[* * *]

While first ladies who embraced an issue used their proximity to the president to lobby for legislation, only three actually testified before Congress concerning their issue—[Eleanor] Roosevelt, Carter, and Clinton. Several tried to use more informal methods to lobby legislators for their pet programs. Ellen Wilson, the first wife of Woodrow Wilson, was the first to have her favorite legislation actually enacted by Congress. In her case, it was a law to add new low income housing in the District of Columbia.

Overt political concerns have encouraged eight first ladies to state their personal policy preferences publicly. Six first ladies actually attended executive policy meetings. Moreover, we found evidence that at least five actually influenced the outcome of certain policy debates. These findings clearly show that first ladies are not only politically active, but that this activity has neglected policy implications.

[* * *]

The office of first lady traditionally has been an alternative route to political influence for a select group of women when most other U.S. women were effectively closed out of many formal positions of leadership. The significance of their potential influence needs to be acknowledged and, as [political scientist] George C. Edwards argues, our traditional concepts of leadership should be refined. A facilitator at what Edwards calls "the margins" may be a more realistic description of leadership than the director of change.

The influence of *unelected* first ladies as policy makers or influencers also has interesting implication for democracy. Americans have long taken for granted the key roles that unelected advisers including White House chiefs of staff, cabinet members, friends, and others play without questioning their unelected status. Many of those presidential confidants, however, are at least subject to Senate confirmation. First ladies, in contrast, do not come to the American electorate as a surprise. Today, they are constantly in the spotlight, interviewed alone and 1996 Republican presidential nominee Bob Dole went so far as to suggest—whether it was humorously offered or not—that his wife Elizabeth Dole and Hillary Clinton actually debate each other.

[* * *]

TOWARD CRITICAL THINKING

1. Laura Bush has never been perceived as a Hillary Rodham Clinton type of First Lady. Yet, during U.S. efforts to end the Taliban's rule in Afghanistan, Laura Bush addressed the United Nations on this issue and delivered a presidential radio address on this topic. Later, she traveled to war-torn Iraq. Do Americans now expect first ladies to take a more active role in significant public policy issues and act as official representatives of the president?

2. Vice President Dan Quayle's wife, Marilyn, was an attorney. Vice President Dick Cheney's wife, Lynn, has a Ph.D. in English, held positions in government, and works full time at the conservative Heritage Foundation. Has the public become sufficiently accustomed to women working outside the home that first or second ladies no longer risk public disapproval for pursuing a career or taking on more activist roles?

READING 45

Political Appointees in the United States: Does Gender Make a Difference?

(2001)

Julie Dolan

Even before Julie Dolan began a series of exhaustive studies on women in the senior executive service, scholars were working to fill the void in our knowledge of the executive branch. But, from the presidency to the Cabinet, to political appointees, to the senior executive service, to street-level bureaucrats in Washington—let alone in regional offices around the United States with their own peculiar hierarchies—the very nature of the executive branch makes its study a daunting task. Yet, this is clearly where there are women with the rank and capability to make a difference in how policy is made, especially as it affects women across the range of federal activities. Still, as Mary Hawkesworth (Reading 35) points out, even women members of Congress often have problems getting credit for legislation that they actually propose. Thus, measuring influence of senior women in the executive branch is particularly problematic.

When President Bill Clinton was elected in 1992, he pledged to appoint women and minorities to high-level positions in his administration, to make it "look like America." As Dolan notes here, in work published in *P.S.: Political Science & Politics*, while Clinton appointed more women than any other president before him, women still were appointed to far fewer positions than were males. This was in spite of the fact that women's organizations vigorously lobbied for the appointment of more women and even set up committees to screen and advance the names of women qualified for those posts.

Although the U.S. government has long been considered one of the better places for women to work, women's salaries in high-prestige federal jobs continue to lag behind those of men, and women still are underrepresented in the senior executive service. A 2004 *Washington Post* survey revealed that women working in the Bush White House earned $59,917 on average, while their male counterparts earned $76,624. Thus, women made about 78 percent of what did men .

Salary data tell us something about women's position within the bureaucracy and the executive branch, but Dolan notes how little research has been conducted on the whos, hows, whys, and impact of women in the executive branch. Dolan points to several areas begging for more research. In a subsequent study, for example, she found that women in the senior executive service of government have almost the same responsibilities as men and even view themselves as more influential than their male counterparts.

With every new presidential administration in the United States, the incoming president is in charge of appointing thousands of individuals to work throughout the executive branch of government and assist him in fulfilling his constitutional responsibility to "faithfully execute the laws of the Nation." When the Center for American Women and Politics (CAWP) first began studying female political appointees in the early 1980s, very few women had ever served in Cabinet positions or other high-ranking executive positions within the federal government. In fact, in 1977, almost two hundred years after the founding of the United States, President Carter appointed only the fourth and fifth women ever to serve as Cabinet secretaries. . . .

. . . [T]he number of women in high-ranking executive branch positions in the federal government has expanded greatly. During the eight years of the Reagan administration, 277 women were appointed to high-ranking positions requiring Senate confirmation. Following Reagan, George Bush appointed 181 women, while President Clinton surpassed both of his predecessors combined, appointing 592 women throughout his tenure, including the first women ever to serve as Secretary of State (Madeleine Albright) and as Attorney General (Janet Reno), positions considered part of the president's inner cabinet. Although George W. Bush's administration is only a few months old as of this writing, he has thus far appointed six women to high-ranking administrative positions. making history by appointing the first female Secretaries of Agriculture and Interior (Ann Veneman and Gail Norton), the first female National Security Adviser (Condoleezza Rice), and the first Asian-American woman to serve as a cabinet Secretary, Elaine Chao (at the Department of Labor).

Despite the recent increases for women into high-ranking, high-profile administrative positions in the federal government, we still know very little about these women. . . . [V]ery little research has systematically explored the careers, policy contributions, or perspectives of these high-ranking executive women. This essay reviews the existing research on female appointees in the executive branch, reflecting on what we know thus far about women's experiences in reaching the top of the federal government and the impact they have upon arrival. The essay focuses primarily upon those women serving in the federal government, but also includes findings from state governments, where appropriate.

Recruitment of Female Appointees

Although President Clinton appointed women to nearly a third of all executive positions requiring Senate confirmation, women remain far from equal with men in the ranks of the president's lieutenants. How do they arrive in their positions? Do they bring different qualifications to their jobs than their male colleagues?

Most early research on women appointed to presidential and gubernatorial administrations examines their backgrounds, finding that female appointees are as well-educated and distinguished as their male counterparts. In fact, there are remarkably few differences in background qualifications between the women and men called to serve. Men are slightly more likely to have an advanced degree while women are more likely to have attended private colleges and universities. Women are also likely to come from more advantaged backgrounds than do their male colleagues, at least as evidenced by their father's and mother's occupations. Among previous Republican appointees, women arrived with greater federal administrative experience than do their male colleagues, while women tapped for the Carter administration brought greater state government experience than did their male counterparts. Female presidential appointees are more often recruited from the Washington, D.C., area than are male appointees, but even so MaryAnne Borrelli argues that female "insiders" (those with previous government experience in Washington) receive more skeptical treatment during Senate committee hearings than do male insiders. Lastly, the agencies and departments in which appointees are chosen to serve vary by gender, with female political appointees more often selected for posts in agencies and departments dealing with stereotypically female concerns (health, education and social services).

Gender and Political Impact

Does it matter if women are presidential appointees? Representative bureaucracy scholars would answer yes, that the demographic makeup of the executive branch of government does indeed affect the substantive outputs of government. According to theory, a diverse public sector is important not only for symbolic reasons, but because governmental decisions are expected to be more responsive to the public when the workforce "looks like America." Individuals from different social backgrounds bring different attitudes, priorities, and perspectives to their jobs. . . .

[* * *]

As presidential appointees, women have likewise used their positions to speak out for and draw attention to problems commonly affecting women in society. Serving as President Carter's Secretary of Commerce from 1977 to 1979. Juanita Kreps encouraged the formation of the President's Interagency Task Force on Women Business Owners, a major initiative to help women increase their numbers in the private sector. Appointed as the first woman to head the National Institutes of Health, Bernadine Healy advocated women's health issues from the beginning of her tenure and proposed a $625 million NIH study involving 150,000 women and studying breast cancer, osteoporosis, and heart disease. Two months after taking office as the first female Secretary of State, Madeleine Albright instructed U.S. diplomats to make "the furtherance of women's rights a central priority of American foreign policy."

Beyond these anecdotes, systematic research examines executive women's attitudes, reasoning that attitudes provide legitimate clues about likely behavior. Women who are attentive to women's concerns on paper are expected to be more responsive to women's policy concerns when opportunity for action arises. Numerous studies confirm that female appointees, both at the state and federal level, are more feminist, liberal and Democratic than their male colleagues. Surveys of presidential and gubernatorial appointees indicate that female Republican and Democratic appointees are more supportive of childcare, abortion rights, and the Equal Rights Amendment than their male colleagues. Thus, the existing attitudinal evidence suggests that female appointees, as a group, respond to the distinct concerns and preferences of the female citizenry.

However, attitudes may not translate directly into policy output that benefits women as a group. For instance, a female appointee may work in a position that offers few opportunities to voice a distinctly feminine perspective. Thus, scholars try to determine how female appointees affect policymaking and the nature and substance of government outputs. To date, most studies focus on women's managerial responsibilities and talents. Within both federal and state administrations, a majority of female appointees indicate that they frequently hire women as staff members, doing their part to facilitate the entry of even greater numbers of women into governmental positions. Conducting personal interviews with male and female appointees in the Departments of State and Defense, [political scientists Nancy] McGlen and [Meredith Reid] Sarkees find that males and females exercise slightly different leadership styles, with female appointees more often expressing greater satisfaction in dealing with subordinates and managing their staffs. Further, when asked to identify their major accomplishments, female appointees more often listed management accomplishments as well as accomplishments that affected women. Although research regarding the impact of female appointees is still preliminary, the influx of women into federal government over the past eight years provides ample opportunities for further study.

Directions for Future Research

As this brief review demonstrates, the literature on women in the executive branch has certainly grown . . . but opportunities for additional research remain. We know a great deal about women's recruitment patterns and qualifications, but considerably less regarding whether policy outputs differ because of women's presence. Scholars studying presidential appointees could draw from legislative studies to identify creative approaches for assessing women's impact in the fourth branch of government. However, much more of legislators' words and actions are preserved on public record (votes, floor speeches, committee membership, etc.) than are political appointees', making it more difficult to isolate and interpret political appointees' behavior.

Another open line of research concerns the salience of race. We know almost nothing about women of color in the executive branch, even though a number of women of color have served in highly visible posts (e.g., Hazel O'Leary, Alexis Herman, Aida Alvarez, Condoleezza Rice and Elaine Chao). Small sample sizes have made it difficult to explore women from different racial backgrounds, but ongoing changes provide us with additional opportunities to ascertain the political responsiveness and career patterns for these women. Doing so will provide a much more comprehensive understanding of gender at the top of the executive branch.

TOWARD CRITICAL THINKING

1. As in the legislative and judicial areas discussed in Chapters 8 and 9, until recently, there have been too few women in the executive branch, especially at the Cabinet level, to allow for systematic analysis. Which areas of inquiry noted by Julie Dolan seem particularly timely?

2. Is it "good politics" or "good administration" to create an executive branch that "looks like America"? Why or why not?

WRAPPING UP

1. Name three women who might make strong candidates for the presidency. Given all that you have read in this volume, what traits do you think a woman must possess for a successful run for her party's nomination and, ultimately, the presidency?

2. Can women at senior levels of the governmental bureaucracy, whether national or state, have an impact on public policy? What difference would it make if more women held senior positions in the executive branch?

Credits

Sapiro, Virginia. From "When Are Interests Interesting? The Problem of Political Representation of Women," *American Political Science Review* 75(1981): 701–713. Reprinted with permission of Cambridge University Press.

Diamond, Irene, and Nancy Hartsock. From "Beyond Interests in Politics: A Comment on Virginia Sapiro's 'When Are Interests Interesting?': The Problem of Political Representation of Women," *American Political Science Review* 75(1981): 717–721. Reprinted with permission of Cambridge University Press.

DuBois, Ellen Carol. From "Outgrowing the Compact of the Fathers: Equal Rights, Woman Suffrage, and the United States Constitution, 1820–1878," *Journal of American History* 74(3), December 1987: 836–862. Reprinted by permission of the Organization of American Historians.

McDonagh, Eileen Lorenzi. From "The Significance of the Nineteenth Amendment: A New Look at Civil Rights, Social Welfare, and Woman Suffrage Alignments in the Progressive Era," *Women & Politics* 10 (2), 1990: 59–94. Reprinted by permission of The Haworth Press, Inc., Binghamton, NY. Copyright © 1990.

Mansbridge, Jane J. From *Why We Lost the ERA*. Copyright © 1986 by the University of Chicago. Reprinted by permission of the author and the publisher, the University of Chicago Press.

MacKinnon, Catharine A. Reprinted by permission from *Toward a Feminist Theory of the State* by Catharine A. MacKinnon. Cambridge, Mass.: Harvard University Press. Copyright © 1989 by Catharine A. MacKinnon.

Welch, Susan. From "Women as Political Animals? A Test of Some Explanations for Male Female Political Participation Differences," *American Journal of Political Science* 21(4), November 1977: 711–730. Reprinted by permission of Blackwell Publishing Ltd.

Costain, Anne N. From *Inviting Women's Rebellion: Political Process Interpretation of the Women's Movement*, pp. 44–78. Copyright © 1992. Reprinted with permission of The Johns Hopkins University Press.

Schlozman, Kay Lehman, Nancy Burns, and Sidney Verba. From "Gender and the Pathways to Participation: The Role of Resources," *The Journal of Politics* 56(4), November 1994: 963–990. Reprinted by permission of Blackwell Publishing Ltd.

Hardy-Fanta, Carol. Material excerpted from "Discovering Latina Women in Politics: Gender, Culture, and Participatory Theory" in *Latina Politics, Latino Politics: Gender, Culture, and Political Participation in Boston* by Carol Hardy-Fanta. Reprinted by permission of Temple University Press. Copyright © 1993 by Temple University. All Rights Reserved.

Carroll, Susan J. From "Political Elites and Sex Differences in Political Ambition: A Reconsideration," *The Journal of Politics* 47(4), November 1985: 1231–1243. Reprinted by permission of Blackwell Publishing Ltd.

Costantini, Edmond. From "Political Women and Political Ambition: Closing the Gender Gap," *American Journal of Political Science* 34(3), August 1990: 741–770. Reprinted by permission of Blackwell Publishing Ltd.

Fox, Richard L., and Jennifer L. Lawless. From "Family Structure, Sex Role Socialization, and the Decision to Run for Office," *Women & Politics* 24 (4), 2003: 19–48. Reprinted by permission of The Haworth Press, Inc., Binghamton, NY. Copyright © 2003.

Palmer, Barbara, and Dennis Simon. From "Political Ambition and Women in the U.S. House of Representatives, 1916–2000," *Political Research Quarterly* 56(2), June 2003: 127–138. Reprinted by permission of the authors and the University of Utah, copyright holder.

Gurin, Patricia. From "Women's Gender Consciousness," *Public Opinion Quarterly* 49(2), Summer 1985: 143–163. By permission of Oxford University Press.

Conover, Pamela Johnston. From "Feminists and the Gender Gap," *The Journal of Politics* 50(4), November 1988: 985–1010. Reprinted by permission of Blackwell Publishing Ltd.

Cook, Elizabeth Adell and Clyde Wilcox. From "Feminism and the Gender Gap—A Second Look," *The Journal of Politics* 53(4), November 1991: 1111–1122. Reprinted by permission of Blackwell Publishing Ltd.

Norrander, Barbara. From "The Independence Gap and the Gender Gap," *Public Opinion Quarterly* 61(3), Fall 1997: 464–476. By permission of Oxford University Press.

Kaufmann, Karen M., and John Petrocik. From "The Changing Politics of American Men: Understanding the Sources of the Gender Gap," *American Journal of Political Science* 43(3), July 1999: 864–887. Reprinted by permission of Blackwell Publishing Ltd.

Schreiber, Ronnee. Excerpted from "Injecting a Women's Voice: Conservative Women's Organizations, Gender Consciousness, and the Expression of Women's Policy Preferences," *Sex Roles* 47(7/8), October 2002: 331–342. Reprinted with kind permission from Springer Science and Business Media.

Boneparth, Ellen. From "Women in Campaigns: From Lickin' and Stickin' to Strategy," *American Politics Quarterly* 5(3), July 1977: 289–300. Reprinted by permission of Sage Publications.

Fowlkes, Diane L., Jerry Perkins, and Sue Tolleson Rinehart. From "Gender Roles and Party Roles," *American Political Science Review* 73(1979): 772–780. Reprinted with permission of Cambridge University Press.

Freeman, Jo. From "The Political Culture of the Democratic and Republican Parties." Reprinted by permission from *Political Science Quarterly* 101(1986): 327–356.

Sanbonmatsu, Kira. From "Political Parties and the Recruitment of Women to State Legislatures," *The Journal of Politics* 64(3), August 2002: 791–809. Reprinted by permission of Blackwell Publishing Ltd.

Darcy, R., and Sarah Slavin Schramm. From "When Women Run Against Men," *Public Opinion Quarterly* 41(1), Spring 1977: 1–12. By permission of Oxford University Press.

Bullock III, Charles, and Susan A. MacManus. From "Municipal Electoral Structures and the Election of Councilwomen," *The Journal of Politics* 53(1), February 1991: 75–89. Reprinted by permission of Blackwell Publishing Ltd.

Huddy, Leonie, and Nayda Terkildsen. From "Gender Stereotypes and the Perception of Male and Female Candidates," *American Journal of Political Science* 37(1), February 1993: 119–147. Reprinted by permission of Blackwell Publishing Ltd.

Kahn, Kim Fridkin. From "The Distorted Mirror: Press Coverage of Women Candidates for Statewide Office," *The Journal of Politics* 56(1), February 1994: 154–173. Reprinted by permission of Blackwell Publishing Ltd.

Dolan, Kathleen. From "Electoral Context, Issues, and Voting for Women in the 1990s," *Women & Politics* 23(1/2), 2001: 21–36. Reprinted by permission of The Haworth Press, Inc., Binghamton, NY. Copyright © 2001.

Werner, Emmy E. From "Women in Congress 1917–1964," *Western Political Quarterly* 9(1), March 1966: 16–30. Reprinted by permission of the author and the University of Utah, copyright holder.

Thomas, Sue. From "The Impact of Women on State Legislative Policies," *The Journal of Politics* 53(4), November 1991: 958–976. Reprinted by permission of Blackwell Publishing Ltd.

Kathlene, Lyn. From "Power and Influence in State Legislative Policymaking: The Interaction of Gender and Position in Committee Hearing Debates," *American Political Science Review* 88(1994): 560–576. Reprinted with the permission of Cambridge University Press.

Rosenthal, Cindy Simon. From "Gender Styles in State Legislative Committees: Raising Their Voices in Resolving Conflict," *Women & Politics* 21(2), 2000: 21–45. Reprinted by permission of The Haworth Press, Inc., Binghamton, NY. Copyright © 2000.

Swers, Michele L. From "Are Women More Likely to Vote for Women's Issue Bills Than Their Male Colleagues?" *Legislative Studies Quarterly* XXIII(3): 435–448. Copyright © by the publisher, Comparative Legislative Research Center. Reprinted by permission of the publisher and author.

Hawkesworth, Mary. From "Congressional Enactments of Race-Gender: Toward a Theory of Race-Gendered Institutions," *American Political Science Review* 97(4), November 2003: 529–550. Reprinted with the permission of Cambridge University Press.

Gruhl, John, Cassia Spohn, and Susan Welch. From "Women as Policy Makers: The Case of Trial Judges," *American Journal of Political Science* 25(2), May 1981: 308–322. Reprinted by permission of Blackwell Publishing Ltd.

Songer, Donald R., Sue Davis, and Susan Haire. From "A Reappraisal of Diversification in the Federal Courts: Gender Effects in the Courts of Appeals," *The Journal of Politics* 56(2), May 1994: 425–439. Reprinted by permission of Blackwell Publishing Ltd.

Coontz, Phyllis. From "Gender and Judicial Decisions: Do Female Judges Decide Cases Differently Than Male Judges?" *Gender Issues* 18(4) (Fall 2000): 59–73. Copyright © 2000 by Transaction Publishers. Reproduced with permission of Transaction Publishers in the format Textbook via Copyright Clearance Center.

O'Connor, Karen, and Jeffrey A. Segal. From "Justice Sandra Day O'Connor and the Supreme Court's Reaction to Its First Female Member," *Women & Politics* 10(2), 1990: 95–104. Reprinted by permission of The Haworth Press, Inc., Binghamton, NY. Copyright © 1990.

Ferree, Myra Marx. From "A Woman for President? Changing Responses: 1958–1972," *Public Opinion Quarterly* 38(3), Fall 1974: 390–399. By permission of Oxford University Press.

Frankovic, Kathleen. From "The Ferraro Factor: The Women's Movement, the Polls, and the Press" in *The Politics of the Gender Gap*, Carol M. Mueller, ed. Reprinted by permission of Sage Publications.

Duerst-Lahti, Georgia. From "Reconceiving Theories of Power: Consequences of Masculinism in the Executive Branch" in *The Other Elites: Women, Politics, and Power in the Executive Branch*, MaryAnne Borrelli and Janet M. Martin, eds. Copyright © 1997. Reprinted by permission of Lynne Rienner Publishers.

Borrelli, MaryAnne. From "Gender, Credibility, and Politics: The Senate Nomination Hearings of Cabinet Secretaries-Designate, 1975–1993," *Political Research Quarterly* 5(1), March 1997: 171–197. Reprinted by permission of the author and the University of Utah, copyright holder.

O'Connor, Karen, Bernadette Nye, and Laura van Assendelft. From "Wives in the White House: The Political Influence of First Ladies," *Presidential Studies Quarterly* 26 (3), Summer 1996: 835–850.

Dolan, Julie. From "Political Appointees in the United States: Does Gender Make a Difference?" *PS: Political Science and Politics* 34(2), 2001: 212–216. Reprinted by permission of Cambridge University Press.